HAND HELD HOLLYWOOD's
FILMMAKING
WITH THE
iPAD & iPHONE

Taz Goldstein

HAND HELD HOLLYWOOD'S
Filmmaking with the iPad & iPhone

Taz Goldstein

Peachpit Press
www.peachpit.com

To report errors, please send a note to errata@peachpit.com

Peachpit Press is a division of Pearson Education.

Copyright © 2013 Taz Goldstein

Senior Editor: Karyn Johnson
Development Editor: Corbin Collins
Production Editor: Myrna Vladic
Copyeditor: Kim Wimpsett
Proofreader: Scout Festa
Composition: Kim Scott, Bumpy Design
Indexer: Valerie Perry
Interior design: Charlene Charles-Will and Kim Scott, Bumpy Design
Cover design: Charlene Charles-Will
Author photo, cover: Eddie Daniels, Little Room Studio
Author photo, interior: Amy Olk

ISBN-13: 978-0-321-86294-5
ISBN-10:   0-321-86294-5

9 8 7 6 5 4 3 2 1

For the crazy ones.

ACKNOWLEDGMENTS

This book would simply not have been possible without the pioneering spirit of app developers and accessory designers who continue to empower filmmakers around the world. I'd like to thank each and every one of these revolutionaries, and perhaps I will in my next book, "Taz Thanks Way Too Many People."

I'm profoundly fortunate to have a loyal group of friends, family, and peers who have all graciously contributed their time and energy to this project. I don't know how I can possibly construct sentences to convey the sheer volume of gratitude I feel. I'll do my best, knowing I can only fall short.

Seth, Judy, Scott, Avery, and Garret. From page 1, you believed in this book and in my ability to deliver it. Thank you for supporting me as only a family can.

Amy, you were my model, my muse, my first reader, and my life support system. Thank you for your encouragement, your patience, your input, and your willingness to join me on the ride. I love you very much.

Joseph, thank you for your unyielding support, for your thoughtful council, and for "minding the store" in my absence. I couldn't ask for a better collaborator, business partner, or friend.

My heartfelt thanks to everyone at Peachpit Press. Karyn, thank you for placing your trust in a first-time writer. Corbin, thank you for being a magnificent advisor. Charlene, Myrna, and Kim, thank you for sharing your formidable skill sets. Special thanks to my agent, David Fugate at LaunchBooks, for helping me navigate the process.

Thanks to Emil Beheshti, Brandon Epland, Darryl Freni, Reese Golchin, Butch Hammett, Bob Levitan, Omar McAllister, Lama Mouawad, Byrne Offutt, Amy Olk, Scott Schirai, and Jona Shreeves-Taylor for gracing so many of these pages. Thanks to Louie del Carmen, Eric Haase, Mark Doering-Powell, and Jesse Rosten for allowing me to share their stories and talents. Thanks to the previously unmentioned members of the DPL for their unwavering support: Tom Mahoney, Billy Woody, Jerry Oh, Joe Nussbaum, Sean Klosky, Keith Ortiz, and Jonathan M. Green.

Thanks to Stu Maschwitz for his time, wisdom, and willingness to participate. Thanks to Kimberly Browning and Jonathan Houser for their honesty, integrity, and level-headed thinking. Thanks to Mat Sansom for his incredibly well-timed encouragement and council from across the pond.

Thanks to Ken Ray, Dan Bérubé, and Michael Horton for generously providing me with platforms from which I could preach the mobile-media-making gospel. Thanks to Jason Benesh for letting me shoot at the Dirt Cheap Sound Stage in Santa Monica, California. Thanks to Rob Moniot for his friendship and for giving me my first iPhone. Thanks to Ric Wolfe for being my most enthusiastic collaborator. Thanks to Sarah Bein for helping me miniaturize the hurdles that felt unjumpable.

And lastly, thanks to my dog, Pixel, and her best friend, Bambi, for agreeing to participate without involving their agents.

CONTENTS

Introduction x

PART ONE
DEVELOPMENT AND PRE-PRODUCTION

**1 Stop Playing "Angry Birds"
and Write That Script! 3**

Mapping Your Mind 4
   iThoughtsHD 4
   MindNode 7
   Corkulous Pro 8
   Evernote 10
Structuring Your Story 11
   Syd Field Script Launcher 12
   Save the Cat! 12
   Contour 14
   Index Card 16
   StorySkeleton 19
   Baby Names + ... 21
Writing Your Screenplay 22
   Celtx Script 22
   Storyist 24
   More Options 26
   Fountain 29
Using External Keyboards 32
   Bluetooth Keyboards 33
   Bluetooth Keyboard Cases 35
   What About Wired Keyboards? 38
Speaking Your Script 39
   iOS Dictation 40
   Dragon Dictation App 41
   Dictabulus 42

**2 Don't Just Sit There—
Read a Script and Sit There 45**

Reading Screenplays 46
   Final Draft Reader 46
   FDX Reader 50
   iBooks 51
Annotating Screenplays 53
   PDF Expert 54
   GoodReader 57
   PDFPen 58
   GoodNotes 60
   Adobe Story 62
Memorizing Screenplays 63
   Rehearsal 2 63
Finding Screenplays 65
   Scripted 66
   The iBookstore 67

3 Here's the Pitch! 69

Presentation Apps 70
   Photos and iPhoto 70
   Magic Bullet Arsenal 73
   Keynote 75
   Presentation Link 77
Where to Find Imagery 79
Following Up 80
   Dropbox 81
   iFiles 83
   FAQ 84

4 Prepping the Shoot **87**

Production Directories. 88
    LA 411. 88
    Doddle 89
Location Scouting 91
    Panascout. 92
    Map-A-Pic Location Scout 94
Tech Scouting 95
    TechScout Touch, Lighting Edition 96
    Camera Order. 97
    List Sender 98
Scheduling. 99
    Movie Magic Scheduling To Go 100
    ShotList 102
    Shot Lister 105
Call Sheets. 107
    DoddlePRO. 107
    Pocket Call Sheet. 109
    FilmTouch 112
    Lua 113
Release Forms and Contracts. 113
    Easy Release 115
    Form Tools PDF 117
    Cinema Forms 119
Digitizing Dead Trees. 121
    Go, Doxie Go 121
    DocScanner 125
A Quick Word About Budgeting 127

PART TWO   PRODUCTION

5 The Director's Toolkit. **131**

Storyboarding for Artists. 132
    Penultimate. 133
    Paper 135
    Previs (Formerly SketchPad Pro) 136
    Jot Pro Stylus 137
    Cosmonaut Stylus 139
    Nomad Brush 140
Storyboarding for Non-Artists. 140
    Storyboard Composer HD. 141
    Storyboards 3D 144
The Ultimate Director's Viewfinder 147
    Artemis Director's Viewfinder
       and Artemis HD 147
Blocking Your Shots 151
    Shot Designer. 151
    OmniGraffle 156
    TouchDraw 160
    MagicPlan. 161
Building a Rodriguez List. 164
    Celtx Scout. 165

6 Lights! Camera! Airplane Mode! . . **167**

Getting the Best Results 169
    Prepping Your Device. 169
    The Rolling Shutter Conundrum 172
    Exposure, Focus, and White Balance . 174
    Light It Up! 174
    Keep It Steady 175

The Best Video Camera Apps 176
   FiLMiC Pro 176
   CinePro 179
   Almost DSLR 181
   What About the Built-in
     Camera App? 183
Unique Video Cameras 184
   CollabraCam 184
   Video Camera (Vizzywig) 187
   SloPro 190
   Luma Camera 193
   8mm and 8mm HD 195
   Vintagio 197
   Super 8 198
   Action Movie FX 199
Audio: Half of Good Video 200
   Pro Audio To Go 202
   Hindenburg Field Recorder 204
   FiRe 2 207
   What About Apple's Voice
     Memo App? 207

7 Mount It, Mod It, and Mic It 209

Gearing Up Your iPhone 210
   Steadicam Smoothee 210
   mCAM and mCAMLITE 212
   The iPhone SLR Mount 217
   Glif 219
   iPro Lens 220
   Olloclip 222
   DiffCase 224
   Holga iPhone Lens 226
   iPhone Lens Dial 227
   GorillaMobile for iPhone 4/4S 229
   Shooting Underwater 230
Your iPad, Only Better! 232
   Movie Mount 232
   Padcaster 233

Awesome Extras 234
   Croma and Micro 235
   mobislyder 237
   Action Cart and Mini Cart 239
   SuctionClip 242
Step Up to the Mic 242
   Adapter Cables 243
   VideoMic Pro 244
   iXZ Microphone Adapter 245
   AR-4i Stereo Microphone 247
   iM2 Stereo Microphone 249

8 The Most Versatile Tools on Set . . . 251

Teleprompters 252
   ProPrompter 252
   Elite Prompter 255
   ProPrompter Wing 257
   ProPrompter HDi Pro2 259
   More Options 261
Creating an Interrotron 262
Camera Calculations 264
   pCAM Film+Digital Calculator 265
   Toland ASC Digital Assistant 268
The Ultimate Slate 270
   Movie★Slate 271
   TimeCode Buddy 275
   T-Slate 277
   Denecke Slate 280
   Where's the MamboFrame? 280
   QRSlate 281
Field Monitors and Instant Dailies 283
   The Cube 283
   DSLR Camera Remote HD 285
Let There Be Light 287
   Pocket Light Meter 287
   Helios Sun Position Calculator 290
   Let's Light with iPads! Yes, Really. . . . 291
   Photo Soft Box Pro 293
   The Kick Plus 294

PART THREE POSTPRODUCTION AND BEYOND

9 From Mess to Masterpiece 299

Importing Footage 300
    From iPhone to iPad 300
    From a Video Camera to iPad 300
    From a Computer to iPad or iPhone . . 302
Color Correcting Your Footage 305
    VideoGrade 306
    Movie Looks HD 308
    CinemaFX for Video 310
    More Options 311
Editing Footage 312
    iMovie 312
    Pinnacle Studio 317
    Drop'n'Roll (formerly V.I.K.T.O.R.) 320
    Other Options 321
Composing the Score 321
    Tabletop 322
    GarageBand 324
Mixing Your Audio 325
    TwistedWave Audio Editor 326
    Auria 328
    Alesis iO Dock 331
Editing Extras 333
    Cut Notes 333
    Timecode 336
    Editmote 337
    AJA DataCalc 338
Learning More 340
    Larry Jordan Training for
      Final Cut Pro X 340
    iKeysToGo: Final Cut Pro 7 341
    EditCodes 342
    Moviola's Pro Video Guide 343

10 It's Done! Now What? 345

YouTube, Vimeo, and Facebook 346
Selling Your Work 347
    Put It in the App Store 347
    PayPal, Square, and Intuit 353
iPhone Film Festivals 354
    The Original iPhone Film Festival 354
    The iPhone Film Festival 355
    The Disposable Film Festival 355
Putting It On-Screen 356
    Apple TV and AirPlay 356
    Video Cables 357
The Last App in the Book 360
Additional Resources 361
    Hand Held Hollywood 361
    Prolost and *The DV Rebel's Guide* . . . 361
    Film Riot 361
    Indie Mogul 362
Everybody Off the Bus! 362

Index 363

INTRODUCTION

If you own an iPhone or iPad, or even an iPod touch, you already possess one of the most powerful and versatile production tools ever conceived.

Nothing like starting a book with a big bold statement. Want another one?

By producing and selling more than 400,000,000 of these devices, Apple has helped demolish the barriers to entry-level filmmaking and has revolutionized the way in which professional filmmakers apply their craft.

Boom goes the dynamite!

I know—you're skeptical. I certainly was. As a filmmaker accustomed to working with truckloads of high-end gear and an army of specialized personnel, the idea that my *phone* could play a significant role on set (other than calling a rental house to get more gear) seemed downright silly.

August 15, 2009, is the day everything changed. That's when I downloaded Hitchcock (later renamed Storyboard Composer), a new app that allowed me to quickly create visually expressive storyboards using my existing photos and my iPhone's built-in camera. I had already started using the Notes app to maintain basic shot lists, but Hitchcock was the first app I had ever found that was created specifically for filmmakers. The next day, I began using the app to work out scenes with my cinematographer. It helped us communicate more clearly, work more efficiently, and quickly construct effective scenes.

Not only did I fall in love with Hitchcock, I felt it represented a significant paradigm shift. iPhones weren't just for playing Flight Control anymore. I knew it was only a matter of time before my iPhone would become my most valued filmmaking tool, and I felt an overwhelming compulsion to share and discuss this revelation with other filmmakers. So, I hunted for websites and online forums that focused on iPhone use in film and video production but found nothing. How could this be? Was I the only iPhone-obsessed filmmaker? I decided to find out by launching a site of my own.

Hand Held Hollywood (HHH) was in beta two weeks later and went live on September 22, 2009. The first posts described apps for reading scripts, an accessory for recording automatic dialogue replacement (ADR), and tools for turning iPhones into pint-sized teleprompters. At the end of the first day, the site had received a total of 24 visitors, and believe me, I was psyched! Weeks later, my joy turned to utter astonishment as the site welcomed thousands of like-minded filmmakers from every corner of the globe.

Since its launch, HHH has taken me on a remarkable journey. I've given lectures at industry events, been interviewed by international news organizations, asked to write articles for major publications, and met many extremely talented filmmakers and app developers.

In fact, it's because of the site's success that I was approached to author this book, and for that reason, I am *deeply* thankful to each and every reader who helped put HandHeldHollywood.com on the map.

About the Book

Like any computer, Apple's mobile devices are only as powerful as the software you add. Fortunately for us, the App Store has become a filmmaker's treasure trove.

The next 350-plus pages explore apps (and accessories) that can help mold your story into a completed screenplay, pitch your project to potential partners, manage your shooting schedule, digitize your production's paperwork, storyboard your shots, block complex scenes, rehearse your actors, shoot your raw footage, record sound effects and Foley, edit and mix your completed work, and even distribute it to millions of potential viewers worldwide.

It's my sincere hope that this book helps you unlock the enormous potential packed into the Apple devices you already own or plan to purchase.

Shooting Video with Your iPhone and iPad

Although I spend only about 20 percent of this book discussing the use of iPhones and iPads as video cameras, it's a topic that tends to spark debate among filmmakers. For that reason, I feel it's important to express my perspective right up front.

Every new iPhone, iPad, and iPod touch comes standard with an HD video camera, allowing anyone to grab high-quality video at a moment's notice. The truth is, these cameras aren't anywhere near as powerful as the professional, high-end gear I typically use on my shoots, but that doesn't mean I consider them any less viable or valuable.

As a filmmaker, I pick my camera based on the stories I'm telling, the environment I'm shooting in, and the resources I currently have (or don't have) at my disposal. Over the past 20 years or so, I've shot on everything from 35mm film to Super-8 and from the Arri Alexa to the Fisher Price Pixelvision. Every camera has its place, and that includes those found in Apple's portable gizmos.

What's that you say? You don't believe a smartphone is capable of shooting video for a serious production?

Searching for Sugar Man (film)
hhhlinks.com/ef50

Night Fishing (film)
hhhlinks.com/i3b8

Don't tell that to Malik Bendjelloul, who recently used an iPhone and a $0.99 app called 8mm (covered in Chapter 6) to shoot a good portion of *Searching for Sugar Man*, a documentary that opened the 2012 Sundance Film Festival and has continued to win awards around the world.

You might also not want to say anything to Chan-wook Park, the internationally renowned director of *Oldboy*, who, along with his brother Chan-kyong Park, used an iPhone equipped with an mCAM mount and EnCinema SLR adapter (both described in Chapter 7) to shoot *Night Fishing*, which won the Golden Berlin Bear for Best Short Film at the 2011 Berlin International Film Festival.

For some filmmakers, the iPhone is the only camera to which they have constant access. It's been said that the best camera is the one you have with you. Well, it just so happens that the one you have with you *rocks the house*.

A Little Lingo

iOS is Apple's operating system for the iPhone, iPad, and iPod touch. It's what gives these devices their distinct personality and provides developers with a foundation on which to construct their apps. When I refer to *iOS devices* throughout the book, I'm talking about iPhones, iPads, and iPod touches.

Apple's third-generation iPad is officially called The New iPad—easily the most confusing title since Howard Jones's 1984 hit "New Song." To make things simple, I'll be referring to the third-generation iPad as the *iPad 3*, as Apple should have done from day one.

Info Boxes

As you flip through the pages of this book, you'll notice info boxes floating in the margins. Each box contains useful information, such as an accessory's name, price, company, and website.

When describing an app, the info box will also indicate the device for which the app was intended. Some apps are designed specifically for iPhones, others are meant for iPads, and many are *universal* (intended to work on both). The truth is, this indicator is a generalization. Most of the nonuniversal iPhone apps described in this book will also work on an iPod touch (possibly with diminished performance) or an iPad (using the built-in iPhone emulator). However, nonuniversal iPad apps will never run on an iPhone or iPod touch. It's always wise to double-check an app's compatibility requirements before making a purchase. I talk about that a little more in just a moment.

FIGURE I.1 Two sample QR codes. One will take you to the Hand Held Hollywood website. The other...um...won't.

Most info boxes also contain quick response (QR) codes (**FIGURE I.1**). These seemingly random patterns are actually shortcuts, designed to whisk you to an app in the App Store or to a particular website.

To make use of these codes, download a free QR code–scanning app to your iPhone or iPad. There are plenty to pick from, but my favorite is called Scan (**FIGURE I.2**). It's absurdly easy to use and requires almost no effort on your part. Just launch it, point your camera at a code, and the app will bring you to the encoded link.

SCAN

| iPad | iPhone |

- QR Code City
- free
- hhhlinks.com/ scan

FIGURE I.2 Scan is my QR code–scanning app of choice.

Ever-Changing Apps

The best developers are constantly updating and enhancing their apps. Each new version brings change, sometimes subtle, sometimes substantial. For example, an app that was once iPhone-only may now be available on the iPad. An app that used to be rock-solid may now crash like crazy (or vice versa). An app that originally sold for $3.99 may now be free, or it may be yanked from the App Store completely.

Although I've done my best to ensure accuracy in this book, apps are a moving target. Make sure to confirm an app's price, compatibility, and available features before making a purchase. I'd also suggest you take a moment to read a few of the most recent App Store reviews of any app you're considering. That's often the best way to determine an app's *current* performance.

Where's Android?

You might be wondering why I chose to limit the scope of this book to iOS devices only. After all, Android is a wildly popular, widely available smartphone operating system.

Even though the Android platform is rapidly expanding, it has yet to be adopted by the filmmaking community at large. Although there are a few decent filmmaking tools available to Android users, it's like comparing a Whitman's Sampler to Willy Wonka's Factory.

As industrious developers extend their reach, I'm sure we'll see some nifty production tools make their way to Android. Until then, I strongly recommend sticking with iOS devices—the iPhone and the iPad.

Contacting Me

Care to share your thoughts? Find a malfunctioning link? Feel like saying hi?

The easiest way to contact me is through the Hand Held Hollywood website at http://handheldhollywood.com/contact. Please understand that my work schedule keeps me extremely busy. So although I may not have time to write you back, I do read every e-mail I receive.

You can also find me in the Twitterverse at twitter.com/hhhollywood.

If you really feel like stalking me, stop by TazGoldstein.com.

Enough jibber-jabber. Let's make movies!

Hand Held Hollywood
handheldhollywood.com/contact

PART ONE
DEVELOPMENT
AND
PRE-PRODUCTION

CHAPTER 1

STOP PLAYING "ANGRY BIRDS" AND WRITE THAT SCRIPT!

I firmly believe that writing a screenplay is the most difficult aspect of filmmaking. It's the only job in the process that requires the creation of something from nothing. Everything begins with *your* words, and the life they contain. You're a screenwriter! You're a god! Behold your mighty omnipotence!

Now quit tossing birds at pigs, and let's get crackin'.

Countless books have been written on the subject of screenwriting. I have 12 sitting on the shelf behind me (and I've even read a couple of 'em). There's no way to boil down every aspect of screenwriting into the pages of a single chapter. So, instead, I'll do my best to introduce some of the more important concepts.

As I mentioned in the introduction, the iPhone and iPad are largely interchangeable, but some tasks are naturally better suited to large or small screens. In this chapter, the device of choice is the iPad. I find that brainstorming and screenwriting are more enjoyable and productive experiences when using a larger display. The iPad's bigger canvas allows me to view things in context, such as graphs of connected concepts or pages of scripted conversation.

That said, you *can* perform many of the same tasks on your iPhone (or iPod touch)—you'll just be squinting a bit more.

MAPPING YOUR MIND

iTHOUGHTSHD

iPad | iPhone

- CMS
- $9.99
- hhhlinks.com/ hqfe

iTHOUGHTS

iPad | iPhone

- CMS
- $7.99
- hhhlinks.com/ vzam

Every film begins with an idea. I suppose some begin with an explosion, but those films are often short on ideas.

But what exactly is *an idea*? Is it the earth-shattering what-if scenario that hit you during a business lunch? Is it the little-known historical event you've always wanted to document? Is it a dirty joke or bit of dialogue that made you giggle during class? Or is it the face of the young protagonist that connects them all?

Answer: Yes.

They are all *the idea*—or portions of it. Often, when we begin to think about our next film, we think of it in fragments—tiny bits of possibility. I don't know anyone who pops out of bed and says, "Hey, I just thought of an entire, properly formatted, well-structured screenplay!" Rather, it usually takes the form of a swirling, disorganized mess. But it is a *beautiful* mess, full of potential. It just needs to be sorted out.

The process of collecting and connecting all of your idea fragments is often called *mind mapping*, and it's the first step toward writing your masterpiece.

iThoughtsHD

Since its release in 2010, iThoughtsHD has become one of the most popular mind mapping apps available for iOS devices, and with good reason. It's stable, powerful, flexible, and easy to use, and it receives constant updates.

Before we create our first mind map, let me explain the basic concept.

Think of a mind map like a tree. Everything starts with a single *seed* (a keyword or idea), which quickly grows and begins to produce many *branches* (related words or ideas). Soon, those branches grow new branches of their own (ideas that relate to the related ideas). This continues until you have a complex, hierarchical network of branches stretching outward. This is an oversimplification, but it's accurate enough to get the ball rolling. In iThoughtsHD, each branch is called a *topic*.

Let's take a look at how you might use this app when brainstorming. It can be a little tricky at first, so I'm going to walk you through it. We'll create a new map and add some characters.

1. Launch the app and create a new map by tapping the + button in the upper-left corner.

2. When prompted, give it a name. I'll call mine "My New Movie." Why? Because I'm insanely clever.

   Tap Save to continue to your new map.

3. The first topic is automatically named the same as your map (**FIGURE 1.1**).

   That will work just fine, but if you want to change it, just double-tap it, edit the text, and then tap the empty canvas once to dismiss the on-screen keyboard.

FIGURE 1.1 The first project's first topic, with a totally awesome name

4. Tap the Child Topic button to create a new topic connected to the first.

   This is one of the many ways to add new branches to your tree.

5. Type the name **Beth**, and then tap the spacebar three times.

   Three spaces are a shortcut to adding a new child topic, and as you can see, a new, blank child topic was added to the right of the Beth topic.

6. Type **Bitter from divorce**, and then tap Return three times (**FIGURE 1.2**).

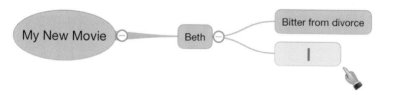

FIGURE 1.2 Sibling topics share the same parent topic. However, they never get along and always fight in the back seat of the car.

   Three returns are a shortcut to adding a sibling topic (one that branches out from the same source). As you can see, there is now a new topic under Bitter from divorce.

7. Type **From Texas**, and then tap the empty canvas anywhere to dismiss the on-screen keyboard.

8. Tap your original topic once to select it again.

9. Tap the Child Topic button on the toolbar, and enter the name **Eric**; then tap Return three times, and enter the name **Devon**.

As your map grows, you'll spot things that should be grouped. For instance, your map now has three character names (**FIGURE 1.3**). Let's clean things up a little.

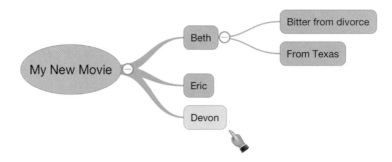

10. Tap your starting topic to select it.

11. Double-tap the empty canvas anywhere to automatically create a child topic. As you can see, there are many ways to create topics.

12. Type **Characters**, and then tap the empty canvas once to dismiss the keyboard.

13. Tap and hold on Beth for a moment, and then drag it over the *right-most side* of the Characters topic until a small, black, right-facing arrow appears. Then release.

    You've just made the Beth topic a child topic of the Characters topic. All of Beth's child topics went along for the ride.

14. Do the same with Eric and Devon.

You now have a well-organized Characters topic, ready to receive more characters, each with their own characteristics (**FIGURE 1.4**).

This example should give you an idea of how flexible this method is. You can create topics for dialogue snippets, locations, visuals, scenes, and whatever else you want.

FIGURE 1.4 You can use parent-child topic relationships to keep things very organized.

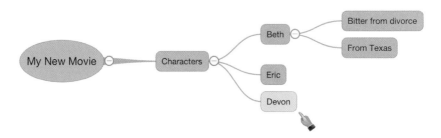

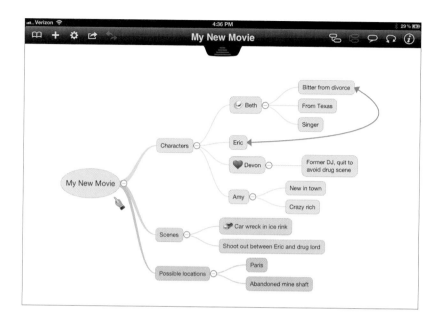

FIGURE 1.5 iThoughtsHD allows you to color topics, add icons, draw arrows between related topics, and do much more.

iThoughtsHD has an embarrassingly long list of features that include the ability to color code topics, add icons and images, draw connecting lines between related topics, and do much more (**FIGURE 1.5**). The app can export to and import from a long list of other applications, file formats, and cloud storage services. iThoughtsHD is also available for the iPhone as a separate app called iThoughts (without the "HD").

MindNode

MindNode is another outstanding mind mapping app that's definitely worth checking out.

The interface is a bit different from iThoughts, but the concepts are the same. For starters, what iThoughtsHD calls topics, MindNode calls *nodes*. You start with a central node and then construct branches of nodes, subnodes, sub-subnodes, super-subnodes, and super-sub-sub-monster-truck-nodes. That's not the official terminology, but it's catchy, right?

MindNode sports fewer features than iThoughtsHD, but sometimes, simple is better! The learning curve is shorter, and having fewer options translates into fewer distractions (**FIGURE 1.6**).

It's not like MindNode is feature-free. In fact, it has the ability to show you your map as a text outline. That's a killer feature because sometimes things just make more sense when viewed as a list.

MINDNODE

| iPad | iPhone |

- IdeasOnCanvas GmbH
- $9.99
- hhhlinks.com/ monf

FIGURE 1.6 Our project mind map as seen in MindNode.

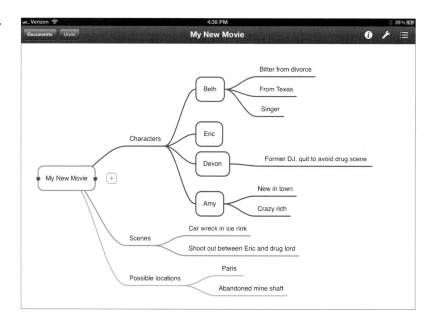

CORKULOUS PRO

iPad | iPhone

- Appigo
- $4.99
- hhhlinks.com/ jzjl

CORKULOUS

iPad | iPhone

- Appigo
- free
- hhhlinks.com/ lg4n

If you have a Mac, check out the *free* desktop version of MindNode in the Mac App Store. The App Store also has a paid premium version with more advanced features, but either version will allow you to share files with your iOS device. Very handy!

Another benefit of MindNode is that it's a universal app—buy it for your iPad and get the iPhone version at no additional cost. And, no additional cost really is the best kind of cost, isn't it?

Corkulous Pro

Corkulous Pro takes a decidedly different approach to collecting thoughts.

Rather than constructing complex, branching maps of related ideas, Corkulous Pro invites you to haphazardly chuck everything up on a digital corkboard…and I do mean everything.

You can pin up virtual note cards, sticky notes, labels, contact cards, photos, tasks with check boxes, and even another entire corkboard (resulting in nested corkboards).

With Corkulous Pro, organization becomes less regulated. You could, for example, include photos of an actress to augment the character description you jotted on a note or make a checklist of characters to ensure you've spent time thinking about each one.

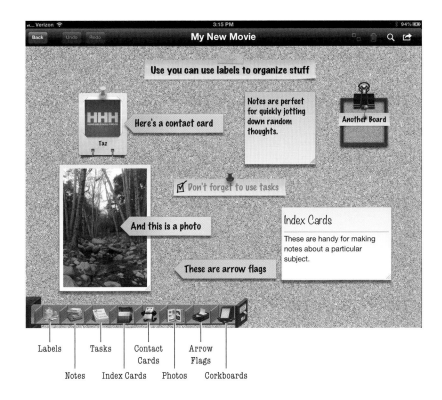

FIGURE 1.7 Corkulous Pro features a variety of items you can add to your corkboard.

Adding new items to your corkboard is obscenely simple. In the bottom left of the interface, there's a pop-out drawer containing all the different types of items you can add (**FIGURE 1.7**). Just tap the item you want, and drag it to your board.

Boards can be pinched, zoomed, scrolled, and searched. If you want to move a single item, just tap and hold it for a moment, and then drag it wherever you'd like. To drag multiple items, tap and hold on the cork background, and then drag out a marquee selection box to highlight the desired items. With the items now selected, you can tap and drag any of them to move the whole group. It's a very slick experience and becomes second nature almost instantly.

My favorite feature in Corkulous Pro is the ability to save boards as templates. That means you can create a board that's well suited to the way *you* like to brainstorm and then save it as a starting point for all your future projects.

Corkulous Pro syncs with iCloud, letting you access the same boards across all of your compatible iOS devices. So, you could build the bulk of your board on your iPad and then add to it via your iPhone (**FIGURE 1.8**), whenever and wherever new thoughts occur!

FIGURE 1.8 Corkulous syncs your files using iCloud, so you can update your corkboards from any iOS device. Here's the same board on an iPhone.

When you're done, you can export your board as an image or as a PDF. You can also export your boards to Dropbox, allowing you to share them with other Corkulous Pro users.

While the app lacks the sophisticated organization of mind mapping, Corkulous instantly feels familiar and therefore intuitive and inviting. That could make all the difference to someone turned off by node-based mind mapping.

In a later section, I'll be discussing the use of virtual note cards to help structure your script. Even though Corkulous Pro may look like the apps I cover later, they work in very different ways and are not entirely interchangeable.

If you'd like to check out the app before handing over your hard-earned $5, you can download a free, heavily crippled version of Corkulous Pro called simply Corkulous. It works well enough for you to determine whether you like the interface, but you'll be limited to one corkboard surface. The free version also prevents importing, exporting, and syncing across multiple devices.

Evernote

Not everyone likes the idea of sorting and organizing their thoughts. Some people simply want to collect them. For example, brilliant screenwriter Ronald Bass once told me that while he's thinking about a new script, he'll always keep a yellow pad handy to jot down everything that pops into his mind—a word, a visual, a scene, a name, anything. He wastes nothing. Then, when it comes time to write his script, he's already built a vault full of valuable inspiration.

Evernote will help you build *your* vault.

EVERNOTE

iPad   iPhone

- Evernote
- free, or $45/ year for bigger upload capacity, more sharing options, and additional benefits
- hhhlinks.com/ am0g

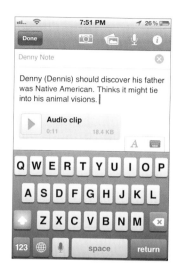

FIGURE 1.9 Creating a note in Evernote

Evernote is a cloud-based, ever-present notebook that syncs between your mobile iOS devices, your desktop computers, and the Web. It allows you to quickly and easily take notes, import photos, and record voice memos (**FIGURE 1.9**). Your entries can then be tagged, sorted into virtual notebooks, searched, and shared with others.

Because all your notes are stored on Evernote's servers, your work will be safe, even if your iPhone falls into the toilet. Yes, I've dropped mine in the toilet.

Using Evernote to collect your thoughts is like writing ideas on small scraps of paper that are thrown into a huge bucket. You've saved everything, and you can search through it, but unless you take the time to tag each item, there really isn't much organization involved.

It should be considered a distant cousin to mind mapping, but in the long run, it does achieve many of the same goals.

Ultimately, the tools you pick are less important than the time you take. Relax, let your creativity flow, empty your brain, and then move on.

STRUCTURING YOUR STORY

Did you successfully pour the contents of your fractured psyche into your iPad or iPhone? Good! Ready to write your screenplay?

Not so fast, Eszterhas!

At this point, there's a chance you grasp the fundamentals of your story. You might have casual relationships with your characters. Maybe you even know how it all ends. But, that's not enough. All you've done thus far is gather the clay. Now it's time to mold it.

The more intimate your familiarity with your story and its characters, the more likely you are to make informed, believable, and emotionally resonant decisions. Fortunately, there are several outstanding story structure apps available. Each works its magic by gently guiding you toward a deeper understanding of your story and characters and by asking a truckload of questions.

The questions, and related writing exercises, differ between apps because each is based on a different structuring method. Whichever method you adopt is a matter of personal preference. I love them all, which isn't at all helpful.

Syd Field Script Launcher

Be careful when walking past the screenwriting section at your local bookstore. You may accidentally trip over the huge stack of books written by Syd Field.

Syd is one of the most respected screenwriting teachers of our age. If you're an aspiring writer, then you've probably already heard his name and maybe even read his seminal tome, *Screenplay*. If not, go get it (http://hhhlinks.com/7ay6).

With Script Launcher, Syd takes you, step-by-step, through his story development process. He breaks everything into easily manageable chunks and provides guidance (both written and audio) along the way (**FIGURE 1.10**).

Once he helps you firm up your subject, he tells you how to properly segment your story into its beginning, middle, and end, otherwise known as the *three-act structure*. This may sound easy, but I can't tell you how often I've worked with writers who seem to have no idea where their acts begin and end.

Moving forward, Syd explains how to create believable, multidimensional characters. To illustrate his points, Syd references several Academy Award–winning films throughout the app.

In the end, Syd explains how to construct a four-page screenplay treatment.

Keep in mind that his app does *not* do the work for you! Instead, it holds your hand, points the way, and tells you everything is going to be all right.

Save the Cat!

Meow hear this! Blake Snyder's Save the Cat! app is an extension of, and companion to, his wildly popular book *Save the Cat! The Last Book on Screenwriting You'll Ever Need* (http://hhhlinks.com/mmn9).

SYD FIELD SCRIPT LAUNCHER

iPad   iPhone

- Syd Field
- $7.99
- hhhlinks.com/ly79

Screenplay (book)
hhhlinks.com/7ay6

Save the Cat! (book)
hhhlinks.com/mmn9

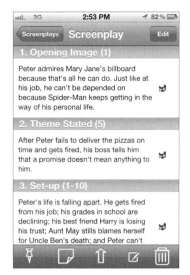

FIGURE 1.10 Syd Field's Script Launcher. First read, then listen, and finally write.

FIGURE 1.11 Save the Cat! uses the same structuring method Blake Snyder teaches in his books.

In his book, Blake teaches his own system for structuring screenplays. His app takes things one step further by providing an interactive template that keeps writers organized, while making sure they adhere to the system. Everything is divided into separate, properly ordered text fields, all based on the rules in Snyder's book.

You begin a new project by entering its name, *logline* (a one- to three-sentence summary of your story), and desired page count. After that, you can pick one of ten genres (descriptions are provided) and begin working on the "beat sheet." I was thinking about inserting a "Beat Sheet 2: Electric Boogaloo" joke here, but I couldn't come up with anything. The Blake Snyder Beat Sheet has 15 stages, and according to his teachings, most stories pass through all 15 of them (**FIGURE 1.11**).

Like other story development apps, Save the Cat! is meant to be used, put away, thought about, and then used again. Give each stage good thought, and don't rush the process.

Once your beat sheet is in good shape, you move into The Board, where you create 40 scenes, one at a time, by tapping the + button in the lower left of the toolbar and entering each scene's relevant information (description, emotional change, conflict, and so on). Once again, these fields require deep thought. But hey, that's the writer's job. Not the app's.

SAVE THE CAT!

iPad   **iPhone**

- Blake Snyder Enterprises
- $19.99
- hhhlinks.com/ivqy

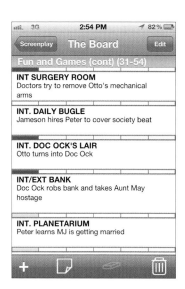

FIGURE 1.12 Track your story's structure on The Board.

You can assign each scene up to six colored tags, each of which has its own meaning. When you're done tagging, you can visually track your story and characters just by following the colors (**FIGURE 1.12**). Scenes can be reordered, deleted, or tucked away into a temporary storage area known as the *litter box*—perhaps not the best visual.

You'll find helpful guidance spread throughout the interface, but the app's true power is revealed only when it's used as an extension to the invaluable concepts taught in Snyder's books.

In some ways, using the app is like filling out a form. But here, every open text box demands thoughtful consideration. Each field poses an important question. Answering the questions doesn't guarantee a great script...but ignoring them nearly ensures a bad one.

The app has a few downsides. It's available only for iPhone (strange, since the app revolves around entering text), it hasn't been updated in more than two years, and its ability to sync with the desktop version of Save the Cat! has had more than its share of technical issues.

So, while the app may be showing its age, I still feel it's a valuable tool for new and existing fans of Snyder's system.

Contour

Contour is another fill-in-the-blanks story development tool, but it follows a different structural path, borrowing a bit from Joseph Campbell's book *The Hero with a Thousand Faces*.

CONTOUR

iPad   iPhone

- Mariner Software
- $14.99
- hhhlinks.com/qy61

Like Save the Cat!, Contour's primary purpose is to give shape to your story and to fill it with well-developed characters whose motivations and reactions have been thoroughly vetted.

After launching the app, creating a new project, and entering some basic information (title, author, genre, and so on), you are brought to the main menu. From here you continue the process by answering The 4 Questions:

> Who is your main character?

> What are they trying to accomplish?

> Who is trying to stop them?

> What happens if they fail?

Don't worry, Contour explains each of the questions in detail and provides plenty of screenplay samples for reference (**FIGURE 1.13**).

Deeper into the app, you are exposed to Contour's central theory: that over the course of your screenplay, your main character will transition between four different archetypes (the Orphan, the Wanderer, the Warrior, and the Martyr). Each has its own distinct characteristics, and Contour makes sure you understand the differences.

You'll be answering questions about each phase of your character's transformation, filling in fields relating to your film's formula and central question, and adding plenty of plot points to flesh out the story (**FIGURE 1.14**).

When you're done, Contour can generate a number of extremely helpful reports, exactly the sort of thing you'll need when you start writing your screenplay.

Like Save the Cat! and Script Launcher, Contour doesn't do the work for you. It simply guides you. The process can be challenging, but if you don't ask yourself

FIGURE 1.13 Contour comes with example structures for nearly 20 well-known movies.

FIGURE 1.14 Contour can teach you the basics, but you'll be the one doing the writing.

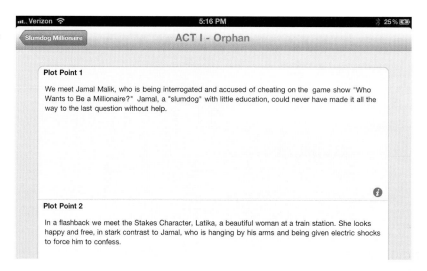

> .ııl.. Verizon 🤖   5:16 PM   🔋 25% 🔋
>
> ◀ Slumdog Millionaire   **ACT I - Orphan**
>
> ---
>
> **Plot Point 1**
>
> We meet Jamal Malik, who is being interrogated and accused of cheating on the game show "Who Wants to Be a Millionaire?" Jamal, a "slumdog" with little education, could never have made it all the way to the last question without help.
>
> ❶
>
> ---
>
> **Plot Point 2**
>
> In a flashback we meet the Stakes Character, Latika, a beautiful woman at a train station. She looks happy and free, in stark contrast to Jamal, who is hanging by his arms and being given electric shocks to force him to confess.

the tough questions, you're destined to author *Bio-Dome 2.* On a side note, if you're actually writing *Bio-Dome 2*, I apologize for my earlier comment. Please write a kick-ass *Bio-Dome 2*, giving it all the love, respect, and attention it deserves.

Index Card

- DenVog, LLC
- $4.99
- hhhlinks.com/9dsz

For years, professional writers have been using index cards to define story structure. Here's how they do it.

Start with a stack of index cards and a large corkboard. On each card, briefly describe a single story point, which might be a scene or a grouped sequence of smaller scenes that share a single story point. The cards are then pinned to the corkboard in the order they'll appear in the film and are split into groups based on the act they belong in (I, II, or III).

Screenwriters will stare at their corkboards for hours, shifting cards from act to act, tossing cards in the trash, scribbling new ones, and changing their order, over and over, until their best structure emerges.

Index Card for iPad lets you re-create that technique digitally!

After creating and naming your new corkboard, you can add a card by tapping the + button in the toolbar. This brings up the card editor. Here, you can add a title and a scene synopsis (**FIGURE 1.15**). Keep each card's synopsis short and sweet, since you'll be looking at up to 16 cards at once. Add just enough info to remind you of the scene.

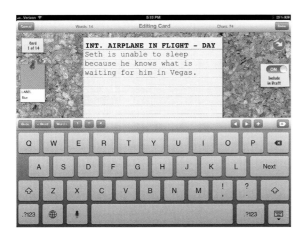

FIGURE 1.15 Card detail view in Index Card

From this screen, you can also change your card's color. Professionals use different colored cards to track individual characters and subplots. By glancing at the colors on the board, they can tell whether characters and subplots are being properly tracked (without having to read each card's synopsis).

Index Card also lets you write on the backs of your cards. This is perfect for keeping extra notes and reminders about each scene.

As I mentioned, each card has a title. This can be something descriptive, like "Susan goes lizard shopping wearing a hat made of meat" or a slug line, like "INT. LIZARD SHOP - DAY." Each has its advantages. Descriptive titles are easier to read and can carry greater meaning. However, slug lines can save you a pile of work when it comes time to writing the script. I'll get into that in a moment.

You keep creating cards in this manner until your entire story (or as much as you have of it) has been added to the board (**FIGURE 1.16**). Remember that each card represents a single story point (also called a *plot point*). Most feature films have between 40 and 60 story points, so you should have about 40 to 60 cards on your board.

With a fully loaded corkboard and a few hours to kill, it's time to start playing!

Cards can be dragged and dropped anywhere on the board, and the rest of the cards will automatically shift to get out of the way. Your goal here is to put your cards in an order that maximizes tension, heightens emotional impact, and maintains believability. No pressure.

The bottom line here is, don't be afraid to try different things! If you decide you need another card, just create it. Naturally, you can edit and delete any existing card. Every scene should push your story forward. If a scene changes nothing, it's pointless and should be ditched.

FIGURE 1.16 You can view up to 16 cards (and stacks) at once. Swipe up or down to see more.

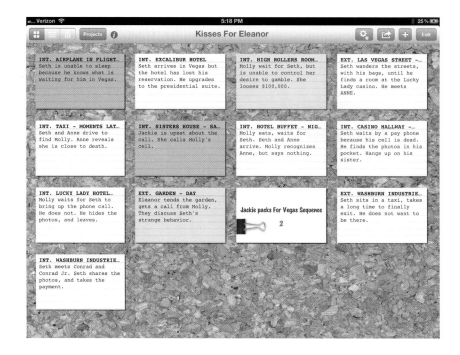

Cards can also be grouped into *stacks*, which is useful for organizing cards by act number. As a bonus, when you switch into Column View, the contents of each card stack are shown side by side, as vertically scrolling lists (**FIGURE 1.17**). This makes it easy to move cards from one act to another and to re-order cards within acts.

Remember I mentioned there was an added benefit to using slug lines for your card titles? Once you've finished with your board, you can export all the data for use inside the desktop version of Final Draft, in which each card title becomes a slug line. Instant blueprint!

In truth, the process isn't quite as seamless as it should be. You begin by exporting your corkboard as an RTF file. Open that file in Microsoft Word (assuming you have it on your computer), and copy the document's contents to the clipboard. Create a new document in Word, and paste in the text from the clipboard. Save that new document as an RTF file, and finally import that into Final Draft. There may be an easier way to do this, but I haven't found it yet.

As I write this, Index Card is an iPad-only app. An iPhone version is in the works, and I'm certain it will be available by the time you read this.

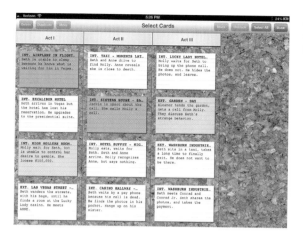

FIGURE 1.17 Stacks of cards can be viewed as scrolling columns.

If you're looking for an alternative corkboard app, check out Index Card Board for iPad. It's not as established, or filmmaker-friendly, but it does sport a slick interface that lets users pinch and zoom the corkboard and flip cards over with a double-tap.

StorySkeleton

Until recently, it was very difficult to find a good index card app for the iPhone. A few came close, but they were more about recipe storage than screenplay construction. Thankfully, that changed a few months ago with the release of StorySkeleton.

Because of the small size of the iPhone's screen, viewing a virtual corkboard filled with cards is somewhat impractical. StorySkeleton knows this and embraces an entirely different metaphor. Rather than pinning cards up on a corkboard, imagine holding a deck of index cards in your hand and then thumbing through them one at a time. That's StorySkeleton.

This approach suffers from not being able to see all your scene cards in context, but the app makes up for it by packaging clever features behind an intuitive interface.

When creating a project, StorySkeleton generates a new deck with a title card and a blank index card. You can move between the cards simply by swiping back and forth. The top of each card shows a running card count and displays two pieces of important information: the card type and the plot point. Tapping the top of a card brings up two editable lists of data—one listing card types, the other listing plot points. Tapping a list item quickly inserts it into the card type or plot point field. For example, with just a few taps, you can quickly set a card

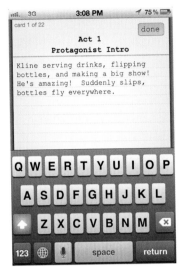

FIGURE 1.18 In StorySkeleton, each card can represent a scene.

FIGURE 1.19 Cards can be viewed as a scrolling list. While you're here, you can also add, delete, and reorder cards.

type to Act I and a plot point to Protagonist Intro. You can also use the pop-up menu to change your card's color.

The contents of each card can be edited simply by tapping and typing in the content area (FIGURE 1.18). New cards are added by pressing the green plus button on the bottom toolbar. Moving cards around is equally easy. Just swipe to the card you want to move, tap the blue arrows on the toolbar, and then swipe to any other card in the deck and tap Drop Card. The original card is dropped at that point in the deck.

As I mentioned, you can't view all the cards at once, but you can view them as a scrolling list (FIGURE 1.19). You can also rearrange cards in list view.

When you're done, you can export your deck to multiple formats, including RTF, text, Scrivener, and Final Draft. Scrivener is an awesome writing application for Mac and Windows that's loaded with research and organizational tools (it's the app I'm using to write this book), and Final Draft is considered to be the industry's standard screenplay application. Being able to export into these two formats is a tremendous time-saver.

Even though this app is designed for defining story structure, I could easily see using this app to prepare for pitch meetings—like story structure flash cards. Plus, anything with Skeleton in its name is automatically kinda cool.

Baby Names +

There's one more app I want to put on your radar. It won't help create realistic characters, but it will help you name them.

When I get bored of naming my characters Bob and Mary, my scripts quickly fill with names like Chip Landmass, Viva LeTruckstop, and Blunter "Golden Fists" Lightswallow III. Granted, while these are clearly brilliant names, drenched in dignity and depth, they may not be right for every project.

For years, I've turned to my trusty, pastel-colored baby name book. I can always flip a few pages and find something unique and evocative. I've been using the same book for the past ten years, and it shows. The cover is torn, too many pages are earmarked, and the binding is in shreds.

I finally decided to trash my book when I found Baby Names +. It includes enormous lists of names, organized by gender and country of origin. It lets you search for names by a bunch of different criteria, including name meanings.

My favorite feature in the app lets users view the top 100 names from any year between 1880 and 2009. If you're writing a period piece that takes place in 1948 and your female protagonist is 23 years old, just move the app's date slider back to 1925 to view the most popular names from when the character was born (FIGURE 1.20).

You can easily tag and recall your favorite names and even e-mail them as a list to your writing partner, who will undoubtedly make fun of you for using a baby naming app.

BABY NAMES +

iPad · iPhone

- Schatzisoft
- $1.99
- hhhlinks.com/ pjvq

FIGURE 1.20 Move the slider in Baby Names + to view popular names from any year.

WRITING YOUR SCREENPLAY

Your story makes perfect sense! You know your characters well enough to dress them for holidays! It's time to write your screenplay!

As you may know, screenplays must be written in a *very* specific format. They are always authored using the Courier font (or a nearly identical variant) and always adhere to a predefined set of indents and margins. If you diverge from industry standards, I guarantee professionals will not take your script seriously. When I first came to Los Angeles, I chose to submit a script formatted in Helvetica. I can still hear the faint echoes of executive laughter. Do yourself a favor: Stick to the standards.

Writing a script is hard enough without having to remember all the formatting rules, which is why writing on an iPad is such a pleasure. All of the following screenwriting apps take control of the formatting in one way or another. All you need to do is tap the right buttons.

Celtx Script

CELTX SCRIPT

| iPad | iPhone |

- Greyfirst Corp
- $4.99
- hhhlinks.com/ g8h6

If Final Draft is the stuffy elder statesman of the screenwriting software world, then Celtx is the coffee-sipping hipster. It's cool, it's slick, and it oozes attitude.

Celtx Script was first released for iOS in 2010, but the Celtx platform has been growing steadily over the past ten years. That may seem like a long time, but consider this—Final Draft was first developed way back in 1986. That's more than a quarter century ago!

As of today, Celtx has grown into a full-service company, offering tools for story development, storyboarding, script breakdowns, production scheduling, and more. It offers screenwriting applications for multiple platforms, including Mac, Windows, Linux, iOS, and Android, as well as a fully functioning web app.

But wait, there's more!

With a Celtx user account, authors can store their scripts in the cloud and access them from any of the Celtx screenwriting applications, on any compatible device. That means you can start you script on your Mac, continue it on the Web, and then finish it on your iPad—all without having to perform any sort of manual file transfers.

Now how much would you pay?!

Celtx is a favorite among new writers and students, likely because you can use several of its applications, including its web app and cloud storage services,

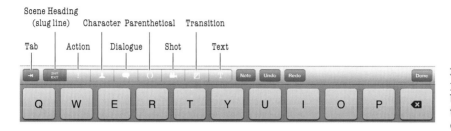

FIGURE 1.21 Celtx provides a handy button bar for easy access to various screenplay elements.

for free! What?! Yup. Free. Celtx offers paid services, but they're optional and largely unnecessary when getting started.

Now that you understand the Celtx Universe, let's focus on its iPad app, Celtx Script.

You begin by creating a new document and picking a template style from a pop-up menu. In addition to Screenplay, the app offers templates for Theatre, A/V, Comic, and Audioplay. We'll be sticking with Screenplay, 'cause that's how we roll.

As soon as the new document is opened, you're immediately immersed in what looks and feels like a word processor that's been fine-tuned to churn out screenplay pages.

Sitting above the on-screen keyboard is a thin toolbar packed with small buttons, each of which represents a different screenplay element (Scene Headings, Action, Character, and so on). Tapping any of these buttons will switch the currently selected paragraph (or empty line) to the corresponding element style. The toolbar also has a Tab button, as well as buttons for adding script notes, undoing, and redoing (**FIGURE 1.21**).

Typing your script is as easy as…um…typing!

For instance, if you're entering a new scene heading (slug line), you'd first tap the Scene Heading button on the toolbar and then begin typing. Celtx does its best to predict what type of script element you'll need next and switches automatically. For example, after you enter a Scene Heading, it assumes the next element will be Action, and after a Character element, it predicts the next will be Dialogue. This saves a lot of time. If Celtx predicts wrong, just tap the correct button on the toolbar.

As you continue writing, Celtx will display lists of context-aware shortcuts. For example, if you're writing a Scene Heading, the app will display shortcuts for **INT** and **EXT**. Tapping a shortcut will insert it into your script, saving you time. And, after you've entered a character name once, it will offer that name as a pop-up shortcut if it sees you starting to type it again (**FIGURE 1.22**).

FIGURE 1.22 Celtx Script remembers character names you've added and automatically suggests them when it senses that you're typing them again.

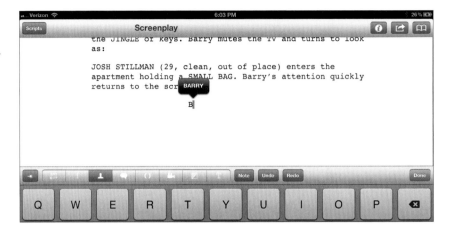

Want more features? How about color-coded script notes? Resizing the page from 50 percent to 400 percent with standard iOS pinch and zoom gestures? Wireless printing with AirPrint? You're never satisfied, are you?

When you're done with your script, you can save it on your iPad and/or sync it with the Celtx servers if you have a user account. Scripts can also be exported as text and PDF files.

If you decide to use Celtx with an external keyboard (which I'll be covering later in this chapter), the on-screen keyboard disappears, and the app's button bar drops to the bottom of the screen. You can also use your external keyboard's Tab key to cycle through element styles.

Celtx is a universal app and provides the best iPhone screenwriting experience I've seen so far. Oh, and in case you were wondering, Celtx stands for Crew, Equipment, Location, Talent, and XML. I got that from Wikipedia, so I'm about 10 percent sure it's 100 percent accurate. Maybe 5 percent.

STORYIST

- Storyist Software
- $9.99
- hhhlinks.com/ r51f

Storyist

Easily one of my favorite apps in all of Applandia, Storyist provides a rich screenwriting toolset that truly deserves its own book.

Note to self: Write a book about Storyist.

Storyist is unique in that it offers features not normally found in a stand-alone screenwriting application. For starters, every project is given its own folder in which you can store multiple screenplay files, story sheets (more on that in a moment), and any other related documents (notes, research, and so on). You can even create nested folders for greater organization.

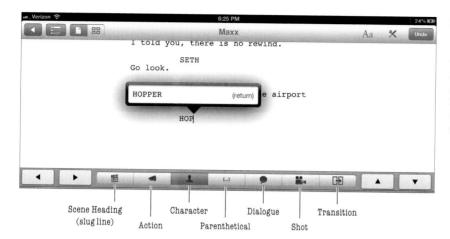

Scene Heading (slug line)   Action   Character   Parenthetical   Dialogue   Shot   Transition

FIGURE 1.23 The Storyist button bar provides quick access to screenplay elements, as well as a full set of arrow keys. Like Celtx, it also offers quick entry of previously used character names.

Storyist has a built-in system for creating *story sheets*. These are premade document templates that help you keep detailed notes about individual characters, plot points, settings, scenes, and sections. Creating a new story sheet is like photocopying a blank form that can be filled out and saved with the rest of the documents in your project folder. For example, a Character story sheet has fields for a character's name, summary, and physical description, as well as a general notes area. If your memory is as bad as mine, you're going to love story sheets.

As you can see, there are a lot of structuring functions in Storyist. In fact, I could have included it in the "Structuring Your Story" section just as easily as this one.

Let's look at Storyist's screenplay functions. The app works very similarly to Celtx, in that it presents a toolbar of element buttons above the on-screen keyboard. You can use the toolbar buttons to switch between element styles as you type. The Storyist toolbar also has buttons for up, down, left and right—very handy when you're not using an external keyboard (**FIGURE 1.23**).

Like Celtx, shortcut lists of slug lines and character names will pop up throughout the process, saving you boatloads of time.

You can insert story notes, pinch and zoom the page (but not below 100 percent), and switch to an index card view that offers some of the same functions as Index Card, the app I mentioned in the previous section (**FIGURE 1.24**).

Every part of this app feels polished. The interface is smooth as silk and clean as a whistle, which brings up an important point. Whistles are not at all clean. They're breeding grounds for germs and bacteria—like little containers of biological evil. Storyist isn't like that. It's actually very clean.

FIGURE 1.24 Storyist features its own index card system, useful for quickly restructuring your screenplay.

Storyist can print wirelessly via AirPrint, easily sync with Dropbox, and exchange files with Storyist for Mac. You can also import from, and export to, the Final Draft format (in addition to text).

Like Celtx, if you use Storyist with an external keyboard, the button bar drops to the bottom of the screen, freeing up valuable screen space.

The bottom line is this: If I could have only one screenwriting app on my iPad, Storyist would be it. While Celtx offers a slightly better screenwriting experience, Storyist's inclusion of research, development, and organizational tools makes it a winner.

More Options

Celtx and Storyist are swell apps, but they're not the only games in town. There are plenty of other interesting and worthy alternatives. Here's a quick look at a few.

Scripts Pro

SCRIPTS PRO

iPad   iPhone

- Inkless Ideas, LLC
- $7.99
- hhhlinks.com/ ezxi

Scripts Pro sets itself apart from the others by *not* providing a toolbar filled with script element buttons. Instead, this app gives you one extra button: a Tab key (FIGURE 1.25). The simplicity of the interface is the app's signature feature. That one key is used to shift between the various element styles of a screenplay.

The app's built-in character manager makes it easy(ish) to change a character's name throughout your script, and finished scripts can be exported in Final Draft

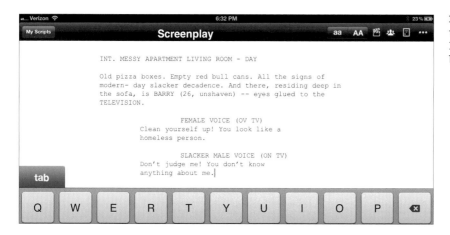

FIGURE 1.25 ScriptsPro uses only a single Tab key instead of a full button bar. Nice and tidy.

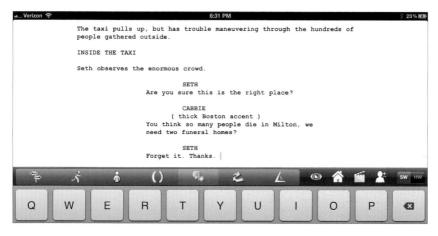

FIGURE 1.26 The ScriptWrite interface uses a button bar similar to Celtx and Storyist.

and Celtx formats. As I write this, Scripts Pro is undergoing a major interface overhaul, but I believe its signature Tab key and clean interface will remain intact.

If you dislike the idea of a button bar eating part of the screen or if you're just a fan of simplicity, check out this app.

ScriptWrite

ScriptWrite puts a row of element buttons above the keyboard and sports a handy list view, in which scenes can be easily reordered (FIGURE 1.26). Other features include an editable character list, multiple import methods, and Final Draft export.

The iPhone version is nicely designed but may have issues with newer versions of iOS.

SCRIPT-WRITE

| iPad | iPhone |

- Filter Apps, LLC
- $3.99
- hhhlinks.com/tld8

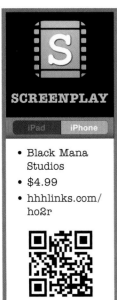

SCREENPLAY

iPad | **iPhone**

- Black Mana Studios
- $4.99
- hhhlinks.com/ ho2r

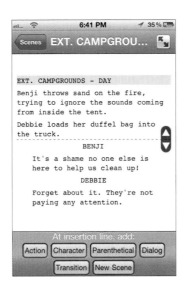

FIGURE 1.27 Screenplay was the very first screenwriting app for iOS.

SCREENPLAY FOR iPAD

iPad | iPhone

- Black Mana Studios
- $8.99
- hhhlinks.com/ 8zvo

Screenplay

I tip my hat to the makers of Screenplay, not because their app is the best but because it was the first. They helped set the iOS stage, not only for other screenwriting apps but for *all* filmmaking apps. I kept Screenplay on my iPhone, even when I wasn't using it, just to show it to all my filmmaking friends.

Perhaps because it was the first, Screenplay takes a different, more modular approach to screenwriting (**FIGURE 1.27**). Elements are added to the script, one at a time, via a series of screens and menus. It's a time-consuming process that feels a bit dated by today's standards. That said, different writers have different tastes. So, if you have different tastes, check out Screenplay (and Screenplay for iPad).

I also want to point out that this app was one of the first to appear on HandHeldHollywood.com years ago. For that reason, I re-tip my hat.

Where's Final Draft?

Good question!

Final Draft is the industry-standard desktop screenwriting application. It has a large and loyal worldwide following. We've been hearing rumblings about an iOS version since 2010. So, where the heck is it?

Well, I'm happy to report it's coming soon. *Very* soon. So soon, in fact, that it might already be here. As I write this, Final Draft has been beta testing its app called, appropriately enough, Final Draft Writer. So, there's a decent chance it will be released by the time you read this. Or this.

Go check it out! Then, come back here and fill in the space below with a comprehensive review of its features and interface. I'll wait.

Thank you.

Fountain

Even with all the impressive script-authoring apps currently available, I can't help but get excited about a new development in screenwriting called Fountain.

Unleashed only months ago, Fountain enables screenwriters to compose their scripts in *any* text-authoring app they'd like, not just screenwriting-specific programs. A quick search in the App Store revealed well over 100 text-editing apps. That's a *lot* of options! To truly understand what Fountain is, you need to know a little about its history.

In 2004, John Gruber introduced Markdown. Part markup syntax, part conversion utility, Markdown was designed to make authoring web pages cleaner, easier, and faster. Instead of having to write long strings of cryptic code, a web author could now write her pages in plain English, within any text application, and include formatting preferences with Markdown's simple syntax, such as beginning a sentence with a number sign (#) to indicate that it should be displayed as a heading or putting a word between two asterisks (**) to have it displayed in italics. When she was finished, she could use the Markdown conversion utility to translate her basic text into the complex HTML code required for proper display in web browsers.

Put simply, Markdown lets users write in English and wind up with HTML. It's a simple idea that changed the face of web authoring. Fountain was developed to do the same for screenwriting.

Just recently, a group of very talented minds (including one of my filmmaking heroes, Stu Maschwitz) came together to define a comprehensive, easy-to-implement screenwriting syntax based on the standards that already exist (most of which you already know or can learn *very* quickly).

With this new syntax, you can write your script as plain text in any iOS text editor, not having to worry about indents, margins, and other formatting particulars. The rule of thumb is, make it look like a screenplay, and Fountain will take care of the rest. When you're finished writing, simply feed your text through a Fountain converter, and presto! You've got a properly formatted script!

Here's a sample of the basic syntax:

> ❯ Start all scene headings (slug lines) with **INT**, **EXT**, or something similar.

> ❯ Write action as you normally would.

> ❯ Keep character names in UPPERCASE when indicating dialogue.

> ❯ Dialogue always follows character names.

> ❯ Dialogue parentheticals should be placed inside parentheses.

Here's a short scene written using the Fountain syntax:

Int. Office Building – Day

Richard is anxiously pacing behind his desk, which is littered with documents. Douglas sits in the corner, his head in his hands. Erica enters.

BOB
Do we know anything yet?

ERICA
No. I'm sure they want to discuss everything with their investors before they make any decisions.
(to Douglas)
Relax. This is not the time to lose it.

Looks like a scene, right? That's the idea!

Here's what the scene will look like when it's been converted:

INT. OFFICE BUILDING - DAY

Richard is anxiously pacing behind his desk, which is littered with blueprints. Douglas sits in the corner, his head in his hands. Erica enters.

                    BOB
          What do we know?

                    ERICA
          Nothing yet. I'm sure they want to
          discuss the merger with their investors
          before making any decisions.
               (to Douglas)
          Relax. This is not the time to lose it.

Naturally, the Fountain syntax includes all the elements you know and love (transitions, dual dialogue, line breaks, centered text, and so on), and you can find a complete list on the Fountain website (http://hhhlinks.com/660w).

Every text editor has a slightly different feature set. And, since Fountain-friendly scripts can be written in any text editor, you'll need to pick the one that best suits your particular needs. Tech guru Brett Terpstra (who also contributed to Fountain) has compiled a comprehensive, interactive list of the best iOS text editors. This should help make the choice much easier. See http://hhhlinks. com/dpsz.

Text documents are app- and platform-independent. This means you can start your project in one text editor and then continue it in a different one. I bounce between iOS text editors all the time, but my current favorite is Writing Kit (**FIGURE 1.28**). Not only does this gem of an app feature a slick interface, powerful researching tools, and a slew of import, export, and sync options, but it also has a Fountain preview mode!

Fountain
hhhlinks.com/660w

Best iOS text editors
hhhlinks.com/dpsz

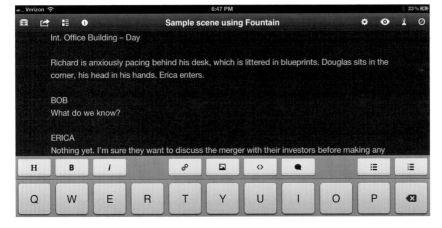

FIGURE 1.28 Writing Kit's clean interface packs a lot of power.

At any point, you can tap a single button and instantly view your text in proper screenplay format (**FIGURE 1.29**). That feature alone is worth the price of admission.

Are there any downsides to Fountain? You bet, Negative Nancy! When writing in a text editor, you don't get the conveniences that come with a dedicated screenwriting app, like pop-up access to slug-line elements (**INT**, **NIGHT**, and so on) or autofilling character names. There are also problems with **MORE**s and **CONTINUED**s, but I suspect these issues are temporary.

WRITING KIT

iPad   iPhone

- Quang Anh Do
- $4.99
- hhhlinks.com/ inip

FIGURE 1.29 Preview your Fountain documents in proper screenplay format.

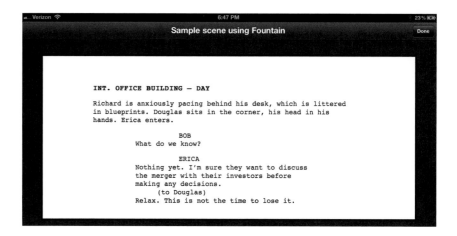

Screenplain
hhhlinks.com/nita

Highland
hhhlinks.com/p16s

Storyist for Mac
hhhlinks.com/22om

Fountain
hhhlinks.com/660w

Once you have your finished script, you need to convert it to proper screenplay format. Fountain is still in its infancy, but a number of conversion methods are already available.

> **Screenplain** is a free website that will convert Fountain documents to Final Draft FDX files, as well as properly formatted HTML files (in case you want to post your script online). See http://hhhlinks.com/nita.

> **Highland** is an application for the Mac platform that can convert between Fountain, Final Draft, and PDF files. As of this writing, the app is still in beta, but I suspect it will be available by the time you read this, and I believe it will be worth the wait. See http://hhhlinks.com/p16s.

> **Storyist for Mac** ($59) is a comprehensive writing tool that features the ability to import and export Fountain documents. Note that this is the Mac version of Storyist, not the iOS version I discussed earlier. See http://hhhlinks.com/22om.

Once again, I direct your attention to the Fountain website for an up-to-date list of conversion utilities and related applications: http://hhhlinks.com/660w.

USING EXTERNAL KEYBOARDS

No matter which applications you incorporate into your creative writing work-flow, you'll always be faced with one potential hurdle—the iOS on-screen keyboard.

While several of the apps I've mentioned improve upon the default on-screen keyboard by adding versatile function keys, they can't do much to improve the overall experience. I've been tapping away on my iPhone's virtual keyboard since the day it was released. The same is true of my iPad's keyboard. Even after all these years, I still feel like a ham-handed brute when I'm punching in a simple text message or trying to search Google for images of dogs in ugly sweaters.

Fortunately for me and my fat-fingered brethren, there are alternate ways to enter text into an iPad or iPhone, the most popular of which is through the use of an external keyboard.

Bluetooth Keyboards

All iPhones and iPads come standard with Bluetooth, a short-range wireless protocol used for connecting nearby compatible devices. You're probably already aware of the most common Bluetooth gear. In fact, you may even be wearing a Bluetooth headset over your ear right now. If you are, take it off. You look ridiculous, and your shouting annoys me while I'm waiting in line for my iced café mocha.

Using Bluetooth, you can easily connect your mobile iOS device to an external keyboard wirelessly and enjoy entering text via actual keys. Not only does this improve the writing experience for anyone accustomed to typing on a computer, but it also frees up around 40 percent of the screen space that was previously devoted to the virtual keyboard.

Bluetooth keyboards come in a wide variety of sizes, shapes, colors, and configurations. Amazingly enough, most new keyboards should work with your Apple devices, since they're all based on the same wireless standard. That said, not all keyboards are created equal. In fact, some are created downright crappy. I strongly advise you to take the time to test every keyboard on your retailer's shelf before making a purchase.

Most Bluetooth keyboards offer the same set of standard alphanumeric characters. However, there are now several keyboards on the market that have been designed specifically for iPads and iPhones and contain iOS function keys capable of triggering iOS events. Those keys typically include Home, Search, Select All, Cut, Copy, Paste, Show Keyboard, Rewind, Play/Pause, Fast Forward, Mute, Volume Up, Volume Down, Picture Frame Mode, and Lock/Unlock. Not all iOS keyboards contain all of these functions.

My favorite Bluetooth keyboard is Apple's own Wireless Keyboard ($69) (**FIGURE 1.30**). It's the same keyboard that comes standard with all new iMac computers. So, if you already have a recent iMac on your desk, you may be in luck! As you might expect, this keyboard lacks iOS-specific keys since it was designed for use with Mac computers. While I miss those extra functions, I

APPLE WIRELESS KEYBOARD

| iPad | iPhone |

- Apple
- $69.00
- http://apple.com

FIGURE 1.30 The Apple Wireless Keyboard. Small but powerful... like Yoda, only smaller and less powerful.

still prefer the feel of this keyboard. It's all about personal taste when picking the perfect option. After all, writing a script can keep you at your keyboard for months. Do you *really* think a Hello Kitty keyboard is the best idea?

Like most other Bluetooth keyboards, you can share the Apple Wireless Keyboard between your iMac and your mobile device, but it will maintain a connection with only one of them at a time. You'll have to manually change your Bluetooth settings every time you switch from your desktop to your tablet, and vice versa. Not fun, and I recommend against it.

Pairing a Bluetooth Keyboard

Once you've picked out the perfect keyboard, it's time to introduce it to your iOS device. This one-time process is called *pairing*, and Apple has made it very simple. The required steps are the same for iPads and iPhones.

1. Make sure your wireless keyboard is on and in a *discoverable* state.

    Most wireless keyboards default to this state when first turned on, but you might have to dip into the keyboard's user guide to be sure.

2. Open the Settings app on your iPhone or iPad.

3. Tap General and then Bluetooth.

4. If Bluetooth is off, turn it on.

5. After a moment, your keyboard will show up under Devices. When it does, tap its name (**FIGURE 1.31**).

FIGURE 1.31 Preparing to "pair" in the iPad's Bluetooth settings panel

6. You'll be prompted to enter a series of numbers on the keyboard, followed by the Return or Enter key. Enter the numbers as instructed.

7. After a moment, the words *not paired* will be replaced by *connected.*

Congratulations, you've been paired. From now on, you'll be able to use your external keyboard to enter text, and the iOS virtual on-screen keyboard will not appear. If your keyboard moves out of range, it will no longer work, and you will once again see the iOS virtual keyboard. As soon as the keyboard comes back in range, it will become active again.

Bluetooth Keyboard Cases

If you dread the idea of lugging around an external keyboard every time you head to Starbucks with your iPad, consider getting yourself a Bluetooth keyboard case. This new breed of case protects your investment and also keeps a thin, light external keyboard available at all times. When opened, these cases reveal their concealed keyboards and position your iPad at an angle for easy viewing.

Naturally, these cases are a bit thicker than others, but not by much. On the bright side, these cases are made specifically for iPads; therefore, their keyboards almost always include the iOS-specific function keys I mentioned earlier.

There are boatloads of keyboard cases on the market, with more arriving every day. They all have pros and cons, and once again, it's up to you to shop around to find what works best for you and your writing habits.

Let's take a look at a few highlights to get you started.

Targus Versavu Keyboard for the iPad 3

The Targus Versavu has the unique ability to swivel your iPad from landscape to portrait orientation (**FIGURE 1.32**).

FIGURE 1.32 The Targus Versavu lets you rotate your iPad into portrait orientation.

TARGUS VERSAVU KEYBOARD FOR THE iPAD 3

iPad   iPhone

- Targus
- $99.00
- http:// targus.com

I prefer to write in portrait, since it allows me to see more of the page. Sadly, most keyboard cases don't accommodate portrait orientation. You're stuck with landscape. On the upside, landscape orientation lets you view your text at a slightly larger size—an important distinction for those with impaired eyesight.

While the Versavu does offer portrait orientation, it does so at the expense of the iPad's viewing angle. The case forces the iPad into a nearly upright position that I find difficult to look at while typing.

The keys feel solid but cramped. Because of the dark character imprints on the physical keys, they are difficult to see in dark environments.

ZAGG Folio for iPad 2

The ZAGG Folio is a hard shell case that defaults to a landscape orientation (**FIGURE 1.33**); however, the keyboard can be removed and repositioned to allow for use in portrait orientation.

The hard shell provides extra protection. The keys are nicely spaced and easy to read (even in darker settings). I do wish it had an iOS Select All function key and a better designed latch. Otherwise, I like this case quite a bit.

- ZAGG
- $99.00
- http://zagg.com

FIGURE 1.33 The ZAGG Folio's keyboard can be removed.

Belkin YourType Keyboard Folio for iPad 2 and 3

The YourType Keyboard Folio is a true transformer. After exposing the keyboard, you can adjust the case to multiple viewing angles (**FIGURE 1.34**). When you're done writing and ready to start watching YouTube videos, the keyboard flips up and hides under the screen, out of sight and out of the way.

It's a neat trick and helpful when you want to hold the tablet in your hand without accidentally tapping keys.

Here's another bonus. The keyboard sports two extra buttons I haven't seen on any other iOS keyboards: a select forward button and a select backward

- Belkin
- $99.00
- http://Belkin.com

FIGURE 1.34 The Belkin YourType Keyboard Folio can hide its keyboard when not in use.

button. These clever additions allow users to expand or reduce their text selections one character at a time.

On the downside, the case functions only in landscape orientation, has dark imprints on the keys (harder to see in low light), and is a bit bulkier than the others because of the extra flap that hides the keyboard.

Kensington KeyFolio Bluetooth Keyboard Case for iPad 1 and 2

Like the Belkin, the Kensington KeyFolio is designed for landscape use only (**FIGURE 1.35**). So, what makes this case unique? Horrible keys. Really bad. It's like typing on Jell-O cubes that have been dipped in Vaseline. Truly mushtacular. Then again, everything is subjective. You may love this keyboard!…if you like mush and mushy things.

Amazingly, this case features the nicest exterior of all the cases I tested for this book. It *feels* high quality. It *feels* rich and smooth. It *feels* like it should have a less mushtastic keyboard. Just sayin'.

KENSINGTON KEYFOLIO BLUETOOTH KEYBOARD CASE FOR iPAD 1 AND 2

iPad   iPhone

- Kensington
- $99.00
- http://kensington.com

FIGURE 1.35 The Kensington KeyFolio Bluetooth Keyboard Case has way too long a name.

LOGITECH ULTRATHIN KEYBOARD COVER

iPad   iPhone

- Logitech
- $99.00
- http://logitech.com

Logitech Ultrathin Keyboard Cover

As I write this, the Logitech Ultrathin Keyboard Cover is not yet available, but the prerelease images look sexy as hell (**FIGURE 1.36**). And someone once told me "sexy" sells books. Not sure if this is what they meant.

The case works very much like Apple's own Smart Covers, in that it protects your tablet by snapping into place with the help of the iPad's internal magnets. When you're ready to do some typing, simply pull the cover off the front of your iPad, place it on a flat surface, and then position your iPad in the cover's narrow ridge. This allows your iPad to be used in both landscape and portrait modes.

By the time you read this, I will own one. Period.

FIGURE 1.36 The Logitech Ultrathin Keyboard Cover snaps onto your iPad like an Apple Smart Cover.

Apple Keyboard Dock
hhhlinks.com/egfq

Apple Keyboard Dock

While not technically a keyboard case, the Apple Keyboard Dock is worth mentioning for readers who are still rockin' the original iPad. Essentially, the Keyboard Dock is a keyboard stuck on an iPad dock.

The dock didn't sell especially well, and the awkward shape made it somewhat impractical. Apple dropped the item, but it can still be found on eBay for around $30.

Here, let me help you find one: http://hhhlinks.com/egfq.

What About Wired Keyboards?

Funny you should ask. There was a time, not too long ago, when you could easily connect a USB keyboard to your iPad.

Back in April 2010, Apple started shipping its Camera Connection Kit for iPad— a set of two adapters intended to facilitate the transfer of photos and videos from external cameras to iPads. One of the two adapters adds a USB port to your iPad.

What Apple failed to realize is that when otherwise sensible people see an open USB port on an iPad, they'll stick things in it! And that's exactly what happened.

Early adopters found that not only did USB cameras connect effectively, so did USB keyboards, audio headsets, and microphones! Sadly, while updating iOS, Apple retooled its power management system, sending less power out to external devices. That change removed compatibility with external USB keyboards… sort of.

Today, if you were to attach Apple's full-size wired keyboard to your iPad, the screen would display an error indicating that there wasn't enough power to drive the device. This is likely because Apple's keyboard contains a mini USB hub and extra USB ports that require additional power.

If you were to plug in a wired keyboard that had no such additional USB ports and didn't require the added power, your iPad would simply indicate that it is unable to use the connected USB device…and then it would work anyway! That's right, it still works. However, that error keeps popping up over and over again, requiring you to dismiss it each time, and that's no way to work.

While preparing this chapter, I took a trip to my local Fry's Electronics (a major electronics chain) and tried every wired keyboard they had on display—and they had a lot. Before getting chased out of the store, I wanted to be sure there wasn't at least one keyboard that worked perfectly, without triggering the error. No luck. Stick with a Bluetooth keyboard or the iOS on-screen keyboard.

SPEAKING YOUR SCRIPT

If external keyboards aren't your thing, how do you feel about speaking?

There have been some stunning advancements in voice recognition over the past few years. It's become freakishly easy to speak to your iOS device and have it instantly transcribe your words into text.

With a little practice, voice dictation can be a terrific addition to your writing workflow, but don't expect it to completely replace your keyboard or touchscreen. For now, that's simply not possible. All of the screenwriting apps I mentioned require some degree of interaction while formatting text.

Naturally, dictation works best in quiet environments. So, if you're working on your screenplay at Starbucks and you're sitting near the register, you might wind up with a few "Mocha Coconut Frappuccinos" scattered throughout your script.

iOS Dictation

With the introduction of the iPhone 4S, Apple sprang intuitive speech recognition on the world in the form of an intelligent personal assistant named Siri. Simply ask Siri to perform a basic function, such as composing an email or a text message, and she will happily obey—no typing necessary (**FIGURE 1.37**).

FIGURE 1.37 Siri won't write your screenplay no matter how nicely you ask.

Along with Siri, Apple added a simple speech-to-text transcription button right next to the spacebar on the iOS virtual keyboard. Several months later, when Apple released the iPad 3, it included that same handy feature. This means that anyone with an iPhone 4S (or newer) or an iPad 3 (or newer) can use their voice to enter data into nearly any iOS app.

Here's how you might use voice transcription while writing a script in Celtx:

1. Move your cursor to the point at which you want to enter some text, preferably a blank line.

2. Tap the icon for the script element you'd like to create (Slugline, Action, Character, Dialogue, and so on).

   In this example, I'll create an Action element.

3. Tap the voice transcription button to the left of the spacebar, and wait for your iPad to beep.

4. Speak the following as written:

   Tom sits under a single swinging light bulb period his hands move at breakneck speed comma frantically cleaning the gun sitting on the makeshift table in front of him period

5. Tap the voice transcription button again.

Your iOS device will begin the transcription process, and a moment later, the text will appear in your script (**FIGURE 1.38**).

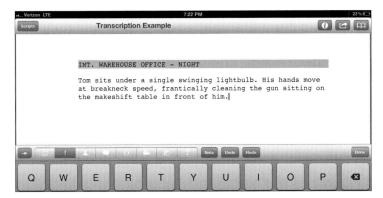

FIGURE 1.38 The transcribed text in screenplay form

By repeating this process, you can use dictation to significantly speed up your writing.

There's one thing worth noting. Speech transcription in iOS and third-party apps is dependent on an Internet connection. After you speak, most of the actual transcription work is done on networked servers. If you don't have Internet service, you won't be able to use voice dictation.

Dragon Dictation App

If you aren't lucky enough to have an iPad or iPhone with built-in dictation, you can still use the free Dragon Dictation app to transcribe your speech (**FIGURE 1.39**).

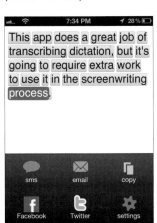

FIGURE 1.39 Dragon Dictation on the iPhone is an impressive transcription app but impractical for most screenwriters.

DRAGON DICTATION

iPad   iPhone

- Nuance Communications
- free
- hhhlinks.com/ 3tgp

Sadly, going this route isn't nearly as seamless. Since Dragon Dictation is a separate app and not built into iOS, the process requires a few extra steps. You'd have to switch from your screenwriting app to Dragon Dictation, record your voice there, copy the resulting transcription, switch back to your screenwriting app, and then paste in the text.

It's not fun, but it is possible.

Dictabulus

Here's a fun one! Dictabulus lets you use your iPhone 4S or iPhone 5 to dictate a screenplay (or anything else) directly into a Mac computer on the same wireless network.

Dictabulus
hhhlinks.com/m51f

To pull off this bit of magic, you'll need to run a tiny helper app on your Mac. It's available as a free download from the developer's website (http://hhhlinks. com/m51f). Once the helper app is installed, it will guide you through a quick, one-time setup to establish the connection between your iPhone and Mac.

The Dictabulus interface is absurdly simple. Once the on-screen keyboard appears, tap the voice transcription button, and speak. Moments later, the transcribed text will appear on your iPhone (**FIGURE 1.40**) and then in your Mac's frontmost application as if you typed it there yourself (**FIGURE 1.41**)!

FIGURE 1.40 The Dictabulus interface or, as I like to call it, a keyboard and some text.

DICTABULUS

iPad | iPhone

- Spielhaus
- $1.99
- hhhlinks.com/
  zzvs

FIGURE 1.41 Use Dictabulus on your iPhone to dictate straight into Final Draft on your Mac.

The workflow is the same as the one I described in the "iOS Dictation" section, with the only difference being that the screenwriting software is on your Mac, rather than your iPad.

As an added bonus, you can also use this form of remote dictation to scare the crap out of your friends and co-workers. That's worth the two bucks right there.

CHAPTER 2

DON'T JUST SIT THERE— READ A SCRIPT AND SIT THERE

Before we all hop on the reading-app tour bus, I think it's worth pointing out that many of the screenwriting apps I cover in Chapter 1 can also be used to read screenplays (assuming you have scripts in a compatible format, such as FDX or Celtx). However, screenwriting apps are far less likely to provide features that enhance the *reading* experience. And make no mistake, reading a script *is* an experience, or at least it should be.

When you're at the local Cineplex, reclining in front of a massive projection, a truly great film can envelop you completely. The moment you lose sight of the screen's edges, are no longer bothered by the obnoxious exit signs and floor lighting, and forget about the sticky substance keeping your feet in place, you know the movie has succeeded in turning a 24-frame-per-second stream of flickering images into *an experience*.

There are plenty of reasons for filmmakers to read scripts. We read to find our next passion project, to give notes to the writers, to learn our lines, and to find inspiration and become better writers ourselves. Some even read for pure pleasure.

Lucky for you, the App Store is bubbling over with powerful apps, packed with features that *can* and *will* enhance your reading experience.

READING SCREENPLAYS

Reading screenplays on an iPad is *wicked-pissah-awesome* (to quote my Boston-dwelling former self). Clearly, the biggest selling point is that the tablet can hold hundreds (if not thousands) of scripts, while weighing just slightly more than one printed one. But, convenience isn't the only factor to consider. Hollywood has been printing and photocopying hundreds of thousands of scripts, 120 pages at a time, since before you were born. That's a lot of trees, my friend. Wouldn't it be swell if we could harness the marvels of modern technology while simultaneously saving a forest?

Read a script. Save the world. Not bad!

Final Draft Reader

FINAL DRAFT READER

| iPad | iPhone |

- Final Draft
- free
- hhhlinks.com/ f6ur

Known around the world for its industry-leading screenwriting software, the Final Draft company surprised everyone by first entering the iOS App Store with a script *reader*, rather than a writer. While this move disappointed some filmmakers who had been patiently waiting for Final Draft to come to the iOS platform (I'm looking at you, me), the fact remains, Final Draft Reader is an impressive script-reading application that should be judged on its own merits.

As you probably guessed, Final Draft Reader plays nice only with screenplays saved in the Final Draft FDX format (introduced in version 8 of its desktop software).

Scripts can be imported into Final Draft Reader using one of two methods.

If the script was e-mailed to you (or if you e-mailed it to yourself), you can bring it in directly from your iOS device's mail application. Here's how:

1. Open the e-mail that contains your FDX screenplay.
2. Tap and hold the FDX icon until Mail's Open In menu pops up.

3. If you see Open in "FD Reader" in the pop-up menu (**FIGURE 2.1**), tap it. Done!

   If you *don't* see Open in"FD Reader" in the menu, tap Open In... instead. Then, find FD Reader in the scrolling list, and tap it.

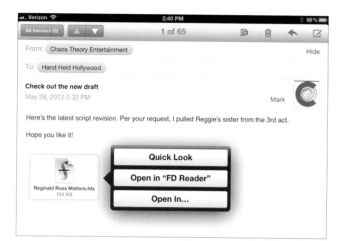

FIGURE 2.1 Tap and hold on the attachment to see additional viewing and importing options.

The second import method utilizes iTunes File Sharing and requires a little more effort. Naturally, to do this, you'll need iTunes running on a Mac or Windows machine.

Here's how it works:

1. Connect your device to your computer, and launch iTunes.

2. Click your device's name when it appears in iTunes under DEVICES.

   You'll be taken to a summary of your device's settings.

3. Next, click the Apps tab (found toward the top of the window), and scroll down to the bottom half of the page.

   Under File Sharing, you'll see a list containing all the apps currently installed on your device that can import and export files via iTunes File Sharing.

4. Scroll through the available apps, and click FD Reader.

   In the Documents box to the right of the Apps list, you should now see all the FDX files currently installed on your device and accessible from within Final Draft Reader (**FIGURE 2.2**).

5. To import an FDX file, just drag it into the Documents box. It will upload in seconds and be ready for reading.

FIGURE 2.2 The iTunes File Sharing interface

Exporting files is equally easy. Just drag the desired FDX file *out* of the Documents box and to any location on your computer.

Take the time to get comfortable with both of these import/export techniques because they'll be coming up a lot throughout the book.

Since Final Draft Reader is made by the same folks who make Final Draft for Mac and Windows, it's not surprising that the app does a brilliant job of accurately displaying script pages on your iOS device. What *is* surprising, however, is how much effort was put into making everything appear realistic. They even went so far as to virtualize the texture of photocopied paper and the obligatory three-hole-punch (**FIGURE 2.3**). When you read a script page in Final Draft Reader, it's like looking at a high-quality photo of an actual script page.

Navigating around the script is natural and intuitive. You can turn pages with a simple swipe, and a single tap calls up additional controls, including a search function and a handy page slider.

Character Highlighting allows users to quickly highlight all the dialogue from one or more characters, each in its own color. This is nifty for performers looking to memorize lines (although I discuss an app later in this chapter that I believe is better equipped to address actors' needs).

Final Draft Reader effortlessly displays tricky script elements such as dual-dialogue (side-by-side dialogue blocks used when two characters speak at the same time) and revision marks (asterisks placed to the far right of any line that has been edited) (**FIGURE 2.4**). It can even display script notes that were created using a desktop version of Final Draft.

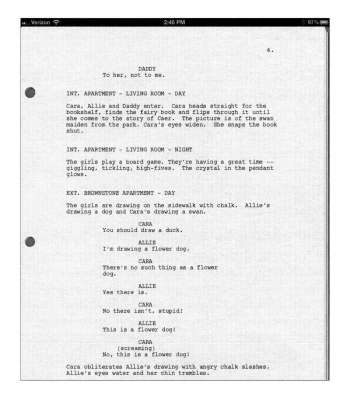

FIGURE 2.3 In Final Draft
Reader, script pages look like
script pages (without the coffee
and ketchup stains).

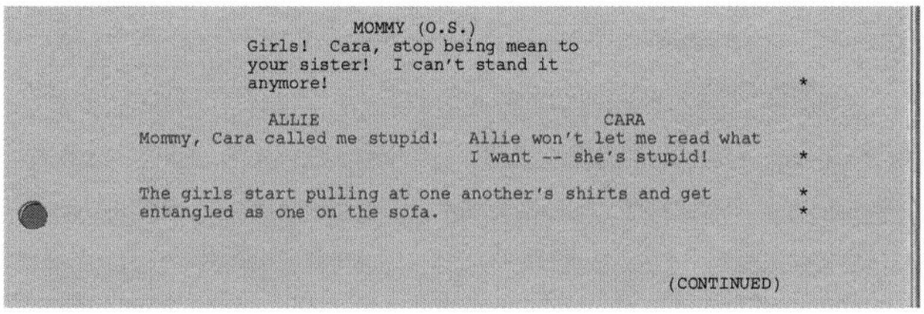

FIGURE 2.4 Final Draft
Reader can display colored
revision pages, dual-
dialogue, revision marks,
and more.

Once a script goes into production (now called a *shooting script*), it gets littered
with new elements such as scene numbers, "A" pages, and colored revision
pages. Once again, Final Draft Reader displays these elements with ease.

A moment ago, I pointed out that Final Draft Reader can display script notes.
What I didn't mention is that by tapping and holding anywhere in the script, you
can also *add* script notes and optionally categorize them as well. The new notes
are saved inside the FDX file and can be shared with others.

Yes, this technically means the app can annotate scripts. But I chose to keep it
in this section because I find Final Draft's script notes to be somewhat inconvenient. For instance, after entering a new script note, it becomes hidden behind

a teeny, tiny, itty, bitty icon [!] in the body of the script. When I'm in a meeting, rapidly flipping through script pages, I prefer to have all my notes fully visible, on the script page, at all times. I get deeper into annotation in the next section.

In the app's defense, it can export all your script notes in a well-organized report (which is pretty sweet) and upload your annotated script directly to a Dropbox account (which is semisweet).

If you find yourself reading boatloads of FDX files or if you need to accurately view shooting scripts or simply enjoy the look of the printed page, Final Draft Reader belongs on your iOS device.

FDX READER

| iPad | iPhone |

- Quote-Unquote Apps
- $7.99
- hhhlinks.com/ 90g7

FDX Reader

Like Final Draft Reader, FDX Reader will display only FDX scripts. Scripts can be imported via iTunes File Sharing or from an e-mail attachment or Dropbox account. Each screenplay listed in the app's document library also includes the date it was imported (vital when you have multiple revisions of the same script) and a percentage counter that displays how much of the script you've actually read (**FIGURE 2.5**). This is especially effective at making you feel horrendously guilty about not reading your friend's script yet.

While Final Draft Reader shoots for realism, FDX Reader puts its emphasis on improving the reading environment. The app feels heavily influenced by Apple's design standards and bears a strong resemblance to iBooks. The colors are warm, the text is clear, and the interface is elegant (**FIGURE 2.6**).

Aside from a button that returns you to the script library, the only other controls are for adjusting font size, and jumping to a desired page. On the iPad, pages are turned with a swipe. On the iPhone, your script appears as a single, continuous scroll. Both methods allow for easy navigation.

FDX Reader does have a few shortcomings. For instance, dual-dialogue isn't displayed properly, and shooting script elements are mostly ignored. Then again, if you're in production, you should probably be using Final Draft Reader instead.

FDX Reader was designed to provide a simple, elegant, and enjoyable way to read FDX files…and that's exactly what it does.

One bit of bad news: Shortly after Final Draft Reader was released, Quote-Unquote Apps, the developer of FDX Reader, announced that the app would not be receiving any more "major" updates. The app still works perfectly on my iPad and iPhone, but it's possible that could change in the future.

FIGURE 2.5 In FDX Reader, percentage indicators show how much you've read.

FIGURE 2.6 FDX Reader hates courier...and now, so do I.

iBooks

Until now, the apps I've been describing load only FDX files, but you're just as likely (if not more likely) to need a good PDF script reader, and the easiest way to read PDF files on your iPad or iPhone is with Apple's very own iBooks.

Let's start with the good news: iBooks is free! Want the bad news? Too bad. Here's some more good news instead. iBooks can read both text-based PDFs (very small files, typically exported directly from screenwriting software) and image-based PDFs (large files created when scanning an original paper screenplay).

You can import PDF scripts into iBooks from an e-mail attachment (using the technique I described in the earlier section "Final Draft Reader") or by first adding it to your computer's iTunes library and then syncing with your device. Surprisingly, you *cannot* import scripts via iTunes File Sharing (also described in the section "Final Draft Reader"). Maybe the Apple developers behind iTunes should walk down the hall to the Apple developers behind iBooks and have a little Apple chat.

Once imported into iBooks, your script will appear on the app's virtual bookshelf. Unfortunately, in this view, you won't see any of your screenplays' titles! This makes finding a specific screenplay next to impossible (FIGURE 2.7). Switching into list view will reveal your titles and prevent excessive swearing.

iBOOKS

| iPad | iPhone |

- Apple
- free
- hhhlinks.com/5dqs

If you're an iCloud user, your documents will sync across all your iOS devices, allowing you to start reading a script on your iPhone and pick up from the same place on your iPad. I'd call that slick and cool, or "slool" for short.

Most Apple products ooze minimalistic beauty, and iBooks is no different. Script pages look terrific in iBooks, especially on a Retina display (**FIGURE 2.8**).

FIGURE 2.7 No titles in iBook's thumbnail mode makes every script a mystery.

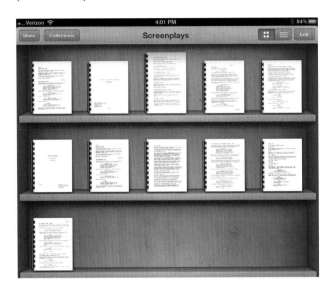

Return to Document Library   Thumbnail View

Print and E-mail

Change Screen Brightness

Search for Word Page Number

Add Bookmark

FIGURE 2.8 A script PDF file in iBooks on the iPad.

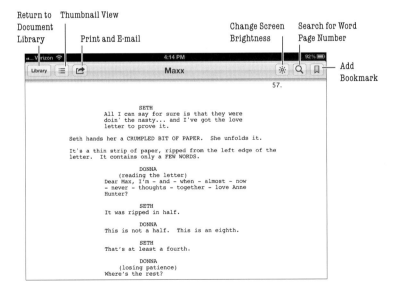

A single tap displays the app's toolbar and a row of tiny thumbnails along the bottom. Another tap sends those elements away, leaving only the script page behind.

You can fly through pages by gliding your finger across the page thumbnails and turn pages with a swipe. The toolbar's buttons allow you to return to your bookshelf, switch to thumbnail view, e-mail or print your script, change the brightness level, search for a word or phrase, and bookmark a page.

If you're looking for a high-quality, free PDF script reader, iBooks offers the perfect combination of power and simplicity.

ANNOTATING SCREENPLAYS

Since moving to Hollywood more than two decades ago, I've found three things to be completely impossible:

> Avoiding traffic

> Eating a truly excellent egg roll

> Entering a cafe in which no one is marking up a script

Let's focus on this last one for now.

Like most filmmakers, when I read scripts, I make notes…lots and lots of notes. I can't remember the last time I read a screenplay without a pen (real or virtual) in hand.

I'll write essential suggestions in the margins, circle favorite scenes, scratch out weak dialogue, doodle storyboards to remember potential shots, and write "HA!" next to anything that makes me laugh. These are all forms of annotation. When it's time to discuss the project, I'll grab my marked-up script and reference the notes. When I'm done, I'll toss it on the absurdly tall pile of annotated scripts already crammed into my closet.

There's nothing groundbreaking about my routine. It's not the *right* way. It's just *my* way. Even though every filmmaker may annotate for different reasons, using different techniques, most of us have one thing in common: a compelling need to scribble our thoughts all over those nice, clean script pages.

I've been doing it the same way for as long as I can remember. But even from day one, I knew there had to be a better way.

I'm not exaggerating when I tell you that I've been dreaming of reading and marking up scripts on a tablet-like device since I first started directing. I imagined a gizmo that held every screenplay I had ever read, along with every note I had ever scribbled. In an effort to create such a device, I burned through way too much cash, buying and selling used tablet computers, and despite my best efforts, the results always sucked—too heavy, too bulky, too short on battery life, too difficult to use.

When Steve Jobs announced the iPad in January 2010, I realized that I had finally found the script reader of my dreams. Even before the iPad was released, I purchased a document scanner so I could digitize every script sitting in my closet. Yes, I was that obsessed.

Today, I only read and annotate scripts in PDF using one or more of the apps listed in this section. I adore this workflow as much as I imagined I would. It's fast, it's simple, and I have all my notes with me at all times. What was my obsession is now second nature, and I'm *never* going back to paper. You're welcome, trees.

Want to be obsessed like me? Sure, you do! Here's how.

PDF EXPERT

| iPad | iPhone |

- Readdle
- $9.99
- hhhlinks.com/
  tOoe

**PDF EXPERT
FOR iPHONE**

| iPad | iPhone |

- Readdle
- $9.99
- hhhlinks.com/
  voju

PDF Expert

Despite its name, PDF Expert can load a variety of different file types, including Microsoft Office files, iWork documents, text files, images, and movies.

Having said that, I've never actually used PDF Expert for anything other than PDFs. Perhaps if the app were called OFFICE IWORK TEXT IMAGE MOVIE Expert, things would be different. But, until they rename it, I'll remain focused on its PDF functionality. Speaking of functionality, this thing has a lot of it! I'll do my best to summarize.

When you're ready to import your PDF screenplay, you'll be faced with far too many options. If you like sticking with the classics, you can import files via iTunes File Sharing or Mail's Open In command. If you're hankerin' for something new, fire up your computer's web browser (on the same wireless network as your iPad) and upload files using PDF Expert's built-in web server. If you're feeling a little disconnected, PDF Expert can connect you to a wide variety of online servers, including Dropbox, WebDav, Google Docs, FTP, SFTP, Readdle, SugarSync, Box, and more. It can even stay in sync with user-designated Dropbox folders.

Imported scripts can be sorted inside nested folders and displayed as a scrolling list or as a grid of thumbnails (**FIGURE 2.9**). You can select one or more to be moved, copied, deleted, e-mailed, and even zipped! Tapping a script opens it (**FIGURE 2.10**).

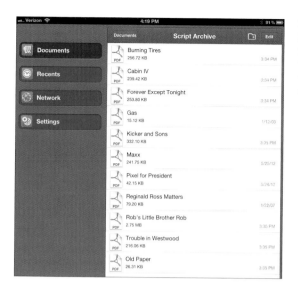

FIGURE 2.9 PDF Expert's list view might not be as pretty as its thumbnail view, but it can display more titles at once.

Return to Document Library

List of Recent Files

Thumbnail View

Toggle Annotation Toolbar

Search

Option and Export Menu

List of Bookmarks, Outlines, and Annotations

Add Bookmark

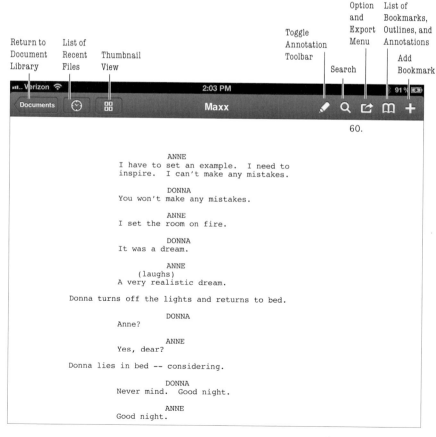

FIGURE 2.10 A script page viewed inside PDF Expert

FIGURE 2.11 Tapping the pencil on the toolbar reveals the dedicated annotation toolbar.

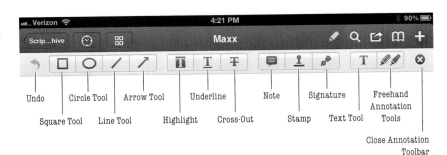

Navigation works as expected. Swiping turns the page, and tapping once reveals the toolbar on top and a page slider at the bottom. The toolbar provides buttons for searching the script's text, exporting to a variety of formats, bookmarking pages, and more.

By tapping the annotation button in the upper right , a second toolbar, loaded with annotation options, slides down. You'll find tools for creating basic shapes, lines, and arrows, as well as options for highlighting, underlining, and crossing out text. You can add pop-up notes, rubber stamps (images and pre-defined bits of text), and even a finger-drawn signature (**FIGURE 2.11**).

When you're ready to scribble, the app provides a palette of customizable pens and highlighters. If your handwriting is lousy, you can use the app's versatile text tool to type anywhere on the screen.

Jot Pro by Adonit
hhhlinks.com/jotp

While reading a script, let's say you want to add a quick handwritten note. Just tap the Pen tool of your choice (I like a thin tip with red or black ink), and then scribble away (**FIGURE 2.12**). If you're not used to writing with your finger, it can help to resize the page first. The usual pinch-to-zoom gestures work just fine. If you cringe at the idea of writing anything with your finger, get yourself a good quality stylus. I use the Jot Pro by Adonit (http://hhhlinks.com/jotp). I discuss styluses in Chapter 5.

Other types of annotations can be added just as easily. To cross out text, tap the Cross-out button and then swipe your finger across the words you want to affect. To add an arrow, tap the arrow button and start drawing. Your arrow will automatically appear as you drag your finger from a start point to an end point. There are plenty of other ways to add annotations, but I don't know enough adjectives to include them all.

When you close a script, all of your annotations are safely stored with it. If you feel like sharing your annotated script (sharing is caring), you can e-mail the original document, which keeps your annotations in an editable state, or a *flattened* copy of the document, which prevents your annotations from being

FIGURE 2.12 Add as
many annotations to
a page as you need.

altered. The app also gives you the option of exporting your script directly to any other PDF-compatible app on your iPad.

I've been focusing on PDF Expert for iPad simply because I prefer to read and annotate on a large screen. If you prefer your scripts shrunkafied, you can buy an equally impressive version of the app made specifically for the iPhone.

Since PDF files are (mostly) universal, you're not limited to using a single PDF reader. So, let's look at some more!

GoodReader

I'm going to keep my description of GoodReader quite short, not because it deserves less attention, but because if I described it in detail, it would seem like I copied almost everything I wrote about PDF Expert and pasted it here. (I'm not above doing that, but I'd rather not get in trouble on my first book.)

GOODREADER FOR iPAD

iPad | iPhone

- Good.iWare
- $4.99
- hhhlinks.com/
  1uw7

GOODREADER FOR iPHONE

iPad | iPhone

- Good.iWare
- $4.99
- hhhlinks.com/
  3cdz

GoodReader and PDF Expert have been duking it out, one-upping each other since the dawn of time (slight exaggeration). They both offer numerous import options, advanced annotation tools, and separate versions for iPad and iPhone. They each have one or two awesome features the other lacks, but when it comes time to make a purchase, it's going to come down to two things: price and ease of use.

Currently, GoodReader is half the price of PDF Expert. But, in my humble opinion, PDF Expert has a far more intuitive interface. I've been a fan of both of these apps for a long time, and I still recommend both to my filmmaker friends. Variety is the spice of life, right? Or is that paprika?

But wait! There's more!

PDFPen

For years, I've been a loyal user of PDFPen for Mac, so imagine my joy when it won Best of Show at the 2012 Macworld | iWorld Expo. If you can't imagine my joy, I'll reenact it for you now: "Hooray!"

Like its desktop counterpart, the iOS version of PDFPen hides serious power behind a friendly interface.

You can import scripts in the usual ways (iTunes File Sharing, Open In from an e-mail attachment), or you can use one of the app's additional network connections, including WebDav, Dropbox, Evernote, FTP, and Google Docs. That's not quite as many import options as PDF Expert, but I think it's more than most filmmakers will ever need. Unlike PDF Expert, PDFPen also allows you to *upload* your annotated script to any of the aforementioned networked servers. Take that, PDF Expert!

In addition, PDFPen effortlessly syncs with iCloud, so any documents you store on your iPad will immediately become available inside PDFPen on your Mac. Likewise, any desktop documents you save to iCloud will instantly appear in PDFPen on your iPad. In summary, iCloud = good.

After opening a script, you'll be met by a sparse toolbar that includes buttons for viewing pages as thumbnails, changing the app's settings, and, of course, adding annotations.

Tapping the toolbar's pencil icon ✎ presents six different types of annotation tools (a highlighter, a freeform pen, a custom shape creator, and tools for underlining, crossing out, and squiggle-underlining text) (**FIGURE 2.13**).

As with the other apps I mentioned, adding annotations in PDFPen is a breeze. Just tap a tool, and then draw on the screen. You can modify an existing

PDFPEN

iPad   iPhone

- SmileOnMyMac
- $14.99
- hhhlinks.com/c5vq

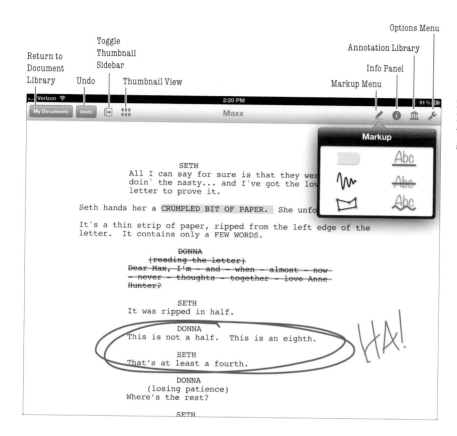

FIGURE 2.13 Don't let PDFPen's minimalistic toolbar fool you. There's gold in them there hills!

annotation by tapping it to select it and then tapping the Info button 🛈 on the toolbar. A drop-down menu offers various editable properties based on the type of annotation currently selected. For example, if you already used the Freeform Pen tool to circle some dialogue, you could now edit the properties under the Info button to alter your annotation's color, thickness, opacity, and line type (solid, dotted, dashed, and so on) (FIGURE 2.14).

In addition to the basic annotation tools, you'll find a plethora of predefined objects, arrows, and proofing characters under the Library button in the toolbar. These objects can be added to your script with a single tap. To save time, you can even store your own custom annotations in the app's library to be used again and again. I created a custom object from a photo of dog poo so I could vengefully stamp any scenes I vehemently hate. Why? Because I'm classy.

I've saved one of the coolest features for last. PDFPen allows users to modify existing text in text-based PDF documents. This means you can fix typos and make corrections without having to return to the original screenwriting software. Hooray! I can't tell you how many scripts I've sent out with horrifically embarrassing typos. Oh, wait, yes, I can. All of them.

FIGURE 2.14 The Info panel can help you modify existing annotations.

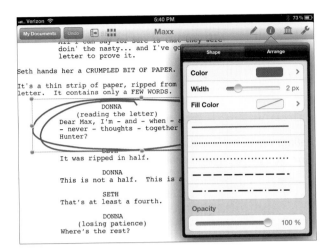

As I mentioned earlier, PDFPen allows you to export your scripts in a variety of ways, and if you don't feel like sharing, you can simply leave your scripts on your iPad, and iCloud, for safekeeping.

If you prefer your app burgers lean and tasty, PDFPen is sure to satisfy. And that, ladies and gentlemen, is the very worst metaphor contained in this book… so far.

GoodNotes

If the elegant simplicity of PDFPen simply isn't elegantly simple enough for you, allow me to introduce GoodNotes, a criminally simple iPad-only app for annotating your PDF scripts.

Files can be imported from e-mail attachments and via iTunes File Sharing, Dropbox, and Box. The app can also pull in images from your photo library and even use your iPad's camera to grab a quick snapshot. I have no idea why you'd want to do that while annotating a script. Boredom, perhaps?

Imported scripts appear atop glass shelves in GoodNote's virtual bookcase. Each script is represented by its thumbnail and title (Hear that, iBooks? Good-Notes displays *titles* in its bookcase view!). For a little extra organization, scripts can be further sorted into custom folders. If you're comfortable in iBooks, you'll have no problem finding your way around GoodNotes.

Once a script is open, you'll see two tiny buttons on the top of your screen. The options menu 🔲 in the upper left opens a scrolling list of page thumbnails, as well as additional buttons for navigating, editing, printing, and exporting your document.

The Pencil button 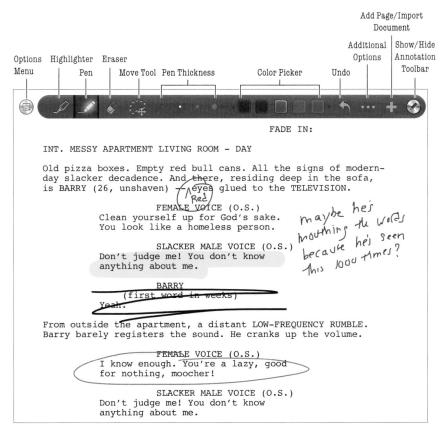 in the upper right reveals a palm guard, a zoom function, and all the annotation tools. And, by "all," I mean a highlighter, a pen, an eraser, and a tool to move existing annotations (**FIGURE 2.15**). You want more tools? Tough. You get four. If you long for a little extra control, you can pick your line thickness and color. That's it.

It's simplicity at its most simple, wrapped in simpleness.

When you're done annotating, you can share scripts via e-mail, iTunes File Sharing, Dropbox, and Box. You can also send your scripts directly to other PDF-compatible apps on your iPad.

GoodNotes will run you five bucks, making it the cheapest of all the PDF annotation tools I mentioned. If five bucks is still too much, you'll be happy to know there's a free version of GoodNotes patiently waiting for you in the App Store. It can hold only two scripts at a time, but that may be good enough for some of you…especially those of you without five bucks.

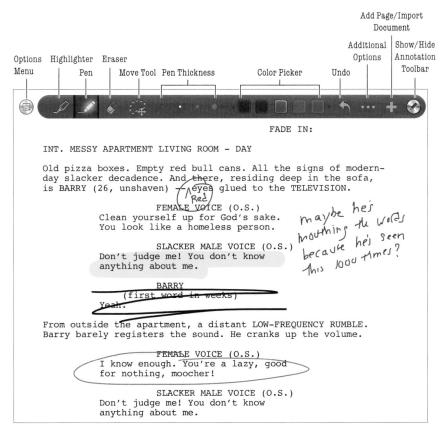

FIGURE 2.15
GoodNotes offers only four annotation tools, but they are smooth and responsive. I wish the other apps had pens this smooth.

ADOBE STORY

iPad **iPhone**

- Adobe
- free
- hhhlinks.com/ f21t

Adobe Story

Adobe Story isn't a script reader, although it can read scripts. And, it isn't an annotation tool, although you can use it to insert comments. So, what is it?

Adobe Story is an iPhone app that acts as an extension of Adobe's online screenwriting/scheduling/preproduction tool, also called Adobe Story, which won't make the rest of this description confusing at all.

The Adobe Story *web app* is a slick, online collaborative environment in which multiple users can simultaneously work on and review screenplays (**FIGURE 2.16**) and their related documents. All of the files are stored on Adobe's servers, so they're accessible from any computer.

The Adobe Story *iPhone app* lets users read and comment on any document they've created, or have permission to share (**FIGURE 2.17**). New comments are instantly available to other users who share the same file. Additionally, by having the Adobe Story app on your iPhone, you'll be alerted when other users have made changes to a shared document, or when new comments have been posted.

In truth, the Adobe Story *iPhone app* is a bit clunky and doesn't feel ready for prime time. However, it exhibits enormous potential, and that's why I chose to include it here.

FIGURE 2.16 Adobe Story running in Safari on a Mac. Very slick!

FIGURE 2.17 Adobe Story running on an iPhone. Not nearly as slick.

MEMORIZING SCREENPLAYS

Remember those people I mentioned earlier—the ones marking up scripts at the corner cafes? I forgot to mention the other people—the ones working behind the counter, serving you scones and taking your money. In Hollywood, these people are called *actors* (pronounced "ak-tors").

Actors are often required to memorize long passages of dialogue (and to cry on cue). While the script readers I've already mentioned are versatile, there's one app in particular that will make every actor spout tears of joy (helpful when having to cry on cue).

Rehearsal 2

Rehearsal 2 is a script-reading app designed specifically for actors who must memorize lines and submit voice auditions via e-mail. The app works only with PDF files, which typically isn't a problem since that's the most common file format actors receive.

Here's how it works.

After installing Rehearsal 2, you have two options for bringing in your scripts. You can import PDF files directly from an e-mail (using the Open In method I described earlier), or you can import them via Rehearsal's online server. This option requires setting up a free Rehearsal online account—it's quick, easy, and can be done from inside the app. Once you have an account, you simply

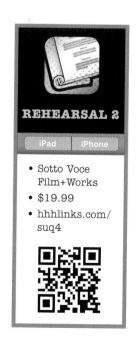

REHEARSAL 2

| iPad | iPhone |

- Sotto Voce Film+Works
- $19.99
- hhhlinks.com/suq4

e-mail your PDF file to the unique e-mail address provided by the app. Once the file has been received by the Rehearsal 2 server, it becomes instantly available from within the app's ADD NEW SCRIPTS screen.

The second method does involve a few extra steps, but it has the added benefit of storing a backup copy of your script on the Rehearsal server (until you choose to delete it). So, if your iOS device ever winds up in a blender, you can simply redownload your scripts on another device. Of course, if your iOS device is in a blender, you likely have bigger problems.

I feel the Rehearsal server is perfectly safe, but if you had to sign a nondisclosure agreement (NDA) before receiving the script or if you have other privacy concerns, you're likely better off sticking with the first import option (iTunes File Sharing).

Typically, when actors receive "sides" (portions of a script containing their scenes), they'll grab a highlighter and color their lines, allowing them to focus on what needs to be memorized. Rehearsal 2 works the same way.

Once users import and open a script, they can use any of the app's four highlighters (pink, blue, yellow, and green) to color their lines (**FIGURE 2.18**).

Once users are confident they have their lines memorized, they can tap the Blackout button **B** , which instantly hides every line that was previously highlighted, forcing them to perform the scene from memory (**FIGURE 2.19**)!

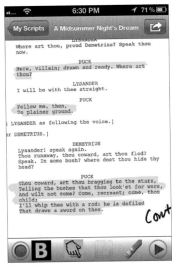

FIGURE 2.18 Color your lines with virtual highlighters.

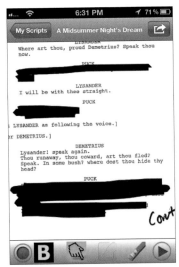

FIGURE 2.19 Think you have those lines memorized? Test yourself in Blackout mode.

Tapping the button once more removes the blackout and reveals the highlighted text again. After seeing the Blackout function in action, I became very upset because I didn't think of this brilliant app first. I'm still not over it.

Rehearsal 2 also has built-in audio capture and playback functions, perfect for actors who need to quickly read, record, and e-mail a voice audition. The audio functions are also useful for actors who want to record the other characters' lines and then play them back while performing their own part. In addition to recording audio, users can insert script notes, photos, and videos.

Rehearsal was developed by professional actor David H. Lawrence XVII (**FIGURE 2.20**) who you might recognize from shows like *Chuck*, *Lost*, *Heroes*, and many more (http://hhhlinks.com/oklm). It's clear that his years of professional acting experience helped him craft what I believe is an indispensable tool for all actors. Furthermore, David's connections in the acting community allowed him to beta-test Rehearsal with A-list talent on professional shoots all over Los Angeles. *Who ever said app development isn't glamorous?*

There are other offerings in the App Store meant to help actors learn their lines, but I have yet to see anything as elegant and intuitive as Rehearsal 2.

FINDING SCREENPLAYS

Sometimes, I enjoy sinking into my favorite leather chair, holding a glass of 1972 Chateau MarGaux in one hand and the screenplay for *Beverly Hills Chihuahua* in the other. If you think that's a joke, you're right. I don't drink wine.

It may seem like a waste of time to read screenplays that have already been produced, but it's these scripts that offer filmmakers the greatest potential education. By studying the written blueprints for films we've already seen, we can identify what moments translated well from page to screen and what moments suffered. We can compare our vision of a particular scene with that of the film's director. We can understand how our favorite visually complex sequences were originally described "on paper."

Let me put this another way. If you want to be a better filmmaker, read more scripts, and if you want to read more scripts, you'll have to find them first.

As luck would have it, our iOS devices have been blessed with an Internet connection and a web browser. Armed with both, filmmakers can visit numerous websites that exist for the sole purpose of sharing scripts. I'll list a few in a moment, but first some words of caution.

Most of the scripts you'll find online are saved in iPad- and iPhone-friendly file types, including plain text, HTML, and PDF. However, there are other, more

David H. Lawrence XVII on IMDB
hhhlinks.com/oklm

FIGURE 2.20 David H. Lawrence XVII: brilliant actor/brilliant app developer.

The Daily Script
www.dailyscript.com

**Drew's
Script-O-Rama**
www.script-o-rama.
com

**The Internet
Movie Script
Database**
www.imsdb.com

Simply Scripts
www.simplyscripts.com

**Screenplays
for You**
www.sfy.ru

obscure file types out there, some of which even require special plug-ins and work only on desktop PCs. Complicating matters further, many of the scripts that are saved in favorite file types may still be problematic because of horrible text formatting. Want some more bad news? Some of the scripts aren't scripts at all. You'll stumble across half-baked transcripts, fan films, and other irrelevant reinterpretations of the original work.

All surly snafus aside, there's one other very serious issue you need to consider. Some screenplays have been made available by their authors, some are in the public domain, but others may have been illegally reproduced and represent copyright violations. I don't advocate crossing legal lines, but sometimes it can be difficult to know where those lines are drawn.

It may sound like a minefield, but that's only because it is. It's a rough landscape, but there are treasures to be found. If you are a brave soul, and *really* want to track down that script for *8 Legged Freaks*, here are a few sites to explore:

> The Daily Script: www.dailyscript.com

> Drew's Script-O-Rama: www.script-o-rama.com

> The Internet Movie Script Database: www.imsdb.com

> Simply Scripts: www.simplyscripts.com

> Screenplays for You: www.sfy.ru

Scripted

Hate surfing the Web? Wish someone else would do it for you? Have I got some good news for you!

Scripted is an iPad app that drapes a fairly pleasant, unified interface over the websites I just mentioned (plus a few others) (**FIGURE 2.21**). After the app pulls in all of the relevant data, you can browse through an alphabetically sorted library of available script titles. The app is even kind enough to point out the scripts most recently uploaded.

When you come across a screenplay you'd like to read, the app downloads it directly into your script library. In addition to marking favorites, users can share scripts with friends via e-mail, Twitter, Facebook, and other online services.

Since Scripted is pulling in screenplays from the websites I mentioned, you'll have to be extra diligent when avoiding copyright infringement. Speaking of which, if you're reading this book as a pirated PDF file, please consider buying the book the next time you pass a bookstore. For you youngsters, a "bookstore" is a building where people used to buy books. It's like a shoe store but for books. Google it.

FIGURE 2.21 Scripted helps you download screenplays to your iPad.

SCRIPTED

iPad · iPhone

- The Appstillery Ltd.
- $0.99
- hhhlinks.com/9lt4

iBOOKS

iPad · iPhone

- Apple
- free
- hhhlinks.com/5dqs

The iBookstore

If you'd rather avoid all the file-type and formatting potholes and you want to ensure that you're downloading scripts from a legit source, take a look in Apple's iBookstore (accessible through iTunes or Apple's iBooks app). There you'll find a bountiful abundance of maybe ten scripts! OK, so it's not the biggest selection, but they do have a few worth reading:

› *Inception*

› *Inglourious Basterds*

› *Casablanca*

› *Star Wars: Episode III: Revenge of the Sith*

Stop snickering. Episode III was decent, right? Hello? Is this thing on?

CHAPTER 3

HERE'S THE PITCH!

In Hollywood, the term *pitch* immediately conjures visions of high-stakes, closed-door meetings in which creative hopefuls desperately tap-dance through elaborate presentations in hopes of winning the attention of influential studio executives. Make no mistake, those meetings *do* occur (I've pirouetted my way through plenty), but they represent only a tiny fraction of the pitches you'll be making throughout your filmmaking career.

Every time you enthusiastically describe your project to a friend or relative in hopes of getting some support, that's a pitch. Every time you persuade a talented actor to accept a meager role in your film, that's a pitch. Every time you beg the owner of the pizza joint down the street to feed your crew in exchange for an executive producer credit, that's brilliant!…and it's a pitch.

If you plan on making movies, plan on pitching.

For new filmmakers, pitching can be unnecessarily intimidating. If you count yourself among the nervous, let me point out that a pitch is nothing more than the adult version of "I have a neat new toy! Wanna play with it?" You'll be amazed how many people love playing with neat new toys.

Whether you're pitching a dramatic feature set in 1920s Ireland or a musical sitcom about a cigar-smoking walrus (copyright Taz Goldstein, all rights reserved), your iOS devices can help transform a solid pitch into a *spectacular* pitch.

PRESENTATION APPS

Film is a visual medium, and yet most pitches don't include a single image. What a waste! I learned early on that including even a few photos can have a profound impact on the outcome of a pitch.

For example, imagine pitching your feature to the owner of a lighting company who may, or may not, donate equipment to your shoot. Halfway through your pitch, you say, "Amy stumbles across a desert oasis." Now imagine that same pitch, but this time you hold up your iPad, which displays a breathtaking photograph of wind-sculpted sand dunes and towering palm trees surrounding a shimmering pool of aqua-blue water. Now you say, "Amy stumbles across a desert oasis." Which do you think will have more impact?

At the most basic level, giving your audience something to look at will engage them and help hold their attention. It quite literally demands they employ another of their five senses. I would include smells in my pitches if I could, although some of my pitches certainly have stunk (*cue rim shot*).

By including imagery that represents your vision of the film, your pitch recipient is far more likely to envision the movie the same way you do. When someone understands your vision, or at least recognizes that *you* understand your vision, they'll have an easier time believing that you can turn 100 typed pages into a successful, cohesive film.

Thanks to iPads, iPhones, and some terrific apps, it's now incredibly easy to incorporate high-quality, visually striking images and film clips into your pitch presentations.

Photos and iPhoto

Sometimes the simplest solutions are the best, and I can't imagine anything simpler than Photos, Apple's default photo-viewing app included on every iPad, iPhone, and iPod touch.

iPHOTO

| iPad | iPhone |

- Apple
- $4.99
- hhhlinks.com/Obuz

If you've spent more than five minutes with an iOS device, you've undoubtedly opened and explored this refined but modest tool. If you're unfamiliar with Photos (has no iPhone owner ever tried to show you photos of their kids, their pets, or their kids with their pets?), I'll do my best to explain the app's intricacies: add photo, tap photo, view photo, swipe left to view next photo, celebrate successful iPhone interaction. There's more to it than that, but not much. And for many pitches, that's all the functionality you'll need.

The most efficient way to load images and video files into your iOS device is by syncing it with a Mac or Windows machine running iTunes and a compatible photo management application, of which there are several. Mac owners can use iPhoto (version 4.0.3 or newer) or Aperture, while PC owners can use Adobe Elements (version 10 or newer) or Adobe Album (version 2 or newer, now discontinued). Each of these apps touts its unique features, but they all allow you to import, sort, edit, and organize your entire image library. More importantly, they offer tools for creating custom photo albums, which can be populated with any imagery pulled from your main library.

To prepare for an upcoming presentation, launch your photo management app of choice, create a new custom album, and fill it with all the pitch-related photos and video clips you've collected (**FIGURE 3.1**). Then arrange everything in the proper order, and finally sync it all back to your iOS device. Your new album will appear inside the Photos app (**FIGURE 3.2**). All you need to do now is start pitching.

Don't have a computer? Not to worry. You can still create custom albums from within the Photos app. Just switch to the Albums tab and tap Edit in the upper-right corner. Now tap New Album (or New, if you're on an iPhone) in the upper-left corner. After giving your new album a descriptive name (such as the name of your project), pick the photos and video clips you'd like to include, and tap Done when you're finished.

If you need to reorder the contents, simply tap the album to open it, and then tap the options menu ⬆. You can now tap and hold any item to select it and then drag it to its new location. Tap Done when you're satisfied with your new arrangement. Keep in mind that this reordering technique will work only within albums you've created directly on your iOS device. To reorder the contents of albums you originally created on a Mac or PC, you'll have to return to your computer to make any adjustments and then sync your changes back to your iOS device.

If you need to make some slight adjustments to your images, the Photos app provides a few elementary editing tools, including Rotation, Auto-enhance, Red-eye Reduction, and Crop. It's not much, but what do you expect from a free app? What's that you say? You hate free apps? Well then, say hello to iPhoto.

FIGURE 3.1 Preparing an album of pitch photos in iPhoto on a Mac.

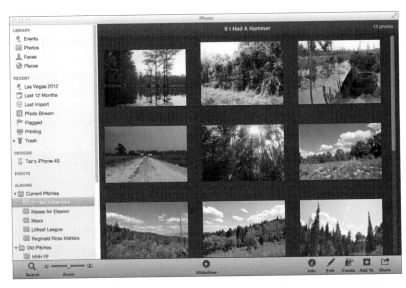

FIGURE 3.2 After a sync, the same album is available on your iOS device.

Apple recently released an iOS version of its popular Mac application, iPhoto. Performing equally well on iPads and iPhones, iPhoto trumps the default Photos app by sporting a significantly slicker interface, a complete set of editing tools (handy if you don't have a computer), and a long list of impressive photo management features. Having said that, these additional features won't do much to help your presentations. So, why bother spending the extra cash for iPhoto? Because iPhoto can create journals.

Similar to albums, journals are used to present collections of selected photos and videos. Although an album's contents are best viewed one item at a time, journals automatically arrange their contents into a tight, elegant, geometric collage, allowing you to view everything in the collection at once (**FIGURE 3.3**). For this reason, journals are not especially well suited for linear pitches, but they're extremely helpful when trying to visually express large, overarching themes.

Part scrapbook and part vision board, your journal might include color swatches, scenic location photos, fabric samples, sketches, actor headshots, needlepoint, and anything else that can help your audience imagine the single,

MAGIC BULLET ARSENAL

iPad iPhone

- Red Giant Software
- $4.99
- hhhlinks.com/ 7nuf

fully formed world in which your story takes place. This sort of thematic presentation is often called a *look book*, and it's more about tone and texture than it is about plot points and act breaks. Using your iCloud account, iPhoto can publish your journals online where they can be shared with anyone you want.

Both Photos and iPhoto offer an automatic slideshow function that will present your images using Ken Burns–styled zooms, pretimed cross dissolves, and accompanying music. It's the perfect way to show Mom your vacation photos and a horrifically embarrassing way to present your pitch. Avoid this cheese at all costs.

Magic Bullet Arsenal

If Photos is the Honda of photo presentation apps and iPhoto is the Toyota, then allow me to introduce you to the BMW.

Magic Bullet Arsenal is a relatively new iPad app designed for photographers wanting to display their portfolios in a more refined manner. The app won't manage your library, edit images, or upload snapshots to Twitter, but what it will do is present groups of photos and videos in a totally professional, minimalistic environment, free from the distractions that typically clutter consumer applications.

When you launch Arsenal, you are presented with an elegant list of your current collections (FIGURE 3.4). Think of collections as groups of photo albums. I use collections to separate my projects by category (television projects, film projects, commercial projects, and so on).

After opening a collection, you are brought to an equally elegant list for strips (Arsenal's version of photo albums; FIGURE 3.5). I create separate strips of

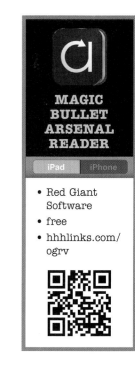

MAGIC BULLET ARSENAL READER

iPad iPhone

- Red Giant Software
- free
- hhhlinks.com/ ogrv

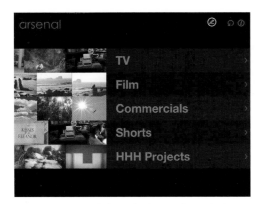

FIGURE 3.4 Red Giant's Arsenal can help give your presentations a professional vibe, even when you're pitching in shorts and a T-shirt.

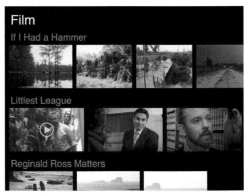

FIGURE 3.5 Thumbnails accompany project names in Arsenal's elegant interface.

each of my pitches. Each strip is represented by a row of thumbnails, one thumbnail for each image or video contained in the strip. Tapping a thumbnail will fill the screen with its corresponding image or movie clip. From here, you can swipe your way forward or backward through the remaining items in the strip.

Want to inject an additional dose of awesome? Arsenal lets you place your logo in the upper-left corner of the Collections screen and the upper-right corner of the Strips screen. That said, if your logo features a pig playing hopscotch, you might want to leave it off of this otherwise tasteful interface.

There's no denying that Arsenal is one classy app. But a polished facade isn't the app's killer feature. That distinction belongs to Arsenal's ability to sync selected strips with FTP servers and Dropbox folders, which makes updating content a snap. One word of warning: Strips that sync with online sources do not allow manual reordering of content. You can reorder imagery only inside nonsyncing strips. Sadly, the FTP features in Arsenal are buggy and not entirely intuitive. If you plan on using the app's syncing functionality, I recommend sticking with Dropbox for now.

When you're in a sharing mood, you can e-mail any of your collection to another iPad owner. If they don't already own Arsenal and don't feel like dropping five bucks, they can open your collection using the free Arsenal Reader app available in the App Store. Here's the kicker: If the collection you've shared contains any strips that are set to sync with an FTP server or a Dropbox folder, they will *continue* to sync while living on your recipient's iPad. That means you can make changes to a presentation even after you've sent it!

Aside from a couple minor annoyances, Arsenal is a solid and stylish media presentation app that should be given serious consideration.

Keynote

If you'd like to add a little customization, interactivity, or visual punch to your pitch, you'll need to move beyond photo viewers and into the realm of full-blown presentation applications. Apple's Keynote is a great place to start, especially if you're already familiar with the Mac version of Keynote or Microsoft's Power-Point software.

Within Keynote, it's easy to build fairly complex presentations, one slide at a time (**FIGURE 3.6**). Each new slide can contain multiple images and video clips, making it behave similarly to a photo viewing app, but Keynote goes much further, allowing you to add text, tables, charts, and custom shapes (**FIGURE 3.7**). For each item you add, you have the option of animating it in and out of the slide. You can choose an animation style from the app's long list of presets. On top of that, you can inject visually striking transitions between each of your slides.

Because Keynote features this wide assortment of easy-to-implement special effects, it takes very little effort to go completely overboard, pushing the boundaries of good taste and professionalism. You might start with a simple animation, perhaps a slow push into the face of your protagonist, but before you know it, you're inserting twirling graphics, unnecessary flying text, and entirely gratuitous Confetti transitions.

KEYNOTE

| iPad | iPhone |

- Apple
- $9.99
- hhhlinks.com/
  1zm5

FIGURE 3.6 Apple's Keynote makes it criminally easy to build slick pitch presentations.

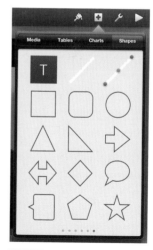

FIGURE 3.7 Add text, lines, and shapes to your presentation. Don't all great presentations include a voice bubble or two? (No.)

FIGURE 3.8 Keynote provides several style options to customize shapes and text.

FIGURE 3.9 Use Keynote Remote on your iPhone to control Keynote on your iPad. Now you have a legitimate reason to own both devices! You're welcome.

If you want to keep your head on straight and your presentation on track, follow my one simple rule: At the point you consider adding extra visual pizzazz for the sole purpose of making your pitch more interesting, close Keynote, open Pages, and write a better pitch. Remember, you're using your mobile device to enhance your presentations, not dominate them.

That doesn't mean you should avoid Keynote's power. Just make sure you use it in moderation. For instance, you could use the animation tools to design a smooth pan across a panoramic location photo or the text tools to insert character names above your cast photos (**FIGURE 3.8**).

Once you've perfected each slide and selected each transition, it's time to check your work. Tap the Play button ▶ to begin your presentation. You can step forward through your slides by tapping the screen or by swiping from right to left (or left to right if you need to return to the previous slide). Slides can also be set to switch automatically after a preset duration, but I generally advise against that.

It's imperative that you run through your entire Keynote presentation, making sure everything plays back properly, before utilizing it during a pitch meeting. All it takes is one missing slide or ill-placed animation to throw you off your game. Once everything is working as expected, you're ready to pitch.

Your audience should not have to strain to see your device's display. There are plenty of iPhone and iPad cases that double as stands, allowing you to quickly position your device at the perfect viewing angle. Typically, when I pitch with my iPad, I'll place it close to my audience, sometimes even inviting them to hold it during my presentation. However, when your iPad is out of reach, controlling your Keynote presentation becomes impossible. Or does it? Thanks to Keynote

KEYNOTE REMOTE

| iPad | iPhone |

- Apple
- $0.99
- hhhlinks.com/ cgvt

Remote, another fine app from your friends at Apple, you can wirelessly control the Keynote presentation on your iPad from your iPhone (**FIGURE 3.9**)! If you're unclear on the definition of sexy, reread that last sentence.

Because Keynote works with Apple's iCloud service, any presentations you create on one iOS device will automatically appear on your other iOS devices. You might question the importance of this feature, but that will surely change the moment you need to make an impromptu pitch and realize that you left your iPad at home. You're sure to exhale a sigh of relief when you remember that iCloud can automatically download a copy of the Keynote presentation to your iPhone. At that point, I advise you to write a little love letter to iCloud, apologizing for questioning its importance.

The iOS version of Keynote can exchange files with the Mac version, although not all features and file types are compatible (always double-check your presentations before pitching). You can import a Mac Keynote file into your iOS device as an e-mail attachment or via iTunes File Sharing.

Presentation Link

I can't tell you how many times I've seen polished, professional pitches go entirely off the rails simply because someone interrupts with a question.

A well-rehearsed pitch is ideal, but one that's been meticulously and inflexibly planned down to the syllable only invites problems. Being intimately familiar with the subject matter, and your vision, is far more important and more impressive than delivering an overly produced pitch. Besides, getting interrupted with questions is a wonderful thing! It suggests your audience is engaged and interested enough to seek clarification. Hooray, interruptions!

All the presentation apps I've covered thus far are linear in nature. You begin with one image, video clip, or keynote slide, then move to the next, and so on. However, if you expect to field a lot of questions that may divert you from your planned sequence or if your pitching style is fluid in nature, take a look at Presentation Link for iPad.

Like the other apps, Presentation Link allows you to construct slide shows from images and movies contained in your photo library. And, just like the other apps, you can easily navigate from one slide to the next. However, Presentation Link offers you the unique ability to insert Link buttons that can be used to construct complex and flexible navigation systems within your presentations.

Link buttons can be resized and positioned anywhere on the screen. For example, I've put a button around the image of the actor on this presentation slide (**FIGURE 3.10**). Buttons can be made visible (appearing as a translucent blue

PRESENTATION LINK

iPad   iPhone

- Zuhanden GmbH
- $4.99
- hhhlinks.com/ 3sd9

FIGURE 3.10 Buttons can be placed anywhere and can link to other slides or web pages. On this slide, I put a button over the actor and linked it to his IMDB page.

FIGURE 3.11 Tap a button's gear icon to view its settings.

box) or kept invisible for a cleaner pitch. New buttons default to being active only on a single slide, but they can be toggled into Master mode, at which point they become active on every slide in the presentation.

Each button can have one of three functions (**FIGURE 3.11**). It can link to any other slide, link to a web page, or serve as a Back button, just like you'd find in a web browser. Using these three simple functions, you can construct some mind-blowing, interactive presentations.

Let me give you an example of how this might be useful.

Let's say you're pitching an ensemble comedy with multiple, intertwining story-lines. For most of your presentation, you're simply swiping from one slide to the next. But then, the development executive sitting across from you says he can't remember which character is which. No problem! Because you anticipated that question, you already added a Master button on the bottom of every slide that links you to another slide containing sketches and descriptions for each character.

Before you can tap the Back button you created in the upper-left corner of the character slide, the executive asks who you see in the role of "Xander Buckswallow." No problem! Because you are one smart cookie, you already positioned invisible web link buttons around each of your character's sketched faces. When you tap Xander's sketch, Chris Pine's IMDB (Internet Movie Data-base) web page pops open and displays his current filmography (this assumes you have an active wireless data connection). The executive nods approvingly, knowing full well he can never afford Chris Pine and asks you to continue. You close the web page, tap the Back button, and are instantly brought right back to where you left off in your pitch.

Knowing that you can easily maneuver around within your presentation will allow you to pitch in a more relaxed and confident state…like Texas. This approach also allows for greater on-the-fly customization of your pitch. Naturally, every pitch changes depending on the audience and the intended goal, but as long as your passion remains consistent and the project is worthy, you stand a decent chance of winning someone over...or at least making a good enough impression that their door will remain open for your next pitch.

WHERE TO FIND IMAGERY

Now that you understand how to use your iOS device to deliver a visually captivating pitch, you might be wondering where to find visually captivating visuals with which to visually captivate.

When hunting for material, I'll usually start by sifting through my own photo library. This inevitably fails since my library is saturated with snapshots of my dog, Pixel. I hope your library is more diverse. After spending way too much time admiring my pooch, I'll fire up Safari and surf over to Google Images, a remarkably thorough image search engine. From there, it's off to Flickr, a popular photo-sharing website. After that, I'll poke around various stock footage sites like iStockphoto and Shutterstock, and finally, I'll dig into my most valued resource, the video rental shop.

If you have a Mac or a Windows machine, there are countless ways to "rip" images and video clips from websites and DVDs. A quick Google search on the subject will get you on your way. However, if you're living in the "post-PC era" and only own an iOS device, your options are far more limited. Here are a couple quick techniques to get you started.

To download still images, begin by launching Safari and surfing to the page that contains the photo or graphic you'd like to grab. Then tap and hold the image until your device asks if you'd like it to be saved to your camera roll (**FIGURE 3.12**). Once saved, the image becomes available to any other app capable of accessing your camera roll; this includes all of the apps I've mentioned thus far in this chapter. Unfortunately, this method of downloading images may not work for all websites. It's simply a matter of trial and error.

Downloading video isn't nearly as easy, and frankly, I suggest you avoid it altogether. But, since you've already decided to ignore my expert advice, here are the absolute basics.

The first thing you'll need is a video-downloading app. There are piles of them in the App Store, all claiming to be able to download videos from "popular video websites." We all know that the only video site that matters is YouTube. Sadly, very few of these apps can successfully download from YouTube. The few that

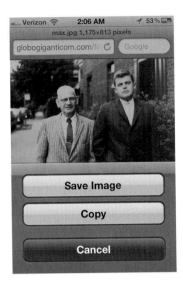

FIGURE 3.12 Download an image from Safari by tapping and holding it until the Save Image button appears.

can do so inconsistently since YouTube is always changing its security proto-cols. If you manage to download a clip, you'll likely want to transfer it into an editing app for trimming (I'll be covering video-editing apps later in the book). After that, you'll render your new clip and export it to your device's camera roll. From there, you can use it in any of the presentation apps I've mentioned that support video. Sounds like a pain, right? It's not. It's a *gigantic* pain.

One final thought about gathering imagery: Resist the urge to include a par-ticular photo or video clip simply because it's *friggin' sweet*. Sure, watching the Death Star explode is immensely dramatic, but does it really belong in your Circus Monkey Retirement Home pitch? Actually, maybe it does, but that's beside the point. Every item you incorporate into your presentation *must* directly represent *your* vision. If it doesn't contribute, don't include it.

FOLLOWING UP

Here's a question for you. What do most successful filmmakers do right after a fruitful pitch? If you answered "drink heavily," you'd be partially correct. The answer I was looking for, however, was "filmmakers follow up."

Let's say you're grabbing lunch at McDonald's and suddenly bump into Bruce Willis. (I know what you're thinking. Mr. Willis probably prefers Taco Bell.) Somehow, while waiting in line, you manage to pitch him your latest project, an action/musical about a blind sushi chef. He loves the idea, gives you his ultra-private e-mail address, and says the four greatest words to ever enter your ear canals: "Send me the script." Without hesitation, you whip out your iPhone, tap a few keys, and presto! You've just e-mailed him your script, bio, and vCard. He's so impressed, he buys you a McFlurry.

Now picture yourself as a struggling actor. You've just met a director at the Laundromat. He's currently casting an indie comedy and asks for your info. You tap your iPhone and instantly e-mail him your latest headshot and resume...all before you take your socks out of the dryer.

In my experience, not only does instant follow-up prevent missed opportunities, but it also impresses the hell out of people (especially if they see you doing it on your iPhone). So, which apps can help? Quite a few, actually. Just about any app that can e-mail files (or links to files) will do the trick.

Let's look at two of my favorites.

Dropbox

Dropbox has rapidly become one of the most popular online file storage and sharing services, due largely to its rock-solid performance, its ability to easily sync with Macs and Windows machines, and its extensive support for third-party iOS apps (including many I've already mentioned).

After installing Dropbox on your computer, the app will create a dedicated Dropbox folder (**FIGURE 3.13**). Anything you place within this folder, or its subfolders, gets automatically synced to the Dropbox servers and to any other computers sharing the same Dropbox account. In other words, after you put something into your laptop's Dropbox folder, it will soon appear in your desktop computer's Dropbox folder, and vice versa. You can even share (and sync) specific folders with other Dropbox users.

Dropbox also makes a terrific, free iOS app that can effortlessly access and e-mail links to any of the files stored in your online account (**FIGURE 3.14**). This includes everything you've placed in the Dropbox folder on any of your linked computers.

Are you beginning to get the picture? Let's bring it into focus.

After you move your important documents (scripts, treatments, headshots, vCards, and so forth) into your computer's Dropbox folder, you can use your iOS device to e-mail links to those files whenever the need arises. Instant follow-up! The app also offers the ability to mark any file as a favorite, making it quickly accessible on the Favorites tab.

DROPBOX

| iPad | iPhone |

- Dropbox
- free
- hhhlinks.com/8exf

FIGURE 3.13 When you first install Dropbox on your Mac or Windows machine, it creates its own simple folder structure.

FIGURE 3.14 Use the Dropbox app to quickly access all your pitch documents on the go.

FIGURE 3.15 The Dropbox app can generate and e-mail links for all your stored files. This is a great tool for e-mailing follow-up documents right after a pitch meeting.

Sending a link is remarkably simple. Just select the desired file within the Dropbox app, tap the Share Link button [link icon], and choose E-mail Link. Dropbox will create a unique URL and drop it into a new e-mail (**FIGURE 3.15**). Add a recipient, edit the subject and body text, and hit Send. Done! Your recipient can use the link to download the file.

Keep in mind that Dropbox links are not private. If your recipient decides to share your link or someone else magically guesses the link (unlikely, but not impossible), there's little you can do to stop them, other than logging into your Dropbox dashboard and disabling the link. For this reason, I don't recommend using Dropbox to share any private or sensitive material.

When using Dropbox, preparation is key. Make sure the files in your Dropbox folder are always up-to-date and complete. The more prepared you are, the more opportunities you can seize.

If you don't already use the Dropbox service, you need to bookmark this page, set this book down, and get yourself a free, 2-gigabyte account right now at www.dropbox.com. If you require more storage, Dropbox will be happy to charge you a small monthly fee.

Dropbox
www.dropbox.com

iFiles

File management isn't the most exciting of topics, especially in a filmmaking book, but I couldn't leave this chapter without mentioning one of my all-time-favorite iOS apps: iFiles (**FIGURE 3.16**).

In short, iFiles lets you manage files and folders on a wide variety of online services, including Flickr, Google Docs, Facebook, Picasa, Box, Dropbox, Rackspace, Amazon S3, CloudApp, and SugarSync. It will also connect with several server standards, such as FTP, SFTP, and WebDAV. Using iFiles, you can upload, download, delete, move, copy, rename, print, zip, unzip, and share any files you choose. It will also brew your morning coffee, iron your shirt, and drive you to set.

Unlike Dropbox, which e-mails links that can be used to download files stored on its servers, iFiles can e-mail the actual files themselves. There are two primary advantages to this approach. First, unlike Dropbox, you can send multiple files at once. This is handy if you want to send someone a copy of your script, along with your resume and bio. Second, and more importantly, by e-mailing the actual files, you don't need to create and share download links that could potentially be discovered and exploited by evildoers (those guys who enjoy leaking top-secret scripts, while twirling their handlebar moustaches). On the flipside, e-mailing large files can be tricky, while sharing download links will remove most file size restrictions.

Dropbox and iFiles are only two of countless file-sharing options. While they are my personal favorites, a quick search in the App Store will reveal dozens

iFILES

iPad   iPhone

- Imagam
- $3.99
- hhhlinks.com/rfcy

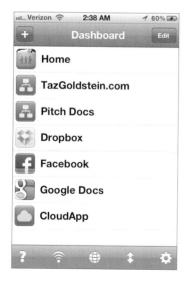

FIGURE 3.16 iFiles lets you access, download, and share your files from a wide variety of online sources.

more. How you choose to share your files is far less important than your ability to share the most recent versions of your documents quickly and easily. After all, you never know who you're going to meet at the supermarket, the gym, or McDonald's.

FAQ

FAQ

| iPad | iPhone |

- Soluble Apps
- $2.99
- hhhlinks.com/yaqk

I've already told you how important it is to send follow-up e-mails. What I haven't told you is how much I despise sending follow-up e-mails. It's not that I harbor disdain for the written word or dread communicating with my peers; I just hate seeing large chunks of my day being sucked into the e-mail time vortex. I've sat down to write a quick e-mail, only to discover I'd grown a full beard and lost 20 pounds.

Unlike the previous two apps, FAQ doesn't facilitate the sharing of files. Instead, FAQ allows you to author a library of text snippets that can be stored and reused when creating a new e-mail. In other words, it helps you generate e-mails quickly, transforming you from an e-mail Luddite into a follow-up ninja.

For example, you might create a few different introductory snippets ("It was a pleasure meeting you today," "It was great seeing you again today," and so on), followed by a variety of snippets for each of your projects ("Thanks for letting me pitch you *Kisses for Eleanor*…"), and finally a handful of closing snippets ("I'm looking forward to your thoughts," "I hope we get to collaborate soon," and so on).

After building your library, you're ready to create your first e-mail. Simply place a check mark next to each snippet you want to include (**FIGURE 3.17**), and then let FAQ assemble your finished message (**FIGURE 3.18**). From there, you should take a moment to tweak the generated e-mail, making sure it's sufficiently customized for your recipient, and then hit Send.

Although I've been discussing FAQ as a tool for generating follow-up e-mails, the app is infinitely flexible and can be beneficial to anyone working behind or in front of the camera. Writers can launch FAQ to swiftly generate query letters. Actors might keep it nearby when responding to casting notices. Producers could call it up when sending out thank-you e-mails (yes, some producers send thank-you e-mails).

FAQ was designed to be as productive as the people who use it, and for that reason, it remains one of my favorite iOS utilities.

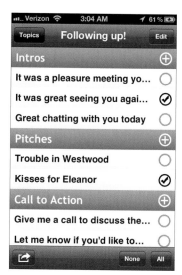

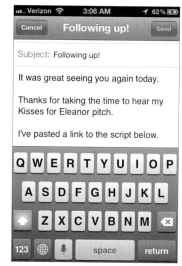

FIGURE 3.17 FAQ helps you build a custom library of text snippets that can be used to quickly generate follow-up e-mails.

FIGURE 3.18 After picking your snippets (which you should never do in public), FAQ builds you a new e-mail!

CHAPTER 4

PREPPING THE SHOOT

A wise person once said, "Failing to plan is planning to fail." It's a little unclear who is responsible for these words (I found the quote attributed to at least five different luminaries), but I can tell you with absolute certainty that whoever said it first was clearly a filmmaker.

Preparation takes many forms. It might be knowing where to look for a hard-to-find prop. It might be having the right tools mastered for your next location scout. It might be understanding the importance of a release form. It all comes down to this: The more you prepare, the greater your chances for success.

Everything in this chapter is about preparation. In some cases, I discuss apps and ideas that could have just as easily been included in Part II, "Production," but I'm hoping that if I inject them here, you'll spend more time getting familiar with them *before* your shoot begins. The last thing you should be doing during production is learning an app. Trust me, you'll be busy with other things.

PRODUCTION DIRECTORIES

"We're setting up the next shot! Quick, we need 300 chickens, a 1963 Chevrolet Impala, and a watermelon-shaped ice sculpture! We also need a stuntman who can jump a 1963 Chevy Impala over 300 chickens into a watermelon-shaped ice sculpture!"

If this has happened to you, I'd really like to see your film. I'd also suggest you download a few of the great production directory apps available for your iPhone and iPad.

It doesn't matter if you're shooting tomorrow or if you're still two months away from calling "Action!"—at some point, you're going to need to track down something, or someone, for a production. Maybe your space adventure will need a laser-pistol prop. Perhaps your sound mixer will get sick and you'll need to secure a replacement. Maybe you'll be looking to rent a hospital standing set, rather than building one from scratch (a standing set is one that remains in place even when not being filmed and is usually available for long and short-term rental). You can find all this in production directories.

Although Google is a great place to search for odds and ends, production directories will save you time by providing well-organized listings of the most commonly requested film production resources and services. Directories make it easy to shop around, research availability, and compare prices.

Keep in mind, these apps access directory content stored in online servers. That means the directory listings will always be up-to-date, but when you're without an Internet connection, you'll also be without working directory apps.

Let's look at a few of the production directory apps patiently waiting for you in the App Store.

LA 411

Known in Los Angeles as *the bible*, the LA 411 is one of the oldest, most trusted production directories around. Long before iPhones, iPads, and the Internet, spiral-bound versions of this behemoth directory could be found sitting on production company desks in offices all over Los Angeles. An updated version was published every year and carried a not-so-small price tag. Owning the latest edition was as much a symbol of status as it was a useful filmmaking resource.

The paper version is still published annually, but most of the filmmakers I know have gone digital. Not only is the LA 411 available online, but it now has its own free, ad-supported iPhone app.

LA 411

iPad **iPhone**

- 411 Publishing
- free
- hhhlinks.com/ we8u

NY 411

iPad **iPhone**

- 411 Publishing
- free
- hhhlinks.com/ 7fdy

FIGURE 4.1 Use the LA 411 app to quickly find a greenscreen stage or about 3 billion other things you might need.

As soon as you launch the app, you can quickly perform a search. If you simply want to browse, the app includes 12 master categories: Ad Agencies & Production Companies; Post Production; Sets & Stages; Location Services & Equipment; Production Support; Camera & Sound Equipment; High Def; 3D & Digital Cinema; Grip & Lighting Equipment; Props & Wardrobe; Crew; City Guide; and National Listings. Within each of these categories and their related subcategories, you'll find a plethora of companies and crew members competing for your business (**FIGURE 4.1**).

The app allows you to share listings via e-mail, bookmark favorites, import any listing's contact information into your iPhone's address book, and quickly pull up driving directions.

You don't have to live in Los Angeles to enjoy the benefits of the bible. There are separate 411 apps for Los Angeles, New York, Florida, and New Mexico.

Doddle

Whereas the LA 411 originated in print and then eventually transitioned online, doddle began its life in the digital era and as a result provides more of what you'd expect from an iPhone application. It's slick, interactive, and far more social.

The app has two flavors: a free version appropriately titled doddle and another version called doddlePRO that will set you back ten bucks. For now, I focus on the free version.

DODDLE

iPad   iPhone

- Mobile Imagination
- free
- hhhlinks.com/ ln2x

To find a listing in doddle, you must first tell the app if you'd like to search by name, by proximity (to you or another contact in your address book), or by country (**FIGURE 4.2**).

Searching by name provides a basic search box with no other filtering. Searching by proximity brings up an extensive alphabetical list of categories and subcategories organized into four main groupings: Vendor, Crew, Talent, and Location. Searching by country lets you start your hunt in a particular geographic region. It may sound a bit confusing, but once you've performed a search or two, it will become second nature.

Let me give you a quick example. Let's say you need to find a food stylist for your next commercial shoot. You'd start by tapping the Find a Listing tab at the bottom of the screen, followed by the Where I Am Now button. This tells doddle that you'd like to find listings in your neck of the woods. Next, tap the Crew button toward the top of the screen to view an alphabetical list of every conceivable film crew position (**FIGURE 4.3**). Scroll to the *f*'s, tap Food Stylist, and watch your screen overflow with names of possible candidates. Search results can be sorted alphabetically, by distance, or by rating.

Tapping a single listing reveals greater detail, including contact info, web links, and reviews left by other doddle users. From here you can initiate contact, mark the listing as a favorite, add your own review, and add the contact info to your iPhone's address book.

If that weren't enough, the app also supplies a thorough listing of U.S. and U.K. film offices, along with a few in South Africa (**FIGURE 4.4**).

Not only is the app free, but you can even add yourself to doddle's directory in up to two categories at no charge. You can post your name, photo, basic contact info, and links to your pages on Twitter, Facebook, IMDB, and more. If you're feeling especially boastful, you can purchase a Premium Listing, which allows you to add a description of your company or skill set, a downloadable PDF of your resume, photos and videos of your work, and more. A Premium Listing isn't cheap, but if it brings you work, it's worth it!

Thus far, I've only discussed doddle's prowess as an interactive, mobile production directory. But there's a whole separate side of this pint-sized powerhouse that I've intentionally left out of the conversation…until now. Doddle users can receive and interact with digital call sheets that have been created with doddlePRO, the paid version of the app! This is a big deal! It's so big, in fact, that you can read all about it in the separate "Call Sheets" section of this chapter. I'm such a tease.

FIGURE 4.2 Doddle lets you search here, there, and everywhere...or by name.

FIGURE 4.3 Doddle's listings are broken into four categories (Vendor, Crew, Talent, Location) and sorted alphabetically.

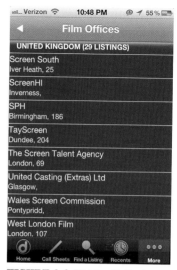

FIGURE 4.4 Need a listing of film offices in the United Kingdom? Doddle has got you covered.

LOCATION SCOUTING

When I was 8 years old, I would wander down the block to my neighborhood park and shoot reel after reel of 8mm film, staging complex battle sequences between platoons of tiny green plastic army men and wind-up robot toys. It was epic! Or at least it *seemed* epic to a person no taller than a mailbox.

The park location had two significant qualities vital to a young filmmaker: It was close, and my parents let me go there alone. However, at the ripe old age of 10, I began to take notice of equally interesting shooting locations further up the street. With each birthday, the geographic range of my location database expanded. Pretty soon I was racing my bike through neighboring ZIP codes, hoping to find a unique setting in which to set my next robot-invasion flick. I had no idea that there was a name for what I was doing, but now I know better. I was *location scouting*!

It wasn't until much later in life when I learned that there are people who make a career out of location scouting. They're called *location scouts*. Clever, right?

When working on a film, a location scout gathers the best options. After that, the *location manager* steps in to handle all the necessary arrangements (contracts, releases, payments, and so on). Granted, I'm simplifying the process, but those are the basics. As a professional director, I have the great fortune of working with many talented location scouts and managers. However, on smaller-budget projects I don't always have that luxury. Sometimes, I'll wake up early, grab my iPhone, and scout a few locations myself. If you're a young or independent filmmaker, I imagine you're in the same boat.

Let's take a look at two of the best location-scouting apps available today. Grab your iPhone, hop on your bike, and follow me!

Panascout

Great news! Every iPhone and iPad comes standard with the most basic location-scouting tool available. It's called a camera, and it works like this: Find a good location, take a picture of it, and, finally, make grand plans to shoot there. As an added benefit, most of Apple's mobile devices will add GPS coordinates to the metadata of each photo. Some apps, including Apple's own iPhoto app, can use this data to present a photo's original shooting location on an interactive map (**FIGURE 4.5**).

Using the standard camera app is a great place to start, but if you're serious about scouting, have a look at Panavision's Panascout for iPhone.

In addition to snapping photos of your desired location, the app will overlay a heap of useful data including your GPS coordinates, the direction you're currently facing (important when trying to predict the movement of sunlight and shadows), the current date and time, the estimated time for sunrise and sunset, and an optional framing overlay that can be set to 2.40:1, 1.85:1, 1.78:1 (16x9), 1.33:1 (4x3), or a custom ratio (**FIGURE 4.6**). All of this data can be incredibly useful when picking your locations and planning shoot times.

FIGURE 4.5 Apple's iPhoto can show you exactly where you took that awesome location photo.

FIGURE 4.6 Panascout automatically adds useful information to all your location photos.

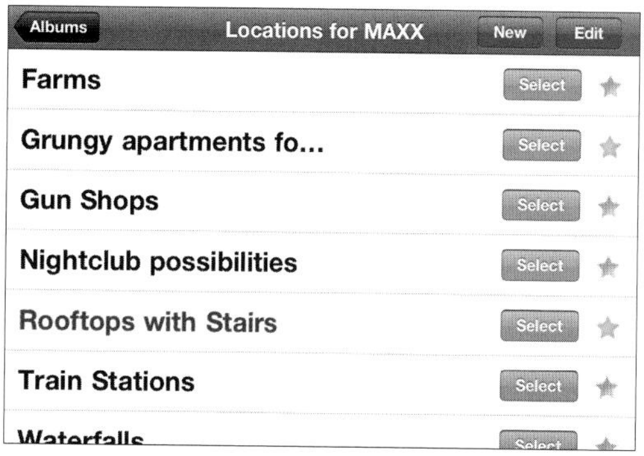

FIGURE 4.7 Use albums and rolls to keep your location shots organized within Panascount.

For example, let's say you've just returned home with an iPhone full of location shots. While reviewing everything, you come across a photo of a dilapidated wooden shack in the middle of a field. Because you took the shot with Pana-scout, the photo includes a variety of information, including compass data. You realize you were facing west when you snapped the image, which means you could return here during *golden hour* to capture the setting sun's rays gleaming through holes in the shack. If you didn't already know, *golden hour* describes a day's last hour of sunlight, which typically provides gorgeous skies and soft, dramatic lighting. Looking back at the photo, you see that sunset is expected at 7:43 p.m. Because this photo was taken today, tomorrow's sunset time shouldn't be much different. You enter the GPS coordinates into your favorite iPhone navigation app, and you're ready to go!

Panascout helps you keep things organized by letting you sort your shots into user-created albums and rolls (**FIGURE 4.7**). You can add text notes to any image, or if you're feeling especially vocal, you can even record an audio note. When you're ready to share, you can e-mail a location shot straight out of the app. In addition to the photo, your e-mail will include any text notes you've entered, along with the sunrise and sunset times, the time and date the shot was taken, and even a link to the location on Google Maps! If you recorded an audio note, it will also be attached to the e-mail as an .m4a audio file.

In addition to stills, Panascout will also record movies, but they won't include any of the app's on-screen data. I'm really hoping this changes in future versions.

Panavision offers a free Lite version of the app that you should completely avoid. It lacks all the important features and doesn't give you any sense of the full app's value. It's a bit like offering a lite version of a popsicle in the form of an empty stick. Mmmm…stick.

**MAP-A-PIC
LOCATION
SCOUT**

iPad   iPhone

- Sea To
  Software, LLC
- $4.99
- hhhlinks.com/
  arwv

Map-A-Pic Location Scout

For the longest time, Panascout was the only location-scouting app I kept on my iPhone. A few other contenders put up a good fight, struggling in vain to secure a position on my home screen. But ultimately, their lack of unique and useful features prevented them from infiltrating my workflow.

All that changed the day I met Map-A-Pic Location Scout.

While Panascout puts its emphasis on capturing information-rich images, Map-A-Pic focuses on providing extensive organization tools tucked neatly masked behind an unintimidating user interface.

You begin by tapping the New Location button and then choosing to snap a new photo or grabbing an existing shot from your photo library. After adding the first photo, you can name the location, confirm your location on a mini Google map, and add up to nine additional photos to this location's record (**FIGURE 4.8**). Tapping the Save button in the upper right brings you to another screen that displays the same information but adds a street address, the current distance to the location, an area for text notes, the location's GPS coordinates, and the record's creation and modification dates.

The *real* power, however, comes from the ability to add any number of user-defined tags to each location record. For instance, after entering a new location

FIGURE 4.8 Each location record within Map-A-Pic can store up to ten location photos.

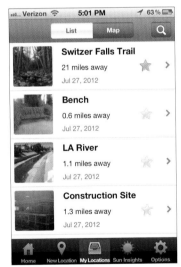

FIGURE 4.9 When you need to recall a location, just scroll through your database. You can also preview your locations on an interactive map.

at the base of a beautiful waterfall, you might assign tags like *waterfall*, *exterior*, *nature*, *romantic*, *forest*, and of course *massive garden hose*. That last tag was suggested by my business partner, Joseph. He has a unique way of sorting things.

As I mentioned, every location record provides a place to enter notes. I use this field to store important contact information associated with the location, such as the property owner's phone number and e-mail address. Remember, whenever you shoot on location, you need to gather all the necessary release forms (I cover how to use your iOS device to collect release forms later in this chapter).

When it's time to find the perfect location, tapping the My Locations tab brings you to a complete list of all your existing location records (**FIGURE 4.9**). To quickly find what you're looking for, you can search names, sort by distance or date entered, and, most importantly, filter by tags. When you have hundreds of locations in your collection, tags will save your butt. The app will also let you mark favorites and view all your locations on an interactive map.

When you need to share a location with your crew, Map-A-Pic will create an e-mail containing the location's name, notes, address, photos, and a link to the location in Google Maps. You can also broadcast locations on Twitter and Instagram…because there's nothing more awesome than hundreds of people unexpectedly showing up to observe your private, unpermitted shoot.

TECH SCOUTING

In addition to location scouts, your career will be peppered with technical scouts, or *tech scouts* as they're more commonly known. Unlike location scouts, tech scouts happen *after* you've secured your locations—typically a few days before you're scheduled to shoot. These are group events, attended by you and many of your department heads.

As soon as you arrive, the questions begin. How much of the location will require set dressing? Can the natural light be incorporated, or must it be contained? Will any departments require equipment not already in their trucks? Where will you put crew parking, catering, and extras holding (the area where extras wait while not in a shot)?

Although the specifics of everyone's agendas may differ, all of the participants share the same goals: to plan effective shots, to maximize a location's existing resources, to identify and solve all potential problems, and to determine exactly what new equipment will be required to pull everything off. It's that last goal that's just now getting a small boost from iOS developers. Current App Store offerings are slim to say the least, but three apps are worth singling out.

TECHSCOUT TOUCH, LIGHTING EDITION

iPad | iPhone

- LiteGear Inc.
- free
- hhhlinks.com/ i2t2

TechScout Touch, Lighting Edition

If you're a director of photography, gaffer, or best boy, you should stop reading this book, grab your iPhone, and download TechScout Touch, Lighting Edition. Really, go get it! Why are you still reading?

As long as you're still here, I suppose I should take a moment and tell you about this nifty little utility. Aside from having one of the longest names in the App Store, TechScout Touch, Lighting Edition can help you quickly compile a complete lighting order (a list of all necessary equipment) right from your iPhone!

After launching the app, tap Create New Job and then enter all the vital information. You can include job title, order number, and production company as well as the pickup, shoot, and drop-off dates.

Once your new job has been created, tap Add Gear to start building the order. Equipment is grouped into categories and subcategories, making it easy to drill down to your desired item (**FIGURE 4.10**). For instance, if you were prepping a glamour shoot and wanted to add an LED Ringlight to your order, you'd first tap the LED Sources category and then the Ringlight subcategory. From there, you'd browse the list of options and pick the one you want. For this example, I'll select the Gekko Kisslite Ringlight Kit. Tapping the ⊕ next to this item would add one to the order (**FIGURE 4.11**). If you change your mind, you can always tap the ⊖ to have it removed. Using this same process, add all the necessary gear until your order is complete.

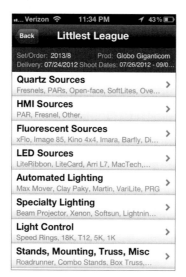

FIGURE 4.10 With more than 3000 items, it's good TechScout Touch, Lighting Edition keeps everything well organized.

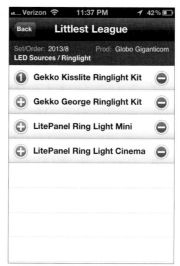

FIGURE 4.11 To add an item to your order, tap its green plus symbol. To remove it, tap the red minus symbol to the right.

When you're satisfied, tap Send Order to e-mail a cleanly formatted, well-organized equipment list to your rental facility, producer, or anyone else (like your mom—you don't e-mail her nearly enough).

The app was developed by LiteGear, a Burbank, California-based company that designs and builds specialty lighting equipment for the film industry. After using their app for a few minutes, I think you'll agree that these guys really know their stuff. The app includes more than *3000* individual pieces of lighting equipment. That said, you might require something that has not yet been added to the app's database. In those rare cases, you can easily add and edit your own items.

The most exciting thing about this app is the last two words in its title. Because the developer chose to call this the *Lighting Edition*, I'm quite hopeful that they have a few more editions up their sleeve. For instance, I believe a *Grip Edition,* a *Special FX Edition,* and even a *Craft Service Edition* would fit very nicely on my iPhone's home screen. A man can dream.

Camera Order

If you just read the description of TechScout Touch, Lighting Edition and said, "I sure wish something like that existed for the camera department!" you should stop talking to a book. It makes you look like a crazy person. Also, you should know about Camera Order, an app made specifically for the camera department.

I'm not going to go into too much detail because this app operates very similarly to TechScout Touch, Lighting Edition, or T.S.T.L.E. (that's what the cool kids call it).

In Camera Order, you begin by creating a new job and then navigating through the various categories of camera gear to find the equipment you'd like to add to your rental list. Equipment is broken up into six main categories: Cameras, Lenses, Filters, Accessories, Support, and Film and Media (**FIGURE 4.12**).

When you locate an item you'd like to add, just tap its ⊕. After you've completed your list, you can e-mail a clean, well-organized order straight from the app to your rental house. You can save and duplicate your jobs for use down the line.

More than just a list of equipment, Camera Order serves as a basic reference guide, providing useful data for lenses (maximum aperture, close focus, and front diameter size) and cameras (weight, lens mount, frames per second, digital camera's native ASA) (**FIGURE 4.13**).

Unlike T.S.T.L.E., Camera Order works equally well on all your iOS devices and doesn't distract you with in-app advertising. However, all this awesomeness comes at a price—20 smackers, to be precise—but it's a small price to pay for the convenience this app provides.

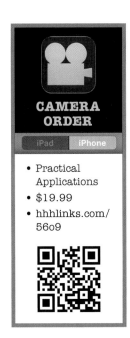

CAMERA ORDER

iPad   iPhone

- Practical Applications
- $19.99
- hhhlinks.com/ 56o9

FIGURE 4.12 Camera Order keeps everything organized within categories and nested subcategories.

FIGURE 4.13 Launch Camera Order the next time you need to know the details about a specific camera or lens.

LIST SENDER

iPad **iPhone**

- Goldplum
- $1.99
- hhhlinks.com/xomd

List Sender

List Sender essentially performs the same primary function as TechScout Touch, Lighting Edition and Camera Order, but while those apps come with huge databases of professional gear, List Sender comes with nothing but a cute icon. It's this total lack of preexisting content that makes the app so versatile. In List Sender, it's up to you to create *templates* (the app's name for databases) and populate them with items.

For instance, if you work in the grip department, you could build a template that includes *all* the grip equipment you might ever require on a typical shoot. Then, when it's time for a tech scout, you could draft an equipment order (or list) on site by selecting desired items from the grip equipment template you created earlier. Adding items to your list works just like it did in T.S.T.L.E. Find the item you want, and then tap the plus symbol to add it. When your list is complete, you can e-mail a nicely formatted copy to your rental house, your producer, or your mom. (Trust me on this; she'll treasure any e-mails you send.)

Using these same techniques, List Sender can be customized for any department. Because *you're* the one creating the templates, there really is no limit to how the app can be used. That said, building templates takes a lot of time, especially if you're particularly thorough. It's up to you to decide whether the effort is worth the reward.

SCHEDULING

Shooting a film, large or small, is very much like participating in an intricately choreographed square dance—large groups of people scurrying in circles, pushing and pulling, all hoping to ace the next Horseshoe Turn (just in case you're not a big square-dancing fan, a poorly executed Horseshoe Turn can easily turn a party into a pile-on).

A smooth production begins with a solid schedule.

As simple as it may seem, scheduling film and video production can be mind-numbingly tricky. As you likely already know, 99.9 percent of all films are shot out of order. Similar scenes are grouped together in order to maximize every dollar spent and avoid redundant work.

For example, if your crime drama includes several scenes that take place in a prison and they require actors who don't appear elsewhere in the film, it makes no sense to schedule those scenes on multiple days, spread across your production calendar. You'd wind up re-renting (or rebuilding) your jail set multiple times and paying actors for numerous days. By scheduling them all for the same day, you avoid all that additional expense.

Another reason to group scenes is to accommodate someone's (or something's) limited availability. For instance, let's say you're lucky enough to land a name actor for a small role. Unfortunately, she's only willing to give you two days of her time. In this case, scheduling her scenes together will become your highest priority. That said, it's still important to schedule those scenes in an order that makes the most sense logistically and budgetarily.

Seems simple enough, but what happens when the weather suddenly takes an unexpected turn? Or a stunt takes much longer to shoot than expected? Or one of your locations backs out?

It's not just a matter of cramming a bunch of scenes into a bunch of days. Shoot schedules are living, breathing organisms that must remain flexible enough to shift and stretch under ever-changing circumstances. Consider it the elastic waistband on the stain-covered sweatpants we call *production*.

So, are you ready to take on some scheduling mayhem? Not so fast, Captain Calendar! Before you can begin scheduling, you'll first need to *break down* your script. I have yet to find any iOS apps that truly contribute to this process, but there are certainly a number of excellent books on the subject. Breaking down a script involves numbering the scenes for easy identification and pinpointing the elements that appear in each scene so you'll know exactly who and what will be needed at each location. You need a script breakdown because you can't schedule what you don't fully understand. If you're not confident you can break down your own script, find someone who can.

Once your script has been broken down, you're ready to rock.

Macs and Windows machines have long dominated the film-scheduling arena. However, with three excellent scheduling tools already available in the App Store, iOS devices may soon be taking over...or at least, sneaking in the back door.

Movie Magic Scheduling To Go

- Entertainment Partners
- $29.99
- hhhlinks.com/75g4

Movie Magic Scheduling for Mac and Windows has been the entertainment industry's scheduling touchstone for as long as I can remember. Although a few other scheduling apps have attempted to crash this Hollywood party, they've never managed to get into the V.I.P. section.

When Movie Magic Scheduling To Go (M.M.S.T.G.) hit the App Store in April 2011, it was a clear sign that Hollywood was taking iOS very seriously. It was also a sign that insanely long app names had somehow become acceptable.

Before I get into the app's operation, I want to give you a quick bit of background. Film scheduling is typically done by the assistant director using something called a *strip board* (sometimes called a *production board*). Strip boards were once made of plastic, cardboard, or wood, but they have since been computerized, although the basic concepts and usage have remained largely unchanged. The idea is simple. Every scene in a film gets its own color-coded strip. The color indicates the scene's time of day and type of shot. For instance, a white strip indicates an interior day scene, while a green strip indicates an exterior night scene. All the strips are then put onto a board, which is why it's called a *strip board.* The strips are then shifted, shuffled, reordered, reorganized, and assigned to specific shooting days, until the entire schedule takes shape.

Movie Magic Scheduling for Macs and Windows machines can help you break down scripts and then virtualize the creation and management of your strip board. M.M.S.T.G. turns your iPad into an extension of the ubiquitous desktop application (**FIGURE 4.14**). It's not a self-contained, stand-alone scheduling app, which is a bit of a disappointment for filmmakers anxiously hoping to see the full application emerge on Apple's mobile platform. So, if you're not using Movie Magic Scheduling on your desktop or laptop computer, you can skip this app. Move along. Nothing to see here.

This isn't a book about traditional computers, so I won't go into detail about the operation of Movie Magic Scheduling. Suffice it to say, it does a wonderful job

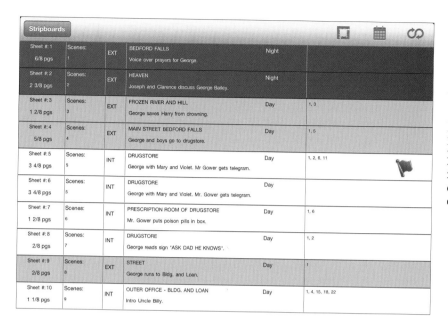

FIGURE 4.14 Movie Magic Scheduling To Go brings strip boards to the iPad. (Screenshot created using Movie Magic Scheduling application owned by DISC Intellectual Properties, LLC dba Entertainment Partners. For more information, http://www.entertainmentpartners.com/scheduling_to_go.)

of building complex schedules using the strip board technique. Assuming you're a Movie Magic user and you have a schedule ready to go, you can import it into M.M.S.T.G. from an e-mail attachment or via iTunes File Sharing.

After opening your newly imported file, you can scroll through the full board by flicking your finger up or down on the iPad's screen. You can also change a few layout options, edit the schedule by dragging strips between days, and move strips to the *boneyard*—what the app calls its holding area for unused strips.

Tapping any strip instantly displays that scene's *breakdown sheet*, a simple form containing all of the scene's required elements broken down by category (Cast Members, Extras, Stunts, Props, Costumes, Vehicles, and so forth) (**FIGURE 4.15**).

You can't generate new scene strips from within the app, but you can create additional days by adding day break strips. You can also incorporate special notes, such as company moves, by adding banner strips. All the changes you make to the schedule will be saved and can be exported via e-mail or iTunes File Sharing.

There are other features to explore, but manipulating existing schedules is this app's primary function. I have no idea if we'll ever see a full-featured version of Movie Magic Scheduling for iOS, but until we do, users of the desktop app can still benefit from this handy app.

FIGURE 4.15 Tap any strip to view that scene's breakdown sheet.

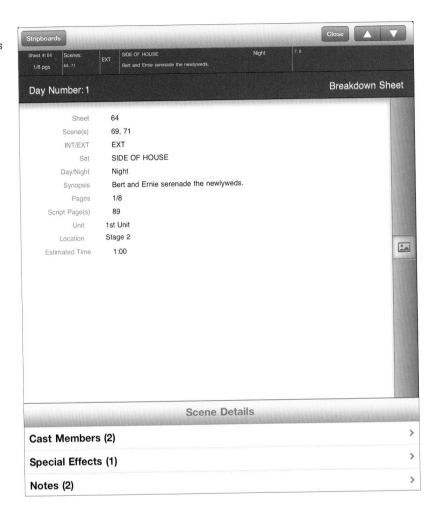

SHOTLIST

iPad   iPhone

- Soluble
- $11.99
- hhhlinks.com/3pd6

ShotList

$499. That's how much you'll have to shell out for the Mac or Windows version of Movie Magic Scheduling. And, of course, that doesn't include the additional 30 clams you'll be dropping for the iPad app! I know for a fact that these professional-grade budgeting applications are worth every penny, but many new filmmakers simply can't afford to fork over that kind of cash.

$12. That's how much ShotList will run you. Things are looking up, right?

Unlike M.M.S.T.G., ShotList is a totally self-contained scheduling app, which is both a blessing and a curse. Although it doesn't depend on an expensive desktop app for its data, it lacks the ability to work with industry-standard file formats (like Movie Magic Scheduling files).

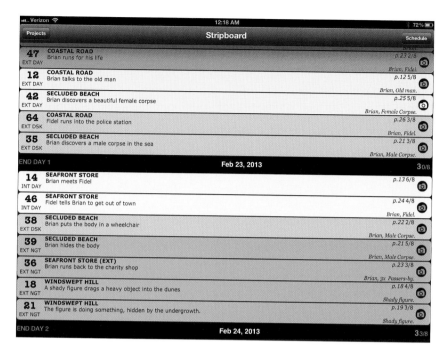

FIGURE 4.16 ShotList embraces the industry-standard strip board metaphor.

Using the app is fairly straightforward. After creating and naming a new project, you need to start adding scenes. Like most production scheduling tools, Shot-List uses the same strip board metaphor I described earlier, with each scene being assigned to its own color-coded strip (**FIGURE 4.16**).

To add a new strip, switch into scheduling mode, and then tap the plus symbol to the left of an existing strip. Your new strip will be created directly underneath. Enter all the vitals, such as the scene number, the location, the time of day, the included cast, and more (this is where a script breakdown really comes in handy). You can also import up to six images per scene strip. These might be storyboard frames or location photos and can be pulled from your photo library or camera.

After turning all your scenes into individual strips, it's time to arrange them into the ideal shooting order. Strips can be dragged up and down, alone or in groups. After organizing a day's worth of shots, add an *end of day* strip. This black divider shows the precise shooting date and calculates how many script pages will be shot that day. Depending on the complexity of your shoot and the talent of your crew, you can expect to shoot anywhere from two to eight pages in a day. Naturally, if you're shooting an effects-heavy action sequence, you might shoot only a half-page. Likewise, if you're shooting a 15-minute conversation between two guys in La-Z-Boy recliners, you might be able to pull off 15 pages.

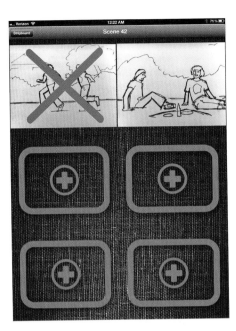

FIGURE 4.17 Every strip in ShotList can store up to six images. This works great when using storyboard panels for reference.

Remember I mentioned that you can import storyboard frames into a scene strip? Once you're in production, those frames can be crossed off one by one as you grab the associated shots (**FIGURE 4.17**). When you've completed the entire scene, you can toggle that strip's status from ToDo to Done. This turns the strip gray and makes you feel all warm and fuzzy.

At the end of your shoot day, if you failed to complete one or more scheduled scenes, return to ShotList and shuffle your remaining strips once again. Like I said, your schedule should always remain flexible, and that's why an app like ShotList will make a powerful addition to your workflow.

ShotList project files can be exported to and imported from a Dropbox account, which makes sharing schedules a painless process. While the app can't export a PDF of your full strip board, it can e-mail a one-line schedule (a condensed version of the full schedule that excludes certain information such as script pages and notes). It's also worth mentioning that the app can't currently print, but the developer is working to add that and other helpful functionality.

ShotList is not going to replace high-end, desktop-based scheduling solutions. But as it turns out, that's just fine by the developer, who describes his app as being perfect for planning smaller shoots in detail. I agree completely.

Shot Lister

The newest scheduling app to materialize in the App Store is Shot Lister. If apps were judged purely on their letter count, Shot Lister would be exactly two letters better (or worse) than ShotList. As it turns out, this is not necessarily the most accurate way to compare apps, so let's look a little deeper.

Although you will recognize a few similarities to the previous two apps, Shot Lister takes an *extremely* different approach to scheduling. Most notably, it's the only app in the bunch that breaks things down to the *shot* level. In other words, if you plan on shooting eight distinct shots for a particular scene, Shot Lister lets you organize those shots into a desired shooting order within any given shoot day. It even lets you schedule those shots across multiple shoot days! That feature alone is worth the price of admission. Although the iPhone and iPad versions don't look or operate exactly alike, both versions perform equally well.

To schedule a film, begin by adding a new project and giving it a name. Then add a scene by tapping ➕ in the upper-right corner and entering all the vital information (scene name, scene description, location, time of day, scene number, script page count, and so on). Add a shot to your new scene by tapping the familiar ➕ and entering the shot's name, a description, its size (close-up, medium, wide, and so on), and more. Repeat this for every shot in your scene (**FIGURE 4.18**). When you're done, return to your scene list, and create your next scene. This continues until all your scenes have been added.

SHOT LISTER

- Reel Apps Inc.
- $13.99
- hhhlinks.com/75xd

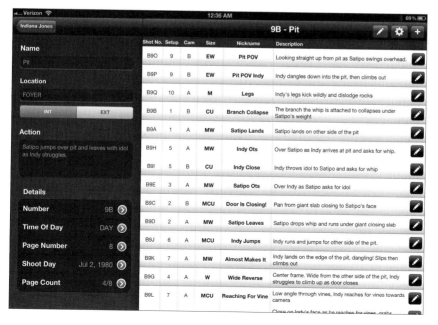

FIGURE 4.18 Shot Lister's Scene view displays every shot that makes up a scene. The app comes with a sample schedule that really helps reduce the learning curve.

FIGURE 4.19 Shot Lister helps you schedule each shoot day, shot by shot, and then informs you when you're running behind or ahead of schedule.

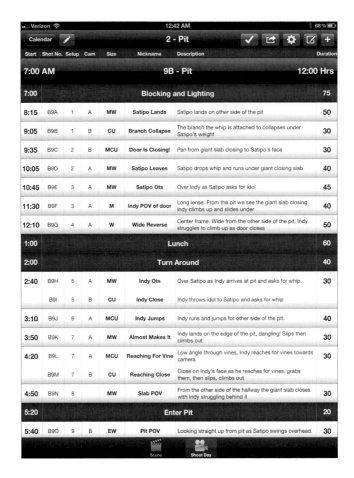

Start	Shot No.	Setup	Cam	Size	Nickname	Description	Duration
7:00 AM					**9B - Pit**		**12:00 Hrs**
7:00					**Blocking and Lighting**		**75**
8:15	B9A	1	A	MW	Satipo Lands	Satipo lands on other side of the pit	50
9:05	B9B	1	B	CU	Branch Collapse	The branch the whip is attached to collapses under Satipo's weight	30
9:35	B9C	2	B	MCU	Door Is Closing!	Pan from giant slab closing to Satipo's face	30
10:05	B9D	2	A	MW	Satipo Leaves	Satipo drops whip and runs under giant closing slab	40
10:45	B9E	3	A	MW	Satipo Ots	Over Indy as Satipo asks for idol	45
11:30	B9F	3	A	M	Indy POV of door	Long lense. From the pit we see the giant slab closing, Indy climbs up and slides under	40
12:10	B9G	4	A	W	Wide Reverse	Center frame. Wide from the other side of the pit, Indy struggles to climb up as door closes	50
1:00					**Lunch**		**60**
2:00					**Turn Around**		**40**
2:40	B9H	5	A	MW	Indy Ots	Over Satipo as Indy arrives at pit and asks for whip.	30
	B9I	5	B	CU	Indy Close	Indy throws idol to Satipo and asks for whip	
3:10	B9J	6	A	MCU	Indy Jumps	Indy runs and jumps for other side of the pit.	40
3:50	B9K	7	A	MW	Almost Makes It	Indy lands on the edge of the pit, dangling! Slips then climbs out	30
4:20	B9L	7	A	MCU	Reaching For Vine	Low angle through vines, Indy reaches for vines towards camera	30
	B9M	7	B	CU	Reaching Close	Close on Indy's face as he reaches for vines, grabs them, then slips, climbs out	
4:50	B9N	8		MW	Slab POV	From the other side of the hallway the giant slab closes with Indy struggling behind it	30
5:20					**Enter Pit**		**20**
5:40	B9O	9	B	EW	Pit POV	Looking straight up from pit as Satipo swings overhead.	30

Ready to schedule? Tapping the Shoot Day tab at the bottom of the screen brings up a list of all your scheduled shoot days, of which you currently have none. Add one by tapping ➕ and assigning it a date and a nickname (which will make it easy to quickly identify later), as well as call, lunch, and wrap times. Your new shoot day will be added to the list. On a side note, when using Shot Lister on an iPad, you can switch between list and calendar views by rotating the tablet between portrait and landscape orientations.

Tap your new shoot day, and you'll be brought to that day's schedule. From here you can add shots by once again tapping ➕ and picking any of the scenes you created earlier that now appear in a pop-up list. Once a scene is added, all of the shots associated with that scene will appear on the day's schedule. Now you can reorder them as necessary, giving each an estimated duration for completion. You can add notes with their own durations, perfect for scheduling setup times, lunch breaks, and company moves (**FIGURE 4.19**).

After you've structured the schedule, the real fun begins. On the day of your shoot, switch Shot Lister into Live Production mode, and you'll be staring at an attractive but unrelenting shot clock that will let you know if you're on time, ahead of schedule, or falling behind. Armed with this knowledge, you can make quick decisions and reorganize the rest of your day if necessary. Sick!

Shot Lister's amazing hour-by-hour control comes at a small cost. It's a *brilliant* tool for planning individual shoot days, but it's not ideal when structuring "the big picture"...at least, not yet. When crafting a master schedule, full scenes are constantly being shifted between days. That's why a strip board presentation is so popular—it allows you to see many days at once and easily slide scene strips between them. Shot Lister does not provide a multiday strip board view. Therefore, it's not as easy to move scenes from one day to another. Is this a deal-breaker? Absolutely not! While Shot Lister may not be the perfect app for an assistant director who is preparing to schedule an entire film, it's the perfect app for keeping directors informed and on track, which typically translates into highly productive shoot days.

CALL SHEETS

You've secured your location and scheduled your shoot day. Now it's time to share that information with everyone else, which means it's time to create a call sheet.

Typically prepared by the assistant director, a call sheet contains all the details pertaining to a particular day of production. It informs the crew where they need to go and what time they are expected to arrive (their *call time*). In addition to listing the day's scheduled scenes, a call sheet also includes useful information such as a weather forecast, times for sunrise and sunset, crew contact details, safety warnings for pyrotechnics and stunts, and the address of the nearest hospital.

For years, call sheets have remained largely unchanged, as have the methods for their distribution: faxing, e-mailing, and being handed out on set. Thanks to the wonders of modern technology and the work of several innovative app developers, call sheets are getting an iOS makeover.

DoddlePRO

I've mentioned doddle, the free production directory that should already be gracing your iPhone's home screen. Doddle's big brother, doddlePRO, has a bit of a split personality. Not only does this ten-dollar app offer the same production directory, but it also grabs paper-based call sheets by the collar and drags them kicking and screaming into the digital era.

doddlePRO

iPad iPhone

- Mobile Imagination
- $9.99
- hhhlinks.com/sOkj

DoddlePRO greatly simplifies the process of call sheet creation and even auto-mates a few of the steps (**FIGURE 4.20**). For instance, when adding a new shooting location, you can type in the address manually, copy it from a list of recent locations, or import it straight from your address book or doddle's own production directory. With your location entered, a map will indicate all the nearby hospitals and police stations. Just tap one, and it's added to your call sheet. Some items are added without any interaction at all, such as the loca-tion's sunrise and sunset times (**FIGURE 4.21**).

This simplicity is mirrored throughout the app. For example, when entering con-tact information for a cast or crew member, you are presented with time-saving buttons that quickly indicate if that person is meant to report to the location, wait for a pick-up, or simply be on call. It's just as easy to dial in unique call times for each person on the sheet (if you don't assign a custom time, the gen-eral call time will be inserted).

When you're ready to share your completed call sheet, you can e-mail it to your entire cast and crew, individual departments, or just a few select people. Only call sheet creators need to spend money on doddlePRO. The free version of the app also functions as a doddle call sheet reader.

FIGURE 4.20 When creating call sheets in doddlePRO, save time by importing information directly from your address book and the doddle online directory.

FIGURE 4.21 DoddlePRO auto-matically fetches the weather forecast for your call sheets, as well as sunrise and sunset times.

FIGURE 4.22 Anyone with the free doddle app can view and interact with doddle's online call sheets.

Wait! What happens when members of your cast or crew don't have doddle or, worse yet, don't own an iOS device? Are they left out in the cold? Of course not! DoddlePRO automatically generates and e-mails a PDF version of your call sheet along with a link to the doddle version, ensuring that everyone gets the necessary information. What happens if members of your cast and crew don't have an e-mail account and insist you *fax* them the call sheet? Fire them. I'm sure they could use the extra time to feed their dinosaurs.

Cast and crew members savvy enough to own the free doddle app can view and interact with your virtual call sheets right on their iPhones. They can tap the weather icon to see the updated forecast (**FIGURE 4.22**) or the map icon to get instant driving directions. They can even tap another crew member to view that person's details and initiate a phone call or text message.

Yes, this is all well and good, but what about a one-line review that doddle's marketing department can stick on a T-shirt? Completely logical question! Here you go: "DoddlePRO is the smart way to create smarter call sheets, smarterly!" Dear doddle marketing department, I wear an XL.

Pocket Call Sheet

After reading all the lovely things I had to say about doddlePRO, you might be wondering why I'd bother recommending another call sheet app. There are two reasons: doddlePRO isn't for everyone, and Pocket Call Sheet is super cool.

DoddlePRO's unique interface comes with a (small) learning curve. I'm sure there are plenty of assistant directors out there who'd rather keep things simple

POCKET CALL SHEET

iPad | iPhone

- Snake Byte Studio
- $6.99
- hhhlinks.com/qadi

and not spend any time providing tech support for crew members frustrated by doddle's newfangled interactive call sheet (filmmakers can be a stubborn bunch).

Pocket Call Sheet is a deceptively simple app with a super-clean interface and surprisingly few controls. It works well on iPhone but is a joy to use on an iPad. Its output looks, feels, and smells like industry-standard call sheets (**FIGURE 4.23**)—the kind that won't trigger cold sweats from crew members who "like things the way they are, damn it!" (filmmakers can be a grumpy bunch).

With Pocket Call Sheet launched, tapping the [+] in the upper-right corner will open the Production page. After entering all of your project's general information (title, studio, shooting days, producers, assistant directors, production office info, and so on; **FIGURE 4.24**), you can move on to your shoot day's particulars (cast and crew call times, locations, and more).

FIGURE 4.23 Pocket Call Sheet makes call sheets that look just like any other call sheets—and that's a very good thing!

PRODUCTION COMPANY: Ernest Pictures
STUDIO: Snake Byte Studio
EXEC PRODUCER(S): Ronald Allen, Isabella Blue
PRODUCER(S): Theresa Breen
DIRECTOR(S): Gigi Burns
PRODUCTION OFFICE: 100 Studio Way, Boston MA 02112
PHONE NUMBER: 555-555-5541
PROD./EPISODE #: 127
GENERAL CREW CALL: 7:00

Dark Days

DATE: Saturday, October 27, 2012
SHOOTING DAY: Day 1 of 45
FIRST SHOOTING DAY: Saturday, October 27, 2012
SUNRISE: 5:24
SUNSET: 20:03
WEATHER: Sunny
COMPANY REPORT TO: Stage 17
COMPANY SHOOTING CALL: 9:00

TODAY'S SCHEDULE

SATURDAY, OCTOBER 27, 2012 - Day 1 of 45

SC#	INT/EXT	SCENE HEADING	D/N	DESCRIPTION	PAGES	CAST	LOCATION ADDRESS	NOTES
49	INT./EXT.	Train Station	D13	David follows Charles into the station.	2/8	1, 2, 5, 6	100 Station Way, Boston, MA, 02112	Parking on Main St.
27	EXT.	Parking Lot	N20	David watches people exit the station.	3/8	1, 3	122 Dark Lane Drive, Boston, MA, 02112	
67	INT.	David's Basement	N30	David releases a snake into the basement.	1 1/8	1, 3	100 Studio Way, Stage 17, Boston, MA, 02112	
	--- END OF DAY 1 ---			TOTAL PAGES	1 6/8			

PROPERTY

SC#	DESCRIPTION	QUANTITY
27	Knife	1
67	Surgical Equipment	1

CAST

#	CAST	ROLE	STATUS	PICK UP	CALL TIME	HAIR & M/U	SET CALL	NOTES
1	Alex Hughes	David	W	7:00	7:30	8:00	9:00	
2	George Innes	Charles	W	7:00	7:30	8:00	9:00	
3	Sarah Morgan	Isabella	W	7:00	7:30	8:00	9:00	

STAND-INS, ATMOSPHERE, MUSICIANS

#	CAST	ROLE	STATUS	PICK UP	CALL TIME	HAIR & M/U	SET CALL	NOTES
4	Background Group #1	Boston PD Officers	H	N/A	10:00	10:30	11:00	
5	Background Group #2	Station Employees	W	N/A	10:00	10:30	11:00	Please wear dark sunglasses.
6	Background Group #3	Train Passengers	W	N/A	10:00	10:30	11:00	

ADVANCE SCHEDULE

MONDAY, OCTOBER 29, 2012 - Day 2 of 45

SC#	INT/EXT	SCENE HEADING	D/N	DESCRIPTION	PAGES	CAST	LOCATION ADDRESS	NOTES
38	EXT.	Field	D40	Det. Charles Brown approaches the crime scene.	5/8	2, 4	199 Open Plains Way, Boston, MA, 02112	
34	INT.	David's Basement	N20	David accidentally leaves a window open. Isabella looks through, notices something inside.	2 1/8	1, 3	100 Studio Way, Stage 17, Boston, MA, 02112	
	--- END OF DAY 2 ---			TOTAL PAGES	2 6/8			

ADVANCE SCHEDULE

TUESDAY, OCTOBER 30, 2012 - Day 3 of 45

SC#	INT/EXT	SCENE HEADING	D/N	DESCRIPTION	PAGES	CAST	LOCATION ADDRESS	NOTES
46	INT.	David's Basement	D33	David composes a letter for the detectives.	1 0/8	1, 3	100 Studio Way, Stage 17, Boston, MA, 02112	
	--- END OF DAY 3 ---			TOTAL PAGES	1 0/8			

This call sheet was produced: Friday, July 27, 2012, 21:27:24 PDT

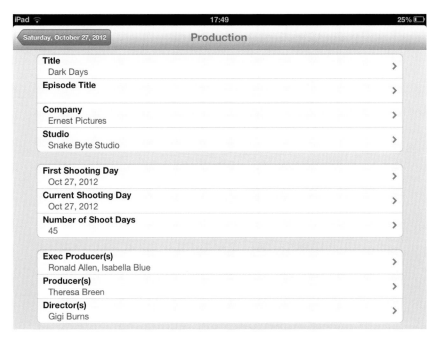

There's no automatic lookup for things like sunrise time, sunset time, and the weather, so you'll have to enter those things yourself. The same is true for emergency contact information such as local hospitals, police stations, and firehouses.

Once all the details are entered, tap Produce Email to generate your finished call sheet. You have the option of sending it to everyone listed on the call sheet, as well as any additional contacts. The call sheet can appear as an HTML-formatted document (the same coding language used to create web pages) and can be attached to the e-mail as a PDF file. There's even an option to add a signature with your finger or a stylus.

When it's time to create the next day's call sheet, the app is smart enough to copy everything over from the previous day's sheet, while advancing the shoot date by one. Naturally, everything is editable in the new call sheet.

Before you start using the app, you should be aware of two things. First, in order to add someone to your call sheet, that person must first exist in your iOS device's address book. There's no way to manually enter a name. Second, while the app is smart enough to replicate a previous day's call sheet information into a new call sheet, it doesn't "remember" things. In other words, if I have Jada, Nick, and Andre all on the call sheet for Monday but then remove Nick on Tuesday because I caught him jumping his skateboard off some tanks marked *Nitroglycerin*, there's no shortcut for putting him back on the call sheet for Wednesday (once I realized the nitro tanks were props). If I wanted him back, I'd have to reenter his details. Neither issue is a deal-breaker, but they are inconvenient.

Minor annoyances aside, Pocket Call Sheet is a well-designed, professional tool that takes call sheets as seriously as you do, maybe more so.

FilmTouch

I can't tell you how this app has changed my life because I just learned about it a few days ago. I can't praise its ease of operation, because I'm still figuring it out. I can't even point out how useful it is, because I haven't used it long enough.

So, why am I bothering to mention a tool I barely know? Because FilmTouch is a *very interesting* app. Very interesting, indeed.

Rather than create call sheets, FilmTouch imports your existing PDF call sheets, extracts all the crew member names and their positions as well as company names, and then stores that data in a massive shared, searchable database. Sadly, the system does not support feature film call sheets, but it works quite nicely with commercial and music video call sheets. Furthermore, it works only with text-based PDF files. Scanned call sheets are a no-go.

You begin using FilmTouch by importing a call sheet. The easiest way to do this is as an e-mail attachment. The app will upload your call sheet to its server for processing, and a few minutes later, a new, properly named project magically appears on the My Jobs tab. If you upload multiple call sheets, the app organizes the resulting projects by year. If you tap a project, you are presented with a scrolling list of all crew members associated with that project or, more specifically, its originating call sheet (**FIGURE 4.25**). By tapping a crew member's name, you get their contact information (as it existed on the call sheet). In other words, you now have a complete record of everyone you've worked with! How sick is that? Wait, it gets sicker.

If you tap the ⬇ next to any crew member's name, you'll be taken to a list of every project they're associated with, even if it originated from someone else's call sheet. It's like having your very own IMDB…for a price.

The app will run you six buckaroos, but if you want to keep uploading call sheets after the initial two-month free trial, you'll have to purchase a subscription extension. They range in price from $2.99 a month to $19.99 a year. Is it worth it? Don't know. But, like I said, FilmTouch is a *very interesting* app. Very interesting, indeed.

FILMTOUCH

iPad   **iPhone**

- MonkSeal Media, LLC
- $5.99
- hhhlinks.com/ 7w35

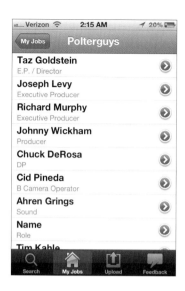

FIGURE 4.25 FilmTouch doesn't *create* call sheets. It *reads* call sheets, extracts their information, and adds the data to its master database. I'd say that ranks about 80 percent awesome and 20 percent disturbing.

Lua

OK, fine. One more.

Lua is not officially available as of this writing, but I thought it was worth sneaking into the chapter. Put simply, Lua lets you set up a private online digital community for your production crew. It invites discussion, streamlines communications, and can even broadcast important crew-wide text messages. With an intuitive web interface that feels like it snuck out of Apple's underground laboratories, Lua is more of a service than an application, although its forthcoming iPhone app is the reason it's on my radar.

I've included Lua in this chapter because it provides a powerful document distribution system, perfect for daily call sheets. In its initial public release, Lua will not help you generate your call sheets. However, during a recent demo, I was told that an assisted call sheet creation tool is certainly in the works.

RELEASE FORMS AND CONTRACTS

I learned a few important lessons during my early years as a filmmaker.

> Never be afraid to ask for free stuff.

> Feed your crew well no matter how small your budget.

> Always, and I mean *always*, get a signed release.

There are several different types of release forms, all of which serve the same general purpose—to cover your butt or, in slightly more mature language, to ensure that you are legally permitted to exploit whatever is being released.

The forms you'll be using most often are the talent and location releases, although there are several others, including crew releases, music releases, photo releases, and more. The specific language in your release depends largely on what you're shooting, as well as any union affiliations you may have.

Let's look at an example. Any time you shoot an actor for your film (with a camera, not a Taser), you must also get their permission to use their likeness in your film. You do this with a talent release. Just because someone shows up to set, lines memorized, and delivers a stunning performance, that doesn't mean they're agreeing to let you include them in the finished film. Even if they stand there at the wrap party, celebratory beer in hand, and announce, "I agree to let you include me in the finished film," they may feel differently the next day, or whenever they sober up. By getting a signed release form, you are guaranteed the right to use their likeness and performance in your film, your marketing, your bonus material, and everything else relating to the project.

"Yeah, but my lead actor is my roommate, so I don't *really* need a release, do I?"

Yeah. You *really* need a release. Let's say you're preparing to submit your recently completed masterpiece to the Sundance Film Festival. Suddenly, you get a text from your roommate/ lead actor. He explains that he just landed a *huge* role in the next Tyler Perry flick (*Medea Eats a Sandwich).* He says he doesn't want your movie coming out and screwing up his chances at stardom. He demands you shelve your film. You don't think much of it until he utters these devastating words: "I never signed a release!" You, my friend, are boned.

Now that I've sufficiently scared the crap out of you, allow me to soothe your psyche with a refreshing cup of reality. Getting signed release forms is no big deal. All you have to do is ask. Most actors don't think twice, probably because they've signed dozens of them already. If someone gives you grief about it, you can always alter the language slightly to accommodate their concerns. If they give you a *lot* of grief, kick them off the project. Do you really want someone that problematic involved with your film?

Even knowing the potential pitfalls, many indie filmmakers *still* make the mistake of not collecting signed releases. Why? The excuse I hear most often is, "I didn't have any forms with me." Clearly, these people don't own an iPhone or iPad. With either of these devices on hand, filmmakers will always have access to release forms. Here's how.

Easy Release

While it's not the first release form tool to grace the App Store, Easy Release is certainly one of the best. It's so good, in fact, that my description of it might lead you to believe I own stock in the company. To prevent any misconceptions, I'll begin by pointing out the app's biggest flaw: It provides release forms only for talent and locations. Considering these are the two release forms you'll be using most, I'm willing to overlook the limitation. With that incredibly harsh critique out of the way, let the love-fest begin!

Working equally well on iPads and iPhones, Easy Release lets you quickly collect and share signed release forms. Even though the included templates are terrific, you may need to make a few alterations in the text or use completely different language. With the app's Custom Release feature, you can duplicate and edit existing templates and create new templates from scratch. Because my company has been using the same talent release form for years, I simply copied its text and pasted it directly into a new Easy Release custom template.

Creating a new release is a fairly quick process. Begin by tapping the ⊞ in the upper right and then tapping either Model (talent) or Property (location). From there, you are presented a list of all releases available in that category—this will include the default, as well as any custom release templates you've created. Pick one, tap Next, and you'll be asked to enter various bits of information about the production, the location (if it's a location release), and some specifics about who will be signing the form. After that, your device's camera will pop up. If you're creating a talent release, take a photo of your actor. If you're creating a location release, snap a shot of the location. Finish up the photo, and fill in the remaining fields, which will vary depending on your settings.

Finally, you'll be brought to the summary screen where you can make any last-minute changes (**FIGURE 4.26**). When everything is up to snuff, it's time to get that autograph! Tap the Signature field, and hand your iOS device to the signer. They'll be given the chance to read through the entire release before signing, which they can do with their finger or a stylus (**FIGURE 4.27**).

Once the form has been signed, you can immediately generate a snazzy-looking PDF of the completed release and e-mail a copy to the signer (**FIGURE 4.28**).

To achieve maximum efficiency on set, create your release forms ahead of time, making sure to input all the vital information, and then save them for later use. Then, when you're ready for a signature, just reopen the appropriate saved release, get the signature, and move right along.

EASY RELEASE

iPad | iPhone

- ApplicationGap
- $9.99
- hhhlinks.com/jqqm

FIGURE 4.26 Double-check all the information you've entered into Easy Release *before* asking your performer to sign. If you change anything afterward, the form will need to be signed again.

FIGURE 4.27 The signer can use a finger or a stylus right on the iPad or iPhone screen.

FIGURE 4.28 After you gather the required signatures, Easy Release will generate a PDF of your completed release form.

Easy Release will run you $9.99 for the basic feature set, but if you prefer a life of luxury, you can spend an additional $3.99 for the Advanced Customization Pro-Pack. The extra green buys you the ability to create multiple brands and assign any of them to new releases. This is especially useful if you work free-lance for several different companies. You also gain greater control over exist-ing fields and the ability to create your own custom fields. Finally, the Pro-Pack allows you to share your custom release templates with other Easy Release users as well as your other iOS devices. For me, the additional purchase was a no-brainer, but if you have no need for the extra customization, don't feel com-pelled to spend the cash.

Form Tools PDF

One of my new favorite apps, Form Tools PDF, employs a fundamentally differ-ent approach to completing release forms.

When filling out a form in Easy Release, you must first enter relevant information into a succession of labeled fields. After that, the app generates a new PDF file containing the completed release form. It's not until the *last step* that your fin-ished form is blinked into existence. Conversely, when using Form Tools (as well as the next app, Cinema Forms), you *begin* with a fully realized form that incor-porates blank lines that must be filled in with the pertinent data. In other words, it works the same as filling out paper forms. I'm not suggesting this approach is better, but I do think it will feel more familiar to those unaccustomed with digital forms.

FORM TOOLS PDF

iPad | iPhone

- Relevantwalk Software
- $4.99
- hhhlinks.com/ szkc

Form Tools PDF was meant to work with your existing forms, and as such, it doesn't come with any of its own. To import your existing forms, you must first convert them into PDF files (unless they're already PDF files, in which case you get a gold star). On the bright side, if your release forms include a custom mast-head or logo, those will be brought along for the ride. On an even brighter note, since Form Tools PDF works with any PDF file, you can use the app for just about any production form that needs filling, not just release forms.

You can import a PDF document from an e-mail attachment, via iTunes File Sharing, or from any app that provides the Open In menu (Dropbox, PDF Expert, and so on). As soon as a PDF is imported, Form Tools PDF immediately turns it into a new form. From there, you can add and position various form ele-ments, including text boxes, date fields, drop-down menus, check boxes, and photo boxes.

Adding new form elements is a snap (**FIGURE 4.29**). Just tap anywhere on the document. You'll be offered three main options: Text Box, Check Box, and Photo Box. Pick the one you want, and it will be added in place. From

FIGURE 4.29 Use Form Tools to turn any PDF into an interactive form.

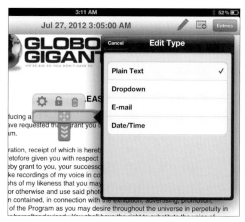

FIGURE 4.30 Each form element you create within Form Tools provides several adjustable parameters.

there, you can adjust its parameters, which vary based on the element type (**FIGURE 4.30**). There's no need to add a special element for signature collection since the app includes a Pen tool that can draw anywhere on the form.

It's worth noting that while the PDF file standard includes its own form elements, Form Tools PDF does not currently support them. Therefore, if you import a PDF document that contains form elements, you'll have to re-create them inside Form Tools PDF.

Once you've added all the necessary elements, it's time to put the form into use. Simply by switching the application's mode from Edit Form to Quick Fill Form, the form is ready to be filled in and signed (**FIGURE 4.31**). When you have a completed form and you need to get another, just tap Entries (which displays a list of every entry associated with this form), and then tap New Entry. The form will be cleared out and made ready for the next signer. Every signer is considered a separate entry, and all entries remain associated with that form.

Exporting and sharing is as easy as tapping [icon]. You can e-mail a PDF of a single entry or a multipage PDF of *all* entries. You can even export your entries as an Excel-compatible CSV file (which won't include photos or signatures). Finally, you can choose to e-mail a FORM file that can be shared with other iOS devices running Form Tools PDF.

Based on its versatility alone, I highly recommend this app.

FIGURE 4.31 This completed release form is ready to be exported.

Cinema Forms

Unlike the previous two apps, Cinema Forms doesn't allow you to import your own release forms, or edit the text of the supplied templates. OK, that's not entirely true. It does come with *one* talent release template that allows you to paste in a block of your own text, but for the most part, this is a take-it-as-it-comes sort of tool. However, what the app lacks in flexibility, it more than makes up for in versatility.

When you buy this $9.99 iPad app, it comes standard with talent and location release forms, but that's not all. Cinema Forms also provides a breakdown sheet, a shot log, a location scout worksheet, an asset inventory log, cast and crew contact lists, a preproduction checklist, and a call sheet (**FIGURE 4.32**). (I originally considered putting Cinema Forms in the call sheet section of this chapter.) That's a total of ten very useful, professional forms. While that may seem like a lot, it's nothing compared to what's available from within the app's built-in form store, which currently offers more than (drumroll, please) 90 film production form templates!

You can buy additional template packs for $3.99 to $7.99, or you can buy the whole catalog for $29.99 (**FIGURE 4.33**). Naturally, that price may rise as the developer adds new forms.

CINEMA FORMS

iPad | iPhone

- Ikan International Corp
- $9.99
- hhhlinks.com/t73s

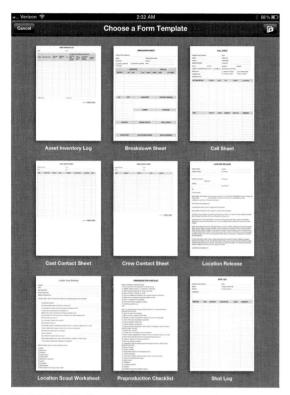

FIGURE 4.32 Cinema Forms comes with a bounty of useful production forms.

FIGURE 4.33 Cinema Forms has its very own form store where it sells nearly 400,000,000 different production forms, or maybe it's around 100. Either way, it's awesome.

To use the app, simply launch it, tap the + in the upper left, and then pick a template. You'll be asked to enter your company name and, optionally, a show name and production number. After that, your desired form will appear on-screen and get automatically geotagged (your current location will be inserted into the form's metadata). All that's left to do is fill in the blanks. It's just like Mad Libs, but instead of filling in fart jokes, you'll need to enter real, far less humorous information.

For a dash of panache, you can customize the forms with your company logo, address, and contact information. If you're creating a release form or any other document that requires a signature, one can be added with a finger or stylus, just like Easy Release. Signed forms can be printed wirelessly via AirPrint (Apple's wireless printing standard) or shared as PDF files via e-mail or Dropbox.

Because the app is tied into iCloud, you can rest assured that your data is safely backed up and protected. By the way, when it comes to releases and other legal forms, *never* believe anyone who says, "You can rest assured that your data is safely backed up and protected." Signed documents are crucial, and you need to ensure your forms are secure (by backing up your iPad to your computer, uploading everything to Dropbox, and so on).

Cinema Forms is a fairly new app, so it still has a few rough spots, but if you have a recurring dream of having instant access to a library full of production forms, you should really consider therapy…and, you should check out Cinema Forms.

DIGITIZING DEAD TREES

When I lean back and let my mind mosey into the infinite fields of possibility, I imagine a utopian society in which everyone picks up after their dog, *Small Wonder* is back on the air, and film production no longer generates piles of paperwork. Sadly, the world does not bend to my will (yet), and filmmakers are a long way from going paperless.

We print piles of talent releases, location agreements, camera reports, call sheets, script revisions, rental agreements, crew contracts, and much more. Some of the apps I've discussed in this chapter will help reduce your dependency on the printed page and the waste it generates, but until every department embraces a digital workflow, filmmaking will continue to generate a cornucopia of documents. Fortunately, our iOS devices can help us collect, manage, and sort through it all.

One enormous advantage of digitizing your production's paperwork is that it all becomes searchable. You'll never have to scale a mountain of contracts just to find a particular form. Instead, whip out your iPad or iPhone, tap in a few keywords, and your desired document will materialize before you.

If you *must* generate paperwork, at least you can now digitize the documents, and then recycle them without fear of destroying anything important.

There are two primary ways of digitizing documents with your iPhone and iPad—with a physical scanner or with a scanning app. Let's look at examples of both.

Go, Doxie Go

Nothing beats the quality of a dedicated hardware scanner. That said, most scanners are large, bulky devices that occupy too much desk space and are never as easy to use as their retail boxes would have you believe.

DOXIE GO PORTABLE SCANNER

| iPad | iPhone |

- Apparent Corporation
- $199.00
- getdoxie.com

If you have a desktop scanner connected to a Mac or Windows machine and you've managed to figure it out (congratulations, by the way), then getting your scanned documents onto your iPad or iPhone is a snap. Simply use your scanner's software to save your scanned documents as PDF files. Then import those files into your iOS devices as e-mail attachments or via iTunes File Sharing. Some iOS apps also support importing PDFs via a cloud storage service like Dropbox or iCloud. I covered a bunch of PDF reading apps, along with various importing techniques, in Chapter 2.

Desktop scanners are fine for office use, but what happens when you're shooting on location? Do you really want to lug around a massive scanner everywhere you go? If you'd like to keep things portable but still be able to scan documents into your iPad, you, my friend, need a Doxie Go ($199).

Unlike other scanners, the Doxie Go was designed to be used *away* from your computer. In fact, its documentation warns against connecting it to a computer during a scan, claiming that such a connection would impede the device's performance. Bottom line, the Doxie Go was meant to be used on the go (**FIGURE 4.34**).

Measuring only 10.5" x 1.7" x 2.2" and weighing less than a pound, this thing is compact! You'll barely notice it in your backpack, briefcase, or shoulder bag. For every two-hour charge, the Doxie's internal battery will power through around 100 scans at its default setting of 300dpi (600dpi is available, but it eats more battery). It's worth pointing out that once the battery is depleted, you'll have to wait until it's at least partially recharged before continuing to scan. In other words, you can't plug it in and use it at the same time. First charge it; then use it. Plan accordingly.

As you might imagine, a scanner this small is meant to scan one sheet at a time, which makes it perfect for things such as talent releases and call sheets. If you have a two-sided document, you'll have to scan one side and then flip it over and scan it again.

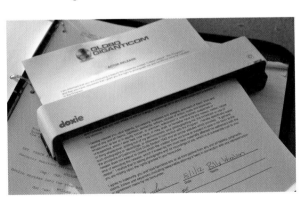

FIGURE 4.34 The Doxie Go scanner is a battery-powered, wireless wonder that can scan production paperwork to SD memory cards, USB thumb drives, and its own internal memory.

Aside from scanning production paperwork, the Doxie Go has another invaluable use for documentary filmmakers—scanning photographs. Recently, I produced a documentary, a good portion of which was shot in a restaurant located in the heart of Balltown, Iowa. The owners of the restaurant had dozens of astounding photos that we knew we wanted to include in the film. Unfortunately, the easiest way to capture them involved the director wasting valuable time by schlepping a full-sized desktop scanner to his hotel room where the images were scanned overnight. I wish we had a Doxie Go at that time! We could have scanned the photographs, imported them into our iPads to double-check the quality, and returned the original photos to their owners, all without ever leaving the restaurant. For this reason alone, my Doxie now has a permanent place in my gear collection.

By now, you're probably wondering how the scans get from the Doxie Go onto your iPad or iPhone. You have great timing, because I was just about to explain that. There are two primary ways to transfer the scans, one more mind-blowing than the other.

The first way is the easiest but will work only with the iPad. Although the Doxie has its own built-in storage, you'll need to plug in your own SD memory card or flash drive in order to pull this off—the Doxie has slots for both. You'll also need Apple's iPad Camera Connection Kit, a set of two adapters that will set you back about $29 (**FIGURE 4.35**). One adapter gives your iPad a USB port, while the other adds an SD card slot.

With either an SD card or flash drive inserted into the back of the Doxie, the device will scan documents directly to your removable media. When you're done scanning, remove the SD card or flash drive from the Doxie, grab the appropriate Camera Connection Kit adapter, and plug your memory card (or stick) into your iPad (**FIGURE 4.36**). All of the scans become instantly available for import from within the Photos app. Each imported scan is added to your camera roll as a separate JPEG file. Now, clear the card, recharge your scanner, and repeat!

FIGURE 4.35 Apple's iPad Camera Connection Kit allows your iPad to access SD memory cards and USB devices.

FIGURE 4.36 I use the Camera Connection Kit to import saved scans from an SD memory card.

- Eye-Fi
- free
- hhhlinks.com/ 56d6

- Evernote
- free
- hhhlinks.com/ am0g

Once you have the scans on your iPad, you can go one step further and upload them to an Evernote account. This will make them available to anyone you choose, and more importantly, it will make them searchable, thanks to the text recognition process Evernote automatically applies to JPEG images. Once you've uploaded your scans to Evernote, they will also become available on any of your other devices, including your iPhone and most desktop computers. Think about that for a moment...you can scan production paperwork on set and have those documents uploaded, sorted, made searchable, and shared with your entire production staff within minutes. In your face, fax machine!

The second method of transferring requires a very cool piece of tech called Eye-Fi, which is basically an SD memory card with a built-in Wi-Fi transmitter (**FIGURE 4.37**).

Once you've used your desktop computer to set up the Eye-Fi card (not the most intuitive process), pop it into the back of your Doxie Go and start scanning. Moments after a document passes through the scanner, the Eye-Fi card will *wirelessly* transmit the image directly to your iPad or iPhone running the free Eye-Fi app. Does that sound awesome? It should! Why? Because it's awesome! Same as before, you can upload your scanned documents to an Evernote account if you'd like them to become searchable. Even better, if your Eye-Fi card is connected to a local Wi-Fi network with Internet access, it can upload scans directly to Evernote all by itself. Then you can access the documents via the Evernote app for iPhone and iPad. I know it's a bit confusing, but that's what happens when you have too many options.

On the downside, using the Eye-Fi card will reduce your Doxie's battery life. Once again, plan accordingly.

You can order a 4GB Eye-Fi card directly from Apparent, the makers of the Doxie, for about $30, or you can grab one at your local Best Buy for around $40.

FIGURE 4.37 The Eye-Fi SD Card turns your Doxie into a totally wireless scanner, capable of transmitting files directly to your iPhone or iPad.

DocScanner

When a new iPhone or iPad is unveiled, it almost always sports an improved camera with higher resolution and updated optics. These hardware revisions do more than simply up the pixel count. They invite developers to create more powerful and versatile *camera-dependent* tools. Document "scanning" apps are a prime example of this. As cameras improve, so do the results of photographed documents. When you need to scan production paperwork and you don't have a physical scanner like the Doxie at your disposal, using a camera-based scanning app is a terrific alternative.

There's no shortage of document-scanning apps in the App Store. They all orbit around the same basic idea—after you take a photograph of a sheet of paper (or whiteboard) with your iOS device's built-in camera, the app crops, rotates, distorts, and color processes your photo to generate a digital re-creation of the original document. Each app caries out this process a little differently. Some do all the work without any interaction, while others let you fine-tune each parameter along the way. Finished documents can be e-mailed, uploaded, printed, and shared depending on the options offered within a given app.

I keep a few scanning apps on my iOS devices at all times, but the one I rely on most is called DocScanner.

Forget for a moment that DocScanner produces the best-looking photo-based scans I've seen from any iOS device. What I find most remarkable about this app is its autodetection features that kick in the moment you launch the app. Simply pointing your iPhone's or iPad's camera at a document will cause Doc-Scanner to automatically identify the edges of the paper, even if it's rotated or skewed. The best edge detection occurs when your document is placed on a surface that's colored differently than the paper you're scanning. In other words, a white document on a white table might make the app gasp in terror, but a white document on a dark table will work wonders (**FIGURE 4.38**).

Before you snap the photo, prepare to witness a second bit of *prestidigitization* (not a real word, but I'm considering petitioning Webster). As soon as Doc-Scanner identifies the edges of the document, it will also attempt to detect the type of item you're scanning, classifying it as either a document, receipt, business card, whiteboard, or miscellaneous. The app doesn't always guess correctly, but I've found it to be surprisingly accurate.

Seconds after you tap the scan button, your document will be scanned and waiting for you within the app's document library (**FIGURE 4.39**). If you'd like, DocScanner can even perform OCR in any of 36 available languages, making your scan fully searchable. If that weren't enough, your scans can also be

DOCSCANNER

iPad | iPhone

- Norfello Oy
- $3.99
- hhhlinks.com/auxv

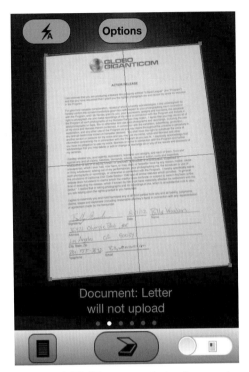

FIGURE 4.38 When scanning a document with DocScanner, the app does most of the work for you, making it your lowest-paid crew member.

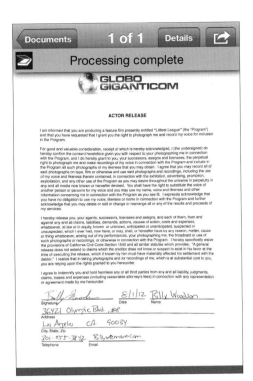

FIGURE 4.39 After DocScanner works its magic, your corrected scan appears on-screen.

automatically uploaded to iCloud and Evernote (allowing you to take advantage of Evernote's awesome sharing tools). There are a few other whiz-bang features, like networking to an external scanner, but I believe I've pimped this app sufficiently.

Like most apps, DocScanner isn't perfect. It can yield some funky results if conditions aren't ideal. Also, because the app just received a *major* overhaul, there are bound to be a few pestering bugs that will need to be squashed. The app's growing pains aside, if you love the idea of digitizing your production paperwork and don't want to carry (or pay for) an additional piece of hardware, take a look at DocScanner.

A QUICK WORD ABOUT BUDGETING

When I was building the outline for this book (using the insanely awesome OmniOutliner for iPad, by the way), I had hoped to include a big fat section on film-budgeting apps.

As a director, I usually leave the budgeting to someone else, but I felt it was a topic that belonged in the book. Plus, I recalled using at least one or two decent film-budgeting apps in the past. As it turns out, one of those apps is no longer available in the App Store, and the other was, in fact, total crap. Sadly, as of today, there are no film-budgeting apps I can comfortably recommend.

Don't fret! There are several terrific, high-quality film-budgeting applications available for your Mac or Windows machine (Movie Magic Budgeting, anyone?). If you truly want to budget your flick on an iOS device, take a look at Apple's Numbers. It's a dirt-cheap, surprisingly powerful spreadsheet app available for iPad, iPhone, and the Mac.

Creating a movie budget from scratch is madness, especially when there are several decent film budgeting templates floating around the interweb. Do a Google search for *Free Excel Film Budget Template*, and you should find a few options. Fortunately, Numbers can import most Excel documents without too much fuss.

In case you have a rare reading condition that forces you to gloss over adjectives, I'd like to point out that I just used the word *decent* to describe those templates. They are most definitely not awesome, and none of them will replace the feature set of a dedicated film-budgeting application.

The moment someone releases a good iOS film-budgeting app, rest assured I'll be yapping about it on HandHeldHollywood.com.

PART TWO
PRODUCTION

CHAPTER 5

THE DIRECTOR'S TOOLKIT

What's in your director's toolkit? Permit me to tell you what's in mine:

> One roll of gaffer's tape

> Two Sharpies (one black and one red)

> A ball-point pen that I fully expect to lose

> Mentos, preferably strawberry

> A copy of *The War of Art* by Steven Pressfield

> My iPad

> My iPhone

> Another roll of gaffer's tape (you can never have enough gaffer's tape)

If it wasn't apparent after viewing my exhaustive list, allow me to summarize. My director's toolkit contains anything that will keep me prepared, proactive, and productive...and Mentos.

To help round out your toolkit, this chapter discusses apps that will help you prepare for an upcoming shoot, be proactive while on set, and remain productive under pressure. Grab your iOS device, and let's dig in.

STORYBOARDING FOR ARTISTS

Storyboards are sketches, drawn to represent each key moment within a given scene. By storyboarding your shots, you have the opportunity to "shoot" your film before you shoot your film.

In other words, when you draw storyboards, you have the freedom to experiment with different angles and camera moves prior to shooting a single frame. You can visualize entire scenes, without wasting time and money on set. Best of all, you can begin the shoot day knowing how you'd like your project to look when it's completed.

When storyboarding a scene, each shot is drawn as a separate panel, although more complex shots can be drawn over multiple panels, demonstrating the shot's evolution. For example, if a shot starts inside a car, then moves out of the car through an open window, and finally floats upward to watch the car as it speeds into the distance, a single storyboard panel can't possibly express the content of that shot.

Storyboard artists include distinct symbols to indicate movement within the panel (for example, an actor walks toward the camera) or movement of the camera (for example, we dolly toward a stationary actor). These symbols may include arrows, lines, frame outlines, and text descriptions.

Storyboards are especially useful when preparing visually unique or logistically challenging sequences. Scenes that contain visual effects (computer-generated effects composited in post), special effects (practical effects executed on set, such as gun shots and breaking glass), or large stunts are almost always storyboarded.

However, if you're shooting two actors sitting outside a cafe, eating bagels and chatting calmly, there's absolutely no need for storyboards (unless the bagels suddenly turn into human-hunting, fire-breathing bagel-bots).

New filmmakers tend to storyboard every shot in every scene, no matter how basic the action may be. I've done it myself. But after a few gigs, you come to learn that not every scene requires boards. That said, having storyboards even for simple scenes can help to quickly communicate desired frame sizes and camera positions. On days when I have to shoot a lot of pages with a new crew, I'll storyboard more aggressively the night before. A little extra preparation goes a long way on days like that.

With its large, touch-sensitive display, the iPad makes a perfect storyboarding canvas. All you need now is an appropriate app and a comfortable stylus. To that end, here are some appropriate apps and comfortable styluses.

Penultimate

The App Store is bubbling over with extraordinary illustration and painting apps that boast a wide assortment of virtual pens, pencils, and brushes. So, you may be surprised to learn that my top recommendation for storyboarding is actually a note-taking app!

Penultimate was one of the first hand-written note takers to emerge after Apple released the iPad, and it continues to be one of the best. In essence, the app turns your iPad into a virtual notebook. When you launch the app and create a new notebook, you're presented with a blank page and all of your drawing tools...all four of them. You've got a pen, an eraser, a selection tool, and a button that clears the page. Tapping the Pen tool twice brings up a palette with ten color options and three line thicknesses (**FIGURE 5.1**). Congratulations! You've just earned your Penultimate PhD.

OK, there's a little more, but it's pretty straightforward. You can turn pages by swiping your finger across the page's margin or view a grid of page thumbnails by tapping ▦ in the lower-left corner. You can insert an image from your photo library or take a new image with the built-in camera by tapping 🖼 . In addition to printing, you can send pages or entire notebooks via e-mail or upload them to a Dropbox or Evernote account.

PENULTIMATE

iPad | iPhone

- Evernote
- $0.99
- hhhlinks.com/ozc3

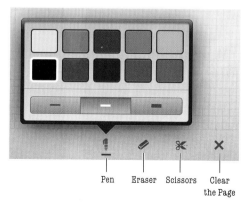

FIGURE 5.1 That's a mighty small toolbar for such an awesome app!

Pen   Eraser Scissors Clear the Page

So, why do I recommend this app for storyboard artists? A few reasons, actually. First, the app is insanely easy to use and has very little in the way of distractions. Most storyboards are drawn with just a pencil, so why waste time with anything else? Second, drawing within the app feels perfectly smooth and realistic. Some of the fancier illustration apps actually lag slightly behind your finger or stylus and feel unnatural. Drawing in Penultimate is smooth. All that's dandy, but it's this next reason that's the most compelling.

Penultimate allows you to use custom-paper backgrounds in your notebooks. The app comes standard with graph paper, lined paper, and plain paper. Sure, that's pretty limited, but there's also a built-in paper shop, from which you can purchase a wide variety of additional paper styles. The first item listed in the store is a free paper pack that contains multiple lined papers, as well as a…wait for it…a storyboard template! As if that weren't cool enough, the app allows you to import your own templates. So, if there's a particular storyboard template you prefer, simply add it as a custom paper and then assign it as the background for your notebook. Awesomeness!

Don't have time to craft custom templates? Filmmaker Stu Maschwitz has already created a versatile series of Penultimate storyboard templates that he shares freely on Prolost, his informative and thoughtful website (http://prolost.com). Professional storyboard artist Louie del Carmen (http://hhhlinks.com/ww2b) uses Penultimate along with Stu's templates while sketching panels for several projects, including *How to Train Your Dragon*, the TV series from DreamWorks Animation (**FIGURE 5.2**). When I asked Louie why he prefers Penultimate, he simply pointed out that when it comes to doing *actual* work, Penultimate is the most straightforward and practical app out there. I couldn't agree more.

Louie del Carmen
hhhlinks.com/ww2b

Prolost
http://prolost.com

FIGURE 5.2 A panel drawn in Penultimate by professional storyboard artist Louie del Carmen.

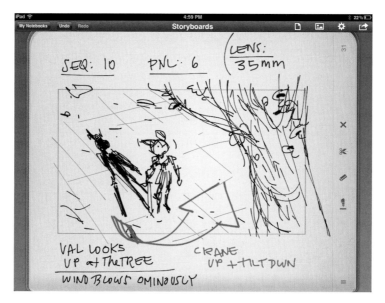

Paper

I almost didn't include this app simply because I couldn't find storyboard artists who currently use it, which is strange considering how highly it ranks on the slick-o-meter. Even though it doesn't have Penultimate's impressive track record, I strongly encourage you to take Paper for a test-drive.

Before I slather on the praise, let me point out that Paper does not allow you to import custom paper backgrounds, so you won't be working with storyboard templates. Instead, each page begins as pure and white as Justin Bieber. It's also worth pointing out that while the app and basic fountain pen tool are free, the other drawing tools are not. Each of the other four tools will run you around $1.99 each (or you can get them all at once and save a buck). While the free fountain pen is nice, you'll probably want to purchase the pencil (**FIGURE 5.3**) and possibly the ink pen for storyboarding purposes. Fortunately, you can test-drive each of the tools within the app before making any purchases.

With the bad news out of the way, I can now safely tell you that Paper is a gorgeous, extremely well-designed app. Use it for five seconds, and it becomes clear that a lot of love and attention went into its minimal interface.

Like Penultimate, you begin by creating and naming a new notebook. After opening said notebook, you come face to face with the app's drawing interface…a totally blank page. To start drawing, just start drawing. To pick a different tool, swipe up from the bottom of the screen to display the very minimal tool set. To turn pages, swipe in from the left or right side. To undo, write to the developer and ask them to add an Undo button, because currently there is none.

PAPER

iPad iPhone

- FiftyThree, Inc.
- free
- hhhlinks.com/
  a3pn

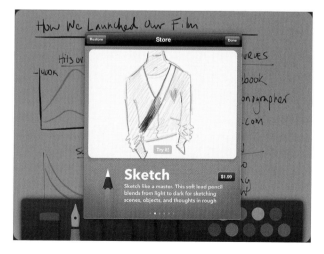

FIGURE 5.3 Paper by FiftyThree is *free*! The fountain pen is *free*! But if you want a pencil… well, that's gonna cost you.

FIGURE 5.4 Despite my horrendous artwork, Paper's interface is elegant and understated.

Instead of an Undo function, Paper offers something called Rewind, and it's activated by placing two fingers on the display and then moving them in a counterclockwise circle (**FIGURE 5.4**). This will rewind time, undoing everything you've done, step-by-step, in reverse order. When you find the point at which you want to continue, simply lift your fingers to end the Rewind. Try it once, and you'll be hooked. I want this feature in *every* app!

Elegance aside, Paper's drawing tools are expressive and realistic. While they can be slightly laggy, they more than make up for it by looking freakishly good. If you prefer to storyboard in pencil (like most storyboard artists I've met), spend two bucks on the pencil, and start drawing. I think you'll like what you see.

When you're ready to share your work, you can e-mail your entire notebook as a PDF file or send a PDF file to compatible apps, like the PDF readers I mention in Chapter 2. Currently, Paper won't allow you to e-mail a single page, so make sure you don't sketch dirty pictures elsewhere in the notebook and then forget about them. That would be…unfortunate.

Previs (Formerly SketchPad Pro)

Normally, I wouldn't tell you about an app that you can't buy, but in this case, I'll make an exception. Artists around the world have been anxiously awaiting the release of Previs, an iPad app that specifically caters to the needs and workflows of the professional storyboarding community. Originally named SketchPad Pro, the developers chose to change the name to avoid confusion with similarly named apps.

After examining the app's interface, it's clear that Previs hopes to become the go-to tool for artists looking to make the transition from paper to digital media (**FIGURE 5.5**). It offers features and an environment that will feel familiar to

In Front Of Your Eyes   SEQUENCE Photo Booth   SCENE 31

FIGURE 5.5 Previs (formerly known as SketchPad Pro) provides an interface to love...if it ever comes out.

most storyboard artists. It provides an array of flexible virtual pens and pencils, along with a host of sharing options. You can e-mail PDFs of your boards, export Photoshop documents, and print six-panel pages up to 11 x 17 inches.

Unfortunately, Previs has been "coming soon" for a very long time. As frustrating as that may be, it's totally understandable considering the enormous expenses involved in iOS app development. In an effort to bring in some additional capital, Previs (the app's developer) tried launching a fundraising campaign on Kickstarter.com. Sadly, the goal wasn't reached. According to TikiBone, the app is still "coming soon." For all storyboard artists out there, I certainly hope so.

I decided to include Previs in the book for a few reasons. I want to help TikiBone spread the word, find needed support, and, I hope, speed up app development. I also wanted to make sure you keep a look out for this app's eventual release.

In the meantime, you can learn more by visiting the app's website at www.previs.co.

Previs
www.previs.co

Jot Pro Stylus

Don't stick that finger on your iPad! You don't know where it's been! Or maybe you do. Uncharacteristically clean or suspiciously dirty, your finger is not an ideal drawing instrument. If you're going to be storyboarding on your iPad, you should consider getting a stylus.

Stroll down the aisle at your local Best Buy, and you'll spot 20 different styli from 20 different companies that all look nearly the same: a metal pen with a round black rubber nub on the end. As you might imagine, they all operate

JOT PRO STYLUS

iPad   iPhone

- Adonit
- $29.99
- www.adonit.net

nearly the same as, well—horribly. In this endless sea of rubber-tipped styli, an entirely new design has floated to the top.

The Jot Pro ($29.99) has done away with the rubber nub and replaced it with a tiny, clear plastic disc that freely pivots on a fine-point tip (**FIGURE 5.6**). This combination allows you to see exactly where you're drawing—something that's not possible with a thick, round rubber nub. Since the clear disc pivots, it remains flush with your iPad's screen even as you reposition your hand into different drawing angles (up to 45 degrees). It is, without a doubt, the best stylus I've ever used.

Being able to see the tip of your stylus directly engaging the screen makes a tremendous difference when drawing fine detail. This is the only stylus I've ever used that permits and encourages precision illustration.

Adonit, the makers of the Jot, recommend using their stylus along with a screen protector, although several are deemed incompatible because of the friction they introduce. They advise avoiding protectors from Ghost Armor, Bodyguardz, Skinomi, and Wrapsol, along with ZAGG's Glossy Invisible Shield, although ZAGG's Smudge-Proof Invisible Shield is said to work nicely.

This aluminum and steel stylus comes in a variety of colors and sizes. The Jot Classic ($19.99) comes in green, purple, red, and turquoise. The Jot Pro ($29.99) comes only in gun metal, silver, turquoise, and red, and it features a comfortable padded grip (**FIGURE 5.7**). It's also magnetized, so it will cling to the side of your iPad 2 or 3. The Jot Mini ($21.99) is a smaller version of the Jot Classic that features a built-in clip. The Jot Flip ($39.99) includes a concealed fine-tipped ball-point pen in addition to the standard Jot stylus. And finally, the Jot Touch ($99) boasts a sound-dampening tip as well as Bluetooth-powered pressure sensitivity and shortcut buttons.

FIGURE 5.6 All models of the Jot stylus utilize a clear plastic disc that pivots on a narrow tip as you draw.

FIGURE 5.7 The Jot Pro has a cushioned grip, making it mighty comfy in my Sasquatch-sized hands.

Regardless of the model, they all work on any capacitive touchscreen, which means they'll work just fine on Android devices as well as your iOS devices.

Fun fact: The Jot began its journey on Kickstarter.com in mid-2011. To bring the Jot to life, the folks from Adonit were seeking a total investment of $2500. They received more than $168,000 in pledges. Not bad. Not bad at all.

Cosmonaut Stylus

Do you remember drawing in kindergarten? Compared to your tiny fingers, the crayon you held seemed enormous, like an extension of your hand. There was something liberating about it. Something natural. Well, that was a long time ago, and your hands have grown quite a bit larger. Wouldn't it be nice if your crayon grew as well? It did. It's called the Cosmonaut ($25) (**FIGURE 5.8**).

From the same company that brought us the Glif (see Chapter 7), the Cosmonaut features a wide rubber grip and fat tip that makes it feel less like a pen and more like a Sharpie or dry-erase marker. The round black tip looks similar to the ones found on every stylus in all of stylusville, but somehow the Cosmonaut feels different. Gliding its tip across the glass screen of your iPad or iPhone feels silky smooth.

All that said, the Cosmonaut isn't appropriate for finely detailed storyboards. After all, you wouldn't perform surgery with a butter knife. Rather, this stylus is perfect for quick, rough sketches you might whip up while on set. It's best used when communicating broad concepts with broad strokes. As odd as it may sound, the Cosmonaut is an excellent choice for artists who work in a rush.

Want a stylus that matches your outfit? No problem…as long as your outfit is black. The Cosmonaut isn't available in different colors, but it does arrive in a very hip cardboard box. That has to count for something, right?

COSMONAUT STYLUS

| iPad | iPhone |

- Studio Neat
- $25
- studioneat.com

FIGURE 5.8 The Cosmonaut stylus is perfect for rough sketches and broad strokes.

Nomad Brush

The Nomad Brush ($26 and up) is a stylus that looks *and feels* like a traditional paintbrush (**FIGURE 5.9**). Although storyboards aren't painted, I thought this stylus might be useful for tablet-toting artists who come from a painting background.

Originally, I assumed this tool was a typical rubber nub stylus camouflaged by brush bristles. But to my surprise, this thing is all bristle and no nub. It glides smoothly across the iPad's glass screen, and makes a terrific partner for painting apps like Autodesk's SketchBook Pro.

Because the iPad is not pressure sensitive, the experience is certainly a little strange at first. But, after an initial "whaaaa?" moment, the Nomad Brush becomes second nature. The developer offers a wide variety of models, ranging in price from $18 to $40. Makes me wish I could paint…which, as you may have guessed, I really, really, *really* can't do.

FIGURE 5.9 The Nomad Brush features natural and synthetic fibers instead of a traditional rubber nub. This is a great stylus for painters making the move from canvas to tablet.

STORYBOARDING FOR NON-ARTISTS

I truly envy storyboard artists. I can't imagine what it must be like to be able to grab a pen or pencil and quickly sketch an image that is not only informative but also emotive. The simple fact is, I break into a sweat drawing stick figures. That's why I embrace any app that can help me effectively communicate the visuals swirling through my head.

Because of my inability to illustrate, I've always shied away from doing my own hand-drawn storyboards. I'll sketch out a few scenes in the margins of a script or doodle a sequence on the back of a napkin, but that's as far as it goes. If I chose to punish my cinematographer by showing him my boards, I'd have to stand over his shoulder and say something like, "This squiggle over here runs up to this other squiggle over here, pulls a gun…or maybe that's a banana…and then speeds away behind the wheel of this blobby thing."

If you share my affliction, you'll be happy to know that there are several terrific iOS storyboarding apps designed specifically for filmmakers just like you and me.

Storyboard Composer HD

If you read this book's introduction, you already know all about my history and love affair with this paradox-shifting application. If you haven't read the intro-duction, you really should. There's a secret code embedded in the text. Not really. Or is there? No. Unless? Who knows?

Like the rest of the apps described in this section, Storyboard Composer HD requires no drawing skills whatsoever. Say it with me, "Hallelujah!" Instead, this app converts photographs into fully animated storyboards right on your iPhone and iPad. The idea is simple, as is the interface. Let's look at the basic workflow.

When you launch the app for the first time, a new storyboard document will automatically be created (**FIGURE 5.10**). Like your film, your storyboard docu-ment will likely contain multiple scenes. To get you started, a single, empty scene will be sitting in your storyboard. By tapping its icon, you will be taken to the Page view in which you can view and rearrange all of the storyboard panels associated with that scene. Since this is a new storyboard, no panels exist yet. So, let's add some!

Each storyboard panel is built on top of a single photo, so you'll need to shoot several photos to build an entire scene. Ideally, your photographs will include your cast and be taken on your film's actual shooting location. If the actors aren't willing to participate, drag along a few friends to act as stand-ins. If your friends are too busy avoiding you and your strange requests, you can add vir-tual actors (male and female silhouettes) to existing photos.

STORYBOARD COMPOSER HD

| iPad | iPhone |

- Cinemek, Inc.
- $29.99
- hhhlinks.com/p718

FIGURE 5.10 Hey look! It's your very first storyboard in Storyboard Composer! I'm so proud of you.

Photos can be taken from within Storyboard Composer HD by tapping  or imported from your device's photo library by tapping . Since the app can import existing photos, you have the option to snap your shots with just about any photography app that will save its images to your photo library, making them available to Storyboard Composer HD. Every photo you snap or import becomes its own storyboard panel within your scene. When you're done, all the panels are displayed as rows of small thumbnails (**FIGURE 5.11**). These can easily be reordered into the correct story order.

Double-tapping any panel brings you into the Panel view. This is where the magic happens (**FIGURE 5.12**). Within this screen, you can create virtual camera moves, record associated audio such as line readings, add on-screen text notes, assign a shot number, dial in the shot length, add arrows to indicate movement, and insert virtual actors. The four icons along the right side of the screen represent the different camera moves you can create. You can add a dolly (moving the camera toward or away from your subject), a zoom (changing

FIGURE 5.11 Imported photos will appear in your storyboard's Page view. Place them in the desired order using simple drag-and-drop gestures.

FIGURE 5.12 Double-tapping a photo opens it in Panel view. From here you can add camera moves, arrows, virtual actors, and more.

the length of your lens to frame more or less of your subject while the camera remains stationary), a truck (moving the camera from side to side without turning it), or a pan (turning the camera from one direction to another around a single axis point). In the real world, these moves are usually combined to capture the desired shot. That said, it's pretty easy to fake it within the app.

Adding camera moves is a snap. For example, to add a dolly, tap the ▣ in the upper left. Two boxes will appear over your photo: a green starting frame, and a red ending frame. The green starting frame automatically includes the entire photo, while the red ending frame can be scaled and repositioned by pinching and dragging right on the photo (**FIGURE 5.13**). By default, the app creates a dolly-*in*, but if you'd prefer a dolly-*out*, just tap ◆. When you're satisfied with your start and end framing, tap Done. Every shot defaults to a duration of three seconds, but it can easily be changed by tapping the ◉ and dialing in a new length.

To view an animated version of your shot, return to the Page view by tapping ▦ on the top menu bar and then tapping ▦ on the bottom left. Your dolly move will be smoothly animated, giving you a good idea of how your completed shot will look. If you had recorded audio with this panel, it would have played back during the animation. After repeating this process for each panel, you'll be able to watch your entire scene play back as one single animated storyboard.

It really is quite awesome to see it in action. I've used this app on set multiple times when discussing shots with my cinematographer.

When you're ready to share your boards, you have a few options. If you want to share your panels as traditional storyboards, complete with your starting and ending framings, you can export and e-mail a PDF straight from the app, or you can upload a PDF to a server maintained by Cinemek, the app's developer, where it will be stored for up to 72 hours. After the file uploads, you will be given a web link so you can easily share your PDF with anyone. But why e-mail a PDF

FIGURE 5.13 Storyboard Composer lets you set start and end framings for each of your camera moves.

when sharing a QuickTime video file of the animated scene is so much cooler?! Rendering your scene as a shareable video file would normally eat up a large chunk of your iOS device's processing power and battery, but fortunately, Storyboard Composer HD can help with that, too. Rather than render the movie on your device, it uploads your project file to a computer array maintained by the app's developer. The servers render your movie, freeing up your device to do more important things, like getting to the tenth island in Tiny Wings—not as easy as it sounds. When the server is done rendering your movie, you'll be given a web link that you can share with anyone, letting them watch your animated storyboard in their web browser.

Now that you've been infused with camera animating super powers, perhaps this would be a good time to remind you *why* we move the camera. (Hint: It's not only for increased production value. I'm looking at you, Michael Bay.) By injecting motion into a shot, you can easily reinforce a particular emotion. For example, dollying toward a character can easily enhance the importance of a moment and amp up feelings of discovery and reflection. On the other hand, dollying away from a character might ignite feelings of isolation, loneliness, and failure. Side note: If you're shooting a music video, camera moves have less to do with emotion and more to do with triggering nausea.

As I mentioned earlier, this app can import images from your device's photo library. A wonderful way to exploit that feature is to preprocess your photos in other apps prior to importing them into Storyboard Composer HD. A terrific example is Red Giant Software's Noir Photo, which lets you add emphasis to certain areas in your photos, making them better subjects for storyboard panels.

On one last note, an older version of the app, simply called Storyboard Composer (no "HD"), still resides in the App Store and is available for half the price of the HD version. If you can afford the HD version, I'd recommend it. Not only does it get updates faster than the non-HD version and permit sharing of Storyboard Composer documents between devices, it also works on the iPad as well as the iPhone. The non-HD version is iPhone only.

Storyboards 3D

Can't draw? Hate taking photos? Do I have a storyboarding app for you!

Storyboards 3D lets you create storyboards from scratch using real 3D models that you can position, scale, rotate, and manipulate in multiple ways. While it lacks some professional features (selectable aspect ratios, flexible arrows and frames, and so on) and its interface is a tad goofy (the adjective, not the Disney character), this app provides an innovative and intuitive approach to storyboarding.

NOIR PHOTO

iPad   iPhone

- Red Giant Software
- $2.99
- hhhlinks.com/03wd

Before going any further, I want to point out something kind of lame, something totally awesome, and something slightly less awesome.

Storyboards 3D will work only on an iPad 2 or 3. Owners of the original iPad are out of luck. *Kind of lame.* The app is totally free and comes with several models to get you started! *Totally awesome*! If you want access to the vast library of additional models and extras, you'll be paying for it. *Slightly less awesome.*

Using a pay-as-you-go model, the app features a "Pack Store" in which bundles of useful items are sold at prices ranging from $0.99 to $4.99. You can pick up new characters, locations, props, character poses, character expressions, and more. Perhaps, one bright and brisk day, they'll offer a subscription plan with access to all their products. Until then, just purchase what you need.

While creating and naming a new board, you will be asked to choose one of three rendering modes (**FIGURE 5.14**). I couldn't find the official names of these modes, so I'll simply describe them as normal, brightly lit color toonish, and black-and-white toonish. There's no correct choice. It's just a matter of taste. However, once you've created your board, you won't be able to go back and change your render mode, so choose wisely! I'm hoping that oversight is corrected in a future version.

With your new board created, you're ready to add subjects to your first blank panel. Tapping the Characters tab at the bottom of the page will present thumbnails of your available virtual actors. The app provides two basic characters by default, but more can be purchased through the app's Pack Store. To add a character, just tap one, and pick its hairstyle. Moments later, your virtual performer will take center stage. You can further refine your character by assigning a pose, a facial expression, an outfit, and accessories. The app comes with a few of these items, but again, you can purchase more through the app's Pack Store.

STORYBOARDS 3D

iPad | iPhone

- Tamajii, Inc.
- free
- hhhlinks.com/ cwc4

FIGURE 5.14 When you create a new storyboard in Storyboards 3D, you can pick one of three rendering styles. Choose wisely!

STORYBOARDS PREMIUM

| iPad | iPhone |

- Tamajii, Inc.
- $14.99
- hhhlinks.com/mlup

Once you're done playing dress-up, tap and drag a character to move him or her into the desired position. Using two fingers, you can scale your character up or down, or rotate it around its z-axis (like a cartwheel). You can spin your character around its y-axis (turning it away from you) by tapping anywhere off your character and dragging from side to side. Do the same thing, with an up and down drag, to rotate the character on its x-axis (like a backflip). The whole thing sounds a bit odd, but I promise you'll get the hang of it very quickly, and if you ever forget, gesture help is available by tapping [?].

In addition to virtual actors, you can insert text bubbles, 3D objects (furniture, props, and so on), and stickers (movement arrows, zoom frames, effects like rain and lightning, and images from your photo library). Naturally, you can purchase more of everything in the Pack Store. You can also record audio that will be played back when viewing that panel. If you want to add a little context, you can import a photo from your photo library and place it in the background (FIGURE 5.15).

When your panel is good to go, you can add a new blank panel and repeat the process until your storyboard is complete. At that point, you can share it with other iPad owners running Storyboards 3D, or you can export and e-mail it as a PDF file.

One last thing worth noting is that Storyboards 3D is a closed system, meaning you can't import your own existing 3D models. So much for creating an intimate scene with models of yourself and _____ (insert hot model of choice).

If you dig the idea of working with premade elements but don't enjoy manipulating 3D objects, take a look at Storyboards Premium (no "3D"), created by the

FIGURE 5.15 This storyboard panel includes two 3D models, a voice bubble, a framing guide, and a background image.

FIGURE 5.16 If you're a 2D sort of storyboarder, check out Storyboards Premium. The interface is better than Storyboards 3D, but the models aren't quite as versatile.

same developer. Rather than using 3D objects and characters, Storyboards Premium provides hundreds of predrawn illustrations (**FIGURE 5.16**). The operation is similar, but the interface is far more professional. If you want to try before you buy, you'll also find a free but limited version of the app simply titled Storyboards.

THE ULTIMATE DIRECTOR'S VIEWFINDER

Imagine walking around your shooting location, trying to find the best possible angle for your next setup. To truly evaluate a possible shot, you can't just look at it with your naked eye. You need to look at it through a lens. This isn't a problem if you're shooting on a small, portable device (like an iPhone or DSLR camera): Just grab your camera and go. But if you're shooting with a professional camera, chances are it's heavy, bulky, mounted to a tripod, and loaded with extra gear, which is not the sort of thing you can easily move around your set.

In those cases, what you really need is a small, handheld viewfinder with its own adjustable lens. That way, you could easily move around set, find your next shot, and *then* move the heavy camera and appropriate lens into the correct position. Fortunately, such a handheld device already exists, and it's called a *director's viewfinder* (sometimes called a *director's finder*).

If you've ever watched behind-the-scenes footage, you've likely spotted someone walking around holding a director's viewfinder up to his or her eye. Now you know why!

Ready for some bad news? Director's viewfinders are expensive, fragile, and not especially light. Ready for some great news? You may already have a virtual one in your pocket!

Artemis Director's Viewfinder and Artemis HD

Artemis Director's Viewfinder is an app that turns your iPhone or iPod touch into a director's viewfinder. Artemis HD does the same for your iPad. Aside from a couple of minor interface differences, the apps perform exactly the same function.

Before using Artemis to line up shots, you should fill it with information about the camera equipment you're using on your shoot. Begin by tapping in the upper-left corner to bring up an extensive list of formats (16mm film, 35mm film, ½" Digital Sensor, DSLR, and so on). Pick the appropriate format, and you'll be taken to a long list of cameras that shoot in that format. In all likelihood,

ARTEMIS DIRECTOR'S VIEWFINDER

iPad · **iPhone**

- Chemical Wedding
- $29.99
- hhhlinks.com/ v6au

ARTEMIS HD

iPad · iPhone

- Chemical Wedding
- $29.99
- hhhlinks.com/ mxr3

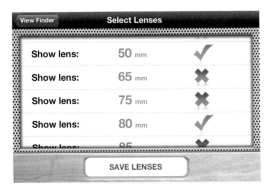

FIGURE 5.17 Prep Artemis by telling it which lenses you have on your shoot.

you'll find your camera in the list, but if you don't, you can create your own custom camera. With your camera selected, you'll be asked to select your intended aspect ratio (4:3, which is standard-definition video; 16:9, which is high-definition video; 1.85, which is standard theatrical presentation; and so on). After picking your ratio, you'll be asked to select the type of lenses you'll be using (Canon EF Compatible, Cooke S4/I, Red Pro, Zeiss Standard, and so on). Lastly, you'll be presented with a list of available lens sizes. Put check marks next to each lens you expect to have on your shoot (**FIGURE 5.17**). That's it!

If that last paragraph droned through your head like the voice of Charlie Brown's teacher, just ask your cinematographer for these details. Once he or she is done openly mocking you, you'll get your answers. On a side note, if your cinematographer doesn't know the answer, feel free to openly mock him or her, and then get a new cinematographer.

Yes, you can use the app and line up shots without entering your equipment information, but doing so will rob you of the app's primary function: to replicate the frame sizes available with your current gear so you won't have to drag your camera all over your set. Still not getting it? Maybe a quick comparison will clear things up. Take a look at these two workflows, and decide which one sounds better.

Workflow 1:

1. Enter camera and lens data into Artemis.

2. Walk around set with your iPhone until you find the perfect shot.

3. To match this shot, move your camera to your current location, and attach the proper lens as indicated by Artemis.

Workflow 2:

1. Don't enter camera and lens data into Artemis.

2. Walk around set with your iPhone until you find the perfect shot.

3. To match this shot, move your camera to your current location only to discover that your camera and lens combo don't yield the same shot.

4. Look sheepishly at the crew member who just lugged the camera over.

5. Apologize to your first assistant camera (A.C.) person, who must now run and grab a different lens because the first lens wasn't the right size.

6. Feel like an idiot as your crew hauls the camera closer to and farther from your subject in a time-consuming attempt to re-create the shot you originally found in Artemis.

7. Take a smoke break while your camera crew curses your name. Sneak behind a tree, and enter your camera and lens details into Artemis like you should have done in the first place.

With the details entered, let's take a quick spin around the app's interface (FIGURE 5.18).

FIGURE 5.18 Each dotted rectangle in the viewfinder represents a different lens size.

The majority of your device's screen is taken up by the actual viewfinder. Over the live camera image, you'll see a series of concentric white-dotted rectangles, each of which represents one of the lens sizes you added earlier. One of the concentric rectangles will be red. This is the currently selected lens. Using the plus and minus buttons on the bottom of the interface, you can cycle through your available lens sizes. As each one is selected, its information is displayed below the viewfinder. This is pretty handy, but it's downright necessary when in full-screen mode. What's full-screen mode, you ask? It's the main reason you're going to want to own this app.

By tapping [icon], you will switch from normal mode to full-screen mode, causing the concentric rectangles to vanish and the currently selected lens size to fill the entire frame (FIGURE 5.19). While in this mode, the plus and minus buttons will

FIGURE 5.19 With Artemis in full-screen mode, you can preview the exact framing for a given lens size. Cycle through your lens sizes by tapping the + and − buttons.

still cycle through your lens sizes, allowing you to get a full-screen view of what each lens would capture if you were to set up your camera in your current location. Because the image is scaled up, the image will get a bit blocky, but that's no big deal since you're using the app for framing, not for focus.

Here's an example of how it all comes together. Let's assume I told Artemis that I have three lenses available: a 35mm, a 50mm, and an 85mm. That means I will see three dotted rectangles on my iPhone's screen, each labeled with the lens size it represents. I enter full-screen mode to get a better idea of what each lens would capture. Let's say I find a shot I like with the 50mm lens. I can now move the camera to my current position and attach the 50mm lens. This will result in my camera capturing the same framing I originally found on my iPhone's screen. Neat!

While in full-screen mode, tapping 📷 will snap a photo of your current view. The photo will include on-screen information, including the lens size, your format and aspect ratio, your current longitude and latitude, and your heading and tilt measured in degrees. All shots taken with Artemis will be stored in your device's camera roll, making them easy to share via e-mail. This provides a fast and convenient way to record and share the details associated with the shots you find.

Here's a cool tip! If you're planning on using Storyboard Composer HD to visualize your scene and you already know the exact camera equipment you'll have on your shoot, consider using Artemis to snap the photos that will eventually be imported into Storyboard Composer HD. This way, you can be sure that your boards are based on imagery you can actually capture with the equipment you will eventually be using. Taking these steps will result in more accurate storyboards and your immediate enrollment into the Society for Extremely Nerdy Filmmakers. As a fellow member, I welcome you with open armatures.

In conclusion, I believe that Artemis should be on every filmmaker's iPhone or iPad simply because it can replace and, in many ways, improve upon traditional, expensive viewfinders. As a bonus, it will help you convince nonbelievers that the iPhone and iPad are legitimate filmmaking tools. I keep the app on hand for both reasons. Therefore, in conclusion of my conclusion, go get this app. This concludes my conclusion's conclusion.

BLOCKING YOUR SHOTS

Simply knowing the shots you'd like to capture isn't enough to ensure a smooth production. You need to know *how* you're going to get those shots, and that's where blocking comes in.

If you've ever played sports in high school or college or watched professional football or basketball games on television, you've likely seen coaches using overhead diagrams to communicate plays. They'll draw *x*'s and *o*'s to represent players and add lines and arrows to indicate paths the players should take. This is blocking! You'll be doing the same thing, but with actors and cameras instead of athletes and other athletes.

Are you required to create blocking diagrams when directing? No, of course not. But I assure you, it's a skill worth learning. When creating your overhead-blocking diagrams, you can choreograph the positions and movements of actors, cameras, and everything else crucial to the successful execution of your shots. As a bonus, your diagrams can also reveal ways to squeeze the most out of every camera setup and reduce the overall number of setups required to shoot a scene. This is priceless any time you have to shoot a pile of script pages in a single day.

Like most aspects of filmmaking, blocking is an art form, one that is learned through experience. Any time you successfully implement a new move on set, you're adding more ammo to your blocking technique arsenal. I've been directing for years, and I'm still learning. With this in mind, it's impossible for me to fully describe every aspect of blocking within a few pages, but by looking at a few of the best blocking apps, I'm sure the basics will come across. So, let's get started!

Shot Designer

When I was preparing to write this chapter, I contacted Per Holmes to see whether he had any thoughts on the subject. Per is a talented director, music producer, and creator of *The Master Course In High-End Blocking & Staging*,

SHOT DESIGNER

iPad   iPhone

- Hollywood Camera Work
- free ($19.99 to unlock pro features)
- hhhlinks.com/ y3e9

the best training for camera and actor blocking I've ever seen (www. hollywoodcamerawork.us). As it turns out, my timing was extraordinarily good. Per was in the process of beta testing Shot Designer, his brand-spankin'-new shot-blocking app.

He let me try it, and within seconds, it had officially blown my mind. After one hour of testing, it went from something I'd never heard of to one of my all-time favorite apps. Even after that brief exposure, I knew *this* was an app that was going to help me become a better director. It's that good. Really.

Let's have a look at the app's basic functionality.

After launching the app and creating a new document, you'll see a red circle and a blue circle (**FIGURE 5.20**). These represent your characters. Like storyboards, blocking diagrams utilize a distinct visual language that relies on symbols and context to communicate meaning. You can identify a character's gender and the direction it's facing by the quantity and position of small lines contained within its circle: one line indicates a male, while two lines represent a female. The red and blue colors are totally subjective and can be changed at any time.

The document can be scaled up and down using the standard pinch and zoom gestures. Likewise, you can pan around the document by dragging anywhere on-screen. To move a character or any object, you must tap it once first to select it. While an object is selected, you can drag it around and change its direction. Tapping once on a blank area of the canvas will deselect the object.

So far, this diagram shows a man and a woman facing each other. Great! And, by *great*, I mean horribly boring. Let's add cameras!

You can add items to the diagram in one of two ways. You can tap ➕ to pull up the object menu that contains characters, cameras, set pieces, props, lighting,

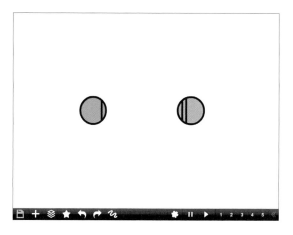

FIGURE 5.20 When creating a new diagram in Shot Designer, you'll always begin with this charming and totally unintimidating couple.

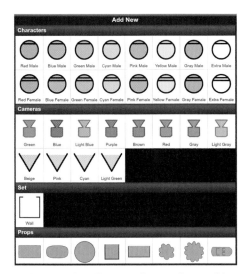

FIGURE 5.21 When you're ready to add objects to your diagram, you'll have a truckload to pick from.

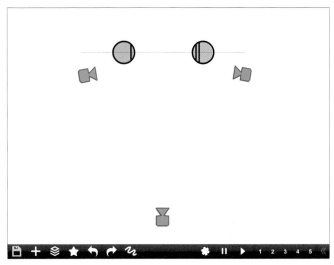

FIGURE 5.22 A basic diagram showing two characters being covered by a pair of over-the-shoulder (OTS) cameras and a wide master.

and annotations (**FIGURE 5.21**). It's worth noting that the object menu screenshot was pulled from a beta version of the app, so it's likely missing many of the objects that will come bundled in the official release. Tap the desired object, such as a camera, and then tap the diagram where you'd like to place it. The second way to add an object is to tap and hold an empty spot in the diagram. In a moment, you'll see a small pop-up that will allow you to add an object or import a background image.

In the example scene, I've added three cameras for a matching pair of over-the-shoulder shots and a wide master (**FIGURE 5.22**). These cameras can be moved and rotated just like the characters objects. I've also added an axis line between the characters. These are equally easy to create. Tap the first character to select it, and then tap again to pull up its Edit menu. Now tap Axis Line To, and then tap the second character. A new axis line appears between the characters.

Being able to view axis lines will help you avoid breaking the *180-degree rule* while placing your cameras. If you just nodded with total understanding, skip ahead a few paragraphs. If you are under the impression that the 180-degree rule refers to the temperature at which water boils, please read on.

The 180-degree rule helps maintain proper screen direction when shooting a conversation between two or more characters, or put simply, it ensures that your actors appear to be facing one another. This is achieved by positioning all of your cameras on one side of the axis line. The moment you stick a camera on the other side of the line (sometimes called *crossing the line*), you risk having a scene in which one character appears to be talking to the back of another character's head. Why is it called the 180-degree rule? Imagine a large 360-degree circle of dolly track wrapped around your characters. Now picture the axis line slicing that circle in half, leaving you with two 180-degree arcs. You can now shoot from any point along one of the arcs while maintaining proper screen direction. In other words, you have 180 degrees of yummy goodness.

There are times when you might want to intentionally break the 180-degree rule in order to startle or confuse your audience. You might even choose to stick your camera right on the axis line, yielding a direct-to-camera style often found in Wes Anderson's films. As your characters move through a scene and more characters are added to a conversation, your axis line will shift. Knowing how to manage and exploit axis lines comes with experience (or intense instruction like Per's training series).

Also, water boils at 100°C or 212°F. You really should know that.

Within Shot Designer, axis lines serve another wonderful purpose. You can forge an invisible connection between a camera and an axis line. Then, when you move one of the characters and its associated axis line, the connected camera moves along with it. In other words, Shot Designer does its best to automatically preserve the relationships between cameras and the characters they're shooting. The app is *filled* with equally brilliant, automatic features just like this.

Let's get a little more advanced. Tap the red man to select him, and then tap again to open his Edit menu. Now tap Walk From, and then tap about 2 inches above his current position. The app automatically adds a new character position and a corresponding motion arrow. Now we're getting somewhere! Tap the camera positioned for the wide master shot, and then tap it again to view its Edit menu. Now tap Track To, and then tap about an inch away from your characters. The app adds a second camera position with an arrow indicating its intended direction. Looking at the full diagram now (**FIGURE 5.23**), it's clear that the wide-angle camera dollys in as the man walks up to the woman and turns to face her. At that point, the conversation is covered by the pair of over-the-shoulder cameras.

Using the same techniques, you can build complex sequences with multiple moving characters and cameras. After fooling around with the diagram for another minute, I created blocking for both characters and added a tracking move to the woman's over-the-shoulder camera so that it transforms into the man's over-the-shoulder shot as he moves into his third position. I also added an over-the-shoulder for the woman that will pan left slightly as the man walks

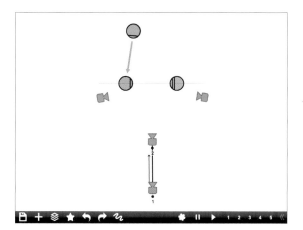

FIGURE 5.23 Getting fancy in Shot Designer. Now the man walks into position, while the wide master dollys in. See? What did I tell you? Fancy!

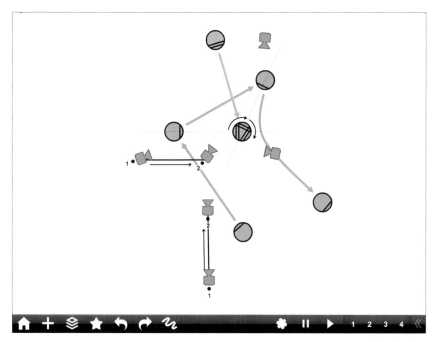

FIGURE 5.24 When blocking a scene, even with only two characters, things can get a bit confusing.

out of frame (**FIGURE 5.24**). *Say what*?! Yes, this is a lot to absorb, especially if you've never blocked before. Don't panic if it doesn't make sense yet. It will with practice.

Once you've mastered the basics, you can add details to your diagrams like walls, vehicles, captions, storyboard frames, and more. The app even includes a built-in viewfinder that can simulate various formats and lens sizes (similar to Artemis Director's Viewfinder).

And when you think your mind has been expanded to its limits, you can bring your diagrams to life! Shot Designer includes a remarkably intuitive animation system that will take you through your entire blocking diagram, one step at a time. This is incredibly useful when working with complex diagrams, helping to make sense out of chaos. Having this kind of power invites creative experimentation, and that's what blocking is all about.

Can you handle some more good news? Sure you can! By the time you read this, Shot Designer should be available for iPhone, iPad, Android, Mac, and Windows machines! Better yet, all of the different versions operate in exactly the same way. Master it on one platform, and you've mastered it on all of them. And, yes, you can exchange data files between all platforms. Want to hear the very best news? The app is *free* to try! However, you'll likely want to pay for the Pro features after you've played with it.

As I write this, Shot Designer is still in beta, and the tool set is still growing. One feature that is expected to be part of its initial release is automatically generated, fully editable shot lists! How sick is that? I wish I could show you this feature and describe how it works, but the truth is I haven't seen it yet. I don't think anyone has. However, based on the elegant implementation of the features I've experienced thus far, I have no doubt that the shot lists functionality will be equally well thought out.

Pssst. Want to know a secret? Here's what's planned for future versions of Shot Designer: script integration (so you can time your moves to the screenplay), the ability to record dialogue or have the app synthesize voices for you, and automatic 3D visualization! What?! Are you kidding me?! The only way you can't be impressed by that is if it's already 2034 and you found this book in the one-dollar bin, in which case Shot Designer has likely already added holographic projection, human cloning, and time travel.

As you can see, Shot Designer is a monster of an app. I have no doubt that it will soon reside on every filmmaker's iPad from Hollywood to Bollywood. And, I remind you: I've only seen the beta! Who knows what wonders await us all in the final version? Only Per knows for sure. You want his number?

OMNIGRAFFLE

- The Omni Group
- $49.99
- hhhlinks.com/ wm85

OmniGraffle

There's no denying that Shot Designer is in a class by itself, but that doesn't mean it's the only app worth adding to your toolkit.

While typically used to create flowcharts and graphs, OmniGraffle's ability to import, manipulate, and connect custom graphic elements make it a wonderful solution for designing blocking diagrams, which is why it's been my tool of choice for nearly a decade.

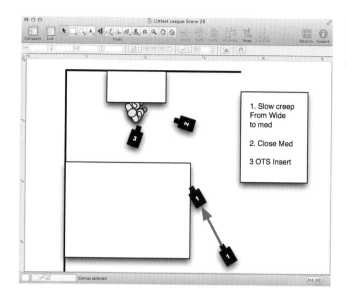

FIGURE 5.25 A shockingly basic blocking diagram created in OmniGraffle on the Mac.

Prior to the launch of OmniGraffle for iPad, I used the Mac version to block my scenes at home (**FIGURE 5.25**) and then print out the finished diagrams to use on set the next day. When things changed during the shoot, as they always do, I altered the diagrams with a pen, and then another pen, and then a Sharpie, and then a highlighter. Before long, my diagrams looked like a test pad in the pen aisle at Office Depot.

When I heard that OmniGraffle was being released for the iPad, I was ready and willing to camp out in line in front of the App Store. Since that's impossible, I just camped out in front of my computer. The day the app was released was the day my workflow started to change. For a while, I still created my diagrams on my Mac, but rather than printing them out, I'd simply transfer them to my iPad. When things changed during production, as they always do, I could edit my diagrams right within OmniGraffle on my iPad. As I grew more comfortable with the iPad version, I stopped using the Mac version for all but the most complex diagrams. I now design, edit, and share most of my blocking diagrams exclusively on my iPad. *Vive la Revolution*!

Let's go over the OmniGraffle basics, and then we can look at designing a blocking diagram.

With the app launched and a blank document created, new objects can be added in one of two ways. You can use the Pen tool to draw a shape by hand, or you can copy a predefined object from one of the app's many stencils. Like the plastic stencils you may have used in elementary school, each OmniGraffle stencil contains multiple premade objects. The stencil's name should give you a pretty clear indication of what it contains. For example, the Shapes stencil includes a circle, square, triangle, star, and so on.

By tapping ⊞ in the upper right, you'll call up a list of all the stencils you currently have installed (you can add more later). Tap any of the stencils to view the shapes it contains. If you wanted to add a circle to your canvas, you would first tap the Shapes stencil (**FIGURE 5.26**) and then drag a circle object from the stencil to your canvas. If you wanted to duplicate that circle, you could reopen the stencil and drag out another one, but instead, I want to share a terrific shortcut: Tap and hold your first circle just for a moment, and then tap Copy on the menu that appears above it. After that, use three fingers to tap anywhere on the canvas, and a duplicate circle will be pasted in that location. It's amazing how many OmniGraffle users don't know that shortcut. Congratulations, you now have permission to be smug.

Next, we'll add an arrow between the two circles. There are a few ways to do this, but since you've already seen stencils in action, let's draw a connecting arrow by hand. Tap ✏️ to switch into drawing mode, and then tap ✎ to select the Connection tool. Now, simply drag from one circle to the other (**FIGURE 5.27**). Done! Go get yourself a brewski. You've earned it. If you're under the drinking age, go get yourself a Coke. You've earned it.

The best part about this lovely new arrow is that it remains stuck to your objects. If you were to move either of the circles around, the arrow would move right along with them.

Hey, are you seeing what I'm seeing? This looks an awful lot like the beginnings of a blocking diagram, doesn't it? Ha-*ha*! I tricked you! I told you we were

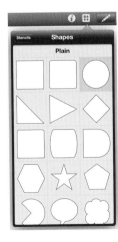

FIGURE 5.26 The Shapes stencil within OmniGraffle on the iPad, because you never know when you're going to need a Pac Man symbol.

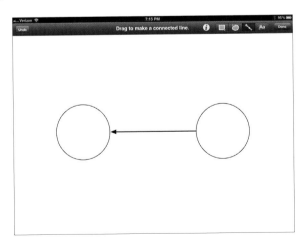

FIGURE 5.27 Connecting two objects within OmniGraffle is as easy as dragging a line. By the way, dragging a line is very easy.

just going over the basics, but in fact, you've already learned how to make a blocking diagram! Granted, we've diagrammed one character walking from one spot to another, facing an unknown direction, without a camera to shoot it, but still…Ha-*ha*! I tricked you! With a little practice and better-designed objects (no offense to plain white circles), you'll be constructing diagrams complete with curved arrows, text labels, color-coded characters, and more.

Previously, I mentioned you can add additional stencils into OmniGraffle, but I didn't say how. The easiest way is to use the search field conveniently located right at the top of the stencil list. Any keywords you enter here will be used to query http://graffletopia.com, a website that manages a huge library of free, user-created stencils. Tap any of the stencils in the search results to open a preview and optionally download it to your library. Sadly, not all of the stencils on http://graffletopia.com play nice with the iPad version of OmniGraffle, so you'll have to do a bit of trial and error.

Since stencils are so readily available, there's no reason to limit yourself to circles and squares. In fact, if you do a search for *camera staging*, you'll find the exact stencil I used to create the diagrams for a Walt Disney movie I recently directed (**FIGURE 5.28**).

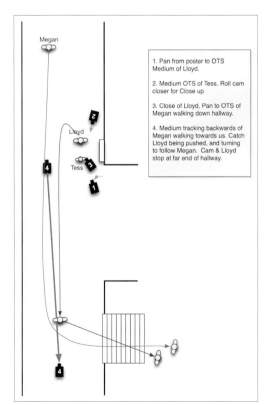

FIGURE 5.28 One of the many blocking diagrams I've created in OmniGraffle for iPad.

As cool as OmniGraffle is, I'm not recommending it over Shot Designer. I'm also not recommending Shot Designer over OmniGraffle. I'm recommending you take a close look at both and grab whichever you feel will best serve your needs.

I believe Shot Designer will be my tool of choice under typical conditions, but there's no way I'd ever let OmniGraffle escape from my iPad. Even though it lacks Shot Designer's blocking-specific functions, it still offers some impressive features. For instance, OmniGraffle has better layer controls, including *shared* layers that can remain editable across multiple diagrams. It allows you to easily create and share your own objects and stencils. And, as I just mentioned, it can access a massive, ever-growing library of premade stencils that will greatly extend the app's usefulness. For instance, if you were to download the Film Lighting stencil, you could use OmniGraffle to design your stage's lighting plan. Not too shabby.

OmniGraffle is as flexible as it is powerful. Once installed on your iPad, I'm certain it will slowly seep into the many crevices of your creative life. Please excuse any unintentional creepiness contained within that last sentence.

TouchDraw

TOUCHDRAW

iPad   iPhone

- Elevenworks LLC
- $8.99
- hhhlinks.com/ b4m5

I wanted to quickly mention this outstanding, less expensive alternative to OmniGraffle. While TouchDraw has a loyal and growing user base, it's a relative newcomer compared to OmniGraffle, which has been enjoying updates for well over a decade. That said, TouchDraw is a finely tuned iPad-only app that allows for quick creation of charts, graphics, and diagrams. Its versatile tool set offers more than enough power to perform all of the tasks necessary to create beautiful and descriptive blocking diagrams (**FIGURE 5.29**).

Like OmniGraffle, TouchDraw allows you to create your own graphic elements (actors, cameras, and so on), link objects together with auto-updating lines and arrows, import images from your photo library, use real-world measurements (inches, feet, yards, and so on), and share your completed diagrams with others.

As much as I dig TouchDraw, I've remained an OmniGraffle loyalist for one primary reason: OmniGraffle for Mac. When I'm faced with a particularly complex scene, I love being able to design its blocking diagram on my Mac and then transfer it to my iPad. Since TouchDraw is an iPad-only app, it doesn't offer that luxury…yet. As it turns out, Elevenworks, TouchDraw's developer, will soon be releasing a Mac version (it might be available by the time you read this). Once that happens, all bets are off. If TouchDraw for Mac provides a more enjoyable and productive experience, I'll be making the switch.

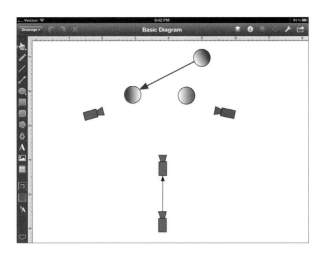

FIGURE 5.29 TouchDraw offers many of the same features found in OmniGraffle but costs about one-fifth the price. However, for the moment, there isn't a compatible Mac version.

While we're on the subject of switching, I believe it's important to remain app-agnostic, or *appnostic* for short. Loyalty to a particular tool is admirable, but if another one comes along that's better suited to a particular project or simply helps you express your vision with greater ease and speed, why wouldn't you use it? You can e-mail your answer to pleasedontemailme@itwasarhetorical-question.whatever.

MagicPlan

Of all the apps in all of apptopia, MagicPlan might be the most appropriately named (except perhaps for Beer! and iFart Mobile). What this app can accomplish truly feels magical. The fact that it's free makes it feel that much more magicalish.

Using only your iPhone's or iPad's built-in camera, MagicPlan can create a surprisingly accurate floor plan of your entire shooting location in seconds (or minutes for multiple rooms). While aiding in film production is not this app's intended purpose, I can't imagine a better use for it. When faced with an especially tricky scene within an equally tricky space, wouldn't it be great to have a floor plan on which to design your blocking diagram? That was a trick question. Of course, it would be great. Here's how it works.

After launching the app and starting a new plan, stand at a central point toward the center of the room where you can see as many of the room's corners as possible. Line up the app's on-screen reticle with one of the corners, and tap the corner button (**FIGURE 5.30**). A virtual traffic cone is dropped right on the spot you captured. Rotate in place to line up every corner in the room, tapping the corner button each time. Do your best to estimate the locations of corners

MAGICPLAN

iPad   iPhone

- Sensopia
- free
- hhhlinks.com/viuc

FIGURE 5.30 A virtual cone is dropped in a corner of the room while using MagicPlan to create a floor plan.

that are obstructed by furniture or other walls (easier than it sounds). Use the door button instead of the corner button when marking the corners of doorways and openings. Finish by rotating all the way around and recapturing the first corner.

Done!

Seconds after you finish, a fully drawn floor plan will pop on-screen, complete with wall measurements (**FIGURE 5.31**)! You will be asked if the plan appears to be accurate. If you tap No, the app will do its best to intelligently fix the plan before showing it to you once again. If your shooting location includes more than one room, you can capture each room and then connect them to form a complete floor plan. While the app's measurements aren't 100 percent accurate, I've found they come amazingly close, usually within a few inches, and that's certainly good enough for a blocking diagram.

Creating the floor plan is the easy part. Getting it into another app for use in blocking can be a little trickier.

Begin by signing up for a free MagicPlan account. You can do that from within the app, and it takes only a moment. Once you're logged into your new account, you can navigate to your floor plan's info screen and tap the big Get Files button on the lower left. Moments later, you'll receive an e-mail containing your floor plan as a JPEG and a PDF file. If you don't mind the tapestry of MagicPlan watermarking on your image (**FIGURE 5.32**), you're good to go. If, however, the watermarking makes you dizzy, you can pay to "activate" the plan on the Magic-Plan website. Activation costs vary depending on how you choose to pay. A single activation will run you around $2.50, but you can save money by purchasing multiple activations at once or subscribing to a monthly plan. After activating a plan, you can have the online service e-mail you the watermark-free files. Open

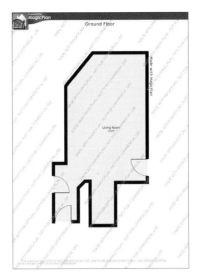

FIGURE 5.31 MagicPlan can spit out a floor plan of your shooting location faster than you can read this sentence. Well, perhaps it takes a little longer…but not much.

FIGURE 5.32 MagicPlan will send you your floor plans for free, but they'll be covered in watermarks. If you pay to "activate" the plan, you'll get a squeaky clean version.

that new e-mail on your iPad, and save the clean JPEG into your photo library by tapping and holding on the image.

When sharing this workflow with other filmmakers, I'll occasionally hear a complaint or two about having to pay for each floor plan. I don't understand this at all. Does a fine artist complain about having to pay for painting supplies? If you are uncomfortable with the idea of paying for watermark-free floor plans, consider it an expendable, like gaffer's tape or makeup. If it still bothers you, just use the free watermarked version!

Having said all that, there is one other way to obtain a watermark-free floor plan without spending a dime. In addition to Twitter and Facebook, MagicPlan can share your completed floor plan with an online service called Floorplanner.com. With a free Floorplanner.com account, you can store, edit, and preview one plan at a time. For most of us, that should be enough. This amazing online 2D/3D floor plan design service can open the floor plan you created on your iPad, but the service itself doesn't work well on iOS devices, so you'll need to access the site with a Mac or Windows machine. Once you have the floor plan open in Floorplanner.com, take a screenshot (Command-Shift-3 on Macs), and then e-mail that screenshot to yourself. Open the e-mail on your iPad, and save the screenshot image into your photo library.

FIGURE 5.33 MagicPlan can create floor plans of your locations, which you can then use as backgrounds for your diagrams. Neat!

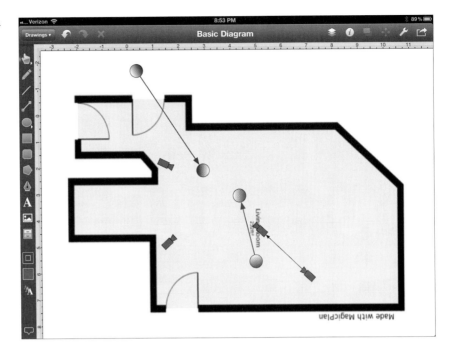

Now that the floor plan is in your photo library, it can be imported into any of the blocking apps I've covered in this chapter (**FIGURE 5.33**). You'll have to resize it relative to the scale of your other elements (actors, vehicles, props, and so on), but that should be relatively easy. Now you can block your actor and camera movements on top of a blueprint of the actual shooting location. I don't know about you, but that makes me giggle with glee. Hehehehehe. That was me giggling. I rest my case.

BUILDING A RODRIGUEZ LIST

When Robert Rodriguez was conceptualizing his breakout film *El Mariachi*, he created a list of every resource he had access to—every location, every vehicle, every prop. He made sure to include all of his own possessions, as well as items belonging to his friends and family. Using this list to guide his writing, he was able to craft a screenplay that exploited every resource. As a result, his film had much higher production value than his ultra-low budget would normally allow.

Around 15 years later, in 2007, Stu Maschwitz authored *The DV Rebels Guide,* what I believe to be one of the greatest filmmaking books ever written. In his book, Stu discussed the resource list Robert had created and lovingly dubbed it "The Rodriguez List." He urged every filmmaker to create his or her own Rodriguez List, suggesting that it is often an excellent source of inspiration and a surefire way to increase your production value. I agree with Stu's advice wholeheartedly and have been maintaining my own Rodriguez list ever since I first read Robert's book, *Rebel Without a Crew*, another seminal filmmaking tome.

Keep in mind, a Rodriquez List need not be in list form. I know one filmmaker who created a wildly elaborate computer database to store records of his resources. I know another who hand-writes everything on scraps of paper and then bundles everything together in categorized binder clips. When you start your own "list," create it in whatever form you believe will work best for you.

Naturally, you could use any number of different apps to store a Rodriquez List on your iPhone. Even the built-in Notepad app would do a swell job. Like most things, however, I find that the easier something is, the more likely we are to do it. With that in mind, I want to introduce you to a free app that makes cataloging resources as easy as taking a picture. Literally.

Celtx Scout

Brought to you by the same company that developed Celtx Script (one of the screenwriting apps I covered in Chapter 1), Celtx Scout is a resource collection tool for your iPhone that effortlessly uploads photos and related information directly into your online Celtx account.

As a reminder, you can sign up for a free Celtx account that comes standard with 2GB of cloud storage, perfect for housing and syncing all of the files relating to your film production.

After launching Celtx Scout for the first time, you'll be asked to enter your account credentials (you have to do this only once). Every subsequent launch will immediately bring up the iPhone's internal camera, which you can use to photograph any resource you'd like to add (**FIGURE 5.34**). After snapping a photo, you'll be given the chance to add comments and a descriptive title (**FIGURE 5.35**). Tapping Done in the upper-right corner uploads your photo directly to your Celtx cloud storage. The fact is, it will take you less time to photograph and upload a new item than it took me to describe the steps.

To keep things organized, tap ⚙ in the lower-left of the camera screen *before* taking a photo, and pick an upload destination folder from your Celtx cloud storage. I recommend setting up separate folders for each type of resource you'll be adding to your "list." For instance, I have folders for Talent, Locations, Vehicles, Animals, Props, Wardrobe, and Equipment.

CELTX SCOUT

iPad | iPhone

- Greyfirst Corp.
- free
- hhhlinks.com/drre

Celtx Scout is a very simple, single-purpose app that does exactly what it claims and nothing more. Use this app to photograph your resources, and before you know it, you'll have your own Rodriguez List from which to pull inspiration and production value.

FIGURE 5.34 Use Celtx Scout to quickly snap photos of any items you can include in future productions.

FIGURE 5.35 Give the item a descriptive name and some useful notes. Everything you enter will be automatically uploaded to your free Celtx account.

CHAPTER 6

LIGHTS! CAMERA! AIRPLANE MODE!

iPhones and iPads aren't going to displace professional video gear any time soon, but Apple's unprecedented amalgamation of video camera and computer has sparked a mobile filmmaking revolution.

Years ago, the biggest barrier to making a movie was finding a decent camera. Now, all you have to do is look in your pocket, backpack, or briefcase.

When partnered with the right apps, iOS devices can duplicate many of the features found in professional video cameras and even pull off a few tricks most other cameras wouldn't dare try. When was the last time you saw someone use a typical video camera to shoot, edit, color-correct, score, and upload a finished project?

While most of the apps in this section were designed for the iPhone, a few are universal and will work just as well on the iPad. Despite the iPhone having slightly better optics, there are plenty of reasons to shoot on both devices. iPhones are small, always available, and easy to hide when shooting without a permit (shame on you). iPads are essentially cameras with built-in field monitors, making it easy for you to check focus and framing. No matter which device you shoot on, it's important to understand its capabilities.

Apple's iPhone 4 and iPad 2 were among the first iOS devices that supported recording 720p, high-definition video. The following generations of each device (the iPhone 4S, iPhone 5, and iPad 3) raised the standard to 1080p. It's only a matter of time before they start shooting in 3D with Smell-O-Vision. If you're still sporting an older model that can't shoot video or is relegated to VGA resolution (640x480), it may be time to upgrade. Scratch that. It's definitely time to upgrade!

TABLE 6.1 breaks everything down, providing each device's maximum resolution and storage requirements. Keep in mind the storage numbers are approximate. Your mileage may vary.

TABLE 6.1 iOS Device Video Capabilities

iOS Device	Max Resolution and Frame Rate	Storage Required for One Minute	Storage Required for One Hour
Original iPhone and 3G*	No built-in video recording		
iPhone 3GS	640x480 @ 30fps	38MB	2.2GB
iPhone 4 and iPad 2	1280x720 "720p HD" @ 30fps	90MB	5.4GB
iPhone 4S, iPhone 5, and iPad 3	1920x1080 "1080p HD" @ 30fps	180MB	10.8GB

*The original iPhone and iPhone 3G can be forced to record video using some third-party apps and jailbreak hacks; however, the results look terrible and will likely make you sad.

You may also be wondering where Apple's iPod touch fits into all this. The most recent generation of this pocket media player shoots 1920x1080 video at 30fps, just like the iPhone 4S, iPhone 5, and iPad 3; however, iPhones typically have better camera systems than iPod touches, capable of shooting higher-quality images, with less noise in low light. That said, a 32GB iPod touch is only $299 and doesn't require any additional expensive monthly contracts. Obviously, since this device lacks the iPhone's cellular connection, it will be able to upload videos to online destinations only when connected to a Wi-Fi network.

Most of the apps I'll be discussing in this chapter will work on the iPod touch, but their capabilities may be limited. Always check in the App Store for the latest compatibility information, especially when using the iPod touch and older iPhone models.

One last thing to keep in mind: Footage recorded on iOS devices is *heavily* compressed in order to keep file sizes small. Considering the limited storage capacities of current Apple devices, this might seem like a good thing. However, heavily compressed footage can suffer from occasional blocky artifacts. This problem becomes especially evident when manipulating and color correcting the footage in postproduction. A couple of the apps mentioned in this chapter allow you to increase the data rates used to record your footage, effectively lowering your compression. Naturally, this means your footage will be eating more storage space than what I indicated in Table 6.1.

With all the technical mumbo-jumbo out of the way, it's time to get our cameras ready to roll. Shooting video on an iOS device is a unique experience, rife with quirks and compromises. The more you know about your "camera," the more likely you are to get the best results. Hey—that just gave me a great idea for a section heading.

GETTING THE BEST RESULTS

Whether you're shooting a narrative feature, a cutting-edge music video, an experimental short, or a corporate sizzle reel, your iOS device can capture some startlingly good footage. All it takes is a little preparation.

So, let's prepare!

Prepping Your Device

Before shooting any important video, the first thing you should do is to switch your iOS device into Airplane Mode. It's incredibly easy to do and always worth the effort. Simply launch the Settings app and then tap the toggle next to Airplane Mode to turn it on (**FIGURE 6.1**). Done.

FIGURE 6.1 Airplane Mode prevents unwanted disruptions while shooting.

While in Airplane Mode, your various radio transmissions will be shut down. This will block disruptive phone calls, text messages, and other unwanted network activity. It will also prevent your recorded audio from getting totally trashed by cellular interference. I can't tell you how many takes I've had ruined by obnoxious digital chirps because I forgot to switch on Airplane Mode. It still happens to me! Even as I write this, I'm considering it a reminder to myself.

When you're done shooting, make sure to switch Airplane Mode off. You don't want to miss any important phone calls from your lead actor demanding a larger trailer. Or, maybe you do.

Making Space

If you plan on doing a lot of shooting, make sure to free up as much storage space on your device as possible. You're going to need it! Even one minute of HD video can easily chew up 180 megabytes—that's more space than is required for many full-blown apps! The more space you empty out, the more recording time you'll have.

To find out exactly how much space each app is eating on your iOS device, just launch the Settings app, tap General, and then tap Usage. You'll be shown a list of all your installed apps, along with the storage space they're currently consuming (**FIGURE 6.2**). Look for large apps you barely use and kick 'em to the curb! Games and GPS applications tend to be the biggest space hogs.

To remove an app, find its icon on your home screen and then press down and hold on it until all the icons begin to shake. Then tap the ⊗ that appears over the app's icon. After you confirm the deletion, that app is history. Remember, you can always redownload an app if you ever want it back, without having to

FIGURE 6.2 Which apps consume the most storage space? Launch the Settings app to find out.

pay for it again (but any in-app purchases will have to be restored from within the app). For that reason, it might be wise to make sure your apps have a "restore purchases" function before deleting them. Lastly, be very careful not to toss any apps that contain irretrievable data.

Next to apps, photos, music, and downloaded movies tend to be the biggest space suckers. If you want to free up some additional space on your iPhone or iPad, consider temporarily removing all three. Here's a basic overview of the steps:

1. Connect your device to your computer.

2. Use iPhoto (or one of the Windows photo apps I mentioned in Chapter 3, under "Photos and iPhoto") to download all the photos and videos you have taken since your last sync or backup.

3. In iTunes, click the name of your device in the sidebar. When the Summary screen appears, you'll find a graph at the bottom of the window clearly illustrating how your space is currently being used (FIGURE 6.3).

4. Sync your device as usual to ensure that your computer has everything it needs to restore your media down the line.

FIGURE 6.3 The Capacity bar in iTunes is telling me that I have way too many zombie games on my iPhone.

5. Click the Music tab and uncheck the box next to Sync Music. Do the same on the Movies tab and the Photos tab.

6. Resync your device.

That's it. Your iOS device should now have more free space for shooting.

Putting everything back on your device is just as simple.

1. Connect your device to your computer.

2. In iTunes, click the name of your device in the sidebar.

3. Click the Music tab, and check the box next to Sync Music. Do the same on the Movies tab and the Photos tab.

4. Resync your device.

Naturally, if you've filled your device with new video files from a shoot, you may have to remove those to make room before restoring your personal media. If your new video files are stored in your device's camera roll, just download everything into iPhoto, and you'll be good to go. I'll also be covering how to move your video files from an iPhone to an iPad in Chapter 9.

It's also worth pointing out that thanks to music-streaming services like iTunes Match, Spotify, Google Play, and more, you no longer need to keep your entire space-devouring music library on your device. Now you can stream your music straight from the Internet, but keep in mind that doing so will eat into your monthly data allotment when on a cellular connection (3G, 4G, and so on).

Freeing Up Memory

Before shooting, I also recommend shutting down any suspended apps to free up memory. While there's some debate about the usefulness of this, I think it's worth taking the extra step to free up memory and avoid unwanted background activity. Start by double-tapping your iOS device's Home button. This brings up a scrolling list of all your suspended apps. Tap and hold on any one of them, until they *all* begin to vibrate. Then simply tap ⊖ next to each application you want to close, until all suspended apps have been shut down.

I'm sure I'll be getting a ton of e-mail from iPhone users informing me that shutting down apps is totally unnecessary. But you know what? So is sacrificing a chicken and lighting candles before every shoot, but we all do that, don't we?! Right? Why are you looking at me like that?

The Rolling Shutter Conundrum

CMOS camera sensors, like the ones found in your iOS devices, shoot video using a *rolling shutter.* Rather than recording an entire frame at once (like film cameras), rolling shutter systems capture a frame by scanning across its surface (from top to bottom). Think of it like the slow-moving sensor bars inside desktop scanners and older photocopy machines. Even with a powerful CMOS sensor and a quick rolling shutter, the scan is not instantaneous. Therefore, your subject is likely to move *while* the rolling shutter scan is taking place and *before* the entire frame has been captured.

While not noticeable in most footage, fast-moving subjects and quick camera pans will result in warped, rubbery video that looks as if the bottom part of your frame is trying to catch up to the top part (**FIGURE 6.4**). If you've ever noticed slanted or stretched subjects in your footage, that's rolling shutter.

Everyone loves Jell-O! Everyone except for me. I despise that bouncy, elastic substance with a hatred usually reserved for clog dancing. So, it comes as no surprise to me that rolling shutter artifacts are now commonly referred to as "Jell-O-cam."

While it's nearly impossible to completely remove the effects of rolling shutter, there are things you can do to reduce it.

FIGURE 6.4 Because of the rolling shutter, even a simple whip-pan can result in serious Jell-O-cam.

First, avoid whip pans. Even fast pans should be limited. Also, try not to have actors or objects zip past the frame (fast-moving vehicles almost always result in nasty Jell-O-cam). When you move your camera to follow a fast-moving subject, try to keep them within the same portion of your frame. That usually helps reduce visible distortion as well.

Naturally, you can't always avoid Jell-O-cam, especially when shooting an action sequence. So, what do you do when you're stuck with wobbly footage? Fortunately, there are several tools available for desktop computers that can help reduce, and in some cases remove, rolling shutter artifacts.

If you have a Mac, get ahold of iMovie! Yes, I said iMovie. This $15 nonlinear editing application, typically associated with amateurs and home videos, is surprisingly powerful and even includes a feature to greatly reduce rolling shutter (**FIGURE 6.5**)! I'm constantly surprised at how much better my iPhone footage looks after being processed through this application.

FIGURE 6.5 Use iMovie on your Mac to help reduce rolling shutter artifacts and increase cheesy page curl transitions.

ROLLINGSHUTTER
hhhlinks.com/kcw7

If you're an Adobe After Effects user, you can purchase (or rent) the Foundry's incredible plug-in called ROLLINGSHUTTER. While this tool is quite expensive (on top of After Effect's already hefty price tag), it might be worth it when you need to rescue some high-priority Jell-O-cam footage. If you'd like to see ROLLINGSHUTTER in action, I covered the plug-in on HandHeldHollywood.com and included sample video of my results. You can find that post at http://hhhlinks.com/kcw7.

Exposure, Focus, and White Balance

One of the key factors separating pro cameras from toys is independent control over your exposure, focus, and white balance. Most consumer-grade cameras set these properties automatically based on what it believes will give you the best overall image. However, this automation comes at a price, and you often wind up sacrificing something important in the process.

Having the ability to properly calibrate color, along with the flexibility to decide what should remain in focus and what should be properly exposed, are absolute necessities for your primary camera app. Fortunately, many apps provide independent control over focus, exposure, and white balance.

Don't take these controls for granted or assume that they must be used to achieve the same boring results you'd expect to get with a consumer camera. Practice *misusing* these controls, and you'll be amazed at what you can learn. By deciding what's in focus and how a shot is exposed, you can make a meaningful, emotional impact on your audience. It's like having mind control but without the theremin soundtrack (if you laughed at that joke, we should hang out).

Light It Up!

As splendiferous as your iOS device's camera may be, it performs horribly under low light. Less than ideal lighting conditions will cause excessive digital noise to dance across your footage. Unless you're filming a low-budget *Tron* prequel in which a guy is trapped inside a crappy camera sensor, you need to learn a bit about lighting.

While the iPhone supplies a built-in LED light, it should be avoided at all costs. It has the habit of transforming beautiful but poorly lit subjects into brightly lit vampires.

Don't get stuck on the idea that you'll need to spend thousands—or even hundreds—of dollars on lighting gear. Even $25 worth of work lights from Home Depot will improve your image (if used correctly). Granted, I typically work with professional lighting instruments, but for situations where I don't have that luxury, I keep a plastic tub of clamp lights in my closet.

Take some time and learn the basics. A little lighting knowledge goes a *long* way. There are plenty of terrific educational sources for lighting instruction, but my absolute favorite is a quaint, little-known website called YouTube. Perhaps you've heard of it? A quick search for something like *video lighting tutorial* will reveal dozens, if not hundreds, of informative videos (along with some total crud).

I enjoy learning about lighting and other filmmaking techniques on YouTube because the site offers a *wide* variety of knowledgeable filmmakers who are eager to share their wisdom. Why learn from one filmmaker, who has one approach to solving a problem, when you can learn from multiple filmmakers and gather a variety of unique solutions?

Here are a couple of lighting videos that will help get you started:

> *Three Point Lighting* by the Frugal Filmmaker (one of my favorite YouTube posters): http://hhhlinks.com/zdih

> *Common Lighting Setups* by Videomaker: http://hhhlinks.com/g1c4

Three Point Lighting
hhhlinks.com/zdih

Common Lighting Setups
hhhlinks.com/g1c4

Keep It Steady

It's almost impossible to get a shake-free shot while shooting handheld with an iPhone or iPad. Regardless of the built-in stabilization now included in new iOS devices, most of the footage coming out of these bad boys is still unbearably jittery. Don't get me wrong; Apple's stabilization technology is actually pretty impressive. It excels at turning total crap into fairly decent crap. But ultimately, this feature is designed to improve home videos, not turn your cell phone into a Steadicam.

I'll be covering a terrific stabilizing app called Luma a little later, but in general, I recommend you pick up one of the tripod mounts or other stabilizing accessories covered in the next chapter (**FIGURE 6.6**).

Now that you know what to expect from your iOS hardware, it's time to examine the wonders that await you in Apple's App Store.

FIGURE 6.6 The Glif is one of many tripod mounts available for your iPhone and iPad. Scenic view not included.

THE BEST VIDEO CAMERA APPS

What makes a truly great camera app? Control.

It doesn't matter how many bells and whistles an app foists in your face. If it doesn't provide control over the basics (focus, exposure, and white balance), you should find an app that does.

Hey look, I already found a bunch! Here are the very best camera apps currently available that specialize in *control*.

FiLMiC Pro

FiLMiC PRO

iPad   iPhone

Cinegenix, LLC
- $3.99
- hhhlinks.com/ 8fqe

If you plan on shooting video with your iPhone, plan on purchasing FiLMiC Pro. In fact, forget planning on it, just do it now. There is no better tool available in the App Store for capturing high-quality video on your iOS device.

From the moment you launch the app and gaze at its clean and intuitive interface, you know you're looking at something with far more gusto than Apple's built-in Camera app (**FIGURE 6.7**).

In the main viewing area, you'll see two shapes hovering over your footage. The first looks like a dashed square. That's the focus reticle, and it determines what part of your frame will be in focus. In other words, if you want your actor to be in focus, tap the focus reticle and drag it over your actor's face. It doesn't get easier than that!

FIGURE 6.7 FiLMiC Pro's main interface and two dudes who are in better shape than me.

Focus Reticle

Exposure Reticle

Audio Meter

Focus Lock | Exposure Lock | White Balance Lock | Light Toggle (for Devices with Built-in Light) | Info | Clip Library | App Settings | Record Button

FIGURE 6.8 FiLMiC Pro uses the exposure reticle's position to set the overall exposure for the frame. By changing the reticle's position, you change the exposure.

The other shape, a circular iris icon, is the exposure reticle. It works just like the focus reticle, but it controls the overall exposure of your image. Just drag it over the part of your frame that you would like properly exposed, and the app will do the rest. For example, if you have an actor sitting in a dark room in front of a bright window and you move the exposure reticle over the actor, the actor will be properly exposed, but the window will be completely overexposed (like the Kardashians). On the other hand, if you move the exposure reticle over the window, the app will adjust the exposure to ensure that you can clearly see what's on the other side of that glass. However, your actor will be thrown into total darkness (**FIGURE 6.8**).

When you have the focus and exposure set to your tastes, you can lock their values by tapping their matching lock buttons on the bottom toolbar. There's also a button for locking the camera's white balance. With all of the values locked, you can safely move your iPhone camera. Without the ability to lock these settings, your footage will be dripping with ugly, unwanted shifts in color, brightness, and clarity. Tap the unlock buttons once more, and your values will once again be defined by the position of the reticles.

On the right side of your iPhone's screen, you'll find a nicely responsive audio meter. Keep your levels toward the top of the green bars, with occasional peaks in the yellow, and you should be all set. If you're seeing a lot of red bars, your audio is sure to be crunchy and distorted. This is why you should always keep an eye on your audio meter.

When you're ready to shoot, just tap the red record button in the lower right, and a running time counter appears, letting you know how long you've been rolling. When you're done, tap the record button again, and your shot is stored in FiLMiC Pro's internal library (or into your iPhone's camera roll, if you prefer). To review your footage, you can tap 🎞 on the toolbar and be taken to the Footage screen. Here you can select a clip, view it, and optionally transfer it to a variety of destinations (your camera roll, YouTube, Vimeo, Dropbox, Facebook, Tumblr, or an FTP server). You can also rename the clip and assign it to a custom project (to keep things organized).

While all of these features sound great, it doesn't necessarily explain why FiLMiC Pro is so universally loved. What is it that makes this app so popular? Open the option-packed Settings screen, and you'll have your answer.

Here, you can switch between front and back cameras, change your shooting orientation, pick your resolution (1920x1080 or 1280x720), alter your camera's frame rate (anything from 1 to 30 frames per second!), switch to a single reticle system (making it slightly more like Apple's own Camera app), flip the image (useful for 35mm lens adaptors like the ones I'll be covering in the next chapter), and turn on GPS tagging.

Wow, those sure are a lot of featur—oh wait, there's more!

You can toggle the audio meter on and off (great when shooting without sound), turn on a thirds guide (terrific for new filmmakers who are just learning to frame using the rule of thirds), add a standard-definition framing guide (in case your footage is going to be center cropped for older televisions), and even flip on a Super 35 matte (if you want your footage to have that extra-wide, Cinemascope look).

Wow, those sure are a lot of featur—*what*? There's more?! Yes. There's more.

FiLMiC Pro gives you the option to change your video encoding rate! The higher the rate, the higher the quality of your video (and the more disk space it eats up). Apple's standard encoding rate on an iPhone 4S and iPhone 5 is up to 24 megabits per second (Mbps). FiLMiC Pro lets you up that rate to 32Mbps, or what it calls FiLMic Quality, and if that's not enough, you can even crank it up to FiLMiC Extreme, which will encode your video at an impressive 48Mbps (**FIGURE 6.9**). If you value quality over drive space, you'll love having these higher rates available. That said, if you would rather maximize your available storage and sacrifice a little quality, you can switch your encode mode to the Economy Rate of 16Mbps.

Wow, those sure are a lot of features!

I can't imagine what features might be added down the road. But why *imagine?* After trading a few tweets with the developer, I know *exactly* what's coming

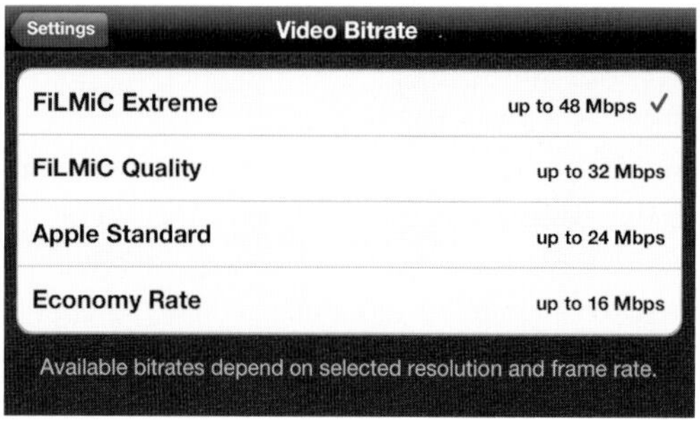

Settings	Video Bitrate	
FiLMiC Extreme	up to 48 Mbps ✓	
FiLMiC Quality	up to 32 Mbps	
Apple Standard	up to 24 Mbps	
Economy Rate	up to 16 Mbps	
Available bitrates depend on selected resolution and frame rate.		

FIGURE 6.9 If you want the best-looking footage, crank up your bit rate. Just remember, higher bit rates mean bigger files.

down the road: variable input and output frame rates, smooth 4x zooming at user-selectable speeds, zooming via pinch and zoom gestures, 60fps shooting, camera setup presets, additional upload destinations, customized file naming with scene and take number indicators, an Event Mode that allows pausing while recording a single clip, and more!

All right, FiLMiC PRO! We get it! You're awesome! Knock it off, already!

Any more features, and this app would need a personal assistant.

If everything goes according to the developer's plan, the new features I mentioned may be available by the time you read this. If not, forget I said anything. There's also a chance that the update will, in fact, be its own app called FiLMiC Pro 2, and not a free upgrade from previous versions.

Either way, FiLMiC Pro is a monster of a video camera app, and it belongs on *every* filmmaker's iPhone, including yours.

CinePro

Just in case one remarkable video camera app isn't enough for you, allow me to introduce CinePro. As the newest member of the "Holy cow, that's awesome!" club, CinePro doesn't have FiLMiC Pro's track record, but this relative latecomer packs a heap of innovation into an absurdly intuitive interface (**FIGURE 6.10**).

FIGURE 6.10 The CinePro interface provides quick access to your camera's most important features.

CINEPRO

iPad | iPhone

- John Clem
- $2.99
- hhhlinks.com/47dv

When you first boot CinePro, you'll instantly recognize the app's biggest strength, which is also its primary difference from FiLMiC Pro. CinePro's interface provides constant, easy access to nearly all of the important user-selectable parameters without having to switch to a dedicated settings screen. Not only does this allow for incredibly swift operation, it also provides users with constant feedback about the camera's current settings. No more guess-work, and no more wondering if you remembered to make an important change.

Along the top of the screen, above the camera's live feed, you'll see buttons to enter the settings screen (more on that in a moment), change the zoom (using virtual focal length measurements such as 32mm, 35mm, and so on), select an aspect ratio for your finished recording, change the shooting frame rate (from 1fps to 30fps, plus an experimental 60fps mode), change the ISO (the camera's sensitivity to light), and lock the white balance, exposure, and focus. There's also a button to toggle your iPhone's built-in LED light (also known as the built-in insta-ugly illumination orb of doom).

On the bottom of the screen, you'll find buttons to play back clips from the app's library, switch between front and back cameras, add and adjust filters, and, of course, start and stop recording.

CinePro comes with a limited selection of interesting filters (**FIGURE 6.11**), but more can be obtained via in-app purchases. The filters are fun and provide a variety of looks, but honestly, I don't recommend their use. I firmly believe you should always record your footage as cleanly as possible and then make your creative color choices in postproduction. But, if you're just making a quick video for the Web and don't anticipate doing any real post, the filters will likely come in handy. To adjust the filters, the app provides a wonderfully simple control system that inserts huge dials on the sides of your device's display (**FIGURE 6.12**).

Let's get back to the settings screen for a moment. Among the available options, you can switch between shooting resolutions, pick your desired encoding bit rate (similar to the option found in FiLMiC Pro), turn on gesture controls for aspect ratio and zoom settings, and toggle a brilliant little histogram overlay that can help you evaluate the distribution of luminance values within your frame.

As much as I enjoy using CinePro, it's not a perfect app. Its biggest flaw is the lack of on-screen audio meters. I'm not the only one to complain about this, so I suspect it's a feature that will be added very soon (and might already be available by the time you flip through these pages). It's also worth pointing out that the app has always been a little buggy. Fortunately, the developer has a solid track record of pushing out updates on a regular basis.

FIGURE 6.11 CinePro offers a wide variety of fun and potentially useful filters.

FIGURE 6.12 Filter settings can be adjusted using one or two large on-screen dials.

Even with its rough spots, I'm a big fan of CinePro. It's clearly worth more than its price tag would suggest, and you're not obligated to buy any of the additional filters.

Almost DSLR

When Almost DSLR was released back in July 2010, it was the first app of its kind—a true replacement for Apple's Camera app that provided individual controls for focus, exposure, and white balance. Before this app hit the scene, most iPhone owners had no idea that such fine-tuned control over the internal camera hardware was even possible.

The app was quickly adopted by the creative community and continues to be a favorite among filmmakers. Granted, Almost DSLR doesn't have the polished interface and intuitive controls found in the other apps in this chapter, but what it lacks in elegance, it *more* than makes up for in features.

When launching the app for the first time, prepare to be slightly overwhelmed. It defaults to displaying its framing guides, along with a bounty of buttons and icons (**FIGURE 6.13**). Nearly every distraction in the app can be hidden, leaving your iPhone's screen nice and clear, but doing so would diminish the app's greatest feature—its ability to display multiple status indicators and option switches while shooting.

The controls are fairly straightforward. To record a movie, tap the video camera button. To take a photograph, tap the still camera button. Tapping the gear takes you to the settings screen, and tapping the filmstrip calls up your video library.

ALMOST DSLR

iPad | iPhone

- Rainbow Silo
- $1.99
- hhhlinks.com/ 6355

FIGURE 6.13 Almost DSLR provides useful tools for both videographers and photographers.

Camera Toggle (Switch Between Front and Back Cameras)

Aspect Ratio

Timer/ Intervalometer (for Photos)

Anti-Shake Mode (for Photos)

Toggle Information View

Rule of Thirds Framing Grid

App Settings

Clip Library

Take a Picture

Start/Stop Movie Recording

ALMOST DSLR FREE

iPad **iPhone**

- Rainbow Silo
- free
- hhhlinks.com/ 7p2d

Like the other two apps I've mentioned so far, focus and exposure can be set individually. To set (and lock) focus, tap once on your desired subject, or tap once and drag to experiment with different points around the frame. To set (and lock) exposure, double-tap the desired location, or double-tap and drag to try different locations. A triple-tap will unlock both settings. On-screen indicators/ switches tell you when your exposure, focus, and white balance settings have been locked.

Among the app's more unique aspects are its options to flip the video and turn off focus control when using your iPhone with an external lens, as well as its ability to wirelessly pair with another iOS device running Almost DSLR, turning one into a remote control for the other. Rather than presenting a graphic audio meter, Almost DSLR displays your current audio level as a decibel (dB) value. Finally, the app also features an interval timer, which can be used to create time-lapse photo sequences, which in turn could be converted into a time-lapse movie within most desktop editing applications.

Because of the app's occasionally confusing, text-heavy interface, Almost DSLR is probably better suited to technically minded filmmakers. Personally, I prefer a more graphic approach, but I know plenty of filmmakers who love seeing the detailed numeric displays this app provides.

If you'd like to "try before you buy," the developer offers a free version of the app, called Almost DSLR Free. It provides exactly the same functionality as the paid version, but also displays distracting banner ads. If you can live with the ads, there's no reason to buy the ad-free version.

What About the Built-in Camera App?

Sure, it works. Sure, it makes fun sounds. Sure, it's a waste of your time.

With so many amazing video camera apps available in the App Store, there's no reason whatsoever to use Apple's elegant but featureless built-in Camera app (**FIGURE 6.14**). That said, if you *must* use the app, I'll give you a very quick overview of its operation. But I do so under protest. And, to make it more interesting for myself, I will be injecting completely made-up features. See whether you can spot them.

Light Toggle (for Devices with Built-in Light)

Camera Toggle (Switch Between Front and Back Cameras)

Photo/Movie Toggle

Record Button

Clip Library

FIGURE 6.14 Apple's built-in Camera app provides very little in the way of high-end features.

After you launch the app, you'll need to make sure you're in video mode by switching the toggle switch from the mini still camera icon to the mini video camera icon. Once in video mode, a quick double-tap at the center of the screen will scale down the live preview, allowing you to see the full 16x9 high-definition frame (if you own an iPhone 5 or newer, your screen is already 16x9, so there's no need to double-tap). A triple-tap will bring up a picture of a monkey.

Tapping the lightning bolt icon lets you control the onboard light; tapping [icon] will let you switch between the back and front cameras, and tapping the banana icon will bring up another picture of a monkey.

Use the record button to start and stop the recording process. Your previous videos await your inspection inside the iPhone's camera roll, which can be easily accessed by tapping the tiny thumbnail of your most recent shot. While reviewing a shot in the camera roll, you have the option to trim its start and end points. As much as I hate to admit it, I really do like that feature.

While not nearly as powerful as the other tools I've mentioned, Apple's camera does have some basic focus and exposure controls. After you line up your shot, tap the frame anywhere to set *both* your focus and exposure. You can lock these settings by tapping and holding on your desired reference point. A square reticle will pulse briefly, letting you know the lock has engaged, and then disappear. Your settings are now locked until you tap elsewhere on the screen. The app has no controls for white balance at all. Enjoy your screwed-up colors!

The app is just fine for shooting home videos, but if you want to shoot professional-looking, cinematic footage, you'll need to stick with an app that provides more control and fewer monkeys.

UNIQUE VIDEO CAMERAS

Now that we've covered the best all-around camera apps, it's time to narrow our sights. It's time to dig deeper. It's time to meet the specialists!

Each of these tools focuses on one particular feature or function above all else. You may not need them all the time; in fact, they may remain dormant for months, but when that moment comes, and you need something special, you'll be thrilled to have these amazing apps on hand.

CollabraCam

COLLABRACAM

| iPad | iPhone |

- Apptopus, Inc.
- $5.99
- hhhlinks.com/ dlmh

While most film productions are shot using a single camera, some situations require the use of multiple cameras shooting simultaneously. For example, you might want to shoot a live event from several different angles. If only there was an affordable, iOS-based, live camera switcher. Oh wait, there is!

CollabraCam is a killer app designed specifically for controlling shoots with multiple cameras, assuming those "cameras" are iOS devices also running CollabraCam and connected to the same wireless network.

It's worth pointing out that while all of your devices need to be on the same Wi-Fi network, that network does not have to be connected to the Internet. In other words, any portable wireless router should do the trick. Even an ad hoc network on a laptop or personal hotspot should be fine, although you might not get sufficient wireless range.

Before going any further, I want to share the app's primary limitation, just so you know what to expect as we go deeper. To pull off its technological magic, CollabraCam must limit the recording resolution to a maximum of 640x480. This means you won't be using CollabraCam for any big-screen productions, but if the Web is your final destination, this app could be just what you need. On the bright side, since resolutions are limited, even an old iPhone 3GS will make a dandy remote camera.

Here's how the app works.

When you first launch the app on your iPad or iPhone, you are given the option of becoming the Director (the one controlling the multicamera session) or a Camera (one of the multiple camera devices that will feed into the Director's control panel). Each session can have one Director and up to four Cameras (think of *sessions* as individual shoots). If you have an iPad at your disposal, I recommend using that device as the Director since the extra screen real estate will be helpful when controlling the session.

When you set a device to camera mode, most of the screen is taken up by the camera's viewfinder. On the side, you'll see a toggle switch for your onboard light (if your device has one) and a status indicator that lets you know when this particular camera is in standby mode or is currently recording (more on that in a moment). While simplicity is awesome, I do hope that future versions of the app will include some much-needed camera controls (focus, exposure, white balance, and so on).

Now for the fun part!

When you set a device to be the Director, you'll be asked to provide a name for your session, as well as any applicable copyright information. After that, you're taken right into the Director's control panel. In the center of the screen are four camera preview windows. At first, each window will display a list of the available "cameras" currently on your network. Tapping one of the cameras will assign that camera to the associated window. Add as many cameras as you have (up to four), and watch their *live* feeds appear before your eyes (**FIGURE 6.15**).

FIGURE 6.15 In CollabraCam's Director mode, you can view live video feeds from up to four networked cameras.

When you're ready to go, tap once on the camera you want to start with, putting it in standby mode. The person operating that camera will also see their status indicator change to standby mode. This lets them know that they will be the next camera to go live.

Tap REC to start the session. The camera that was in standby instantly begins to record. That camera's operator will see their status indicator change from *Standby* to *Recording.*

Now, as the Director, you can examine the live feeds from the other cameras and decide which camera you'd like to cut to next. Tap that camera's window to put it into standby mode (alerting that camera operator), and then tap REC again to make the cut. The first camera stops recording, and the second starts.

During the shoot, you'll likely want to communicate with your camera operators and give them specific instructions about the shots you'd like to see. Collabra-Cam makes that a quick and intuitive process. Simply tap one of the ten camera direction buttons located on the sides of the screen, and then tap a camera window to send the desired instructions to the camera operator's screen (**FIGURE 6.16**). Easy! There are camera direction buttons for pans, tracks, dollies, tilts, and low and high angles.

That's about all there is to it!

When the Director ends the session, all of the clips that were recorded on the remote cameras are wirelessly transferred to the Director's device. Once they've been collected, they are automatically assembled into a single multi-camera rough cut, complete with end credits. That cut can be played back and exported to your device's camera roll. You can also export each of the individual clips to the camera roll as well.

While the app does an amazing job, it's not perfect. You may see occasional black frames between shots, and the cuts are not necessarily frame accurate

FIGURE 6.16 Camera operators receive on-screen instructions from the Director.

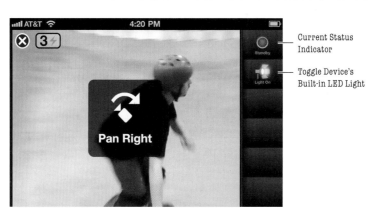

Current Status Indicator

Toggle Device's Built-in LED Light

(resulting in slight jumps in the action). It's also worth noting that since audio switches with picture, there's no way to have one continuous audio track. This makes shooting concerts especially tricky.

All that said, CollabraCam gives you access to all of the original clips. You can easily import these into your desktop editor of choice and then recut the piece, giving it a more professional finish.

Video Camera (Vizzywig)

Video Camera (soon to be renamed Vizzywig) is a bundle of creativity, wrapped in innovation, dipped in a bubbling broth of originality. When I first saw this app, it had just won *Best of Show* at the 2012 MacWorld | iWorld Expo.

The feature that sets this app apart is called live nonlinear editing, or LiNE for short, and it allows you to edit *while* you're shooting. Before I go any further, I want to first cover the basics.

When you first launch the app, you'll see only a few miniature buttons in the corners of the screen (**FIGURE 6.17**). In the upper left, you have access to the settings page and a help button that takes you to an instructional website (that includes video tutorials). In the upper right you'll find buttons that control the onboard light and toggle between your device's front and back cameras. The button in the lower left takes you to your library, and the buttons on the lower right are for recording, adding elements (I'll come back to that), and snapping

- i4software
- $19.99
- hhhlinks.com/ra5e

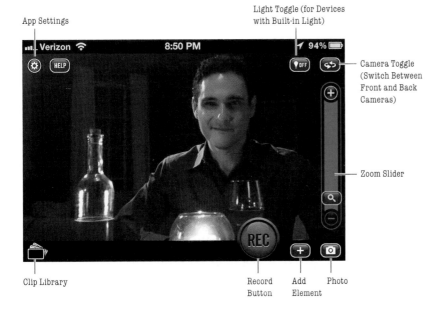

FIGURE 6.17 Video Camera's interface features many elegant but tiny buttons.

FIGURE 6.18 A triple-tap summons Video Camera's independent exposure, focus, and white balance controls.

photos. There's also a slider on the right side of the screen that cleverly controls wonderfully smooth zooms. This slider is one of the app's many innovations.

Triple-tapping the preview area brings up the interface for independently controlling focus, exposure, and white balance (**FIGURE 6.18**). Much like the controls in FiLMiC Pro, you have separate movable reticles for focus and exposure. You can lock a setting by tapping its tiny padlock icon. Speaking of tiny...

It feels like Video Camera was developed by people with tiny hands, for use by filmmakers with tiny fingers, who love tapping tiny buttons. Every button in the app is minuscule. My (admittedly oversized) paws never hit the right button on the first few tries. I *really* wish there were an option to increase the size of *every* button in the interface. OK, rant over.

When I asked the developer why the focus, exposure, and white balance controls were hidden at first, he told me because he wanted the app to be unintimidating for new users, who would eventually become more experienced and willing to dig deeper for the advanced controls. It seems logical enough, although as a pro, I would prefer that those controls be always on-screen.

Tapping the big red record button starts the shot, and a second tap ends it. It's at this moment when you will be introduced to the app's headline feature. A pop-up box will give you two options: Export Clip and Build Movie. If you choose to export the clip, it will be saved to your device's camera roll, essentially making the app work like any other video camera app. However, if you tap Build Movie, you'll then be asked to pick a transition. What?!

Video Camera has reinvented the editing process by making it part of the shooting process! Every time you finish recording a shot, you will be asked how you would like that shot to transition to the next shot (**FIGURE 6.19**). Your transition

FIGURE 6.19 After every shot, Video Camera prompts you to pick a transition. What, no heart wipes?!

FIGURE 6.20 After picking a transition, your shot gets added to the mini timeline at the bottom of the screen.

options are Fade Black (which adds a dip to black between your shots), Fade White (which similarly dips to white), Dissolve (which adds a cross-dissolve between your shots), and None (which will result in a simple cut).

Once you've picked a transition, your clip will be added to a mini timeline that appears at the bottom of the screen (FIGURE 6.20). Then you're ready to capture your next shot and repeat the process until you're done. At any point, you can tap any of the clips in the mini timeline to call up an intuitive shot editor. Here you can reorder, trim, split, or delete your clips. The app provides an adjustable degree of control, even letting you edit on a frame-by-frame level! When you're done editing, the updated shot appears in the mini timeline. What's especially nice is that you've never left the camera interface. If you need to quickly grab a shot while the shot editor is being displayed, just tap the still-visible record button, and you're rolling.

Remember I mentioned a button that can add elements? While you're build-ing your movie, you can use this button to inject titles, photos (complete with Ken Burns–style pans), video clips, and background music (the app provides a library of royalty-free tracks). You can also add a "remote camera." Similar to CollabraCam, Video Camera lets you tap into and wirelessly control other iOS devices running the app while connected to the same Wi-Fi network. The setup is a little clunky, but the results are swell. You can start and stop recording on all controlled devices at once. Then, after you've finished a shot, Video Camera can wirelessly collect all the recordings from the other devices and place them sequentially in your mini timeline. However, you don't have the option to cut between cameras while recording like you have in CollabraCam. It's not a perfect implementation, but it's still fun to see it in action. Just as before, these new shots can be edited and given transitions without having to exit Camera mode.

I don't know about you, but the whole idea of editing while shooting blows my mind. It means that when you're finished shooting your footage, you're essentially done and can export a completed, fully edited video. Don't get me wrong—I'd never suggest using this technique for shooting and editing professional productions. But this is a *fantastic* way to quickly visualize sequences while on set!

You can save your sequences for later, refine your edits in a dedicated editing mode, render the whole thing out, and upload it to a variety of destinations (Facebook, YouTube, Vimeo, and CNN iReport).

Additional app options are accessible on the settings screen. Here, you can change the recording resolution, turn on and off grid lines, add an on-screen time and date stamp, set the app to automatically start recording as soon as it's launched, have the focus automatically lock as soon as you hit record, and a whole bunch of other neat stuff. However, half of the settings screen is reserved for links to the developer's other apps—a pretty tacky design choice. Points off! To the developer's credit, there is a nice big button for quickly submitting feature suggestions via e-mail.

While Video Camera has the necessary features to make it a contender for your primary camera app, its focus is a bit too consumer-oriented to be called a pro solution. That said, it's a brilliant tool for on-set experimentation. If you have the room on your device and some bucks to burn, you should grab this app.

SLOPRO

- Sand Mountain Studios
- free
- hhhlinks.com/ c61d

SloPro

Slow motion is like filmmaker's chocolate syrup. You wouldn't put it on everything, but when you do treat yourself, it's friggin' sweet!

There are plenty of reasons to use slow-motion footage in your project. It's possible you want to add extra emphasis or clarity to an action. Maybe you're employing it as part of a visual effect. Or, perhaps you're using it to make Bruce Willis walk dramatically slower, letting your audience know without a shadow of doubt that he and his crew are ready to drill a hole in that damn asteroid.

Other slow-motion apps have come and gone, but none has been as impressive or as flexible as SloPro.

When you launch the app, you're brought to a fairly standard-looking video camera screen. You can toggle the onboard LED light (especially appealing if you enjoy morgue lighting), set your focus, and lock your exposure. The only truly unique thing you'll see is a little button in the upper-right corner that reads `SLO: OFF` Great! What's SLO?

While you're recording video, you can toggle the SLO button on and off to define regions within your shot that will eventually include speed changes. It's like setting markers for later use. For instance, while recording your actor playing baseball, you might turn on SLO just before he swings his bat and turn it off right after he sends the ball over the fence. You've just told the app what portion of the clip should be played back at an altered speed. You're not limited to one speed-change region. You can set as many regions within a clip as you'd like.

One of my favorite features in the app is the ability to start and stop recording with the iPhone's volume-up button and toggle SLO mode on and off (generating speed-change regions) with the volume-down button. While this is super convenient, you must remember that your iPhone's internal mic *will* pick up a faint click sound every time you press a volume button.

SloPro was the first iOS app for the iPhone to officially shoot 720p HD video at *60fps* (frames per second), rather than the usual 24, 25, and 30fps speeds found on most video cameras. This is sometimes referred to as *overcranking* (a holdover from the days when film was manually cranked through a camera). As I mentioned earlier, CinePro also offers 60fps (but only as an "experimental" and "unsupported" feature), and FiLMiC Pro is planning on adding 60fps shooting in future versions.

So, why is shooting 60fps significant?

When shooting footage for a slow-motion effect, the more frames a camera can capture per second, the slower and smoother the resulting footage will appear when played back at a standard frame rate. Because SloPro can shoot 60fps, it has more frames to work with when slowing down your footage, and as a result, your slow-motion shots will look as silky as a silky thing that's very, very silky.

Right now, 60fps shooting is limited to the iPhone 4S (iPhone 5 support coming soon). As new iOS devices emerge, with more powerful processors, this feature will likely spread.

When you've finished recording a clip, it will instantly open in the app's edit window. Here you can trim the clip's in and out points, as well as modify the start and end points of the speed-change regions you defined while recording. You can also add new speed-change regions and delete existing ones (**FIGURE 6.21**).

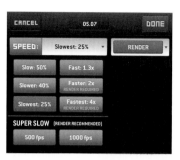

FIGURE 6.22 Pick your speed from SloPro's many options. It appears they left off DMV Speed, which usually runs at about 2 percent. Thank you, I'll be here all week.

FIGURE 6.23 Pick a rendering method based on the nature of the source footage and your desired result.

FIGURE 6.21 SloPro's edit screen allows you to define regions for slow-motion and high-speed effects.

Each speed-change region can be assigned one of eight different playback speeds (which are organized into three separate categories) (FIGURE 6.22). You can assign a Slow Motion speed (50 percent, 40 percent, or 25 percent), a Super Slow speed (500fps or 1000fps), or even a high-motion speed to radically speed up your video (1.3x, 2x, or 4x). Your speed changes are never set in stone, and you should feel free to experiment.

Each of your speed changes can be rendered in one of three different ways: Ghosting (fast to render, but least impressive), Frame Blending (not as fast to render but looks better on dynamic shots), and Optical Flow (slow to render but looks spectacular, especially at 1000fps) (FIGURE 6.23). It's worth pointing out that in the past, Optical Flow processing was available only in high-end compositing systems costing thousands of dollars. Now, it's in your pocket-sharing space with Facebook and Hipstamatic. Crazy.

What if you want to slow down (or speed up) a shot you've already taken using another camera app? No problem! SloPro can import and alter any clip stored in your device's photo albums or camera roll.

When you're finished, SloPro can send your clips to your camera roll and export them via iTunes File Sharing or e-mail.

While I consider myself a big fan of SloPro, I do have two minor complaints.

> My iPhone 4S shoots its videos with a data rate that falls around 24Mbps. However, after importing a shot into SloPro, treating it with some speed changes, and then exporting it back to my camera roll, the resulting clip has a data rate just under 19Mbps per second.
>
> Yes, the footage still looks lovely, but I know something is being thrown away in that process. It doesn't exactly fill me with warm fuzzies.
>
> When shooting 720p video at 60fps, frame clarity suffers, and aliasing is visible in areas of high contrast, especially on diagonal lines. It's annoying, but manageable.

I want to share one other complaint, but it's not mine.

Like many apps these days, SloPro uses the "freemium" business model. The app is completely free to download and try, but if you want to do anything meaningful with your footage, you'll need to fork over $3.99 for an in-app purchase of Pro Mode. This upgrade removes the watermark, lets you e-mail videos, and allows you to export videos to your device's camera roll—this includes your 60fps raw footage. Clearly, you'll want Pro Mode.

I've heard many filmmakers complain about freemium pricing, labeling it as "bait-and-switch" or worse. I suppose there's some truth in this point of view, but I tend to be less skeptical. Apple's App Store makes it difficult for developers to offer *upgradable* demo versions of their apps. Freemium pricing is a workaround. The way I see it, SloPro is actually a $4 app, with a limited, free demo mode. See? Doesn't that sound better?

These are minor gripes that are easily forgiven as soon as you see the app's output. SloMo provides enough slow-motion awesomeness that I urge every filmmaker to plant this app on their home screen.

Luma Camera

As I mentioned earlier, a wide range of hardware accessories exist to help stabilize your shaking camera, and I'll be covering many of them in the next chapter, but for now let's assume it's just you and your iPhone or iPad out there. No additional hardware. So, what's a filmmaker to do?

The way I see it, you have two choices.

> You can find an app that will help stabilize your footage.
>
> You can stick to shooting films about earthquakes.

LUMA

iPad   iPhone

- elyxa
- free
- hhhlinks.com/ 14aa

Light Toggle (for Devices with Built-in Light)

Stabilization Toggle (and Indicator)

FIGURE 6.24 Luma's simple interface hides a powerful stabilization engine.

Clip Library

Filter Switch

Record Button

Camera Toggle (Switch Between Front and Back Cameras)

App Settings

If you picked the first option, you need Luma (**FIGURE 6.24**). This outstanding video-stabilizing camera app is designed to capture silky-smooth footage, even when you're shooting in less than ideal circumstances. It even helps greatly reduce the rolling shutter artifacts I mentioned earlier. When the app is used in conjunction with a hardware stabilizer (and a steady hand), the results can be downright astounding. But even all by itself, Luma does a fantastic job of reducing jitters.

Putting its marquee feature aside for a moment, I want to mention that Luma is one of the only universal camera apps in this chapter, meaning it looks just as good on an iPad as it does on an iPhone. If you're shooting on an iPad, this is reason enough to add Luma to your bag of tricks.

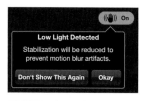

FIGURE 6.25 Luma works best in daylight. When things get a little too dark, you'll be given this polite reminder.

Turning on stabilization is as easy as tapping ((👋)) in the upper-right corner of the screen. The results are instantaneous. There's no need to wait for a rendered preview. In Luma, stabilization happens in *real time!*

Shooting in low light limits the app's ability to properly stabilize your footage (**FIGURE 6.25**). It still does a decent job, but more light will allow for better results. The app displays a warning indicator when your light falls below the app's preferred limits.

Like Apple's own Camera app, Luma allows you to tap your screen to set focus, exposure, and white balance. Although the app lacks independent controls for these properties, it does give you the option to automatically lock them all in place as soon as you hit the record button. This isn't a perfect solution, but it's certainly a great start.

As an added bonus, Luma gives you the ability to smoothly zoom in and out *while you're recording* using standard pinch and zoom gestures. Awesome!

As an *added* added bonus, the app provides you with several real-time filters with which to decorate your footage. These are fun but unnecessary. Unless you have specific reasons for locking yourself to these exaggerated color schemes, I recommend keeping your footage nice and clean and then applying color changes in postproduction.

Among Luma's other, less glamorous features, you can use either your rear- or front-facing camera. You can easily send your videos to your device's camera roll and share them on Facebook or Twitter. You can even play back your recorded videos with and without stabilization!

Shooting with Luma demands one significant trade-off. Like most stabilization software, Luma must zoom in to your footage slightly to work its magic. That means your footage will be slightly less crisp. It doesn't make a huge difference, but image purists will notice the change. For many filmmakers, however, the minor degradation of the image will be worth the gain in stability. To compensate for the loss, you might consider applying a mild sharpening filter in your desktop editing application.

On a side note, I completely ignored this app for months simply because of its name. In the world of film and video production, *luma* is short for luminance (a measure of light), so I had no idea that this was a camera app. I assumed it was a tool for gaffers. Had I known this app's true purpose, I would now have far fewer shaketastic videos in my collection.

8mm and 8mm HD

I don't know about you, but I'm sick and tired of beautiful, detailed, colorful footage that reeks of quality. I mean, really. Haven't we had enough perfection? Thank goodness there's 8mm!

This app can effortlessly transform your iPhone into a completely realistic, vintage 8mm film camera, complete with jitter, discoloration, icky edges, and framing nightmares. Thank goodness!

When you launch the app, you're instantly brought to what looks like the back of a vintage film camera (**FIGURE 6.26**). A small box in the upper-right corner lets you switch between multiple nasty vignetting and framing effects. A dial in

8MM

iPad | **iPhone**

- Nexvio Inc.
- $1.99
- hhhlinks.com/ p2dr

8MM HD

iPad | iPhone

- Nexvio Inc.
- 1.99
- hhhlinks.com/ rznk

FIGURE 6.26 8mm transforms every shot into an instant antique.

Change Lens

Record Button

Import Video

Change Film Stock

Add Frame Jitter

Information

Clip Library

Camera Toggle (Switch Between Front and Back Cameras)

Light Toggle (for Devices with Built-in Light)

Sound Toggle

the lower right lets you switch between the app's eight film types (1920s, 70s, Sakura, XPro, Noir, 60s, Pela, and Siena). At the center of the dial is a small button that introduces frame jitter, adding to the overall illusion. The red record button does exactly what you'd expect it to do.

Below the main viewport, you have buttons to get help, view your previous recordings, switch between front and rear cameras, turn on the built-in light, and switch between multiple audio recording modes (silent, projector sound, or your device's microphone mixed with the subtle sound of an 8mm film camera).

The most amazing thing about the app is that it performs its visual magic live. You'll see the effects as you're shooting. It sounds cute, but in fact, it's unnervingly addictive. Furthermore, you're not limited to *shooting* video. The app can import an existing video from your device's library and apply any of its vintage effects.

Your finished clips can be e-mailed, uploaded to Facebook and YouTube, and sent to your device's camera roll.

Sadly, 8mm is not universal, which means you'll have to pay for two separate versions if you want it on your iPad as well as your iPhone.

Overall, 8mm's results are top-notch, and I'm not exaggerating when I describe its output as looking completely authentic. I wouldn't hesitate to use 8mm on any of my professional projects.

Vintagio

Do you yearn to become the next D.W. Griffith? Are you itchin' to release your inner Chaplin? Vintagio (formerly Silent Film Director) turns your iOS device into a retro-style movie camera capable of churning out footage that feels like it belongs in a 90-year-old film tin.

The app operates in two different modes.

In Express Mode (FIGURE 6.27), you begin by picking one of seven different vintage effects (Classic B&W, Classic Sepia, 20s Newborn, 50s Sepia, 60s Hippie Hair, 70s Crazy Grooving, and 80s Disco Ball). You can select between multiple resolutions ranging from 192x144, all the way up to 1920x1080. And, for some extra retro fun, you can pipe in a little vintage music (like an old-timey piano ditty) or add a sound effect (such as an old film projector). Take your creation one step further into the past by altering its speed. The app will even allow you to start the clip at one speed and then end at another.

Once you've dialed in all of your settings, you can either shoot a new clip or load an existing clip from your device's photo library or camera roll. The moment you're done recording a clip (or selecting an existing clip), the app immediately goes to work, processing and rendering your final video.

Rendering is the app's only downside. It can take quite a while on a long clip. It can take so long, in fact, that the developer has included what seems like an endless list of "amazing facts" that are presented on-screen to help pass the time.

With rendering complete, you can view your work, export it to your camera roll, and upload it to YouTube, Facebook, and Twitter.

VINTAGIO

iPad | iPhone

- MacPhun LLC
- $1.99
- hhhlinks.com/
  91iy

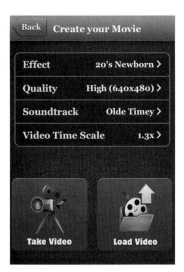

FIGURE 6.27 Vintagio's Express Mode lets you pick your settings before shooting (or loading) a single shot.

FIGURE 6.28 Pro Mode includes some great tools for adding vintage title cards.

Vintagio's Pro Mode adds even more features. Here you can create a new project; pick your effect, quality, soundtrack, and time scale (just like Express Mode); and then build a basic timeline consisting of multiple clips, still images, eight different retro transitions, and awesome vintage title cards (**FIGURE 6.28**). All you need now is a villain with a handlebar moustache.

If you feel like sharing, the app features a social component as well as ongoing contests. If you don't feel like sharing, the app features an antisocial component that forces you to stay inside and eat a pint of ice cream by yourself.

Super 8

Things that are better in "threes": bears, stooges, little pigs, amigos, and vintage-style camera apps. With this in mind, I thought I'd briefly mention one more option.

To promote *Super 8*, J.J. Abrams' Spielberg-esque alien invasion retro-flick, Paramount Digital Entertainment unleashed a vintage "film" camera app, also called Super 8 (**FIGURE 6.29**).

Designed for iPhone, Super 8 helps you shoot video that looks like it just spooled through a classic, cartridge-loading camera. The app also provides some decidedly nonclassic, non-super-8 filters (in the form of switchable lenses) that include Chromatic, Sepia, X-Ray, Negative, Infrared, Posterize, and Fisheye.

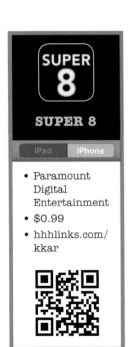

SUPER 8

iPad   iPhone

- Paramount Digital Entertainment
- $0.99
- hhhlinks.com/ kkar

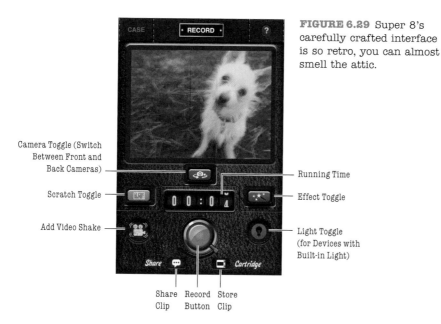

FIGURE 6.29 Super 8's carefully crafted interface is so retro, you can almost smell the attic.

Camera Toggle (Switch Between Front and Back Cameras)

Scratch Toggle

Add Video Shake

Running Time

Effect Toggle

Light Toggle (for Devices with Built-in Light)

Share Clip

Record Button

Store Clip

In addition to the color and filter settings, you can add fringe effects (such as dirty vignettes and light leaks), dirt and scratches, and even add a little jumpy sprocket trouble (what the app calls *video shake*).

Among Super 8's other features, you can post your clips to all the standard social networks, drop your films in an e-mail, and even string a few clips together, allowing for some basic editing.

For me, the best thing about Super 8 is its interface. The developer has clearly gone to great lengths to make this app look and feel like a classic camera that never existed.

Action Movie FX

I wasn't sure about including Action Movie FX in this book (for reasons I'll explain in a moment), but I decided to keep it for one reason. It's a total blast, figuratively and literally!

Action Movie FX lets you add incredible, prerendered Hollywood-style effects to your videos. For example, while shooting some footage of your actor walking down a calm, empty street, you're just one tap away from dropping a full-sized car into your scene! It crashes down, bounces with the sounds of twisting metal, and then careens out of control right toward the camera! Not bad for a free app!

ACTION MOVIE FX

| iPad | iPhone |

- Bad Robot Interactive
- free
- hhhlinks.com/ 3yvc

FIGURE 6.30 Action Movie FX lets you drop stuff on other stuff...and blow it all up, too.

The process is extremely simple. You begin by picking your desired effect. Missile Attack, Car Smash, Demolition Rock, and Rough Terrain come with the free app, but additional effects can be purchased in pairs for $0.99 (**FIGURE 6.30**). With your effect selected, you're taken to a basic video camera interface. Tap the record button to start shooting, and tap it again when you're done. At that point, you'll be taken to the FX Timing screen where you can tell the app *when* you'd like the effect to begin within your clip. After that, the app renders your finished video and plays it back. When you're done, the new clip can be posted on Facebook, exported via e-mail, or saved to your iOS device's camera roll.

Action Movie FX is a *very* slick app and an absolute pleasure to use. So, why did I consider excluding it from the book? Because every person on the planet who owns the app is using the exact same effects as you. Naturally, this doesn't matter when making goofy videos with friends, but don't even consider using this app for your legitimate work. Do you really want to present your latest film, knowing that millions of other filmmakers are essentially using the same shots? I'm sure there are also plenty of copyright and clearance issues to contend with.

All that said, Action Movie FX is absolutely worth downloading. I've purchased several of the additional effects and have thoroughly enjoyed blowing up my friends, dropping helicopters on them, and crushing them under giant meteors. After all, what are friends for?

AUDIO: HALF OF GOOD VIDEO

A film begins with a heated discussion between two rival mob bosses. Tensions flare, accusations are made, and guns are drawn. Suddenly, a silver-caped vigilante smashes in through a window and speaks the most profound words ever uttered on any screen, anywhere, ever. Unfortunately, the audio is so bad that the audience hasn't been able to understand a thing.

No matter how good your visuals may be, your film is doomed without good (or at least decent) audio. Distorted, distant, and unintelligible dialogue is the hallmark of student and amateur filmmaking. That's why most professional film-makers consider good audio to be "half of good video."

While all of the camera apps I've mentioned can record audio, I'm going to spend a little time talking about audio-only apps. Why? *One word*: dual system sound. Three words! I meant *three* words.

On most film and DSLR shoots, audio is recorded separately from picture and then synchronized in postproduction. By recording audio separately, you can utilize dedicated systems for picture and sound, with dedicated power for each. This is known as dual system sound.

The apps described in this section will turn your iOS device into a portable audio recorder, ready for use in a dual system setup. For example, if you're shooting an interview and your subject is sitting too far away from your camera's micro-phone, just boot up one of these apps on your iPhone, hit record, and stick the device in your subject's shirt pocket with its mic facing upward (**FIGURE 6.31**). You can even use the small microphone attached to your iPhone's earbuds as a wired lavalier mic (although you'll have to hide the rest of the cable inside a shirt or jacket).

Since these apps don't make use of timecode (as normally used in profes-sional dual system recording setups), you'll have to employ another method to prep your recordings for synchronization in postproduction. May I recommend a movie slate? I'll be covering slates in greater detail in Chapter 8 (in "The Ulti-mate Slate" section). Even without a slate, many desktop editing applications now offer the ability to automatically synchronize audio and video files.

In addition to dual system sound, you might be using your iOS device to record atmospheric sounds, wild lines (dialogue recorded without video), and Foley effects. You can even use these apps to record live music for use in your films (assuming you have the correct permissions). No matter how you plan on using these apps, each can help your production sound its very best.

FIGURE 6.31 Hide your iPhone inside your interview subject's shirt pocket. Just remember to keep the microphone facing up.

- Weynand Training
- $29.99
- hhhlinks.com/ 2z6z

Pro Audio To Go

Pro Audio To Go turns your iPhone into a professional recorder that effortlessly saves uncompressed, 48kHz AIFF audio files. Kilohertz, abbreviated as kHz, refers to a file's sample rate—how many times an audio source is sampled per second. Most audio recording apps on the iPhone top out at 44.1 kHz (the same rate used on audio CDs). Because Pro Audio To Go has a higher sample rate of 48kHz, the audio sounds that much better. While not as good as the 96kHz and 192kHz sample rates found in some high-end audio gear, 48kHz is a video industry standard and will work great in nearly every situation. Because the files are saved as AIFFs, they likely won't need to be transcoded into some other format before being imported into your nonlinear editor.

The interface is as simple as it gets. The main screen includes an editable file-name (which defaults to a name based on the current day and time), a pop-up menu containing EQ presets, a running time display, an indicator showing your remaining free space, and a great big record button (**FIGURE 6.32**).

Aside from its ease of use and its 48kHz sample rate, the app's claim to fame is its ability to quickly switch between custom EQ presets, each of which contains separate equalization adjustments for lows, mids, and highs, as well as an overall gain attenuation. This feature's true power comes when you create your own presets based on the different microphones you regularly use with your iPhone (**FIGURE 6.33**).

FIGURE 6.32 Pro Audio To Go lets you quickly record high-quality audio.

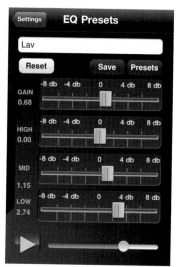

FIGURE 6.33 Create custom EQ presets for each of your microphones.

Let's say you have an external lavalier microphone that needs a little help on the low end. Simply make a preset that increases the low end, and name it Lav. If you have a handheld mic that always comes in a little soft and tinny, create a preset that raises the gain and dips the high end. Name that one Handheld. Before starting your recording, pick the preset named after the mic you're currently using, and the corresponding gain and EQ settings will be applied to your audio file right after you stop your recording. Keep in mind that when the app applies its EQ and gain changes, your original audio file is being altered. If you are an audio purist and would prefer your audio files remain untouched (perhaps you plan on EQing everything in post), just select None from the preset pop-up.

When you're ready to retrieve your audio files, you have three options. You can extract them using iTunes File Sharing (what I believe is the easiest method), you can e-mail them (which may be problematic if your e-mail server hates large files), and you can upload them to an FTP server straight from the app. I really like this last option because it means you can collect audio in the field and then make it accessible to your editorial staff even before you get back to the office. Along these same lines, I'd love to see Dropbox integration in a future version.

On the downside, Pro Audio To Go can record only a mono signal, even when attached to a stereo microphone like the Fostex AR-4i that I'll be covering in the next chapter. I'm hopeful that future versions will add stereo recording.

There's one other issue that you need to be aware of. When creating a new recording, your audio file is given a default name based on the current date and time. However, if you create two new recordings, one after the other, during the same minute on the clock, the files will be named identically, and the second recording will *overwrite* the first! Imagine being out in the field, grabbing short recordings for your film's sound effects library (a door squeak, a bicycle horn, and so on) only to discover that several of your recordings were erased. Eeek! Naturally, you can change the default name before recording to avoid the issue.

The developer is aware of the issue and is already working to add additional safeguards to the app (which may already be available). In the meantime, be careful when capturing *short* recordings!

If I didn't think Pro Audio To Go was a killer app, this naming issue would have prevented it from being included in this book. But I *do* think it's killer, and the problem seems easily correctable (as I mentioned, the developer is already all over it).

If you need a simple, high-quality audio recorder, Pro Audio To Go is a great choice.

HINDENBURG FIELD RECORDER

iPad | iPhone

- Hindenburg Systems ApS
- $29.99
- hhhlinks.com/w3Oo

HINDENBURG FIELD RECORDER LITE

iPad | iPhone

- Hindenburg Systems ApS
- free
- hhhlinks.com/t7u5

Hindenburg Field Recorder

If you like to keep things simple, stop right here, back up, and reread Pro Audio To Go. However, if you're looking for something that packs more punch, a pile of features, and an elegant interface, it's time for the Hindenburg Field Recorder.

There are two distinctly different areas within the app, one for recording and the other for playback and editing.

The Record screen (**FIGURE 6.34**) reflects the very definition of "intuitive." From your first glance at the interface, you'll likely have a pretty clear idea of how it works. Toward the top of the screen is a running time display. Below that is an ultra-responsive level meter, with a gain slider to raise and lower the input volume. Below that is a *huge* record button next to a Marker counter.

FIGURE 6.34 Hindenburg's interface is simple, slick, and sawsome. Sorry, I ran out of *S* words.

As soon as you tap the record button, it cleverly transforms into an Add Marker button (in addition to actually starting your recording). To pause recording, you have to run your finger across a sliding switch at the bottom of the screen (it's just like unlocking an iOS device). By requiring such a deliberate action to pause the recording, the app has greatly reduced the likelihood of accidental stops.

Once you pause your recording, you can pick up where you left off by tapping the record button again. Each time you pause and then restart the recording, you are actually creating a new, separate audio file. However, all of these individual files are still considered to be part of the same session (or project).

While recording, you can easily add markers to your timeline by tapping the Add Marker button. Tapping ▤ in the upper-left corner brings up a list of your

FIGURE 6.35 The app lets you view and edit your marker list, even while recording!

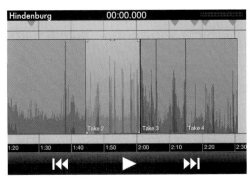

FIGURE 6.36 Switch to Play mode to review and edit your recordings.

saved markers (FIGURE 6.35). From here, you can delete and rename your markers, all without pausing your recording. Very handy!

Tapping Play on the bottom toolbar brings you to the app's playback and editing screen (FIGURE 6.36). Here, you'll find all of the individual audio clips from your session arranged on an easy to navigate timeline that also includes any markers you set while recording.

You can play back your session or perform a wide variety of editing tasks. You can manipulate entire clips or just a desired range on the timeline. Naturally, the app provides the basics of cut, copy, and paste, but that's just the beginning. Audio can be trimmed, faded in and out, crossfaded with other regions, and repositioned on the timeline. You can add, delete, and jump between markers for quick navigation and even scrub backward and forward in your timeline by dragging your fingertip under the audio waveforms. If you want to give your recordings a little extra punch, the app also features a built-in compressor/limiter. All of the editing is nondestructive, meaning you can undo and redo changes without fear of losing the original audio. Even more features await the truly appventurous!

When you're satisfied with your session, a single rendered audio file can be shared via e-mail, uploaded to SoundCloud or an FTP server, and exported via iTunes file sharing. Your session can also be shared with the desktop version of the app if you happen to own that as well.

Before rushing to use all of the incredible editing functions jammed into Hindenburg Field Recorder, I need to issue one word of warning. If you are using the app in a dual system setup (meaning, the app is recording audio *while* a separate camera is simultaneously recording video), you should not perform any editing that changes your audio's timings. Any changes made to clip timings can make synchronizing audio and video in postproduction much more difficult (if not impossible). That said, feel free to edit the heck out of audio that doesn't require 100 percent perfect synchronization during the edit (such as voiceovers, wild lines, natural sound, and Foley effects).

In case you're wondering, here's how I use the app in a dual system situation. I create a new session for each scene and then record each take separately by using the record and pause functions on the Record screen. Remember, each time you pause the recording and then tap the record button to start again, the app is creating a new audio file within the session. At any point, I can switch into Play mode and listen to all of my takes, one after the other on the timeline. When I'm done shooting for the day, I hook my iPhone to my computer and use iTunes File Sharing to access all of the raw, individual audio files that the app stores within session folders (named after the date and time they were created) (**FIGURE 6.37**). I copy all the files to my project drive, rename them as necessary, import them into Final Cut Pro, and then get ready for the next day of shooting. I know this may be a lot to take in, but once you've done it once or twice, it becomes second nature.

Hindenburg Field Recorder works equally well with mono and stereo files (stereo recording requires an external stereo mic) and records at 44.1 kHz. It's a terrific app that requires very little effort to use. And, when you find yourself needing some real editing horsepower, the app delivers. Big time.

If you'd like to give the app a spin, the developer offers a free lite version that automatically stops recording after one minute.

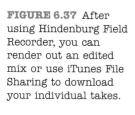

FIGURE 6.37 After using Hindenburg Field Recorder, you can render out an edited mix or use iTunes File Sharing to download your individual takes.

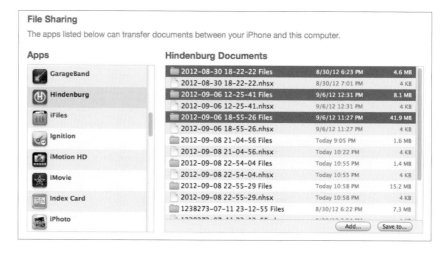

FiRe 2

While I really dig the two audio recorders I've just mentioned, the App Store offers plenty of other options, most of which perform the same basic functions.

One standout is FiRe 2. It's a solid, popular, well-priced app with a good track record. It records 48kHz audio files in either mono or stereo (with an external stereo mic) and features a large set of advanced editing tools, filters, and export options.

Before purchasing either of the previous two audio apps (or any other audio apps for that matter), I encourage you to visit the App Store and read a little more about FiRe 2.

FiRe 2

iPad   iPhone

- Audiofile Engineering
- $5.99
- hhhlinks.com/ 1vy3

What About Apple's Voice Memo App?

When it comes to recording audio for film and video production, the only good thing about Apple's free Voice Memo app is its price.

While it provides a stylish and intuitive interface, typical of Apple's software, it compresses your audio into the AAC format. Like the blocky artifacts that can appear when compressing video, audio compression can result in similar signal loss. Your tracks may sound a little crunchy or have less tonal range.

Granted, the difference is negligible, but with easy access to apps that record uncompressed audio while providing additional professional features, it makes very little sense to use an app that discards valuable data.

CHAPTER 7

MOUNT IT, MOD IT, AND MIC IT

When filmmakers first started using their iPhones as video cameras, it marked the beginning of the mobile filmmaking revolution. At that time, there was no support gear or accessories to speak of. Eventually, a few small companies and start-ups emerged offering one or two wildly innovative products that helped support the rapidly growing iPhone community.

As I write this, the revolution is now in full swing! iPhones and iPads are being geared up by some of the biggest names in the business. We're seeing companies like Steadicam and Schneider Optics jumping into the mobile accessory marketplace. There's even a rumored iPhone product coming from the production-gear giant Manfrotto.

Today, millions of mobile filmmakers can outfit their iOS devices with mounts, lenses, audio gear, stabilization tools, and more.

This, my friend, is the future of mobile filmmaking, and the future is now! I can't stand it anymore! *Let's go look at stuff*!

GEARING UP YOUR IPHONE

Let's start where it started: with the iPhone. Before we roll, there's one thing I want to point out.

Buying accessories isn't like buying apps. While apps come at a fixed price, hardware prices can vary wildly from dealer to dealer. Quite often (but not always), a manufacturer's suggested retail price (MSRP) is significantly higher than the price you'll actually find while shopping. For example, the RØDE VideoMic Pro (an external shotgun mic covered later in the chapter) retails for $329. However, as I write this, you can buy it at Amazon.com for $229. Before dismissing something you want as being too expensive, make sure to check its current street price on a few websites.

With that out of the way, let's strap on our jetpack and blast off to the *future. future. future.* That was the best simulated echo I could muster in print. It would have sounded better in person.

Steadicam Smoothee

STEADICAM
SMOOTHEE

iPad   iPhone

- Tiffen
- $149.00
- hhhlinks.com/
  z13a

I have to admit, when I first laid eyes on the Steadicam Smoothee at the Consumer Electronics Show (CES) in January 2010, my initial thoughts were, "That's totally absurd! Who in their right mind would pay good money for a smartphone stabilizer?" These days, I can't imagine shooting complex traveling shots on my iPhone without it. So, what changed? The iPhone changed.

At the time of the Smoothee's release, iPhones were still shooting video at a paltry resolution of 640x480. Yes, the footage was shaky, but perhaps not enough to warrant the purchase of an external stabilizer. As iPhone cameras improved, the devices also grew lighter. Now, *every* new iPhone contains an HD camera and weighs slightly more than a deck of playing cards. As a result, even the smallest twitches while shooting can create jarring jumps. In short, Apple's improvements have led to the need for external stabilizers, and the Smoothee is the best of the bunch.

Bearing a striking resemblance to a 1950s sci-fi weapon (**FIGURE 7.1**), the Smoothee is an extremely well-designed, easy-to-learn stabilizer, which is not surprising considering it comes from Steadicam, the same company that produces professional camera stabilizers for use in film and television productions around the world.

Setup is a breeze. Your iPhone snaps into an included bracket, which then clips (and locks) into the top of the Smoothee. Just by grabbing the device's handle, your iPhone suddenly feels like it's floating. Before shooting, you can adjust the

FIGURE 7.2 Stick your iPhone in a Smoothee to get incredibly smooth shots.

FIGURE 7.1 Don't point that thing at me! Oh, it's a Steadicam Smoothee. Never mind. You can point it at me.

dials and front-mounted counterweight to bring your iPhone into perfect balance. With everything properly calibrated, you can now walk and move around while keeping your iPhone stunningly stable.

At first, your iPhone will likely float around a little too much and not remain pointed in the desired direction. By using your thumb to apply a *very* slight pressure to the back of the handle's gimbal connector, you can further steady and even steer the Smoothee (FIGURE 7.2). The more you use the device, the better you'll get at controlling it. It took me a couple hours to become comfortable controlling the Smoothee. Having now used it on several shoots, it feels totally natural.

For even smoother shooting, consider using it in conjunction with Luma, the stabilization app I mentioned in Chapter 6. The resulting footage will feel as smooth as a stick of butter wrapped in butter and dipped in butter sauce.

Unlike a few other "camera" mounts I'll be covering in this chapter, the Smoothee works alone. It's not meant to support lights, microphones, and other gear. If you need an onboard light, consider wearing one on your head… and then dismiss that idea for fear of looking like an insane person…and then try it anyway.

Several of the accessories in this chapter are customized for the shape and size of a particular iPhone model. If you upgrade to a new iPhone with a different form factor, those old accessories become obsolete and will need to be replaced. This is not the case with the Smoothee (for the most part).

Because the mounting bracket that holds your iPhone is not permanently con-nected to the Smoothee, it can be swapped out. In other words, the next time Apple changes the shape of the iPhone (as it did with the iPhone 5), you'll only have to purchase a new mounting bracket. Currently, brackets are available for the 3GS, 4, 4S, and fourth-generation iPod touch, with a version for the iPhone 5 being released shortly (perhaps by the time you read this). The company also offers mounts for the GoPro Hero and Hero 2 and the Flip Mino HD. As an added bonus, when it's not connected to the Smoothee, you can use the bracket as a standard tripod mount. Handy!

The funny thing is, even now that I've become completely attached to my Smoothee and the amazing results it generates, I still look at it and think, "That's totally absurd! Who in their right mind would pay good money for a smartphone stabilizer?" Except, now I know the answer: me.

mCAM and mCAMLITE

mCAM

iPad | iPhone

- Action Life Media
- $169.95
- hhhlinks.com/ mcam

On HandHeldHollywood.com, I've described the mCAM (previously known as the OWLE Bubo) as the coolest camera grip ever made (**FIGURE 7.3**). I stand by that proclamation but must now regretfully report that the mCAM is headed to the chopping block. Fear not, dear reader, for the mCAM name lives on in the slick new (but slightly less cool) mCAMLITE.

Before covering the differences between the mCAM and mCAMLITE, let's review what they have in common.

Both are built from incredibly sturdy billet aluminum. Just in case you skipped metal shop, when something is made from billet aluminum, that simply means it has been machined from a single piece of aluminum (rather than being molded from molten aluminum) and is significantly stronger as a result. In short, both the mCAM and mCAMLITE are drop-them-from-the-roof-hit-them-with-a-hammer-drive-a-monster-truck-over-them strong.

mCAMLITE

iPad | iPhone

- Action Life Media
- $159.95
- hhhlinks.com/ mcam

Both come with a silicone iPhone case that protects your Apple device while allowing it to fit snugly inside the aluminum frame (**FIGURE 7.4**). Once inserted, your iPhone is not going to fall out...at least it's never fallen out of mine, and I've been pretty rough with my mCAMs.

Both the mCAM and mCAMLITE add the perfect amount of additional weight to help keep your shots steady, although certainly not as steady as a tripod. Speaking of tripods, Both mCAMs include multiple standard 1/4-20 mounts on the top and bottom. In addition to making your iPhone tripod ready, these mounts allow you to attach external hardware such as lights and microphones.

FIGURE 7.3 The mCAM (formerly known as the OWLE Bubo) stabilizes your iPhone while adding a wide-angle lens and a forward-facing microphone.

FIGURE 7.4 The mCAM and the mCAMLITE hold your iPhone nice and snug.

During my initial testing of the mCAM, I tried attaching a monopod to one of the 1/4-20 mounts on the *top* of the aluminum frame. This way, I was able to walk around, keeping the mCAM only inches off the ground, simulating a dog's point of view. You can check out that footage right here: http://hhhlinks.com/0wz9.

mCAM on HHH
hhhlinks.com/0wz9

Just in case you were wondering, *1/4-20* refers to a bolt (or in this case, a threaded hole) that is a quarter of an inch in diameter and has 20 threads per inch. In addition to the 1/4-20 mounts, both mCAMs also feature a single cold shoe for mounting additional equipment.

Both mCAMs feature a 37mm wide-angle conversion lens that allows your iPhone to capture a far greater field of view (**FIGURE 7.5**). In simpler terms, it lets you see more without backing up. Screw off the 37mm lens to reveal the included macro lens, perfect for shooting extreme close-ups. If you feel like splurging, Action Life Media (the makers of the mCAM), also sells a 2x telephoto lens, useful for capturing tighter shots, at around $35.

iPhone Camera (Without Additional Lens)   Wide Angle   Macro

FIGURE 7.5 The mCAM and mCAMLITE come with a wide-angle/macro combo lens. Sadly, they don't come with dogs.

When talking with iPhone filmmakers, I always recommend using an external microphone. Fortunately, both mCAM models come with an external, adjustable mic that can be inserted into your iPhone's headphone/microphone jack and twisted to face toward your subject. While it's not the greatest mic I've ever used, it does provide a noticeable improvement over the iPhone's built-in microphone. In situations where outstanding audio is required, I highly recommend using a professional external lavalier or shotgun microphone (I discuss a few options later in the chapter).

Considering how much the mCAM and the mCAMLITE have in common, you may be wondering why I initially called the mCAMLITE "slightly less cool." That leads us to the only meaningful difference between the mCAM and the mCAMLITE: their shapes.

While the mCAMLITE is essentially a professional-looking, rounded metal shell (**FIGURE 7.6**), the mCAM is a curvy, totally unique-looking mount that bears a strange resemblance to an Owl (which is where it got its original name, OWLE). Having large hands, I really appreciate the oversized grips found on both sides. Furthermore, the mCAM never fails to grab people's attention. Is that a good thing? I suppose it depends on what you're shooting.

Out of curiosity (and boredom), I decided to conduct an unscientific, unprofessional, and wholly unnecessary experiment. I brought both the mCAM and mCAMLITE to the Third Street Promenade, a bustling three-block stretch in Santa Monica, California, that's always packed with local shoppers and international tourists. I walked around and shot footage with my iPhone mounted in the mCAM. Over the course of 15 minutes (I don't have a lot of time for useless experiments), I was approached and asked about the mCAM six times! Then, I spent the next 15 minutes doing the exact same thing with my iPhone mounted in the mCAMLITE. I was approached exactly 0 times. So, what does this tell us? Nothing at all important, other than the fact that mCAM users get interrupted more often than mCAMLITE users...which isn't necessarily a good thing. If you enjoy making new friends, get the mCAM. If you're trying to remain incognito, the mCAMLITE is clearly the better option. Yes, I just wasted a full paragraph on the social aspects of a camera mount.

FIGURE 7.6 The mCAMLITE hanging out, looking all cool.

As I write this, the mCAMLITE is available for the iPhone 4, 4S, and 5. The original mCAM is still available for the iPhone 3G, 3GS, 4, and 4S (as well as the fourth-generation iPod touch); however, it will not be updated for use with the iPhone 5, and I'm *very* sad to see it go.

Whichever mCAM model you choose, you'll be rewarded with more stable imagery, wider angles, better sound, and terrific options for mounting additional accessories.

EnCinema SLR Lens Adapter for the mCAM and mCAMLITE

One of the biggest complaints I hear from filmmakers (including myself) is that the iPhone's camera is incapable of shooting anything with a shallow depth of field. Put simply, it's difficult to keep your subject in focus while pushing everything else out of focus.

Without getting too technical, the iPhone's inability to shoot with a shallow depth of field comes from its inability to use professional SLR lenses and the tiny size of its digital camera sensor. This is why so many low-budget filmmakers prefer shooting on DSLR cameras (with their large sensors and professional lens mounts).

Enter EnCinema, a lens adapter that aims to close the gap between DLSRs and the iPhone. This amazing gadget attaches to your mCAM or mCAMLITE and allows you to connect most Canon-compatible SLR lenses (**FIGURE 7.7**). (Nikon-compatible lenses require an additional adapter ring.)

Just to clear up any possible confusion (or perhaps, add to it), most of the other lenses discussed in this chapter are *conversion* lenses. They are meant to sit on top of and alter the optical properties of existing photographic lenses (think of them as lens *accessories*). SLR lenses, on the other hand, are photographic lenses normally used to focus light directly onto a camera's internal optical sensor (or a piece of film). That's why SLR lens adapters are so cool; they allow SLR lenses to behave more like conversion lenses. I hope that made sense because it was tough making all of it up.

ENCINEMA LENS ADAPTER

- Vid-Atlantic
- around $210
- hhhlinks.com/ci6a

FIGURE 7.7 Use the EnCinema lens adapter to mount Canon and Nikon compatible SLR lenses to your mCAM or mCAMLITE.

FIGURE 7.8 It's easy to get shallow depth of field when shooting with the EnCinema lens adapter.

Once your SLR lens is properly attached to the EnCinema adapter, you can shoot footage on your iPhone with far more control over depth of field, focus, and exposure. Naturally, you'll also be able to take advantage of the SLR lenses' length (short lenses for wide angles, long lenses for telephoto shots, and zoom lenses for greater flexibility). The results can be surprisingly filmic (**FIGURE 7.8**).

SLR lens adapters are nothing new. They've been around for years, helping filmmakers shoot more cinematic footage on consumer and professional video cameras. Most work the same way: Light enters the SLR lens, and the resulting image is focused on a piece of frosted glass or plastic (sometimes called a *focus screen*) that sits in front of the video camera's lens. This focus screen is essentially simulating a large camera sensor. So, in reality, the video camera isn't actually shooting the scene. Rather, it's shooting a projection of the scene off the focus screen.

Professional SLR adapters keep their focus screens vibrating at all times. This prevents the video camera from seeing the natural grain and texture of the focus screen itself. It also helps keep dust from settling on the focus screen. Since the EnCinema lens adapter uses a fixed (nonvibrating) focus screen, you will likely see traces of its texture in your footage, as well as an occasional moiré pattern. You may also spot large bits of dust. This is why you should always keep your adapter as clean as possible and have a can of compressed air on hand to blow out the adapter in between setups. Keeping your footage 100 percent dust free can be a bit of a challenge.

In addition to the texture and dust issues, you should be aware of four potential gotchas when using any SLR lens adapter.

> The additional optics in the adapter and the connected SLR lens will reduce the quantity of light that actually makes it all the way to your iPhone's video camera sensor. What does this mean? Get more lights!

> Some lenses will produce a slight vignette (darkened corners) on your footage. This can be corrected by zooming in slightly (either while shooting or in postproduction). Make sure to run plenty of camera tests *before* your first shoot day.

> The image will appear upside-down. This means you need to shoot with a camera app that can flip everything right-side-up while shooting. FiLMiC Pro and Almost DSLR offer this option.

> Automatic lenses (lenses that are controlled by a camera) may not provide enough manual control. You're far better off using fully *manual* lenses.

To be perfectly honest, I don't often shoot with an SLR adapter on my iPhone, but when I do, I'm consistently surprised and impressed by the gorgeous imagery they can capture. As video-capable DSLR cameras come down in price, the need for an iPhone SLR adapter diminishes. That said, even the Canon D60 (a popular, low-cost, video-shooting DSLR) still runs around $1000. If you already own an mCAM and a few SLR lenses, the EnCinema provides an affordable way to bring them all together.

More mCAM-Related Goodness

If you're already an mCAM, mCAMLITE, or OWLE owner, here's a short posting that demonstrates how to add a neck strap to your mount for just a couple bucks: http://hhhlinks.com/w2g1.

If you're wondering what an mCAM (or OWLE) looks like when mounted in a car, take a spin over to the FilmTools website: http://hhhlinks.com/ydd3.

And, if you're looking for an alternative to the mCAMLITE, check out the Phocus Accent. It's a bit less expensive, provides similar features, and recently won a lens shootout in *Wired* magazine. I haven't tried this camera mount yet, but it's on my to-do list for sure; see http://hhhlinks.com/0yz9.

The iPhone SLR Mount

Hey, remember when I mentioned that iPhone SLR lens mount a few paragraphs ago? Boy, those were some crazy times. It seems like almost 30 seconds ago. You know what? I'm feeling nostalgic. Let's celebrate our memories of that iPhone SLR mount by briefly discussing another iPhone SLR mount. This one is called the iPhone SLR Mount (**FIGURE 7.9**). Catchy!

Setup is fairly painless. First, your iPhone is mounted inside the included case, which consists of two rugged metal pieces secured in place together by a single large screw. Considering how much extra protection this case is providing to your iPhone, the extra effort seems justified. Currently, the case will only

mCAM Neck Strap
hhhlinks.com/w2g1

OWLE Car Mount
hhhlinks.com/ydd3

Phocus for iPhone
hhhlinks.com/0yz9

iPHONE SLR MOUNT

iPad   iPhone

- Available from Photojojo.com
- $249.00
- hhhlinks.com/7bw8

FIGURE 7.9 The iPhone SLR Mount is a dedicated lens adapter for your iPhone.

- Turtleback
- free
- hhhlinks.com/ojes

FIGURE 7.10 The shallow depth of field is awesome. The moiré patterns are slightly less awesome.

fit an iPhone 4 or 4S, but there's a chance an iPhone 5 version will be coming out soon.

Next, the adapter is screwed into the case, right in front of your iPhone's built-in camera. Finally, your Canon- or Nikon-compatible lens is attached to the adapter. That's it! In addition to creating lovely filmic imagery (**FIGURE 7.10**), the iPhone SLR Mount has a very slick fit and finish. It's a beauty.

To make shooting easier, Turtleback, the mount's developer, has also released a free iPhone app called TurtleHead that will calibrate the adapter's focus while flipping its image right-side-up. Because the app has a limited feature set, I avoid using it, instead sticking with FiLMiC Pro and Almost DSLR.

Since this adapter operates in much the same way as the EnCinema adapter, all the same gotchas and focus-screen issues still apply, although I did notice slightly more of the moiré patterning and focus-screen texture in this adapter.

While the EnCinema adapter is ideal for current mCAM owners who want to add to that device's existing feature set, the iPhone SLR Mount is perfect for anyone who doesn't own an mCAM and prefers single-purpose accessories.

The iPhone SLR Mount is just one of the many bizarre, awesome, ridiculous, and incredibly useful camera accessories available from Photojojo.com (one of my favorite websites). I'll be discussing two other items I've obtained from this site (the Holga iPhone Lens and the iPhone Lens Dial) a little later in this chapter.

Glif

If you're looking for an inexpensive, simple, and elegant way to mount your iPhone on a tripod, you're looking for a Glif (FIGURE 7.11).

The Glif is a tiny rubberized plastic mount that easily connects your iPhone to a standard 1/4-20 tripod connector. When it's not helping to steady your shots, it can be used to prop up your iPhone, in either landscape or portrait orientation, on your desk or tabletop. When it's not in use, it's small enough to toss into your backpack or go unnoticed in your pocket (unless you strangle your defenseless legs in skinny jeans with embarrassingly small pockets).

Because the Glif is designed to fit snugly over your phone's hardware, and not over a bulky case, your iPhone will need to remain buck naked. That will likely turn off a few filmmakers who prefer to keep their phone safely encased in rubber, plastic, or metal at all times. While I typically keep my iPhone in a simple case, I'll go bareback on days when I expect to be shooting for any length of time.

At $20, the Glif is a must-have purchase. I adore mine. If $20 seems a little low to you, whip out an extra $10 and get yourself the Glif+! It's like a Glif but with a +, and who doesn't like +s?

GLIF

iPad **iPhone**

- Studio Neat
- $20.00
- hhhlinks.com/ka7f

GLIF+

iPad **iPhone**

- Studio Neat
- $30.00
- hhhlinks.com/ka7f

FIGURE 7.11 Use the Glif to quickly attach your iPhone to a tripod.

FIGURE 7.12 The Glif+ package adds two additional items for more secure mounting and easy storage.

In addition to the Glif itself, the $30 Glif+ package includes the Serif, a small piece of plastic designed to help keep your iPhone securely seated in the Glif, and the Ligature, a tiny key-ring loop that screws into the Glif's 1/4-20 tripod mount (**FIGURE 7.12**). While I've never used my Ligature, I've made use of my Serif multiple times. It's great when sticking your iPhone in a Glif that's attached to a 6-foot monopod that's being held in the air, over your head, to shoot a high-angle, establishing shot. Been there, done that.

I first heard about the Glif during its Kickstarter.com fund-raising campaign back in October 2010 (coincidentally, this was also the first time I'd ever heard of Kickstarter.com). The developers set out to raise $10,000 in capital, but by the end of their 30-day campaign, the project had raised more than $137,000! If that's not a testament to mobile filmmaking, I don't know what is.

Two versions of the Glif are currently available: one for the iPhone 4 and 4S and another for the iPhone 5. When I was calculating the purchase price of a new iPhone 5, I automatically raised it up another $30 because I knew I'd be upgrading my Glif as well. Total no-brainer.

iPRO LENS

iPad iPhone

- Schneider Optics
- from $199
- hhhlinks.com/ 6xhl

iPro Lens

Schneider Optics is a well-known and extremely respected company that has been providing high-end lenses to the industrial, photographic, and motion-picture markets for decades. With the introduction of the iPro Lens in early 2012, Schneider Optics officially entered the iPhone filmmaking market.

To use the iPro Lens, you begin by snapping your iPhone 4 or 4S into the included plastic case (**FIGURE 7.13**) (an iPhone 5 version is in the works and may be available by the time you read this). This protective shell provides your phone with a custom lens mount and a small hole into which you can attach the included handle—a round plastic grip that gives your camera a little extra stability. The handle also sports a standard 1/4-20 mount, allowing the whole shebang to be attached to a tripod.

FIGURE 7.13 An iPhone 4S mounted in the iPro Lens case.

FIGURE 7.14 Quickly attach any of the lenses using the custom lens mount built into the case.

But, wait! Where are the lenses? They're hiding in the handle!

In a clever bit of engineering, the handle can unscrew into multiple sections, each containing one of the included lenses. The best part about a system like this is that if you later decide to add a lens, you can simply screw another storage section into the handle (increasing its size by about 1 inch). After doing a quick bit of useless math, I figured out that if you added another 70 lenses, the handle would become so long it could be used as a monopod. This, of course, is ridiculous and will never happen, but I'm willing to bet $20 that someone in the iPro Lens manufacturing plant has already done it…and then been fired.

The $200 iPro Lens system comes with a wide-angle lens and a fish-eye lens. To use either of the lenses, just remove it from its storage compartment in the handle, and then twist it into the custom lens mount on the back of the iPhone case (**FIGURE 7.14**). If you feel like handing over an extra $100, you can add the company's 2x telephoto lens to your iPro Lens arsenal. Like the other two, the telephoto lens quickly twists onto your iPhone case or into its own handle segment when not in use.

As you might expect from an established optics company, the images these lenses produce are gorgeous (**FIGURE 7.15**). However, like most conversion lenses of this size, you will find that your edges go soft, dramatically so with the 2x telephoto lens. It can certainly be frustrating at times, but it's not unexpected.

2X TELEPHOTO LENS

- Schneider Optics
- from $105
- hhhlinks.com/ 6xhl

Telephoto Lens

iPhone Camera (Without Additional Lens)

Wide Angle

Fisheye

FIGURE 7.15 By switching lenses you can radically alter your field of view.

Whenever I shoot with small conversion lenses, I use my camera app's digital zoom to push in a little and clip off some of the softness. It helps, but it's not a perfect solution. Then again, to expect *perfection* from a cell phone camera, even with hundreds of dollars of accessories attached, is just shy of totally bonkers. If you keep your expectations in check, you'll be delighted with your results.

Olloclip

If you dig the idea of adding conversion lenses to your iPhone but don't feel like stuffing your filmmaking toolbox with bulky accessories, you are going to love the Olloclip (**FIGURE 7.16**).

Unlike the other lens accessories in this chapter that require the use of a companion case, the Olloclip simply slides over the corner of your iPhone when needed and slides back off (and into your pocket) when you're done. Like the Glif, the Olloclip is meant to slip over a naked iPhone. If you have a case, you'll have to remove it before using this particular gizmo.

OLLOCLIP

iPad | iPhone

- Olloclip
- $69.00
- hhhlinks.com/ollo

FIGURE 7.16 In addition to being a great lens accessory, the Olloclip may be the most adorable iPhone accessory ever made.

iPhone Camera (Without Additional Lens)

Wide Angle

Fisheye

Macro

FIGURE 7.17 Sample shots comparing the Olloclip's multiple lenses.

Using the Olloclip is absurdly simple. When you crave a fish-eye look, just slip on the Olloclip with the fish-eye lens facing outward. If you want to switch to a more subtle wide angle, slide off the Olloclip, flip it over, and slide it back on (**FIGURE 7.17**). On those occasions when you need to capture some extremely extreme close-ups, you can screw off the wide-angle lens to reveal a fantastic macro lens underneath. As an added bonus, the miniature microfiber carry bag can also be used as a lens cleaning cloth. Clever!

The only hitch with Olloclip's diminutive stature is that it can easily be misplaced or forgotten at home. Because I've often left mine on my desk when running out the door, I now keep a second Olloclip in my car's center console. I adore this accessory and feel naked without it.

Much like the Glif, the Olloclip burst on the scene as the subject of a Kickstarter fund-raising campaign. Inventor Patrick O'Neill and designer Chong Pak were looking to raise $15,000 in order to initiate the manufacturing process. When the campaign ended in June 2011, they had raised more than $68,000—more proof that there are plenty of photographers and filmmakers who take their iPhoneography seriously.

While the Olloclip began its life as an iPhone 4/4S accessory, the developers are already hard at work on a new version made specifically for the iPhone 5. In fact, there's a decent chance it's already available.

If you fancy yourself a filmmaker, do yourself a favor and keep an Olloclip in your pocket at all times. Put plainly, it's a must-have.

DIFFCASE

iPad | **iPhone**

- DiffCase
- around $85
- hhhlinks.com/diff

DiffCase

A relative newcomer of the bunch, not only does the DiffCase (**FIGURE 7.18**) bring interchangeable conversion lenses and tripod mounts to your iPhone, it also offers a brilliant feature none of the other accessories have thought to add. I'll get to that in a moment.

The second you encase your iPhone in the custom DiffCase shell, you'll gain two standard 1/4-20 tripod mounts, one on the bottom and another on the *side*. Hang on! Let's stop the bus here for a moment. This is the second time I've mentioned a case with a tripod adapter on its side. You may be wondering why any self-respecting filmmaker would want to shoot video in portrait orientation (tall rather than wide). I can think of two reasons…well, three if you include wanting to annoy everyone on YouTube.

FIGURE 7.18 The DiffCase gives your iPhone multiple tripod mounts and a custom lens system.

First, you might be shooting footage that will eventually appear in vertically mounted screens, like the ones popping up in retail locations around the world. Or, perhaps you're shooting a stationary person against a green-screen—by turning your camera on its side, you can fill more of the frame with your actor and therefore take advantage of more pixels, which will result in a cleaner green-screen key. This is a terrific technique to use when shooting with *any* camera.

We now return to this accessory chapter already in progress.

The DiffCase also features a *hole*! Since when is a hole a feature? Since you can use it (with a carabiner key ring) to attach the case to your backpack or handbag. If you're feeling especially precautious, you can also run a safety line through the hole to connect the case to your tripod (or monopod). Never underestimate the power of a small hole. Anyone? Anyone? Never mind.

The DiffCase comes with three lenses—a fish-eye and a wide-angle/macro combo lens. Each lens locks into the case with a simple twist (**FIGURE 7.19**). To access the macro lens, you must first unscrew and remove the wide-angle lens sitting above it (similar to the Olloclip). It's a simple system and takes only a moment to master. While the Diffcase uses a proprietary mounting system, the company also sells mounting adapters for your existing 15mm-wide lenses.

iPhone Camera (Without Additional Lens)

Wide Angle

Fisheye

Macro

FIGURE 7.19 Here are some sample shots showing off the DiffCase's included lenses.

FIGURE 7.20 This is my favorite feature of the DiffCase: a built-in sunshade. Brilliant!

However, since the DiffCase comes with no means of securing or storing lenses that are not in use, extra care should be taken to avoid misplacing them.

Didn't I say something about a brilliant feature? I sure did! If you've ever tried shooting on a sunny day, you know how difficult it can be to properly view your iPhone's screen because of excessive glare and reflection. By attaching and repositioning the included sunshade, the DiffCase can shield your screen from excess light, making it significantly easier to view and line up your shots (FIGURE 7.20). When not in use, the sunshield can be completely closed to protect your device's touchscreen.

Rejoice iPhone 5 owners! According to the manufacturer, an iPhone 5 version of the DiffCase will soon be joining the current iPhone 4/4S model.

Holga iPhone Lens

Sick and tired of perfection? Look no further than the SLFT-IP4, otherwise known as the Holga iPhone Lens (FIGURE 7.21).

Best known for their legendary line of plastic toy cameras (renowned for their ability to produce horribly imperfect yet beautiful photos), Holga has resurfaced nearly three decades later to inspire a new generation of photographers.

Even if you've never heard of Holga, you've certainly experienced their influence in apps like Hipstamatic, Instagram, Plastic Bullet Camera, and the countless other "vintage" iPhone camera apps currently flooding the App Store. Now, Holga has brought everything full circle by introducing its own iPhone case, complete with a rotating turret of fun and funky lenses (FIGURE 7.22).

By inserting your iPhone into the case and then turning the attached dial, you can switch between the nine included lenses (Dual Image, Triple Image,

HOLGA iPHONE LENS

iPad   iPhone

- Available from Photojojo.com
- $30.00
- hhhlinks.com/f4lm

FIGURE 7.21 The Holga iPhone Lens is the least professional accessory in the book and, perhaps, in existence.

FIGURE 7.22 Turn the dial to call up a variety of silly effects.

Quadruple Image, Macro, Red Filter with Clear Heart—which is unfortunately sideways when shooting video—Red Filter, Green Filter, and Yellow Filter with Clear Center).

Granted, something like this isn't going to get a lot of use during typical narrative filmmaking, but it sure will come in handy the next time you shoot a dream sequence, ultra-low-budget music video, or drunken journal entry.

iPhone Lens Dial

Like the Holga iPhone Lens, the iPhone Lens Dial equips your iPhone 4 or 4S (and perhaps soon, your iPhone 5) with a rotating turret of additional lenses—and that's where the similarities end. Unlike the Holga, this accessory is no toy (FIGURE 7.23).

Designed by Turtleback, the same company that created the iPhone SLR Mount mentioned earlier in the chapter, this iPhone add-on is built from the same sturdy aircraft-grade aluminum. And, like the SLR Mount case, the Lens Dial case must be screwed into place around your iPhone before use.

Once your iPhone is installed, you can now gently lift and turn the lens dial to select any of the three optical-quality conversion lenses (a 0.7x wide angle, a 0.33x fish-eye, and a 1.5x telephoto). If you'd prefer to shoot with the native lens, just rotate the dial to an empty slot.

iPHONE LENS DIAL

iPad   iPhone

- Available from Photojojo.com
- $249.00
- hhhlinks.com/h5es

FIGURE 7.23 The iPhone Lens Dial provides speedy access to a variety of useful lenses.

Need to mount your iPhone to a tripod? Like the SLR Mount case, the Lens Dial case sports two standard 1/4-20 tripod mounts: one on the bottom and one on the side.

The thing I like most about the iPhone Lens Dial is the speed at which you can switch lenses. One moment you can capture a medium shot, and the next you can grab a wide (**FIGURE 7.24**). When I'm in a particularly good groove, I can change lenses within two to three seconds!

Telephoto Lens

iPhone Camera (Without Additional Lens)

Wide Angle

Fisheye

FIGURE 7.24 More sample shots! This time you're looking at all of the options available on the iPhone Lens Dial.

There are some very clear pros and cons with this bad boy. On the upside, it feels rock solid, you never have to hunt for a lens attachment, and dual tripod connectors make it easy to mount. On the downside, the wide-angle and fish-eye lenses go a little soft toward the frame's edge. That said, if super-speedy lens switching and a rugged case are more important than crystal-clear edges, the iPhone Lens Dial is a great choice.

There's one other thing about the Lens Dial worth mentioning. Like the mCAM, this thing attracts attention. When shooting in public, prepare to be interrupted, especially if you shoot anywhere near hipsters.

GorillaMobile for iPhone 4/4S

It's a tripod! It's a clamp! It's an iPhone case! It's the GorillaMobile for iPhone 4/4S, and it's the perfect accessory for those times when you wish you could mount your iPhone camera to a tree branch, a door frame, a rusty pipe, or your nephew's head.

This mounting system provides a plastic iPhone case, similar in appearance and purpose to Apple's own Bumper case. Aside from protecting the edges of your iPhone, the case is designed to quickly slide into and out of its companion tripod—a flexible rubber-and-plastic stand that measures around 8 inches tall (with the iPhone attached). While it can be used as a standard (but short) tripod, the real purpose of the GorillaMobile is to be mobile.

This tripod's stiff but bendable legs can be wrapped around all sorts of stuff: balcony railings, stop signs, and parked cars (can you tell I'm looking out my window?). Simply put, the GorillaMobile turns the world into your iPhone mount (FIGURE 7.25). There's not much more to say about this doodad. Um....it's black, and um…it's neat. Yeah, that's pretty much it.

GORILLAMOBILE
FOR iPHONE
4/4S

iPad   iPhone

- Joby
- $39.95
- hhhlinks.com/
  joby

FIGURE 7.25 The GorillaMobile lets you stick your iPhone just about anywhere.

Shooting Underwater

I've got a very serious question for you. How do you expect to shoot your film's pivotal shark attack sequence with an iPhone? As anyone who's ever dropped their iOS device into the toilet can tell you (myself included), iPhones don't like water.

Not to worry! Your aquatic masterpiece can be shot in safety thanks to these two waterproof iPhone cases.

The MarineCase

MARINECASE

iPad   **iPhone**

- Keystone Eco
- $39.99
- hhhlinks.com/ 0lyg

Safe for use at depths up to 20 feet, the MarineCase is a waterproof, form-fitting plastic shell for your iPhone 4 and 4S (**FIGURE 7.26**). It features a clear silicon cover that allows you to continue using your device's touchscreen above water (as soon as you submerge, your taps and swipes won't do a thing).

It's not a huge problem since you can simply start recording before heading downward. But, it does mean you won't be able to manually change your exposure and focus points while shooting. So, hooray! And boooo.

In addition to water protection, the MarineCase can also protect your beloved device in snow. That means your sharks can now attack while riding snowmobiles! I love your movie already.

Keystone Eco, the makers of the MarineCase, have just announced an updated version (called MarineCase II) and claim it can accommodate a wide variety of smartphones. Will it hold the taller iPhone 5? Not sure yet. But, if you're planning a film (or vacation) that involves a large volume of liquidy liquid, it's probably worth a trip to the company's website to find out.

FIGURE 7.26 Shoot underwater with the MarineCase.

The DryCASE

It's time to go deeper. How deep? How does 100 feet strike you?

The DryCASE takes a very different approach to waterproofing your iPhone. Rather than using a form-fitting shell, the DryCASE looks more like a small plastic bag with a vacuum seal. Perhaps because that's exactly what the DryCASE is (**FIGURE 7.27**).

After dropping any model iPhone into the clear, flexible bag and closing it up, you attach a small hand pump to the side and pump out all the air, creating a tight vacuum seal. This causes the case to wrap itself tightly around your phone. This vacuum seal also extends your phone's freshness and flavor (which is not at all true).

Like the MarineCase, the DryCASE allows you to continue using your touchscreen even while the device is sealed inside. As an added benefit, the DryCASE will also let you store clothing in a space-saving, vacuum-sealed bag under your bed (this is also entirely untrue).

As I mentioned, the DryCASE has been tested at an impressive 100 feet under water for a full hour. So, the next time a great white shark is torpedoing in your direction at only 75 feet down, you can stay calm and shoot some awesome iPhone video! I'm sure it will come in handy when the coroner's office is trying to identify your body.

DRYCASE

iPad   iPhone

- DryCASE
- $39.99
- hhhlinks.com/ 20py

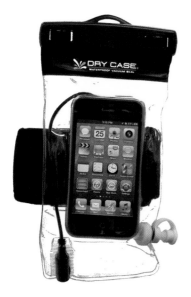

FIGURE 7.27 The DryCASE protects your iPhone in a waterproof bag.

YOUR iPAD, ONLY BETTER!

Every camera accessory we've looked at so far has been specifically designed for use with the iPhone (or a similarly sized camera). I bet your iPad is feeling pretty neglected right about now. Thankfully, that's about to change in a big way.

MOVIE MOUNT (HARDWARE ACCESSORY)

iPad | iPhone

- Makayama
- $69.95
- hhhlinks.com/09t3

MOVIE MOUNT (APP)

iPad | iPhone

- Makayama
- free
- hhhlinks.com/u68j

Movie Mount

In an endless sea of iPhone cases and contraptions, Makayama was the first company to offer filmmakers an oasis for the iPad in the form of the Movie Mount.

This molded plastic frame lets you attach your iPad to a tripod while also providing two cold-shoe mounts (one on the top and another on the side), perfect for connecting additional accessories (**FIGURE 7.28**). For instance, when I take my Movie Mount out for a spin, I'll typically add an external mic (such as the RØDE VideoMic Pro) and a compact light (like the Litepanels Micro). I'll be covering a few audio and lighting options a little later in the chapter.

While the Movie Mount doesn't come with any lenses of its own, it will accept a wide variety of existing 37mm conversion lenses (wide-angle, telephoto, and so on). Just screw in a lens, and you're good to go! When you'd rather shoot some footage without the additional lens, there's no need to unscrew it. It simply slides out of the way (**FIGURE 7.29**)! When you want it back, slide it back. I truly love this feature.

While the developer offers a free iPad video camera app, I've never used it for more than a few minutes at a time. I'm sure it's perfectly capable, but I prefer the feature-rich camera apps I've covered in Chapter 6.

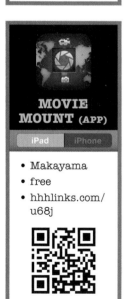

When not connected to a tripod, the Movie Mount can also serve as an upright or reclined tabletop iPad stand—a nice touch.

My only gripe with the Movie Mount is its thin plastic construction. While it feels a bit flimsy, I should point out that I've never had a problem with mine, and it's never wobbled on my tripod. So, perhaps it's more of a grumble than a gripe.

If you shoot video on your iPad and don't feel like spending more than $100 to jazz up your device ($70 for the mount + $30 for a low-cost conversion lens), cruise over to the Movie Mount website.

FIGURE 7.28 Here's my iPad mounted in the super-cool Movie Mount with a bunch of accessories (that aren't included).

FIGURE 7.29 After attaching your own lens to the Movie Mount, it can slide out of the way when not in use.

Padcaster

I haven't had the Padcaster in my possession for very long, but it's already one of my favorite items included in this book, not because of what it is, but because of what it enables.

The Padcaster is a lightweight but sturdy aluminum frame that houses a ure-thane insert designed to tightly grip an iPad 2 or 3 (FIGURE 7.30). Standard 1/4-20 and 3/6-18 threaded holes are scattered all around the frame's edge, making it compatible with a wide variety of mounting gear (tripods, monopods, shoulder mounts, and so on) and accessories (lights, microphones, transmitters, and more).

So, when you really think about it, the Padcaster doesn't do that much on its own. But, it enables and empowers filmmakers to place their iPads at the center of an entirely customized shooting rig. I think I'm in love.

PADCASTER

iPad   iPhone

- Padcaster
- $149.00
- hhhlinks.com/ 73m9

FIGURE 7.30 The Padcaster may be the ultimate accessory for filmmakers shooting on their iPads.

FIGURE 7.31 This Padcaster is totally decked out with an iPad (not included), an LED light (not included), a shotgun mic (not included), and a conversion lens (not included). The tripod, however, is also not included.

PADCASTER WITH LENSCASTER

| iPad | iPhone |

- Padcaster
- $189.00
- hhhlinks.com/ 73m9

If you feel like adding a mount for conversion lenses and you can part with a little extra cash, you can pick up the optional Lenscaster. Essentially, this is a customized bracket that attaches to the corner of your Padcaster and adds a 72mm conversion lens mount (although smaller lenses can be used with additional step-down rings). *The Lenscaster doesn't come with any lenses*, so make sure you budget for those as well.

During my brief experiments, I attached a Litepanels Croma and a Sennheiser shotgun mic to the Padcaster (**FIGURE 7.31**). I also played with the optional Lenscaster and a pair of conversion lenses (a x.06 wide-angle lens and a x1.4 telephoto lens). Finally, I tried mounting the whole rig on a monopod so I could move around quickly. Everything worked perfectly, and it was a load of fun to boot. It was the first time in months that I truly enjoyed shooting video with my iPad (rather than my iPhone).

The Padcaster is portable, is versatile, and is well made, and it reminds me why iOS filmmaking excited me in the first place.

AWESOME EXTRAS

Once you have your iPhone and iPad camera accessories squared away, it's time to accessorize those accessories! Here are a few of my favorite *extras*.

Croma and Micro

If you flip back to Chapter 6, you'll notice I stressed the importance of having extra lighting gear on hand when shooting with iOS devices in low-light environments. As I mentioned, there are plenty of low-cost solutions out there (some more practical than others), as well as several do-it-yourself guides for building lighting rigs from scratch.

Truthfully, I *love* using homegrown gear. Their limitations often spawn creative thinking. However, I know from experience that there are plenty of situations in which professional lighting gear is a must. For these occasions, I highly recommend grabbing a small LED lighting panel. Two of my favorites, the Micro and the Croma, are both made by Litepanels, located in Van Nuys, California.

The Micro

This compact panel (**FIGURE 7.32**) produces bright, flicker-free light that can be easily dimmed to any level by turning the only control on the device. At full brightness, the luminance is roughly equivalent to that of a 25-watt bulb. The multiple banks of LEDs are colored for daylight shooting (5600K); however, by inserting the included gel, the light's color can be adjusted for indoor shooting under typical tungsten bulbs (3200K). The Micro also comes with a diffuser to help soften the light.

Because the Micro runs on four AA batteries, the unit is entirely self-contained—which is ideal when shooting with an iPhone or iPad. Alkaline batteries will last about one and a half hours, but Energizer e2 Lithium Ion batteries last substantially longer (up to eight hours on a good day). If you run out of batteries, the unit can also be powered by an optional AC adapter.

Since the Micro is an LED-based fixture, it never heats up. So, you'll never have to worry about burning yourself or waiting for things to cool down before packing up.

THE MICRO

- Litepanels
- $220.00
- hhhlinks.com/67bh

FIGURE 7.32 The miniature but mighty Micro light from Litepanels.

The Micro comes with a standard, adjustable mount that fits into any available cold-shoe connector, like those found on the mCAM, mCAMLITE, and Movie Mount. If your camera rig has a 1/4-20 threaded connector, like those found on the Padcaster, you can add a cold-shoe adapter (like I mentioned in the Video-Mic Pro description) to mount your Micro.

My business partner and I have been using a Micro on corporate shoots for nearly three years, and it's never failed us once. If you're on a tight budget and don't require anything especially fancy, I highly recommend the Micro.

By the way, Litepanels also offers something called the Micro Pro. This larger fixture provides the same features but outputs double the amount of light (around 50 watts). This is ideal for people who love things that are double the size of other things…and need more light.

The Croma

I've used this fixture only for a brief time, but so far, I'm mighty impressed. Like the Micro, this battery-operated LED light easily mounts to existing equipment, remains cool during use, and is a snap to use.

About twice the size of the Micro, the Croma (**FIGURE 7.33**) outputs about twice as much soft, beautiful light. No surprise there. So, what makes this fixture so special? Is it the dimmer dial that lets you control the light's level? Nope. Is it the fact that it can mount on a light stand (using its 1/4-20 connector) or in a cold shoe, like the Micro? Nahh. How about its ability to run off of an optional AC adapter? Not even close. Perhaps it's the Croma's ability to read your mind and bring your dreams to life? Um…it can't do that, although at $650, perhaps it should. So, what's the big deal?

The Croma has a second knob (perched above the dimmer knob) that lets you control the light's color temperature! You can set it to tungsten balanced

THE CROMA

- Litepanels
- $649.00
- hhhlinks.com/ zvyb

FIGURE 7.33 The awesome Croma lets you adjust the light's color temperature.

(3200K), daylight balanced (5600K), or any temperature in between—no gels required. This is an awesome feature for filmmakers who never know what sort of lighting conditions they're going to face (I'm looking at you, documentarians and wedding videographers). Because the color temperature is controlled by a knob, not a switch, you can carefully dial in your color to match just about any typical lighting source.

Make no mistake, this kind of flexibility doesn't come cheap, but in this case, you get what you pay for. Litepanels, the makers of the Micro and Croma, have been making LED panels for a long time. Their high-end lighting fixtures can be found in studios and on locations all around the world. In short, this company makes quality stuff, and the Croma is no exception.

mobislyder

One of the fastest-growing trends in film and television production is the use of *sliders*. These compact mini-tracks provide filmmakers with an easy way of giving their camera subtle movement, even in tight locations, without having to set up large segments of track or rent (and transport) cumbersome dollies. Sliders are especially useful to filmmakers working without a crew, since they can easily be operated by a single person.

Now, thanks to the mobislyder, any video camera–equipped iPhone (or similarly sized smartphone) can get in on the action.

Created by Glidetrack, a company known for its excellent, high-end camera sliders, the compact mobislyder looks more like a toy, thanks largely to its bright lime-green accents (perhaps not the best choice). Regardless of its appearance, the mobislyder feels completely solid and can definitely help you capture smooth, elegant shots (**FIGURE 7.34**).

The slider consists of a foot-long metal rail sitting between two plastic end caps. Four round, rubberized feet keep the unit firmly positioned on most surfaces, flat and angled. Sliding back and forth across the rail is the interchangeable camera mount. While the mount can rotate to help you position your camera, it's not meant to turn while capturing shots.

The mobislyder comes with multiple mounts (along with a small plastic articulating arm), allowing you to use it with a variety of different equipment. For instance, the padded clamp is perfect for gripping your iPhone, while the 1/4-20 mount is great for attaching many of the iPhone mounts I've mentioned in this chapter (such as the Glif or DiffCase).

MOBISLYDER

- Glidetrack
- $129.95
- hhhlinks.com/5oit

FIGURE 7.34 The mobislyder will help you get smooth slider shots on flat surfaces as well as inclines.

Just about anything, even talking head interviews, can benefit from subtle movement. Because this slider isn't motorized (like some high-end models), you must manually control your moves by gently pushing the camera mount along the rail. Pressing the small button on the side will increase the amount of applied friction, helping you create slower, smoother moves. It takes a little practice, but the results are worth it. Since the mount generates a little noise as it slides, it may be best to record your audio separately.

Consider for a moment that professional dolly track comes in sizes ranging from 4 to 8 feet. With that in mind, you may be wondering whether mobislyder's comparatively tiny 12" track can actually help you capture interesting shots. The answer is yes…and no. It all depends on how you utilize it.

For example, if you were to use the mobislyder to shoot a city skyline with nothing in the foreground, your viewers are unlikely to notice any motion at all. On the other hand, if you were to capture that same shot on the same slider but this time you included multiple items in the foreground at various distances to the lens (plants, signs, people, and so on), *even a 6" move can result in a dynamic shot*. Why? Because objects in the foreground will appear to move faster than objects in the background, creating a greater sense of depth and movement. This is known as *parallax*, and it's a necessary component when creating any effective moving shots (slider-based or otherwise).

I have no doubt that any industrious filmmaker could achieve similar results with homemade gear. Plainly put, the mobislyder is not a complex piece of equipment. That said, this self-contained mini-slider is slick, simple, and ready to use the second you pull it from your bag. If you want an easy way to breathe a little life into your shots, the mobislyder may just be your new best friend.

Action Cart and Mini Cart

Having just discussed the MobiSlyder, I'm sure you understand and appreciate the value of a moving camera. But, what happens when you need to make a bigger move than a slider can support? Sure, you could move all the way up to a full size (and full price) dolly or borrow grandma's wheelchair (she'll forgive you), but perhaps all you really need is a *table dolly*.

Imagine a skateboard built specifically for film and video production. That's a table dolly, and there are a *lot* of them out there. They go by many different names, such as skater dollies, DSLR dollies, micro dollies, and "that thing that looks like a skateboard." They come in all shapes and sizes, with different wheel configurations. Some have three wheels, while others have four. Some can go only straight, while others can roll in an arch. The crappy ones start at around $25, and professional versions can easily climb into the hundreds.

As you can see, there are table dollies for every circumstance and budget. So, which are the best ones? How the hell should I know? There's a ton of these things! I haven't tried them all. Personally, I wouldn't believe anyone who says they have. That said, I *can* tell you about the two I currently use, rely on, and trust: the Action Cart and the Mini Cart from Action Life Media (ALM), the same company that brought us the mCAM and mCAMLITE.

Before I go into detail about each, I'll first tell you what the two have in common. They both sport super-strong aluminum chassis and four butter-smooth urethane wheels. They both come with a single 1/4-20 mounting screw and provide plenty of locations to attach additional equipment. And, of course, they can both be used to capture some awesome moving shots. Naturally, you'll get the best results from both when using them on a clean, smooth surface (unless you're looking for a bumpy shot). Any smooth surface will do so, look around your shooting location and get creative.

Now that you know their shared qualities, let's look at what makes each unique.

Action Cart

Got a lot of gear to mount? Meet the Action Cart (**FIGURE 7.35**). Measuring somewhere in the neighborhood of 12" long, 8" wide, and just under 2" tall, this is the bigger of the two carts. Like its smaller sibling, the Action Cart provides a smooth, controllable roll while supporting a pile of gear.

The Action Cart features adjustable wheels that allow it to roll along a straight path or in broad curves.

ACTION CART

- Action Life Media
- $159.95
- hhhlinks.com/alm1

FIGURE 7.35 The Action Cart, ready for action!

Its larger size makes it a very flexible bit of kit. I've used the Action Cart when shooting with my iPhone and iPad, as well as my DSLRs and small video cameras. I've rolled it across tabletops in restaurants, on floors in office buildings, and even along the edge of a building (in that instance, I had to lay down a smooth piece of pressboard first).

As you can see in **FIGURE 7.36**, the Action Cart can hold quite a bit of gear. Here I've loaded it up with a PadCaster sitting on a ball-mount (with the Croma LED light sitting on top), along with an articulating arm holding an mCAMLITE (with the EnCinema SLR adapter and a Canon lens). I'm sure I could have stuck a few more items on there if I tried. I'll admit, the gear was a little bouncy in this configuration. I guess I got carried away…again.

There's plenty of surface space to work with, but if you need more, you can attach an ALM Cheese Plate—a rectangular aluminum plate with a variety of 1/4-20 and 3/8 mounting holes. At $40, it's not the cheapest add-on, but it has saved my butt on more than one occasion.

FIGURE 7.36 The Action Cart loaded up with multiple accessories

Mini Cart

Looking for something a little smaller? Perhaps even *mini*?

The Mini Cart is a little over half the size of the Action Cart and provides a variety of 1/4-20 and 3/8 mounting holes, but the real charm of this adorable dolly is its adjustable wheels. Two top-mounted bolts easily unscrew to loosen the front and rear wheel axles. By angling both axles slightly inward, you can send the Mini Cart in a wide circle around your subject—perfect for product shots and tabletop work.

While the Mini Cart is undeniably small, it's certainly big enough to carry multiple pieces of gear. For instance, in **FIGURE 7.37**, I've used the adjustable ball mount that came with my Litepanels Micro, along with a Crossbar (another handy ALM accessory) to mount both my Micro and a Glif (holding my iPhone 4S). I used this exact setup when grabbing a product shot for a recent corporate project that had a *very* small budget and had to be turned around within two days.

Want to know the funniest thing about that shoot? I asked the company if I could include a sample shot in the book, and they said no. Why? Because they didn't want the book's readers to know they've used iPhones on their shoots. I guess there's an iPhone stigma out there. Ideally, that will soon change (as it did for DSLR cameras).

As I said, there are plenty of table dollies out there. Make sure to shop around and find a dolly that best serves your particular requirements. In my case, the Action Cart and Mini Cart were exactly what I needed.

MINI CART

- Action Life Media
- $69.95
- hhhlinks.com/alm1

FIGURE 7.37 The Mini Cart's adjustable wheels make arching dolly moves a breeze.

SUCTIONCLIP

iPad | iPhone

- SuctionClip
- $12.99
- hhhlinks.com/ f8ij

SuctionClip

I'll do my best to describe this complex piece of equipment. It's a clip…with some suction cups on it (**FIGURE 7.38**). Whew. I hope you got all that, because I don't have the energy or page space to repeat it.

Using the SuctionClip, you can "stick" any model of iPhone to any smooth surface (such as a window, a tabletop, a picture frame, and so on) and let your camera roll. For example, you could stick your iPhone to your car's rear view mirror for some driving shots of you and your passenger (**FIGURE 7.39**)—a move that is likely extremely illegal, dangerous, and not at all recommended. But, since you're going to do it anyway (which you shouldn't), you can make the shot even more interesting by throwing on the Olloclip's fish-eye lens.

The SuctionClip is also a clip, as its name implies, useful when needing to attach an iPhone to something without a slick surface. While the SuctionClip should be used with care (don't let that sucker fall off!), at $13 there's really no reason not to have one in your iPhone filmmaking bag of tricks.

FIGURE 7.38 This is either the super-handy SuctionClip or the ugliest cufflink ever made.

FIGURE 7.39 I've used the SuctionClip to mount my iPhone in various dangerous places. Don't try this at home.

STEP UP TO THE MIC

Can you see that tiny microphone built into your iPhone and iPad? Cute, right? Sadly, it also kinda sucks. While that's a slight exaggeration, the truth is that when recording audio for film and video production, the internal mic is far from ideal.

Fortunately, there are boatloads of audio accessories available for your iOS devices, with more arriving every day. Generally speaking, two types of microphone accessories are available for your iPhone and iPad: those that allow you to connect existing external microphones and those that *are* external microphones. Let's take a look at a few highlights from both categories.

Adapter Cables

When shooting with my mCAMLITE (and my iPhone) in the field, I often bring along my Sennheiser G3 Wireless lavalier microphone. The wireless receiver, which usually sits in my pocket or on the cold-shoe mount of my mCAM, comes with an audio cable that is meant to run from the receiver's audio-out port to my video camera's audio-in port. However, if I were to simply plug the cable into my iPhone's 3.5mm headphone/microphone jack, my iPhone would not receive the signal. That's because Apple's mobile devices employ a slightly atypical connector (TRRS vs. TRS) and signal path. If you're curious to learn more about this sort of thing, Wikipedia has an excellent article on the subject: http://hhhlinks.com/j4jl.

To make use of my Sennheiser mic, I must connect it to a *microphone adapter cable*, which is then plugged into my iPhone (or iPad). The adapter makes all the necessary signal path adjustments, provides the correct connector type, and allows my iPhone to receive and record the mic's audio signal.

The cable I use is called the 3.5mm TRRS 4-Pole Right Angle Male to 3.5mm 4-Pole Female Cable (**FIGURE 7.40**) from KV Connection. I use this same cable when connecting my RØDE VideoMic Pro to my iPhone or iPad. I've even used it when working with a battery-powered shotgun mic. Since it had an XLR connector, I had to pick up a couple extra converters at my local RadioShack (**FIGURE 7.41**).

Now, before you run out and buy the same cable I did, you need to understand that there are *many* different types of microphone adapter cables available. The one *you* should get is totally dependent on the type of microphone you have, the connectors it provides, and your intended use.

FIGURE 7.40 This little cable is the key to using external microphones with an iPhone or iPad.

FIGURE 7.41 It's a good thing RadioShack is open late.

TRRS on Wikipedia
hhhlinks.com/j4jl

3.5MM TRRS TO 3.5MM FEMALE ADAPTER CABLE
iPad iPhone

- KV Connection
- $18.11
- hhhlinks.com/h1xr

G3 WIRELESS LAVALIER
- Sennheiser
- $629.95
- hhhlinks.com/59pr

KV Connection
www.
kvconnection.com

**Action Life
Media**
www.
actionlifemedia.
com

**VIDEOMIC
PRO**

- RØDE
  Microphones
- $329.00
- hhhlinks.com/
  5urh

Fortunately, there are a few terrific online cable stores with support staffs who are more than willing to help you select the correct cable for your particular situation. Here are two of my favorite online shops:

> KV Connection: http://www.kvconnection.com

> Action Life Media: http://www.actionlifemedia.com

VideoMic Pro

Since I just mentioned this microphone a moment ago, I thought I'd give you a little more information about it.

The VideoMic Pro is a small, mono, camera-mountable shotgun mic (**FIGURE 7.42**) that employs a 1/2" condenser capsule to record high-quality audio. *Shotgun* microphones are used to focus on and record sound sources that are positioned in front of them, rather than off to the sides. This is often referred to as a *super-cardioid* recording pattern—which is often forgotten because *super-cardioid* is a truly awful name that sounds like an unwanted medical condition.

Using its standard shoe mount, the VideoMic Pro can easily be attached to many of the cases and mounts I've already described in this chapter. For devices that don't offer a cold-shoe mount, such as the Padcaster, "1/4-20 to cold shoe" adapters can be purchased at your local camera store for somewhere between $10 and $20. The VideoMic Pro also comes standard with a 3/8" threaded mount for use with standard boom poles.

To keep vibration noise to a minimum, the actual mic component of the VideoMic Pro is cleverly *suspended* in place by small rubberized cords (extras are provided). It's like a mini shock mount for a mini mic. Adorable.

Keeping things nice and simple, the VideoMic Pro has only two controls (**FIGURE 7.43**). The first is a switch with three settings: Off, On, and High Pass Filter. When in that third position, the mic will do its best to prevent low-frequency noise (such as air conditioners and traffic) from mucking up your otherwise excellent recordings.

The second control is used to adjust your audio level. In addition to a default 0dB, you'll find -10dB and +20dB settings. According to RØDE, the mic's manufacturer, the -10dB setting is ideal for loud sounds (live music, motorsport, close-to-camera interviews, and so on), while the +20dB setting boosts the output for use with DLSR cameras, which can in turn lower their own input gain (and the noise that goes along with it). Which setting is best for iOS devices? When I shoot interviews with the VideoMic Pro attached to an mCAM or Movie Mount, I'll almost always use the 0dB setting. That said, I have switched to

FIGURE 7.42 The VideoMic Pro is a small, camera-mountable shotgun mic.

FIGURE 7.43 With only two switches on the VideoMic Pro, there's not many ways to screw things up. Believe me, I've tried.

-10dB when recording in particularly loud environments. I've yet to use the +20dB setting with my iOS devices.

Because the VideoMic Pro outputs its signal to a standard 3.5mm connector, you'll also need a microphone adapter cable, like the one mentioned in the previous section. On the bright side, since the mic adapter is being plugged into your iOS device's headphone/mic jack and doesn't rely on a 30-pin dock connector (as some external mics do), it's already compatible with the iPhone 5 and will likely remain compatible for some time to come.

RØDE, the legendary microphone company behind the VideoMic Pro, claims its microphone will keep on chuggin' for more than 70 hours on a single 9-volt battery. While that's an impressive statistic, I *strongly* urge you to bring backup batteries (for *all* of your battery-powered gizmos). Simply forgetting to turn your mic off on a Tuesday can totally screw you on a Wednesday. Besides, not all batteries are created equal. Extra batteries are *never* a bad idea. It's like my grandmother once said, "Everything in this restaurant tastes like crap!" I know that doesn't apply, but I just thought I'd share.

iXZ Microphone Adapter

Sometimes an adapter cable simply isn't enough to connect an external microphone to your iOS device. For example, many professional mics, such as my trusty Sennheiser ME66/K6P shotgun microphone, require *phantom power*. This simply means that the recording device must supply power to the microphone in order for the mic to work. Power is delivered over the same cable that's used for transmitting the audio signal. Simple enough, right? The problem is, the iPhone and iPad can't and won't provide phantom power.

iXZ

iPad   iPhone

- Tascam
- $69.99
- hhhlinks.com/
  uq0x

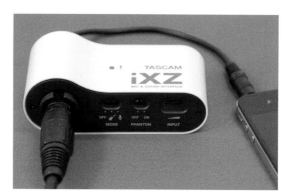

FIGURE 7.44 Use the iXZ to connect your iOS devices to professional mics that require phantom power.

Does that mean you can't use professional phantom-powered microphones with your iPhone and iPad? Nope! You'll just need to get your hands on the Tascam iXZ (**FIGURE 7.44**).

ME66/K6P SHOTGUN MICROPHONE

- Sennheiser
- $499.95
- hhhlinks.com/
  8q9y

Not only does this battery-powered bundle of audio connectivity offer a combo XLR / 1/4" audio input jack, it will also supply phantom power to any mic that needs it. In addition, it provides a guitar mode (for recording guitars), an input level control, and a headphone jack. The whole thing plugs into your iOS device's 3.5mm headphone/mic port.

A quick side note just in case you haven't worked with phantom power mics before: If you find your recordings have an inordinate amount of hiss, you're likely supplying phantom power to a microphone that doesn't require it. Just turn off the iXZ's phantom power switch and rock on.

On the bright side, the iXZ will help you capture clean audio recordings from most professional mics with minimal fuss. On the slightly less bright side, the device's headphone jack provides audio only during playback or while recording with applications that support audio loop-through (most don't). On the not-at-all-bright side, the iXZ is very oddly shaped. It's not quite right for your pocket and doesn't provide any standard mounts. That just means you'll have to find your own way to mount the unit to your rig (or belt). I've used a professional mounting clamp…and gaffer's tape. Both worked wonderfully.

I'm already a fan of the iXZ, but it's not the only device of its kind. As I write this, a similar doohickey is about to be released from IK Multimedia called the iRig PRE. I haven't seen it, tried it, or heard it, so I can't recommend it…yet. That said, it might be worth a look.

AR-4i Stereo Microphone

As I was once told by a supremely creepy sales dude who worked at my local Circuit City, "Everything is better in stereo." At the time, I had no idea what he was talking about (since I was shopping in the appliance department), but I *remembered it* because, like I said, he was supremely creepy. It wasn't until I started shooting movies with my iPhone that I finally understood what he was talking about.

Despite the iPhone's status as one of the most advanced mobile devices on the planet, it still records audio in mono. How sad is that? Thanks to the AR-4i from Fostex, that is about to change. Unlike all the other audio solutions I've covered thus far, the AR-4i doesn't plug into your iPhone. Instead, your iPhone plugs into the AR-4i (**FIGURE 7.45**). Whoa! That's crazy talk!

By sliding your iPhone 4 or 4S into this somewhat bulky but well-built contraption, it will lock into place and make a connection via its 30-pin dock connector (I'm told that an iPhone 5 version of the AR-4i with a Lightning connector is in the works).

The moment your iPhone is in place, the AR-4i automatically springs to life. On the right side, you'll find two microphone inputs, a cold shoe for mounting additional accessories (such as a video light), an input volume dial (to adjust gain), and a small LED meter that provides visual feedback, letting you know if your audio signal is too quiet or too loud.

On the left side of the AR-4i, you'll find a third microphone input, a headphone jack with volume dial, a DC power connector, and a standard 1/4-20 tripod mount. On the bottom, you'll find a second standard 1/4-20 tripod mount. As

AR-4i

iPad   iPhone

- Fostex
- $199.00
- hhhlinks.com/ f90r

FIGURE 7.45 The AR-4i wraps your iPhone in stereo goodness.

you may have already guessed by the multitude of microphone ports and tripod mounts, the AR-4i can be used in either portrait or landscape orientation.

Let's start with landscape (wider, rather than taller), since that's how you'll typically be shooting video. In this orientation, the cold shoe is now on top where it belongs. From here you can insert the two supplied microphones into the two mic ports on the top of the AR-4i. Point the left one toward the left and the right one toward the right. Finally, launch a stereo-compatible video camera app (like FiLMiC Pro). Presto! You now have a stereo-capable video camera (**FIGURE 7.46**)!

Now, turn your iPhone back into portrait orientation (taller, rather than wider). Then, pull the mic out of port 2 on the right side, and insert it into the open mic port on the left side. Finally, launch a stereo-compatible audio app (such as Hindenburg Field Recorder). Presto, again! You now have a stereo-capable audio field recorder (**FIGURE 7.47**)!

Since the mics are adjustable, you can even point one toward your subject and the other toward yourself—a perfect setup for conducting interviews. If you'd rather leave your tripod behind and go handheld, the AR-4i comes with a handy metal handle that can be screwed into either of the two 1/4-20 threaded mounts. Powered by a pair of AAA batteries, the AR-4i adds a bit of heft to the iPhone, but I don't mind since the extra weight can help stabilize shaky shots.

FIGURE 7.46 Using the AR-4i's included microphones, you can finally record videos with stereo audio.

FIGURE 7.47 Just by moving one of the mics you can capture stereo sound in either landscape or portrait orientation.

To tweak the AR-4i's settings, just install and launch its free companion app. Use it to change input panning assignments, activate the built in low-cut filter and audio limiter, adjust various headphone settings, and more.

I really like this gizmo, especially for casual and outdoor shooting. I've also used it to capture atmospheric sound effects for multiple projects. Stereo audio isn't ideal for every situation, but it never fails to breathe a little life into your recordings.

Tascam iM2

The Tascam iM2 is a compact stereo mic for the iPhone, iPad, and iPod touch. Like the AR-4i, iM2 connects directly to your iOS device's 30-pin dock connector (**FIGURE 7.48**). This means any devices with Apple's new Lightning connector will have to sit this one out (I'm looking at you, iPhone 5 and fifth-generation iPod touch).

For a tiny little thing, this puppy packs a lot of power.

After connecting this gizmo to your iOS device, a small blue LED lights up, letting you know all is good in the hood. From then on, the iM2's pair of somewhat directional condenser microphones will soak in the stereo sound and create some terrific recordings. I say "somewhat directional" because the microphones are capable of rotating a full 180° (from facing you to facing away). While this can help you focus in on a particular sound source, don't expect the iM2 to provide the same sort of directional sound isolation you'd get when using a shotgun mic.

iM2

iPad | iPhone

- Tascam
- $99.99
- hhhlinks.com/ c37z

FIGURE 7.48 The iM2 is a pocket-sized stereo microphone for your iOS devices.

The iM2 also provides an input level adjustment (**FIGURE 7.49**), a stereo audio level limiter, and a mini USB port that allows you to power and charge your iOS device even while the iM2 is occupying the 30-pin dock connector—a thoughtful addition.

I don't recommend using the iM2 while shooting video because while your iPhone or iPad is in the landscape orientation, the microphones on the attached iM2 would be positioned one on top of the other (rather than side-by-side; you know, like ears). That said, the iM2 is an excellent choice for recording live music, sound effects, and basic atmospheric background tracks.

FIGURE 7.49 The two condenser mics can be rotated toward your subject for better recordings.

CHAPTER 8

THE MOST VERSATILE TOOLS ON SET

Now that you've made the decision to shoot your next masterpiece on your iPhone or iPad, it's time to face a very harsh reality. While your iOS device is busy making other video cameras feel inadequate, it won't be available to do anything else. By now you must know that this is totally unacceptable!

What if you need to view revised script pages in Final Draft Reader or obtain a signed release form in Easy Release or update your blocking diagram in Shot Designer? It's just not practical to keep yanking your iPhone or iPad off its tripod. Clearly, you need another iOS device. Maybe two. Possibly three. I'd get five to be safe.

All joking aside, I'm not joking.

Once you bring your iOS device to set, you'll quickly realize that it outshines every other piece of gear in terms of flexibility and functionality. It's a production chameleon.

Not convinced? Maybe that's because you haven't read this chapter yet.

Let's explore a few of the astonishing ways in which iOS devices will reinvent your on-set production workflow. You might want to hide your credit cards for now. You have been warned.

TELEPROMPTERS

A teleprompter is an electronic device that sits next to or in front of a camera lens and displays a script as scrolling text. Think of it as a digital cue card. It allows your talent to read their lines off a screen, while *appearing* to look directly into the lens. Anyone who's ever had to deliver long passages of text without looking away from the camera understands the value of a teleprompter (I'm looking at you, local news guy).

Can you guess which two mobile devices are capable of transforming into portable, feature-packed teleprompters? If you guessed Optimus Prime and Megatron, you clearly picked up this book by accident.

There are oodles of teleprompting apps hiding in the App Store, but in my opinion, only two are currently worth closer inspection. Each has its advantages, and each will set you back about ten bucks—less than the cost of a movie ticket. Therefore, if I could buy only one of these two apps…I'd still buy both.

PROPROMPTER

| iPad | iPhone |

- Bodelin Technologies
- $9.99
- hhhlinks.com/ wk3n

ProPrompter

Available for both the iPhone and the iPad, ProPrompter is a completely professional teleprompting solution that boasts a lengthy, ever-growing list of unique and powerful features.

To use the app, simply launch it, create a blank script file, and enter your text (**FIGURE 8.1**). Since the app doesn't offer any word processing functionality, it might be easier to construct your script in another iOS application (or on your computer) and then copy and paste it into ProPrompter. You say you want more text input options? OK! If your Apple device supports the transcription features built into newer versions of iOS, you could simply read your script directly into ProPrompter's text field. Still not satisfied? Bodelin Technologies, ProPrompter's developer, offers a free, web-based service called ProPrompter Producer that lets you upload, manage, and edit text files that will easily sync with your iPhone and iPad.

Once your script has been entered, tapping its name will switch you into teleprompter mode. Tap once more, and your script will begin to slowly scroll up, filling the entire screen (**FIGURE 8.2**). Easy, right?

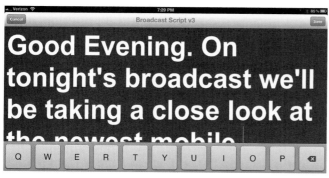

FIGURE 8.1 Type your script into ProPrompter's script editor, or simply copy and paste it from an e-mail.

FIGURE 8.2 As your script plays back, you can adjust your speed, pause, and jump between bookmarks.

While in use, a single tap will pause the crawl. A swipe-up gesture will speed up the crawl, and a swipe-down gesture slows it down. Swiping to the left and right allows you to instantly jump to bookmarks you've placed throughout the text.

The default settings are swell, but once you start using the app on a regular basis, you'll find that every shoot has slightly different requirements. For instance, you may be shooting a fast talker. That means you'll need a speedier crawl. On another shoot, you might have someone with poor eyesight. That means you'll need a larger font. Under some lighting conditions, it might be difficult to read white text on a black background. That means you'll need to change the font and background colors. All of these settings, and *many* more, can be adjusted on ProPrompter's settings screen (**FIGURE 8.3**).

In addition to the text's font, appearance, and starting speed, you can also add a countdown of a customized length, decide whether to autostart or loop the script, and change the text's orientation, which is useful when using Pro-Prompter with external teleprompting hardware (which I'll be covering later in the chapter).

Different people read at different speeds, and those speeds change even while you're shooting. That means you'll need to constantly adjust your teleprompter's speed *while shooting*. You can't use on-screen gestures, because your hand would block the screen. What you really need is a remote control. This is where ProPrompter really shines.

If you have two iOS devices running ProPrompter, they can wirelessly connect, letting you control one device with the other! When I'm shooting, I'll use my iPad as the teleprompter and my iPhone as the controller. The same gestures I described before work on the remote device. So, a single tap will start and stop

FIGURE 8.3
ProPrompter provides a plethora of customization options.

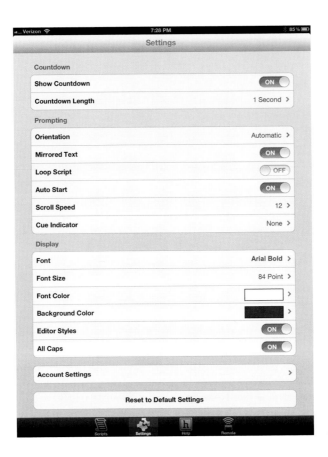

PROPROMPTER REMOTE CONTROL

iPad | iPhone

- Bodelin Technologies
- $69
- proprompter.com

the prompter. It's so natural, you don't even have to look at the iPhone while using it. On a couple occasions, I've even given my iPhone to the performer who held it just out of frame and controlled their own prompter speed!

The only downside to this solution is that occasional interference in tech-heavy locations can disrupt the wireless connection between your devices. It's happened to me a few times, and it will eventually happen to you. For that reason, Bodelin Technologies sells a $69 backup solution. It's a remote-control cable that plugs into the headphone jack on your iPad or iPhone (**FIGURE 8.4**). If you've ever used the squeeze-style buttons on an iPhone's earbuds to control music playback, you'll feel right at home with this remote. The buttons can be used to start, stop, speed up, and slow down the crawl, as well as bounce between bookmarks. The remote comes with a heavy-duty 25-foot extension cable. It's this extension that is responsible for most of the remote's expense. If you don't need the extra distance, you can simply control ProPrompter using the buttons on the earbuds/mic cable that came with your iPhone.

FIGURE 8.4 Bodelin Technologies offers a ProPrompter remote-control cable that connects to your device's headphone jack.

The app works equally well on iPads or iPhones. The iPad's large screen lets it accommodate more text on the screen at once, making it easier for talent to know what's coming next. It also facilitates the use of larger font sizes, making your prompter easier to read at greater distances. However, there are just as many benefits to running ProPrompter on the iPhone. For instance, the iPhone is much lighter, is more portable, and requires less support gear, which means it can be used in situations where an iPad rig simply isn't practical. More importantly, your iPhone is *always* with you (isn't it?)!

Having a teleprompter app on your iPhone will absolutely save the day when working with someone who turns out to be uncomfortable on camera. For example, let's say you're shooting a promotional video for the Sucksalot Vacuum Cleaner Company, and you're about to record the CEO's direct-to-camera sales pitch. Just because she regularly addresses packed rooms filled with vacuum-obsessed executives doesn't mean she won't have a total freak-out panic attack when placed in front of a camera. In those instances, even a mini teleprompter will calm nerves, protect reputations, and rescue your production.

Elite Prompter

There's more than one way to skin a cat! Wow, that is a truly disgusting expression. You don't realize stuff like that until you write it down. Gross.

Like I was saying, there's more than one way to transform your iOS device into a teleprompter. May I turn your attention to Elite Prompter, a nifty iPad-only app developed by ikan Corporation? This is the same company that developed

ELITE PROMPTER

iPad   iPhone

- ikan International Corp.
- $9.99
- hhhlinks.com/je2p

FIGURE 8.5 When using Elite Prompter's rich text editor, what you see is what you get.

Cinema Forms (mentioned in Chapter 4) and produces high-quality field monitors, lighting gear, and support systems.

Unlike ProPrompter, Elite Prompter provides a well-organized rich text editor in which to enter and edit your scripts (FIGURE 8.5). In this app, what you type is what you get. If you want larger text, a thinner font, or different colors, all of those alterations, and many more, are made directly within the app's script-editing window. You can even add properly formatted bullet points. All this control makes Elite Prompter feel much more like a traditional word processor.

As the "official teleprompter of Adobe Story," Elite Prompter can easily import any scripts you might have stored on Adobe's servers. If you're not an Adobe Story user, don't fret: The app can grab files from Dropbox and import e-mail attachments just as easily. As a bonus, the app can even import and filter dialogue from Final Draft and Final Draft AV documents. This is a tremendous time-saver.

When you're ready to play back your script, just tap Play Script in the upper-right corner of the script editor, or tap the Play button on the bottom of the screen. The app immediately switches into presentation mode and begins scrolling your script. A single tap toward the bottom of the screen brings up the playback controls. From here you can pause and unpause the scroll, change the scrolling speed (and its direction), flip the text's orientation, skip between saved cue points, and restart the scroll from the beginning. You can quickly navigate through your script by simply swiping up or down.

From the script edit screen, you can also toggle several playback options, including your initial scroll speed, an optional countdown, on-screen timers, and more.

Unfortunately, Elite Prompter doesn't allow you to control the playback of one iOS device with another, but there are a couple of easy ways to keep your scroll under control. If you have a Bluetooth keyboard, pair it with your iPad, and use a set of eight predefined keys to pause playback, control your speed, navigate between cue points, and flip your text's orientation. Looking for a more elegant solution? Check out the Elite Remote ($79), ikan's Bluetooth remote control (FIGURE 8.6). It's small, it's professional-looking, and it includes dedicated buttons for the functions I just mentioned. I much prefer using the remote, but it's nice to know the Bluetooth keyboard option exists.

ELITE REMOTE

iPad · iPhone

- ikan International Corp.
- $79
- eliteprompter.com

FIGURE 8.6 The Elite Remote provides Bluetooth-based simplicity for remotely controlling your prompter's playback.

ProPrompter Wing

Now that you've turned your iPhone and iPad into teleprompting powerhouses, it's time to figure out where you're actually going to position them! To get the best results from a teleprompter, it needs to be placed right next to, or ideally in front of, your camera lens. We'll start with the "next to" approach since it's significantly less expensive.

The ProPrompter Wing, designed by the same company that developed the ProPrompter app, lets you easily mount your iPhone directly next to your camera's lens (FIGURE 8.7). This $149 accessory is absurdly simple to set up and is perfect for use with small video cameras and DSLRs.

You begin by mounting your camera to the mounting bar and then popping your iPhone into the mobile device clip. After that, you position the swing-out arm and the device clip so your iPhone is sitting as close to your lens as possible without obstructing it. You can mount the whole contraption on a tripod

PROPROMPTER WING

iPad · iPhone

- Bodelin Technologies
- $149
- proprompter.com

FIGURE 8.7 The ProPrompter Wing turns your iPhone into a portable prompting powerhouse.

or attach the included grip for handheld work. Total setup time: four minutes if you're moving slowly, or two minutes if you've had a couple Red Bulls.

If you'd prefer to use your iPad, mount it to a spare tripod using one of the iPad tripod mounts I covered in Chapter 7 (Bodelin Technologies also sells one for $129 called the iPad Bracket). Then position the tripod so your iPad sits directly under or next to your camera's lens. Done! Naturally, this setup won't work for handheld shooting.

Now your talent can read the script and appear to be looking into the lens.

With this sort of setup, you need to follow two *very* important rules:

1. Make sure your talent always looks at the iPhone, even when there's nothing to read, and *never* looks directly into the lens.

   The moment your speaker shifts his or her eyes from the iPhone to the camera lens (even if they are an inch apart), the audience will see (or feel) the sudden change, and the illusion will be shattered. Trust me on this. Even the slightest eye shift is a dead giveaway. Don't believe me? Watch a few local low-budget TV ads. It's an eye-shifting horror show out there!

2. Have your talent stand as far away from your camera as possible while still being able to read the words on the iPhone's screen. This is usually somewhere between 6 and 10 feet.

   Because your talent will be looking slightly off-camera, you run the risk of introducing a disconnect between your talent and your viewers. The further off-camera your talent looks, the greater the disconnect.

   By moving your talent farther away from the lens, you're actually decreasing the visible distance between the lens and the iPhone so the actor doesn't have to look as far off-camera to read the prompter.

Naturally, you'll need to zoom in on your actor to compensate for the distance.

If you're having trouble getting your head around this concept, take a moment and watch a short video I posted on Hand Held Hollywood a while back. It explains the fundamentals in greater detail and includes a descriptive animation as well as several example shots taken at different distances. See http://hhhlinks.com/js7z.

The Wing is one of the first accessories I ever acquired for my iPhone, and it's still one of my favorites. You can find it, along with a boatload of other iPhone mounting accessories, on the ProPrompter website.

ProPrompter HDi Pro2

When you're ready to graduate to the big leagues, it's time to get a "through-the-glass" teleprompter, also known as a "see-through" teleprompter and sometimes referred to as a "direct to lens" teleprompter but usually called "one of those teleprompters that sits in front of your lens."

Through-the-glass prompters provide the most professional results because your talent is reading text that's positioned directly in front of your camera's lens. Your performers appear to be looking right into the lens, because they are! Unfortunately, these types of prompters tend to be fairly expensive. If there's room in your budget, the results are worth the price. If not, you'll find some do-it-yourself alternatives under "More Options."

Here's how through-the-glass prompters work: A teleprompter screen (an iPad running ProPrompter, for instance) is mounted under the front of the camera, facing up. A special piece of coated glass, often referred to as "beam splitter" glass, is mounted at a 45-degree angle directly in front of the camera lens and right over the teleprompter screen. The words displayed on the teleprompter screen are reflected on the angled glass and into the eyes of your talent. The lens shoots through the glass and does not see the reflected text. As a result, your talent can read their script *and* look into the lens at the same time (**FIGURE 8.8**).

When the text is reflected in the glass, it appears backward to the talent, which is why all teleprompter apps have the option to flip, or "mirror," the text. With mirroring engaged, the words will appear backward on the iPad screen but will be reflected in the correct orientation on the glass.

Normally, teleprompter rigs use LCD screens to display the text, but those are quickly being replaced by iPads running the apps I've already mentioned.

Wing Demo on HHH
hhhlinks.com/js7z

PROPROMPTER HDI PRO2

iPad   iPhone

- Bodelin Technologies
- $1195
- proprompter. com

FIGURE 8.8 This handy-dandy diagram explains how through-the-glass prompters work their magic.

1. Video Camera
2. Teleprompter Housing
3. Video Monitor Displaying Scrolling Script
4. Beam Splitter Glass That Reflects the Script
5. Subject Looks into Lens, Reads Reflected Script
6. Script Reflects Off Glass Toward Subject

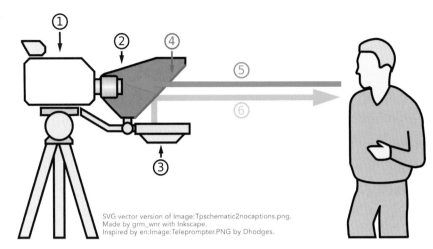

SVG vector version of Image:Tpschematic2nocaptions.png.
Made by grm_wnr with Inkscape.
Inspired by en:Image:Teleprompter.PNG by Dhodges.

FIGURE 8.9 The ProPrompter HDi Pro2 is a top-notch, professional, through-the-glass prompter.

My teleprompter rig of choice is the ProPrompter HDi Pro2 (**FIGURE 8.9**), a professional through-the-glass prompter that supports the iPad 1, 2, and 3 and costs just under $1200.

Setup is a breeze because the HDi Pro2 is mostly self-contained and is stored in an assembled state. It's ready for use seconds after you remove it from its military-grade, waterproof, airtight case.

If you're using it with a small or medium-sized camera, you can mount it on the included camera bar, which attaches directly to the HDi Pro2's mirror box. The included detachable hand grip makes the whole thing portable. When using the HDi Pro2 with a larger camera, the prompter can easily be attached to standard 15mm rails (which you'll have to provide).

Once your camera and prompter are mounted, simply line up your lens within the prompter's 150mm lens opening, and attach the lens sock and antireflection

FIGURE 8.10 After attaching the ProPrompter and snapping your iPad into the bracket, you're good to go!

hood to keep out extra light. Snap your iPad into the included iPad bracket, and you're done (**FIGURE 8.10**)!

The supplied bracket supports the iPad 1, 2, and 3. Since the bracket is removable, I'm guessing they'll soon be releasing replacement brackets for other devices, such as the Android-based Nexus 7, Kindle Fire, and the iPad Mini. Because your iPad is mounted under the mirror box, it can be difficult to access. This is why teleprompter remote controls are so important and why both of the apps I covered earlier include multiple remote options.

I've been using my HDi Pro2 and its predecessors since the moment they were released. They've proven themselves time and time again on shoots massive and micro. I often use my HDi Pro2 when working with professional performers who aren't given enough time to memorize lines. For example, a few years ago I had the pleasure of directing a commercial spot that featured that year's top ten *American Idol* finalists. Since they were rehearsing around the clock, I was given only a few minutes to shoot each of them. Thanks to my prompter rig, each finalist was able to step under the lights, read the script straight off the screen, and get right back to work.

There aren't many accessories I can recommend without any reservations or conditions, but the ProPrompter HDi Pro2 is one of them. I truly love mine. It works well, and therefore, so do I.

More Options

While I believe I've shown you some of the best teleprompting gear available, plenty of other companies offer vast arrays of nifty prompting accessories, and more are popping up every day.

Prompter People
prompterpeople.com

ikan
ikancorp.com

DataVideo
datavideo.us

Indy Mogul DIY Part 1
hhhlinks.com/diy1

Indy Mogul DIY Part 2
hhhlinks.com/diy2

If the prompter mounts I've shown you don't whet your whistle, fire up your web browser, zip over to the Prompter People website (http://prompterpeople.com), and take a look at the Ultralight iPad Teleprompter, as well as the adorable Ultralight iPhone Teleprompter.

If those don't float your boat, swing by the ikan website (http://ikancorp.com), and check out its Elite iPad Teleprompter kit.

If that doesn't shine your shoes, stop by the DataVideo website (http://datavideo.us) and have a gander at its through-the-lens TP-100 teleprompter for the iPhone. Small but sassy!

If that doesn't flip your flapjacks, you can always make one yourself! Indy Mogul (http://indiemogul.com) posted a pair of terrific videos on YouTube, explaining how to construct a prompter mount for around $35. See http://hhhlinks.com/diy1 and http://hhhlinks.com/diy2.

And, if that doesn't (last one, I promise) plant your petunias, you can always watch Dave Kaminski fashion a $5 prompter mount out of an iPad box, a paperclip, and a stick of gum. I may have lied about the paperclip and the stick of gum. See http://hhhlinks.com/kp6n.

CREATING AN INTERROTRON

Since launching HandHeldHollywood.com, I've had the pleasure of meeting brilliant filmmakers from all over the world who are pushing the boundaries of what is possible with iOS devices. Eric Haase is one such filmmaker.

Eric is an extremely talented, Los Angeles–based cinematographer who needed to capture several interviews for Imagine 300, a fundraising project intended to support endangered art, music, and physical education programs at his daughter's elementary school. He made the decision to shoot the interviews *direct-to-camera* (an interview style in which subjects look directly into the lens while answering questions). When done correctly, direct-to-camera interviews can feel intimate and honest and can help forge an emotional bond between your subject and your audience.

The problem is, direct-to-camera interviews are rarely done correctly, especially on low-budget productions. Most people can't and won't make an emotional connection with a camera lens. And yet I see this mistake being made time and time again. The results are always the same: a shot of someone who is clearly uncomfortable looking at us uncomfortably while saying something uncomfortable.

To capture direct-to-camera interviews in his own work, renowned documentary filmmaker Errol Morris turned his attention to the teleprompter. Rather than use the device to display scrolling text, Morris used his teleprompter to present a live feed of his own face. That way, the subject was no longer talking to a dark, lifeless lens. They were talking to Errol! Behind the scenes, Errol would be talking into a second camera, also equipped with a teleprompter that displayed a feed from the primary interview camera. Essentially, Errol used two cameras and two teleprompters to create a two-way, interview-ready videoconference. He called his contraption the Interrotron.

DIY $5 Prompter
hhhlinks.com/kp6n

Having used an Interrotron on many commercial productions, Eric knew the system would be ideal for shooting his required interviews. Unfortunately, this low-budget shoot didn't have the funds necessary to rent the device.

That's when Eric was struck with an idea for a low-cost alternative.

After extensive experimentation and some careful planning, Eric was able to transform a pair of iPad 2s and a borrowed iPad-based teleprompter rig into his very own makeshift Interrotron. He used Apple's free videoconferencing technology, FaceTime, to bring everything together. Brilliant! Here's how he did it.

Eric installed the first iPad in his ProPrompter HDi Pro2 (the same rig I use), which was mounted to his primary camera, a Canon 5D DSLR. Behind the scenes, Eric positioned a second iPad in front of his field monitor that was displaying the 5D's output. Naturally, he couldn't place the iPad *directly* in front of the monitor since it would block his view, so he experimented with various positions until he found one that worked, which was slightly off-center (**FIGURE 8.11**).

FIGURE 8.11 Eric Haase backstage with his iPad propped in front of his field monitor.

Using FaceTime, Eric "called" one iPad with the other and established a two-way videoconference. The second iPad (in front of Eric's field monitor) captured Eric's face and transmitted it to the first iPad, where it was presented on the teleprompter. The interview subjects didn't see a lens; they saw Eric!

The real beauty of Eric's idea is that it's completely scalable. You don't need two iPads and a teleprompter (although using a teleprompter will provide the best results). If you have an iPad and iPhone, position the iPad as close to the camera lens as possible, and use the iPhone behind the scenes for your half of the video conference. Or reverse them if it makes more sense for your shoot. You're not even limited to iOS devices! You could use an iPhone (or iPad) and a Mac laptop. Any combination of two FaceTime-compatible devices will get you on your way.

If you're thinking of trying Eric's idea on your next shoot, there's one more thing to keep in mind. Version 5 of iOS supports FaceTime only over Wi-Fi. That means you'll need an Internet-connected wireless router on your shoot, or you'll have to upgrade your Apple device to iOS v6, which supports FaceTime over cellular networks (assuming your phone carrier supports it). Either way, make sure you research your location's network options *well before* your shoot.

As it turns out, there was no Wi-Fi network available at Eric's shooting location, so he brought along a Verizon Wireless 4G Wi-Fi Hotspot. His solution worked like a charm, and after a full day of shooting interviews, he even managed to remain below his 5GB monthly data allotment.

I want to thank Eric for sharing his experiences with me. I've used his iPad-based Interrotron setup several times since he first described it to me, and I'm *extremely annoyed* that I didn't think of it first. So, instead, I'll be the one to name it. From this day forward, it shall be known as the *InterroPad*. So there.

To view Eric's work, visit his website at ericjhaase.com, and follow him on twitter (@ericjhaase). You can visit the Imagine 300 website at imagine300.com to learn more about the great work they're doing to provide kids with a well-rounded education.

CAMERA CALCULATIONS

Sit back, close your eyes (figuratively speaking), and imagine a young cinematographer in 1963 stepping out of his chrome-sided Ford Galaxy and into his homemade time machine. In one hand, he clutches a jumbled stack of paper scraps that includes old depth-of-field charts, exposure graphs, and hand-drawn lens calculations. He rotates a dial to "2013" and punches a large button

Eric's website
ericjhaase.com

Eric's twitter
@ericjhaase

Imagine 300
imagine300.com

labeled LAUNCH. The machine emits a blinding light, drones mechanically, and disappears in a cloud of improbability.

He emerges from the rematerialized, ooze-covered contraption and spots you standing on set next to your camera holding your iPhone. He approaches slowly, gazing in amazement at the technological marvel in your hand. He looks down at his disorganized bundle of hand drawn calculations and formulas and then back to your iPhone.

Eventually, he says, "Wow."

Thanks to the fantastic calculation apps described in this section, you can confidently reply, "Yup!"

Wasn't that a great story? No? Well, who asked you? Whatever. Never mind.

pCAM Film+Digital Calculator

pCAM is an award-winning, multifunction calculator for film and video production.

It's also totally absurd.

It provides so many different, vital cinematography-related calculations that it's almost impossible to explain succinctly (**FIGURE 8.12**). It's like trying to describe a supermarket by discussing every item on the shelves.

Making things more difficult is that I don't understand half of what it does. And by *half*, I mean *most*. pCAM is clearly meant for pros and smarty-pantses.

iPad | iPhone

- Thin Man Inc.
- $29.99
- hhhlinks.com/pcam

FIGURE 8.12 I'd show you all the calculations contained in pCAM, but I don't have the page space.

To make things easier, I decided to invite one such pro/smarty-pants to the conversation.

Mark Doering-Powell is a brilliant, two-time Emmy-nominated director of photography whom I first had the pleasure of working with more than a decade ago. As a member of the International Cinematographers Guild, the Television Academy, and the Visual Effects Society, Mark has photographed a wide variety of feature films, television programs, and commercial spots. Certainly with a resume like that, he'll know a thing or two about pCAM.

TAZ: So, Mark, when did you start using pCAM?

MARK: I've been using it since the days of my old Handspring Visor and Palm Tungsten.

TAZ: Whew! Thank goodness you know the app. If you didn't, I'd have to end the interview here. So, do you have any favorite calculations? Side note: I believe that's the first time I've ever asked anyone that question.

MARK: One of pCAM's best features remains its Field-of-View/Angle-of-View calculator (**FIGURE 8.13**). Say you're shooting a head-to-toe shot of an actor. Someone might say, "Put an 8×8 flat behind them." pCAM is a great tool for calculating the exact background dimensions required for any given focal length or aspect ratio. It even illustrates precisely how the background's size must increase when moving it farther away from camera. The Relative Size feature is also very helpful with so many different sensor sizes on the market.

FIGURE 8.13 pCAM's Field-of-View calculator contains information for Angle-of-View as well.

The Color-Correction tool is very useful. It helps you find the exact camera filters required to match an existing color temperature. The Mired Shift tool does the same thing for lighting instruments, providing you with the exact gels needed to match a color temperature.

There are many other tools packed in there such as Running-Time to Length, Screen-Time, Time-Lapse, conversions for Kelvin to Mireds, Footcandles to Lux, and more. Everything is thought out in great detail. For example, in the Focal Length Match tool, you can match two focal lengths using either horizontal or vertical values depending on your aspect ratio. It's very thorough.

TAZ: Has pCAM helped you while working with specific equipment?

MARK: I've used the HMI Safe tool to double-check shutter angles. pCAM tells you which angles/fps will grab full peaks, and not full and half peaks like you'd normally get at 24 frames per second with a 180-degree shutter.

On a recent series we shot in Paris and London, I knew that we'd be shooting 172.8° shutter to get the flicker out of the street lights at 24 fps. The thing is, we now shoot 23.976 fps, so pCAM let me nail down a good starting point more precisely: 172.63° (or 258.94° for some "available night/exts").

TAZ: That's awesome! I have no idea what you just said.

MARK: Also, the Exposure calculator is useful when you're under-caffeinated and need to double-check the stop compensation of various frames per second, shutter angles, and NDs on each of the five plus cameras covering a stunt.

Yeah, I call out a base-stop for all cameras, and I checked it on my fingers and toes, but I've been hurt by mistakes before. Therefore, when I have time, I'll double-check. Plus, I might realize that one camera has too deep or too shallow a final f-stop and make adjustments to the ND or shutter angle.

TAZ: I'm not entirely sure, but I believe you just told me some awesome stuff that I should now pretend I understand. Hey, have I shown you the InterroPad?

My thanks to Mark for reminding me why I'm not qualified to be a cinematographer.

The amazing truth is that Mark and I have barely scratched pCAM's surface. The app includes several other calculators, framing previews, a Siemens Star test pattern, and even an insert slate. Of all the things I don't understand within the app, my favorite is the Underwater Distance calculator. Why? Because it includes an image of a shark (**FIGURE 8.14**).

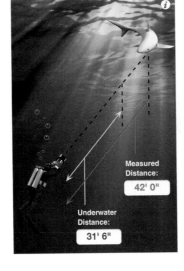

FIGURE 8.14 Shooting under water requires a focus adjustment. pCAM helps you calculate the change, while its background image suggests an imminent shark attack.

Measured Distance:
42' 0"

Underwater Distance:
31' 6"

Mark's website
markdoeringpowell.com

If you are a cinematographer or plan to be one, give pCAM a go…and then explain it to me. If you'd like to view some of Mark's outstanding work, head on over to his website at http://markdoeringpowell.com.

Toland ASC Digital Assistant

Chemical Wedding, the same company that gave us the indispensable Artemis Director's Viewfinder (covered in Chapter 5), teamed up with the American Society of Cinematographers (ASC) and produced one of the most unique and engaging camera calculation apps I've ever seen.

The app covers some of the same ground as pCAM but does so in a *very* different fashion. While pCAM is essentially a collection of individual calculators with shared parameters, Toland provides a virtual representation of your complete photographic system (camera, lenses, filters, shooting speed, and so on) (**FIGURE 8.15**). To get the most out of the app, you must first tell it all about the gear you're using and the format you're shooting. By stepping through a series of nested menus, you can quickly and easily add all the relevant data. You even have the option of adding multiple cameras.

Once Toland knows your setup, it displays *all* of the pertinent information in a lovely, tightly packed, easy-to-navigate interface. With Toland, you don't ask for the answer to a specific question. Rather, you simply make a desired change to a given parameter and instantly see how all other aspects of the system are affected.

TOLAND ASC DIGITAL ASSISTANT

iPad   iPhone

- Chemical Wedding
- $39.99
- hhhlinks.com/msOw

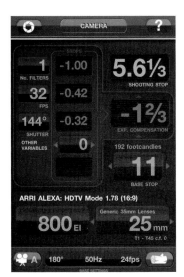

FIGURE 8.15 Everything in Toland is connected. Changes made to one parameter instantly affect all the rest. It's alive!

FIGURE 8.16 Toland's logging screen keeps track of all your vital camera settings. This is especially useful for visual effects teams that may need to digitally re-create your setup.

For example, if you were to switch to a longer lens (by swiping left over the lens size field), the Depth of Field and Field of View displays would instantly update, reflecting the change. You don't have to ask for the calculation. It just does it.

Once you have all of your parameters properly set, tap [image] to switch to the logging screen (**FIGURE 8.16**). From here you can log all of the current settings for each shot. When you've wrapped for the day, you can e-mail a nicely formatted, comprehensive camera log.

Part calculator, part logging system, part living organism, Toland goes well beyond simply supplying data: it helps you understand the connections and interactions between your data.

Ultimately, Toland's unique interface and even more unique methodology won't appeal to everyone. I suspect some filmmakers will dig Toland's kitchen-sink approach, while others will prefer pCAM's individual calculations. Either way, cinematographers win.

In case you're wondering, the app is named after legendary cinematographer Gregg Toland, the man who lensed *Wuthering Heights*, *The Grapes of Wrath*, and his seminal work, the breathtaking *Citizen Kane*.

Speaking of the breathtaking *Citizen Kane*, I have a question. Am I the only film-maker in the world who dislikes *Citizen Kane*? Aside from the gorgeous photography and brilliant work by the art department, it makes me want to scratch my own skin off. In fact, I once traded a copy of it for a six-pack of root beer. You know, I probably shouldn't be telling you all this. I guess it's too late to turn back now. Let's move on.

THE ULTIMATE SLATE

If you poke around the iTunes App Store long enough, you'll find an abundance of two things: apps that generate disturbingly realistic fart sounds and virtual movie slates (also known as markers, clappers, clapboards, clapperboards, clapsticks, and clapper sticks). Let's focus on slates for now and save the fart apps for my follow-up book, *Hand Held Hollywood's Losing Friends with the iPad and iPhone*.

With well over a dozen slate apps to choose from, the first question to ask yourself is, "Do I need *any* of them?" To answer that question, you must first understand the two purposes they serve.

A slate is used to display important logging information that will be filmed at the head of each take. Typically, the second assistant cameraperson (AC) will use a dry-erase marker to write all of the relevant information (such as the scene and take numbers) on the acrylic surface of the slate and then hold it up in front of the lens (**FIGURE 8.17**). As soon as the camera and audio recorder are rolling, the second AC recites the scene and take number for the audio department, then says "marker," and then finally slaps the top hinged portion of the slate closed, creating that loud "clap" sound we all know and love.

On typical film and DSLR productions, sound and picture are recorded separately. Naturally, there needs to be a way to synchronize these elements together in postproduction. That's what the clap sound is for. By lining up the

FIGURE 8.17 An example of a typical slate found on most film and television shoots.

exact frame in which the slate closes with the corresponding clap sound on the audio recording, your picture and sound can be synchronized.

Slate use remained largely unchanged for nearly a century. But you know, a funny thing happened on the way to the future. A company named after a fruit gave us the iPhone and the iPad. As a result, movie slates have been reinvented.

Movie★Slate

As I mentioned, there are *many* movie slate apps in the App Store. Some of them distinguish themselves by including goofy sound effects. Others let you write on them with virtual chalk. Obviously, these are features that will appeal to all professionals. Excuse me. That was a typo. I meant to write "Obviously, these apps are a total waste of time and money."

As far as I'm concerned there's only *one* app that deserves to be called a movie slate, and it's called Movie★Slate®. I'd award it a gold star for its descriptive name, but it appears the developer has already done that.

Compatible with both the iPhone and iPad, Movie★Slate is a professional, feature-packed virtual clapboard that comes from a knowledgeable, reputable, and forward-thinking developer. It's been a longtime favorite of the filmmaking community and was even featured in one of Apple's own iPad television advertisements.

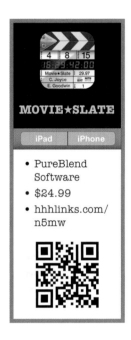

MOVIE★SLATE

| iPad | iPhone |

- PureBlend Software
- $24.99
- hhhlinks.com/ n5mw

To properly explore every feature in this app, I'd have to write a separate book on the subject, which is a bit impractical at the moment since I'm already quite busy writing this one. Instead, I'll give you a tour of the app's highlights. It will be like taking a tram ride around Graceland but without the tram or Graceland.

The first thing you'll notice about Movie★Slate is that it looks just like a traditional movie slate (**FIGURE 8.18**). The app provides editable fields for all the data typically contained on a slate, such as camera roll, scene, take, FPS, Date, Camera ID, and more. To change the contents of any field, just tap it and start typing. Many of the fields can be advanced or rewound simply by swiping up or down. For a little extra pizzazz, you can easily hide the production, director, and DP fields and replace them with your company or show logo.

So, what's up with that timecode display? That, my friend, is the window to the app's true power. If you're not already familiar with timecode, it's a running clock used by cameras and audio recorders to provide a precise means of identifying specific frames, synchronizing media and devices, and calculating durations. Movie★Slate offers several ways in which to input, control, and utilize timecode.

FIGURE 8.18
Movie★Slate mimics traditional slates but adds a whole bag of whiz-bang.

Movie★Slate
movie-slate.com

To see how timecode comes into play, let's step through a basic Movie★Slate workflow. For this example, let's assume you're shooting your project on a timecode-capable camera set to record-run mode (the timecode progresses only while the camera is recording). On a side note, if you're shooting to digital files (rather than tape), you should start by entering your camera's file naming convention into the app's Camera Optics tab. More information can be found on the application's website (http://movie-slate.com).

Before rolling on your first shot, copy your camera's current timecode into Movie★Slate by tapping the app's timecode strip and then punching in the correct numbers on the data entry pop-up window (**FIGURE 8.19**). When you're finished, tap Done while *simultaneously* hitting the record button on your camera. Ideally, the timecode on your slate and the timecode on your camera should be fairly close. Forget getting it exactly right for now. Performing a manual "jam-sync" like this never provides perfect results.

Now, hold your iPad up for the camera, call out the details for the sound department, and then tap the clap sticks at the top of the screen. The virtual clap

FIGURE 8.19 Use the timecode entry pop-up to manually enter your timecode and initiate timecode syncing with other devices.

sticks open, you'll hear a few countdown beeps, and then the virtual sticks will slap shut and you'll hear a loud, simultaneous clap sound. The screen may flash red or freeze depending on the app's settings. Moments later, the app shifts into what it calls the Shot in Progress mode. Here you can enter additional details about the take (**FIGURE 8.20**). For instance, you can rate it, mark it as a circle take (considered one of the best takes), give it a title, add notes or keywords, and more. When the take is done, tap End the Shot. That take is now logged, complete with all the details you've entered along the way. Repeat this process for each take. At any point, you can hop over into the app's History tab to review your shot log and make any necessary changes (**FIGURE 8.21**).

FIGURE 8.20 After marking a shot, Movie★Slate lets you add valuable metadata that will be included in your history log.

FIGURE 8.21 In the History tab, you can manipulate existing shots and export everything for use in multiple nonlinear editors including Final Cut Pro (7 and X), Premiere Pro, and Avid.

If you feel like making things a little easier on yourself, you can set your camera to generate time-of-day timecode (timecode that is always running and is based on the actual time of day). This way, you can manually jam-sync your iPad to your camera once, and it will remain in sync for a while, although it's wise to re-sync every so often. The only reason *not* to use time-of-day mode is if your editing software can't handle timecode breaks. If this paragraph reads like total gibberish, it might be worth spending a little time nuzzled in the user guides for your camera and editing app.

Once your shoot is complete, Movie★Slate can export your shot log in one of multiple formats including HTML, Final Cut Pro 7 XML, Final Cut Pro X XML, Avid ALE, Premiere, and others. Importing the resulting file into your nonlinear editor will create well-organized bins and reference clips with names based on your slate information. Use these reference clips to automatically batch import your footage from tape or to reconnect your media files if you shot to hard drive or memory card. In other words, by matching your camera's timecode (as best you can) while slating with Movie★Slate, your finished clips can be easily imported and automatically organized within your nonlinear editor, saving you an enormous amount of time.

This example worked because the timecode you manually entered into Movie★Slate was pretty darn close to the timecode on the camera. However, some workflows require timecode that is *perfectly* synchronized with a camera, audio recorder, or other external device. In these cases, manually entering time-code will not do. You'll need something more reliable, something more professional. That's where Movie★Slate's Timecode Sync Plugin comes in. Available as a $49.99 in-app purchase, this plug-in adds a bunch of impressive timecode syncing options. For instance, you can use an audio cable to patch your camera's timecode-out port to your iPad's headphone jack (treating it like an LTC-IN port). Using the incoming audio signal, the app can achieve a perfect timecode lock. The cable can be left in to ensure constant accuracy, or it can be pulled out, sending the app into an auto-sync mode that should keep code in sync for hours (assuming the camera's timecode does not stop for any reason).

Another brilliant feature that comes with the Timecode Sync Plugin is the ability to wirelessly transmit timecode and slate data over Wi-Fi or Bluetooth between multiple iOS devices running Movie★Slate. Why is this cool? Imagine shooting a live event with multiple cameras positioned all around your shooting location, too far apart to shoot the same slate. Now imagine each cameraperson having his or her own iOS device running Movie★Slate. The main camera operator's device sends its data over Wi-Fi, allowing the other iOS devices to receive it. Now, each of the other camera operators has his or her own slate displaying the correct, current information (such as scene and take numbers) and synchronized timecode. While each camera is rolling on its respective slate, the master device can trigger a remote clap for all the devices, making it easy to sync everything up in post.

After all that, we've seen only a small percentage of what this app can do. Among the features I don't have the page space to tell you about are tail slates, custom text snippets for quick note taking, test charts and color bars, six additional custom data fields, timecode synchronized audio playback for music videos, using the app as a timecode generator for external gear, an optional Sound Department plug-in to generate outstanding reports for the sound department, and much more.

Movie★Slate is a surprisingly flexible application, capable of accommodating different workflow styles. If you crave customization, this app will certainly satisfy. There are a bounty of options waiting in the app's preferences screen that allow you to alter the slate's appearance and operation. It's clear the developers spent a lot of time with a variety of professional filmmakers throughout the app's development and testing phases. With every new version, the developer continues to expand the app's synching and networking features, while making it even easier to share data among different departments.

So, is using Movie★Slate on an iOS device truly better than using a traditional, physical slate? Yes! And no.

Traditional movie slates (usually made from acrylic, wood, or both) are easy to use, store, and ship. They last for years, don't require charging, and won't get damaged in a rainstorm. They are completely reliable and have been used by pros for much longer than you've been alive. That said, traditional movie slates won't log your footage, synchronize remote cameras, work hand-in-hand with your nonlinear editor, or let you play Cut The Rope during your lunch break.

I've been using Movie★Slate since the day it was released, and I've never regretted it. I've said it on HandHeldHollywood.com, and I'll say it here: Movie★Slate is the Rolls Royce of clapboard apps and one of the best reasons for filmmakers to own an iPad.

TimeCode Buddy

While Movie★Slate offers quite a few methods for syncing timecode, each has its drawbacks.

> Entering timecode manually guarantees inconsistency. I've never seen anyone use manual entry to achieve a perfect timecode lock.

> Jam-syncing timecode from a camera via an audio cable works wonderfully until the cable is removed and the camera's timecode subsequently pauses or changes. Each time that happens, you have to reattach the

TIMECODE BUDDY: WIFI MASTER

iPad   iPhone

- Timecode Systems
- £675 (around $1000)
- timecodebuddy. com

cable and jam-sync Movie★Slate once again. This isn't because of any fault in the app or the iPad. In fact, high-end timecode slates costing thousands of dollars require the same steps to put themselves back in sync. It's just the nature of the beast.

❯ If you jam-sync Movie★Slate to your camera via an audio cable and then remove the cable and make sure your camera's timecode *doesn't* change or pause, Movie★Slate will keep sync quite well. However, it will eventually drift ever so slightly out of sync over the course of the day since it's relying on your iDevice's imperfect internal clock to maintain its sync. It's a *very minor* drift, but it's enough to prevent the code from being 100 percent accurate 100 percent of the time.

I'm happy to report that a new, far superior method has emerged!

Thanks to a partnership between Movie★Slate's developer, PureBlend Software, and Timecode Systems, the makers of an awesome new gizmo called the Timecode Buddy: WiFi Master (**FIGURE 8.22**), your iPad slate can now display accurate timecode at all times! Want to know the best part? The entire setup requires very little setup and practically no effort during your shoot.

The Timecode Buddy: WiFi Master packs a ton of timecode deliciousness into a small, sleek, battery-operated device that easily connects to a professional camera or audio recording device (via its built-in standard shoe mount or optional bracket).

It provides BNC timecode in and out ports, as well as a standard five-pin Lemo connector. It can wirelessly receive and transmit timecode over radio frequency (RF), but more importantly, it can transmit timecode over its own built-in Wi-Fi

FIGURE 8.22 Hey there, little buddy! The Timecode Buddy: WiFi Master receives, generates, and transmits timecode to a variety of devices, including your iPad and iPhone.

network (or another existing Wi-Fi network) to up to 10 iOS devices simultaneously! Think about that for a second…always-accurate timecode floating wirelessly over your entire set via Wi-Fi! Neat!

Topping it all off is the Movie★Slate app, which can automatically and wirelessly sync to the Buddy's timecode feed (**FIGURE 8.23**). You can even use the app to wirelessly configure the Timecode Buddy's settings. Please note that all of this additional functionality requires the Timecode Sync Plugin I mentioned previously.

FIGURE 8.23
Movie★Slate can easily sync with a Timecode Buddy: WiFi Master.

Because it can receive timecode as well as transmit it, the Timecode Buddy can be used in a wide variety of production scenarios. For instance, to keep multiple DSLR cameras in sync with an audio recording, have your Buddy provide timecode to your audio recorder while simultaneously transmitting it to multiple iPhones and iPads, each being used to slate a different DSLR camera. What if you want to sync a consumer camera to a professional camera? No problem. Just attach the Buddy to your professional camera's timecode out port, and have it transmit that code to an iPad slate that's being shot by the consumer camera. Bottom line, the Timecode Buddy: WiFi Master is built to be flexible.

Fortunately, the Timecode Buddy is a breeze to set up. It provides easy-to-navigate menus on its bright blue display, and if you ever get lost, the Buddy hardware contains a complete manual that can be accessed with any Wi-Fi connected web browser!

Costing around $1000, the Timecode Buddy: WiFi Master is clearly targeting professional filmmakers. For those of us who regularly require dependable and unflappable timecode, it's a small price to pay.

T-Slate

Despite the industry's newfound love of Movie★Slate and its ability to wirelessly receive 100 percent accurate timecode, I still hear two gripes from filmmakers.

"That clap is too quiet!"

The problem isn't with the app, it's with the iPad itself. As I mentioned earlier, one of the slate's primary functions is to provide visual and *audible* cues that can be used to synchronize picture and sound in postproduction. However, when using an iPad, the clap sound is never quite loud or crisp enough to make the sound department happy. The iPad speaker simply can't replicate the loud clap created by a traditional clapboard.

"How do we know if it's really accurate? I mean really, *really* accurate."

T-SLATE

iPad iPhone

- ikan International Corp.
- $99.95
- ikancorp.com

FIGURE 8.24 The T-Slate looks (and operates) like any other acrylic and wood slate, but looks can be deceiving.

Because of the lack of tangible, physical sticks slapping shut, there have been concerns about the timing accuracy of the replicated "clap" sound. Filmmakers have questioned whether the digital sound always falls on the correct frame *without fail*. This likely comes from years of doing things one way and not feeling terribly comfortable with change.

These two gripes aside, there's one more important issue most people seem to forget about. There's no denying that using your iPad as a virtual movie slate is awesome. Would you like to know what is significantly less awesome? Using your iPad as a virtual movie slate only to have its battery conk out right before the cameras roll.

Thanks to the T-Slate (**FIGURE 8.24**), all three of these issues have vaporized.

At first glance, the T-Slate ($99.95) appears to be nothing special—just another acrylic and wood clapperboard. But upon closer inspection, you might notice what looks like a manufacturing mistake—a long, thin slot right under the wooden clapsticks. Make no mistake, that mistake is no mistake! It's part of a very clever design that can transform this fully functional, traditional slate into an iPad slate.

Genius Pro
zoogue.com

To initiate this metamorphosis, you'll need any iPad, along with a high-quality case that holds your iPad snugly and features a flip-over cover. Apple's Smart Covers won't work since they disconnect from the tablet with a gentle tug. There are plenty of swell options available from the usual suspects like Incase, Griffin, and Targus. My personal favorite is the $50, black-leather Genius Pro from ZooGue (http://zoogue.com).

FIGURE 8.25 The T-Slate instantly transforms into a digital clapboard the moment you attach your iPad.

With your iPad secure in its case, flip open the cover and slide it through the long slot at the top of the clapboard, and then let your iPad hang down over the front. If your case has any sort of elastic strap or band, wrap it around the back of the T-Slate to secure the iPad in position (**FIGURE 8.25**). Launch the Movie★Slate app, and *presto*, instant iPad slate! Now, when you slate a shot and slap the T-Slate's sticks shut, the app automatically detects the clap and begins to log the shot at the current timecode, just as if you tapped the virtual sticks on-screen.

You might be wondering how the app knows when the physical clapsticks have shut. Thanks to a bit of spectacular engineering, Movie★Slate detects the closure by waiting for a loud sound (picked up by the iPad's built-in microphone) and a simultaneous, sudden vibration (picked up by the iPad's built-in motion sensors). Granted, this is not a perfect solution since it can lead to a few false triggers, but it's still pretty amazing.

When clapping the T-Slate's real sticks, the sound department will have no trouble recording a full-volume smack, and editors will be able to sync up the recording with the visual reference of the physical sticks slamming shut. All this, and the iPad is still recording accurate logs that can be used in postproduction.

If you find yourself in a situation that makes iPad use impractical or if your battery simply dies, just remove the iPad from the T-Slate, and you're right back where you started: a traditional, standard movie slate, totally capable of getting the job done.

Denecke Slate

There's another iPad slate frame currently in development; however, I suspect it won't be available when this book hits the shelves. So, why am I bothering to include it? Because of the company that's developing it!

Denecke
denecke.com

Denecke (http://denecke.com) is one of the most respected names in clapboard creation. It produces a line of electronic "smart slates" that feature digital timecode displays like the one found in Movie★Slate. Now, Denecke is making the move into tablet territory by developing an iPad clapper frame for use with Movie★Slate!

The Denecke frame will contain a small circuit board that can generate timecode or jam-sync code from an external source via a standard five-pin Lemo connector. The circuit board will feature Denecke's temperature compensated crystal (TCXL) to keep its timecode rock solid. Along the same lines, the frame will connect to the iPad's docking port. This implies that it will yield a more precise clap trigger than the one obtained using the sound and motion detection method.

From what I hear, Denecke is still experimenting with different construction materials. I'm sure they're doing their best to keep the price down while maintaining their high standards.

All that said, this product is still being developed. So, there's a decent chance that everything I just told you is now wrong. You're welcome.

Keep an eye on Denecke's website and HandHeldHollywood.com for updates!

Where's the MamboFrame?

Before Denecke's iPad frame became the subject of rumor and speculation, and prior to the T-Slate bursting onto the scene, there was the MamboFrame (FIGURE 8.26). Created by Pomfort, a German company known for their outstanding film production software, the MamboFrame made headlines for finally bridging the gap between virtual slates and traditional hardware.

Built from PMMA lexiglass and anodized aluminum, the $479 MamboFrame was an incredibly rugged iPad slate frame built to withstand the rigors of film production. Unlike the T-Slate, you couldn't just slide your iPad in and out of this monster. You had to use the included hex wrench just to open the frame.

Pomfort was integral to the creation and early implementation of the sound and motion detection technology now living in the Movie★Slate app. There's no denying that they started the ball rolling and paved the way for similar slates. It's disappointing to see them depart from an arena they helped create.

FIGURE 8.26 Pomfort's MamboFrame was the first iPad slate frame on the market. It's solid, sturdy, sexy, and sad. Why sad? Because it's no longer being made.

You might be able to track down a MamboFrame by combing filmmaker websites, but I suspect that anyone lucky enough to have one of these bad boys will most likely be hanging onto it. I won't be giving up mine anytime soon, so don't even ask.

QRSlate

For years, Movie★Slate has dominated the virtual slate landscape, and with good reason. While that app's status is not likely to change any time soon, there's another slate app that has been turning quite a few heads, including mine.

When you launch QRSlate, it has the appearance of a stripped-down version of Movie★Slate (**FIGURE 8.27**). It displays all the standard information you'd expect to find on a slate, such as camera roll, sound roll, scene number, take number, and more, along with a time-of-day timecode display.

While the app provides some basic automation, such as auto-incrementing take numbers, QRSlate won't sync with external timecode sources or allow you to add your own metadata fields. It won't let you customize its appearance and has no options for generating sound department reports. Furthermore, it won't play nice with any external clapboard frames.

If it can't do any of these things, why is QRSlate so impressive? Because it offers one totally unique feature, and it's a show-stopper.

When you hold your iPhone or iPad in front of the camera and then tap the virtual slate's virtual clapsticks, your device's screen is momentarily filled by

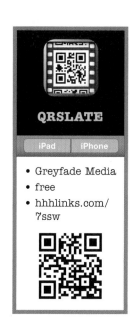

QRSLATE

iPad | iPhone

- Greyfade Media
- free
- hhhlinks.com/ 7ssw

FIGURE 8.27 QRSlate's simple interface hides a very impressive trick.

FIGURE 8.28 Every time you mark a shot, QRSlate fills the frame with a unique QR code to be identified later by the QRSlate Desktop software on your Mac.

a large QR code (those square, seemingly random code boxes that are now popping up on everything from movie posters to soda cans and even in the margins of certain iOS filmmaking books) (**FIGURE 8.28**). After the QR code disappears, the app emits a loud beep (its version of a clap sound) and then displays its Take Editor, in which you can input additional information about your shot, including comments, circled takes, markers, and more. After entering the desired data, the shot is logged, and you're returned to the main slate screen. When your shoot has wrapped, you can e-mail a completed log.

It all seems perfectly normal, except for that whole QR code thing. Speaking of the whole QR code thing, what was that whole QR code thing about?

QRSlate has a companion app for the Mac platform called QRSlate Desktop Importer. After importing all your movie files (only QuickTime videos are supported as I write this) and the QRSlate log file into the desktop app, it quickly analyzes everything, automatically identifying the appearance of any QR codes! Every time the app discovers a code, it recognizes it as the start of a new shot. The app deciphers the slate information contained within the code, blends it with the metadata you entered into your log, and assigns it all to the newly found shot. An app that reads QR codes from footage? I don't know about you, but that blows my mind.

Once your scan has been completed, you can export XML and AFE files that are compatible with Final Cut 7, Final Cut X, Premiere Pro, and Avid Media Composer. Simply import the appropriate file into your nonlinear editor of choice, and then watch as your clips magically appear, *presorted by scene and take number*! All of your metadata and markers show up as well. As a result of all this magnificent automation, you've just organized your edit, avoided hours of additional work, and saved a wad of cash. You've also put an assistant editor out of work. I hope you're happy.

Because the desktop app is scanning your footage for codes, it doesn't require timecode to perform its magic. This means you can use QRSlate with cameras that don't offer native timecode functionality, including most DSLRs. Naturally, if you're recording your audio to a separate device and plan to sync in post, you'll still benefit from the app's sync beep and simultaneous screen flash.

QRSlate for iPhone and iPad is free, but the Mac companion app will run you $49.99 (http://hhhlinks.com/0dgy). Yes, it's a tad pricey but not nearly as expensive as the assistant editor whose job you obliterated. Shame on you.

QRSlate for Mac
hhhlinks.com/0dgy

FIELD MONITORS AND INSTANT DAILIES

Since launching HandHeldHollywood.com, one question has percolated up through my inbox more than any other: "Can I use my iPhone or iPad as a wireless field monitor for my camera?" It's a perfectly reasonable question, and one that I had been asking since the day I first held an iPhone. After all, iOS devices feature beautiful screens and an inherent ability to play back full-screen videos with ease. Sadly, even with all of Apple's cutting-edge technology and Elfin magic, iOS devices simply couldn't be used as wireless field monitors.

But grab your calendar and circle 2010, because that was the year everything changed. It was the year director Kevin Smith was booted from a plane for taking up too many seats. It was the year Ke$ha assaulted a defenseless nation with "Tik Tok." And, it was the year that a company called Teradek unveiled an amazing little gizmo called the Cube.

TERACENTRAL APP

iPad   iPhone

- Teradek
- free
- hhhlinks.com/ ougi

The Cube

Put simply, the Cube (**FIGURE 8.29**) is a camera-mounted video encoder that is capable of wirelessly transmitting a video signal from your camera directly to your iPhone or iPad running the free TeraCentral app, turning it into a wireless field monitor (with a tiny, tolerable lag). Hooray!

Equally impressive is a feature called Remote Proxy Recording. While your camera is recording your shot, the Cube is simultaneously encoding the camera's

THE CUBE

iPad | iPhone

- Teradek
- $1000+
- teradek.com

FIGURE 8.29 Adding the Teradek Cube to your camera rig will record proxy movies to a networked computer and turn your iOS device into a wireless field monitor.

Light Iron
lightiron.com

LIVE PLAY

iPad | iPhone

- Light Iron Digital
- $9.99
- hhhlinks.com/u5qv

output and saving an h.264 QuickTime movie to a wirelessly networked computer. This means you now have instant, wireless access to your completed shots. You can play them back from the computer or from any properly configured iOS device on the same network. It's like getting instant dailies…or what I shall now refer to as *instanties*.

Since those instanties are being saved to a networked computer, you could, in theory, have someone assembling a first cut on that computer *while you're still shooting*! I imagine there would be technical issues to work out, but I think it's worth a try.

If you want to take your on-set instanties to the next level, get your hands on LIVE PLAY, a $10 app from Light Iron that works hand-in-hand with the Cube and lets multiple crew members independently view, share, tag, and comment on video clips directly from their iPads (**FIGURE 8.30**). To make this work, you'll need to download the free LIVE PLAY Video Server app from Light Iron's website (http://lightiron.com) and install it on the same computer that's being accessed by the Cube. Currently, the LIVE PLAY Video Server app is Mac compatible only.

If you're already planning on spending a grand or more on a Cube, there's no reason not to try LIVE PLAY on your next shoot. It's a powerful system that can easily scale to any size production. I highly recommend it to all Cube owners.

Since it's not truly relevant in an iOS filmmaking book, I won't bother mentioning the Cube's ability to record proxy movies directly to SD memory cards or its support of multiple Internet transport protocols (RTMP, RTP/RTSP, RTP Push, MPEG-TS, and HTTP Live Streaming) and its related ability to stream your live

FIGURE 8.30 Using LIVE PLAY on your iPad, you can wirelessly add and share important metadata after every shot. (Screenshot courtesy of Light Iron Digital, LLC.)

video signal to sites like UStream, Livestream, Justin.TV, and others. Nope. I'm not going to mention any of that stuff.

Since its initial release, the Cube has received a significant update and has been placed at the center of an entire product line. As I write this, there are eight different models that range in price from $1000 to $2000, depending on the desired networking options (Ethernet, Wi-Fi, or cellular modem) and video connection type (HDMI, HD-SDI, or composite). Some of the Cube's features are available only with certain camera models. Before plunking down your hard-earned dough, make sure you have a camera that can take full advantage of the Cube's awesomeness.

DSLR Camera Remote HD

Let's have a quick reality check. The Cube is expensive. While I believe it's worth every penny, I imagine most indie filmmakers would wince at the idea of dropping over $1000 for the luxury of turning an iPad into a field monitor. If you count yourself among the wincing, I have another possible solution, and this one will cost you only $25.

DSLR Camera Remote HD is an iPad app that can wirelessly connect to and control your DSLR camera (FIGURE 8.31). While primarily intended for still photographers, the app supports video mode on several Canon cameras (including my personal favorites, the 5D MkII and the 60D) as well as a few

DSLR CAMERA REMOTE HD

iPad   iPhone

- onOne Software
- $24.99
- hhhlinks.com/i6n1

FIGURE 8.31 DSLR Camera Remote wirelessly transmits your DSLR's video feed straight to your iPad. You can even start and stop recording remotely.

OnOne Software
ononesoftware.com

DSLR CAMERA REMOTE

iPad   iPhone

- onOne Software
- $9.99
- hhhlinks.com/luc2

Nikon cameras. OnOne Software, the app's developer, provides a complete list of compatible cameras on its website (http://ononesoftware.com).

To use the app, not only must you be shooting on a compatible camera, but you must also have a Mac or Windows machine connected to your camera via USB, on the same Wi-Fi network as your iPad, and running the free DSLR Camera Remote Server software (available from the developer's website). With the server app running on your desktop, launch DSLR Camera Remote on your iPad. After connecting the two, you will now be able to see your DSLR camera's live video feed on your iPad!

Not only can you view the camera's feed, but you can start and stop recording from your tablet's touch screen. Want more good news? By default, every time you end a shot, the free server app automatically downloads each new video file from the camera straight to your computer's hard drive. Once again, you have instant dailies (or *instanties*), ready for editing.

This is *far* from a perfect solution. The live frame rate is very slow, the long lag time can be frustrating, and your camera must remain tethered to your computer's USB port at all times. But, hey, did I mention this solution costs only $25?! It costs even less ($10) if you opt to go with the iPhone version of the app!

If you're already using a compatible camera and you already own a Mac or Windows laptop and you can deal with the app's shortcomings, DSLR Camera Remote will be a useful addition to your camera setup.

LET THERE BE LIGHT

Filmmakers have a love/hate/love relationship with light.

When we're not positioning silks to smooth out harsh shadows or mounting flags to block distracting reflections, we're tweaking kickers to define our subjects and chasing orange glows revealed during golden hour. It seems like 75 percent of our time is spent measuring, tracking, calculating, mixing, reflecting, and controlling light.

I believe iOS developers understand this complex and evolving relationship. Why else would there be so many fantastic light-related apps in the App Store?

Pocket Light Meter

A light meter is arguably one of the most essential gizmos used in film production (**FIGURE 8.32**). It quickly measures the amount of light hitting a subject or scene and suggests an f-stop for your lens that will help your camera capture the best possible exposure. Without a light meter, filmmakers run the risk of under- or overexposing their footage.

Naturally, this becomes an issue only when shooting with professional equipment, since most consumer cameras contain auto-exposure circuitry and typically don't provide many controls for aperture settings. Let's take this scenario a little further. If you're already shooting with professional gear, then you are most likely a professional filmmaker who is most likely already using a professional

POCKET LIGHT METER

iPad | iPhone

- Nuwaste Studios
- free
- hhhlinks.com/w4q5

FIGURE 8.32 I've been using my trusty Minolta Auto Meter IV F for years.

light meter. That leads us to this perfectly logical question: If the only people who truly need light meters are already using professional light meters, who would actually benefit from having a light meter app on their iPhone?

The way I see it, there are three distinct audiences for a light meter app.

> Film students and studious amateurs who want to learn more about light meters, f-stops, and proper exposure. After all, knowledge = power, and power turns on lights, and lights require proper exposure. See what I did there?

> Professional filmmakers who like the idea of having a backup meter with them at all times.

> Anyone who'd rather spend $0 on a light meter app as opposed to $200 on a professional light meter.

If you fall into any of these three groups, place a bookmark on this page and go download Pocket Light Meter. This clever, simple-to-use, ad-supported app will convert your humble iPhone into a fully functioning light meter for the low, low cost of nada, zip, zero. At that price, why wouldn't you grab it?

Before I get into the app's operation, I think a light meter overview is in order. If you already understand the basic differences between the three most common types of meters, feel free to skip ahead. If you don't, consider these next few paragraphs the world's least expensive film school.

> An *incident light meter* measures the amount of light falling directly onto your subject. These meters typically provide the most accurate measurements since their readings are taken right in front of (or next to) your subject.

> A *reflected light meter* measures the total amount of light being reflected back from your subject or scene. These meters provide very general readings that don't take specific subjects into account. Most consumer-grade cameras utilize this type of meter.

> A *spot meter* is a variation of a reflected light meter. Rather than measuring the light reflecting off an entire scene, a spot meter measures the light reflecting off a small and specific portion of your frame. For this reason, it's able to provide greater accuracy when metering your subjects. Though not as accurate as an incident meter, professionals use spot meters all the time. They are especially handy in situations where using an incident meter is impractical (like metering a distant subject).

The Pocket Light Meter app is essentially a virtual spot meter, and it can be surprisingly accurate (**FIGURE 8.33**). Here's how it works.

 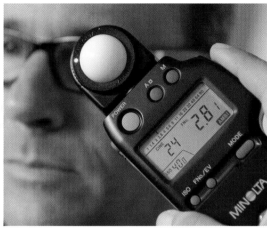

FIGURE 8.33 While not 100 percent accurate, Pocket Light Meter's readings are close enough for many situations.

Like any light meter, you begin by dialing in your ASA (the speed of the film stock you're shooting on, or the relative setting in your digital camera) and your shutter speed, which is typically double your intended frame rate. For example, if you were shooting 24fps (frames per second), you'd set your shutter speed to 48. That might be tough at first, since the app's shutter speed dial doesn't provide 48 as an option. Why not?

By default, the app is set up for use on a photo shoot and doesn't display film- and video-related shutter speeds. A quick visit to the app's settings page reveals a toggle switch labeled "Cinematic Speeds." Flip it on to add 48 and other film-related choices to the shutter speed dial.

With your numbers dialed in, all that's left to do is take a reading. Stand next to your camera, point your iPhone at your scene, and tap directly on the subject you want to meter. Within seconds, Pocket Light Meter displays your target f-stop. Set your lens to the indicated f-stop and celebrate a job well done. Your selected subject should now be perfectly exposed.

Pocket Light Meter can also be used to observe differences between multiple light levels that may exist within your frame. For example, let's say you're lighting a green screen for visual effects work. Ideally, a green screen should be evenly lit across its entire surface, making the job of removing it in postproduction that much easier. Use Pocket Light Meter to double-check your levels at various points on the green screen, and relight when inconsistencies are found.

While first learning to use Pocket Light Meter, I compared its results to those from my Minolta Auto Meter IV F, the light meter I've been using and trusting for years. Much to my surprise, Pocket Light Meter consistently matched my Minolta or came within one stop. While I don't suggest relying on the app completely, I do feel it's accurate enough for basic setups.

Wait. Stop. Let's take a brief moment to ponder how wondrous this all is. You can have a free, accurate light meter with you at all times…on your cell phone! Your *cell phone*. That's insane! OK, pondering over. Let's get back to the book.

If you find Pocket Light Meter useful and feel like showing the developer a little love, I urge you to make one of two *optional* in-app purchases. For $0.99 you can remove all the ads. For $4.99 you can remove the ads and buy the developer a pint of beer! Why didn't I think of that? Note to self: Include a beer-buying button in my next book.

Helios Sun Position Calculator

HELIOS SUN POSITION CALCULATOR

iPad   **iPhone**

- Chemical Wedding
- $29.99
- hhhlinks.com/wa2o

Any time you're facing an outdoor shoot, you need to plan for the constantly changing character of sunlight. To truly maximize your location's natural illumination while avoiding difficult lighting situations, you'll need to know the sun's exact path, elevation, and angle. More importantly, you'll need a way to predict how those details will change throughout the course of your shoot day. What you need is a sun position calculator!

While there are several such calculators residing in the App Store, my long-time favorite is Helios (**FIGURE 8.34**). This iPhone app presents its data within six distinct and graphically rich modes.

> The Heliometer indicates the sun's direction on a compass dial. This view also provides information about the sun's elevation and the lengths of shadows its light will produce.

> The Virtual Sun View turns your iPhone into an augmented reality super scope, which is a fancy way to say that it overlays the sun's path directly over a live feed from your iPhone's camera (**FIGURE 8.35**). As you reposition and rotate your iPhone, the app recognizes the change and instantly updates the display. It's like looking through a window in time. Simply awesome! This is my favorite view by far, and the one I really enjoy sharing with other filmmakers while on set. What can I say, I'm a sucker for "oooohs" and "ahhhs."

> The Map View is extremely practical and easy to understand at a glance. It displays the direction of the sun over a map of the shooting location.

> The Sky View provides a representation of the sun's path across the sky. Of all the views in the app, this is the one I have the most difficulty with. No idea why. Thank goodness there's the Virtual Sun View. Did I mention how much I love that view?

FIGURE 8.34 The Heliometer is just one of several useful (and shiny) calculators within Helios.

FIGURE 8.35 The Virtual Sun View transforms your iPhone's camera into a window to the future.

> The Inclinometer helps you determine when the sun will arrive at a given elevation. For instance, if you need to determine when you'll lose the sun behind a nearby building, the inclinometer will help you find your answer.

> The Compass will display the sun's *azimuth*, which is the horizontal angle between magnetic north and the sun. While it may not be as exotic as the Inclinometer, it is equally useful.

Naturally, you don't *need* an app like Helios to predict the sun's path. You could just stare at the sun for a year, from every location on earth, while taking copious notes. However, it's very likely that you'd be totally blind by the time those notes would come in handy. Therefore, I recommend sticking with Helios.

Let's Light with iPads! Yes, Really.

Want to hear a crazy idea? Flavored thermometers! Want to hear another crazy idea? Using your iPad as a lighting source! Think it can't be done? Meet Jesse Rosten, a Northern California–based filmmaker who's as crazy as he is talented…and he's very talented.

Late one night while unable to sleep, Jesse fumbled for his iPad, clicked it on, and was temporarily blinded by the tablet's overwhelming illumination. At that moment, when most people would cover their eyes and shout obscenities, Jesse hopped out of bed and grabbed his light meter. After taking a reading, he was convinced he had found a viable light source.

Knowing full well that lighting a scene with iPads is completely absurd, totally impractical, and ridiculously expensive, Jessie decided to try it anyway, if for no other reason than to flex his creative muscle. He collected eight additional iPads from friends (giving him a total of nine) and mounted them in sets of three to sheets of plywood small enough to be portable. With his home-made iPad light fixtures ready to go and his friends willing to help out, Jesse set up a test shoot (**FIGURE 8.36**).

The results were surprisingly spectacular (**FIGURE 8.37**)!

Jesse's website
jesserosten.com

Jesse wrote about these iPad lighting escapades on his blog and even created a fun behind-the-scenes video. You can check out both, along with his other work (including his celebrated mock commercial for Adobé Fotoshop) on his website at http://jesserosten.com.

While Jesse chose to test his theory with a photo shoot, there's no reason it wouldn't have worked just as well if he were shooting video. Admittedly, I have yet to try this experiment myself, largely because I don't have eight friends willing to let me mount their iPads to sheets of plywood. I can't say I blame them.

However, I have used my iPad and iPhone as small fill lights when shooting close-ups in extremely dark environments. On one occasion, I even used my iPad as a reflection source for an *extreme* close-up on an actor's eye. For that shot, I loaded my iPad with various video clips of fire and then placed it directly under my actor's nose. The flames reflected in the actor's eyeball and made it appear as though he were closely observing a roaring fire. Granted, this effect could have easily been achieved in postproduction, but where's the fun in that?!

FIGURE 8.36 Jesse and his team use nothing but iPads to light their model.

FIGURE 8.37 Just one of the many beautiful photos Jesse snapped during his iPad-illuminated shoot.

Photo Soft Box Pro

If Jesse's story inspired you and you'd like to try using an iOS device as a lighting source, believe it or not, there's an app for that.

Photo Soft Box Pro provides a useful sets of tools for customizing the colors and patterns being displayed on your iOS device's screen. By fine-tuning the content on your display, you can achieve some pretty interesting and artistic results. Need to add a little warmth to your shot? Dial up the orange. Need to add some detail to a reflection? Load up a preset pattern, and position your device next to your subject. Need an interesting surface on which to shoot a close-up of your product? Pick a unique texture, and turn your tablet into a customized, illuminated tabletop.

While you can achieve the same results without this app, it offers speed and convenience that will be appreciated when working under stress, and let's face it, if you're using an iOS device as a light source, you're probably already working under stress.

Photo Soft Box Pro HD is a universal app that works on both iPhone and iPad (FIGURE 8.38), and it can be remotely controlled via Photo Soft Box Pro Remote, another app by the same developer.

PHOTO SOFT
BOX PRO

iPad   iPhone

- Light Paint Pro
- $2.99
- hhhlinks.com/vak5

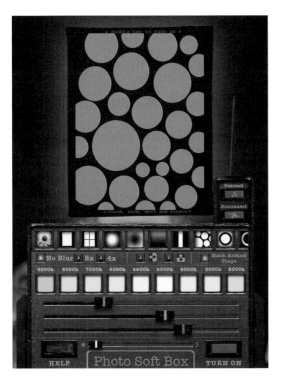

FIGURE 8.38 Photo Soft Box Pro HD can generate a wide variety of colors, patterns, and confused looks from spectators.

THE KICK PLUS

- Rift Labs
- Around $180+
- riftlabs.com

The Kick Plus

The most obvious drawback of using your iOS device as a light source is its limited output. It can get only so bright, and that's usually not bright enough. If only there were a small, powerful, and portable LED lighting instrument that could be *remotely controlled* by your iOS device. Oh wait, there is, and it's called the Kick Plus (**FIGURE 8.39**).

Slightly larger than an iPhone, the Kick Plus is a battery-operated, Wi-Fi connected LED light source that can be wirelessly controlled and programmed via your iPhone running the free companion Kick app. The Kick Plus has a lower-cost sibling called the Kick Basic. It lacks nearly all of the awesome features I'm about to describe and should be ignored…unless you are allergic to awesome features, in which case, the Kick Basic should be on your Christmas list.

Naturally, the Kick Plus can emit straight white light. From there, you can use the app to add warmth to the light or cool it down. In fact, you can pick any color you want from the app's color picker. Nice, right? We're just getting started!

The Kick Plus really begins to shine once you engage its animation features. There are several built-in effects, including Rainbow, Strobe, and Fire. Imagine being able to quickly illuminate your subject with the animated bursts of a lightning storm! Normally, you'd have to set up a complex system of dimmers and

FIGURE 8.39 A 3D rendering of what the Kick will look like once it goes into production.

flags to achieve the same results. The Kick's animated lighting features will save you a ton of time while helping you attain dramatic results.

Still not impressed? Wow, you really are a tough audience. OK, how about this?

Using the Kick's iPhone app, you can load up any video clip and then pick any spot on your device's screen as a color source. As the movie plays back, the Kick's color will animate based on the changing color in the movie! There are a few more bells and whistles packed into the Kick Plus, but I'll let you discover those on your own.

Like many innovative iOS filmmaking gizmos, the Kick light began its march toward fruition with a fundraising campaign on Kickstarter.com (http://hhhlinks. com/50q5). Rift Labs, the Kick's developer, needed $115,000 in order to move the Kick into production, but its Kickstarter campaign pulled in an astounding $210,597! As it turns out, this was an idea that appealed to a *lot* of filmmakers, including myself.

Based on the original shipping estimates, I'm hoping the device will be available by the time you read this. If it hasn't hit the shelves yet, it should be released in the very near future. Keep an eye on the Rift Labs website and on HandHeldHollywood.com for details.

The Kick on Kickstarter
hhhlinks.com/50q5

Hand Held Hollywood
handheldhollywood.com

PART THREE

POSTPRODUCTION

AND

BEYOND

CHAPTER 9

FROM MESS TO MASTERPIECE

When the cameras stop rolling, it can mean only one of three things.

> The police shut down your production after you attempted to shoot an unpermitted action sequence inside your local Ikea's dishware department.

> You ran out of coffee on the craft service table (an unforgivable sin during production).

> You've finished your shoot, and you're ready for postproduction!

In this chapter, we'll be looking at apps that can transform your iPhone and iPad into multitalented postproduction phenoms, capable of correcting your color, editing your scenes, sculpting your sound, and bringing it all together.

Whoa, that's a lot! We better get started.

IMPORTING FOOTAGE

As you'll soon see, iOS devices are uniquely capable of creatively postprocessing all the footage they've captured. What you may not realize is that these same devices can also manipulate footage that has been shot on *other* equipment (such as video cameras, still cameras with video modes, and even other iOS devices). All you need to do is import the footage. Here's how.

From iPhone to iPad

If you're lucky enough to have access to both an iPhone *and* an iPad, here's a great way to maximize the combo. Since your iPhone has better optics, use it to shoot your video (using one of the killer camera apps I mentioned in Chapter 6). When you're done, transfer that footage to your iPad and take advantage of its big-ol' screen during postproduction.

Transferring footage from one device to another is a piece of cake. If you have a computer at your disposal, begin by importing your footage from your iOS device into iPhoto on a Mac or Adobe Elements (or Adobe Album) on a Windows machine. Then, follow the numbered steps outlined in "From a Computer to iPad or iPhone" later in this section. Easy peazy.

Don't want to use a computer? No problem! All you need is Apple's Camera Connection Kit (the set of two adapters I mentioned in Chapters 1 and 4) and the 30-pin to USB cable that came with your iPhone or iPad. If you are using an iPhone 5, or any Lightning-compatible iOS device, you'll need a Lighting-to-USB cable instead.

After shooting your footage, connect the cable to your iPhone, and attach the USB end to your iPad with the help of the Connection Kit USB adapter. Your iPad should instantly launch the Photos app and display all the media currently living in your iPhone's camera roll (**FIGURE 9.1**). If you want to import everything to your iPad, just tap Import at the bottom of the screen. To be more selective, tap the items you want to transfer, and then tap Import .

After your footage has been transferred, it will appear inside your iPad's All Imported album where it can be accessed by the postproduction apps discussed in this chapter.

From a Video Camera to iPad

I have some good news and bad news. Which would you like to hear first? Good news? Excellent choice.

FIGURE 9.1 Using Apple's Camera Connection Kit, you can transfer videos from an iPhone to an iPad.

Using Apple's Camera Connection Kit, you can import footage from compatible video cameras straight into your iPad. To perform the transfer, first attach your video camera (or video-capable still camera) to your iPad using your camera's USB cable, along with the USB adapter found in Apple's Camera Connection Kit. From there, simply follow the same steps I outlined in "From iPhone to iPad."

Working this way practically eliminates the need for a desktop computer when creating small projects with limited amounts of footage.

Ready for the bad news?

Not all video cameras are compatible with iOS and the Camera Connection Kit. Worse yet, I don't know of a single website that maintains a list of compatible cameras, not even Apple.com. Since there are hundreds of consumer and professional cameras on the market (with more arriving weekly), it seems absurd for me to try to tell you which are compatible and which aren't. Instead, I'll pass along the technical specifications that seem to work best, and *then* I'll mention a handful of cameras that have been used successfully in the past.

Forget importing clips from any camera that records in the popular AVCHD format. iPads prefer videos encoded with h.264, Motion-JPEG, or MPEG-4. These files typically have an .m4v, .mp4, or .mov extension, but not always. And, not all files with these extensions are automatically compatible.

Making matters worse, some cameras record audio in 44.1 kHz, while others record in 48 kHz. It seems that iPads prefer 44.1 kHz, but people have argued both sides of this topic, most likely because different people have had different experiences with different cameras on different versions of iOS.

Some cameras can shoot compatible files only in standard definition, even though they're capable of shooting HD video as well. Other cameras that *seem* incompatible at first may offer the ability to switch recording modes. Hint: Look for *Motion-JPEG* in your camera's menu.

If all this weren't enough to make your head spin, allow me to twirl it like a top. Even after you've successfully imported some footage into the Photos app on your iPad, it may not load properly into other apps like iMovie.

All of these factors seem to vary from company to company, from camera to camera, and from day to day. Good times!

I've had success with my Canon 60D and Nikon D90. Other iPad owners have reported positive experiences with the GoPro Hero2, the Samsung DualView TL220, the Panasonic GH1 & Lumix DMC-GF2, the Canon PowerShot S100 & IXUS 220 HS, and the Flip Mino HD & Ultra.

Don't take that list as gospel! If you're considering the purchase of a video camera (or video-capable still camera) with the intention of transferring its footage to your iPad, *make sure you try before you buy*. The same is true if you're thinking of grabbing Apple's Camera Connection Kit for use with your existing camera. Take your iPad, camera, and dock cable into an Apple Store (or Apple reseller) and ask whether they'll let you try the Connection Kit's USB adapter. If it doesn't work, you've just saved $29! Go buy yourself something pretty.

From a Computer to iPad or iPhone

Before describing the steps involved with moving footage from your computer to your iOS device, let's look at *why* you might want to do this in the first place.

As you already know, iOS devices are *extremely* compact, even more so than the smallest, lightest laptops. By transferring your raw footage to your iPhone or iPad, postproduction becomes portable. Not long ago, I watched a woman edit a video project on her iPhone, with *one* hand, while *standing* on the subway!

Before you ask, yes, I offered her my seat but she declined. I guess she was too busy producing content to relocate.

Even after shooting all of your footage *on* an iOS device, you may *still* find a need to import a few video elements from your computer. For example, imagine you're preparing to shoot a weekly web series on your iPhone or iPad. To give the show some polish, you want to create a snazzy graphic open that will appear at the head of each episode. You create your graphic within a high-end, computer-based animation tool like Adobe After Effects or Apple's Motion. After it's been rendered, you transfer that video file from your computer to your iOS device where it can be accessed by your favorite editing app and placed at the beginning of each episode.

Whether you're transferring a pile of footage or just a few clips, the process is the same. We'll get to the actual steps in a moment, but first let's look at *preparing* your footage for use on an iOS device.

As I mentioned in the previous section, iPads are picky about the clips they will import and play. iPhones are no different. To import clips successfully, you must first convert them into an iOS-compatible format. Naturally, if your footage already exists in a compatible format, there's no need to convert it.

Dozens if not hundreds of video conversion tools are available for download— some free, some not so free, and some really, *really* not free. I'd like to recommend two applications in particular.

HandBrake is a free, open source, wildly popular video converter available for Mac and Windows. While its interface can be intimidating for new users, the application provides quick access to presets for iPhones and iPads. Even with the presets, expect a slight learning curve.

If you're using a Mac and don't mind spending a few bucks, take a look at Permute (available in the Mac App Store). This incredibly simple application allows you to convert clips just by dragging them into its primary window (**FIGURE 9.2**) and selecting a preset from a pop-up menu. Like HandBrake,

HANDBREAK

Mac | Windows

- free
- handbrake.fr

FIGURE 9.2 Permute for Mac offers video conversion with drag-and-drop simplicity.

PERMUTE

Mac | Windows

- Fuel Collective, LLC
- $14.99
- hhhlinks.com/cjg4

Permute offers presets for iPhones and iPads, along with a long list of other options.

It's worth noting that the presets offered in most conversion applications (including the two I've mentioned) are meant to provide the broadest compatibility and best *playback* performance. They don't necessarily ensure the highest quality or largest resolutions. To maximize quality and keep your footage at its original resolution, you may have to experiment with your conversion application's settings.

Once your footage has been converted, you're ready to transfer it to your iOS device.

Using a Mac

If you're working with a Mac desktop or laptop computer, here are the steps to follow:

1. Add your converted video clips to your iPhoto library.

   Notice I said *iPhoto* and not *iTunes*. Even though iTunes handles video (movies, TV shows, podcasts, and so on), it's not meant to store your raw footage and custom clips.

2. Connect your iOS device to your computer, and launch iTunes.

3. Under Devices, click the name of your iOS device, and switch into the Photos tab.

4. Make sure Sync Photos From is checked and that iPhoto is selected in the pop-up menu.

5. Pick either "All photos…" or "Selected albums…," depending on your personal preference.

6. Most importantly, make sure "Include videos" is checked.

   Forgetting to check this box is the biggest mistake new users make.

7. Click Sync (or Apply).

Using a Windows Machine

Working in Windows? Here's how you can transfer your videos:

1. Add your converted video clips to Photoshop Album or Photoshop Elements.

   If you don't use either of these photo library applications, you can also store your video clips within a desired folder on your computer.

2. Connect your iOS device to your computer, and launch iTunes.

3. Under Devices, click the name of your iOS device, and switch into the Photos tab.

4. Make sure Sync Photos From is checked and that the name of your photo application or desired folder is selected in the pop-up menu.

5. If you've stored your videos in one of the two applications I mentioned, pick either "All photos…" or "Selected albums…," depending on your personal preference.

   If you've chosen to store your clips in a folder, your options will be slightly different. Pick either "All folders" or "Selected folders."

6. Most importantly, make sure "Include videos" is checked.

   Forgetting to check this box is the biggest mistake new users make.

7. Click Sync (or Apply).

After the Sync

Your video clips should now be viewable within the Photos app on your iOS device and should also be available to most of the postproduction apps in this chapter.

COLOR CORRECTING YOUR FOOTAGE

Color correction, sometimes called *color grading*, serves two equally critical purposes. The first is to literately *correct* the footage. This might include removing unwanted color tints, properly distributing luminance levels, recovering missing detail from shadows and highlights, and bringing consistency across multiple shots in a scene. In other words, it's about *making it all look good*.

The second, but equally essential, purpose is to define your project's *look.* By carefully manipulating the color and contrast, you can alter and enhance the emotional impact of your footage. In other words, you can *give it all meaning.*

For instance, in the *Matrix* trilogy, the film's directors added a slight green tint to all of the scenes that take place within the matrix. This created a subtle but powerful separation between the simulated and "real" worlds.

Adding a *look* to your footage can also help give it consistency. When two shots simply aren't relating well, treating them with the same look can help them connect.

Naturally, a *look*'s effect is also dependent on your source footage. For example, if you were to add a light golden tint to a beauty-shot of your lead actress smiling warmly, she may appear friendlier, happier, and safer. However, if you add a similar but stronger golden tint to footage of your lead actor desperately stumbling across endless sand dunes, you've just added 20 degrees to an already scorching desert.

Some directors choose to go with a particular look simply because of its cultural popularity. For instance, a few years ago, nearly every action film coming out of Hollywood was heavily tinted toward teal and orange. Now, thanks to the mass appeal of iPhone apps like Instagram and Hipstamatic (a personal favorite), today's films, TV shows, and commercials are beginning to take on a retro, vintage look. Imperfect is the new perfect! Next year, it will be something else.

While I'm all for making it look hip, cool, and current, I highly recommend you choose a look that serves your story above all else. I also highly recommend that you kids get off my lawn.

VideoGrade

VideoGrade is the best low-cost color *correction* app currently available for iOS. Notice I emphasized the word *correction*. That's because, of the three apps in this section, VideoGrade is the only one that provides the necessary tools to isolate and fix basic color problems. While it performs equally well on iPhones and iPads, the latter's large, 9.7" screen (measured diagonally) provides a more useful preview.

VIDEOGRADE

iPad iPhone

- Fidel Lainez
- $4.99
- hhhlinks.com/qc7w

After launching VideoGrade and selecting a clip from your device's camera roll or photo library, it appears within the app's primary interface, ready to be modified. Along the bottom of the screen is a scrolling list of icons, each representing a different color correction tool (**FIGURE 9.3**).

Tapping any tool brings up its easy-to-use controls. For example, tapping ☀ brings up a single brightness slider. Move it left, and your image gets darker. Slide it right, and it gets brighter. If you need to make a small, more precise adjustment, simply tap and hold on the slider, drag your finger up, and *then* slide it left or right as before. Doing so decreases the rate of change, giving you far greater control over the effect.

If you're not happy with a change you've made, just tap ⟲ to return a tool to its default settings. You can toggle any tool on or off by tapping the small circle that appears next to its name. A ◉ means that effect is active, and a ● means it's inactive. Three of the tools (Brightness, Saturation, and Tint) even offer extra controls for applying separate corrections to the shadows, mid-tones,

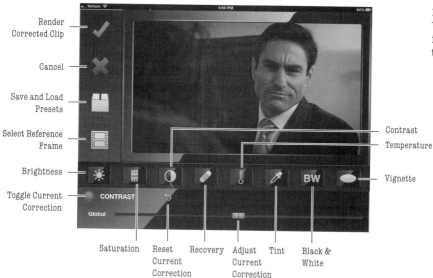

Render Corrected Clip

Cancel

Save and Load Presets

Select Reference Frame

Brightness

Toggle Current Correction

Contrast

Temperature

Vignette

Saturation   Reset Current Correction   Recovery   Adjust Current Correction   Tint   Black & White

and highlights of your image (**FIGURE 9.4**). By adjusting each of the tools, you can turn drab, discolored shots into punchy, meaningful footage, capable of expressing a mood or simulating an environment.

After creating a correction, you can save it as a preset for later use. This is a great way to achieve consistent results across multiple similar shots, although you'll likely have to make some small adjustments to compensate for each clip's particularities. Once your shot is complete, you can export it to your camera roll in a variety of different sizes.

VideoGrade does have a few minor drawbacks. The app lacks color-wheel controls (an interface element typically found in color correction systems) and still-store functionality (the ability to save reference frames that can help when trying to make one shot look like another). It's also worth noting that VideoGrade performs *primary* color corrections only, meaning any changes you make will affect the entire image. You can't select a specific portion of the frame for isolated corrections (known as *secondary* corrections).

While these limitations can be frustrating, may I remind you that professional color correction tools start at around $100 and can quickly run into the thousands. VideoGrade costs about the same as a can of Coke, and it won't rot your teeth. I'd say that's a heck of a good deal!

While VideoGrade is certainly capable of designing some great looks, I tend to rely on it more for correcting footage, rather than crafting it—not because it lacks the necessary power but because of the availability of two terrific look-generating tools.

Let's take a look. A *look*. Get it? A *look*. Hey, they can't all be winners.

Movie Looks HD

MOVIE
LOOKS HD

iPad iPhone

- Red Giant
  Software
- $1.99
- hhhlinks.com/
  b8ub

Created by Red Giant Software, the same company that gave the world Colorista II and Magic Bullet Looks (two much-loved plug-ins for desktop editing and compositing applications), Movie Looks HD borrows heavily from its older, color-correcting siblings.

After launching Movie Looks HD and selecting a video clip from your device's camera roll or photo library, you can quickly browse through the app's 40 cinematic presets (**FIGURE 9.5**). To keep things organized, the presets are broken down into multiple categories, including Quick, Essential, Popular Film, Black & White, and Blockbusters. Many of the app's looks are inspired by popular films or specific genres. For example, the Neo look will dip your footage in a great big vat of moody, green awesome-sauce, letting it appear as though it just stepped out of the Matrix. Applying the War look gives your footage an intense, desaturated vibe suitable for the battlefield.

Based on the variety and complexity of the presets, it's clear they were designed by professionals. However, at their default settings, they can all be a bit heavy-handed. Fortunately, Movie Looks HD lets you lower each effect's overall intensity while adjusting your clip's brightness (**FIGURE 9.6**). I recommend removing the effect completely by lowering the Strength slider and *then* slowly raising it back up, in small increments, until the intensity seems appropriate. In the end, it's simply a matter of taste.

FIGURE 9.5 MovieLooks HD provides previews of its looks, letting you look at how each look looks. Look!

FIGURE 9.6 After you pick a look, you can adjust its strength and overall brightness.

After picking a look and adjusting its settings, prepare for a lengthy render. Because this app is doing far more than simply throwing a color wash over your clips, it can take a while to crunch the numbers. How long? It depends on the look you've applied. For example, a five-minute clip rendered at full resolution with the Ohio look applied took just under 30 minutes on my iPhone 4S. That same clip with the Cold Day look applied rendered in just under 15 minutes. If you're in a rush and quality is less of an issue, you can tell the app to render your results at half-resolution, dramatically cutting down your render time.

While rendering, Movie Looks HD presents a series of helpful tips, not just for getting the most out of the app but also for improving your shooting in general. It's a nice touch. While using other apps, I'm always afraid to get a phone call during a long render because I know I'll have to return to the app to restart the process. Not so in Movie Looks HD. This app is smart enough to pause your render if you get a call or switch to another app. When you return to Movie Looks HD, the render picks up right where it left off. Good stuff right there!

While I really enjoy using Movie Looks HD, it can be a bit buggy. While the app claims it can process clips only up to five minutes in length, I've had it apply its magic to clips as long as ten minutes. Admittedly, the app crashed several times while I was trying to set it up, but it *did* render. I advise keeping your source material under five minutes, but don't hesitate trying something longer if necessary—just don't expect rock-solid performance.

If you're looking for professional and dramatic results and you have the time to spend rendering, Movie Looks HD does a terrific job.

CINEMAFX FOR VIDEO

iPad | iPhone

- Nexvio Inc.
- $1.99
- hhhlinks.com/sxyl

CinemaFX for Video

I'm a big fan of this app and have enjoyed it since the day it was released.

Taking a build-it-yourself approach, CinemaFX for Video provides you with the building blocks necessary to construct your own cinematic looks, rather than using canned presets. While this added flexibility increases your chances of creating something unique, it also increases your chances of creating something hideous. Like all good color correction, *moderation is key.*

You begin the process by picking a clip from your device's camera roll or photo library. From there, your clip video is opened in a screen with very few visual distractions. By tapping ⊕ in the lower left, you are brought to a scrolling list of visual effects (including Black & White, Sepia, Negative, Vignette, and so on), each represented by a preview icon (**FIGURE 9.7**). If you can't find a specific effect, just keep looking! The app contains more than 50 different visual effects broken down into four separate categories, including Essential, Cinematic, Toy-Cam, and Vintage.

While these may seem like presets, each of these effects is actually an individual building block. By chaining multiple effects together (up to three at a time), you can create entirely new, custom looks for your footage.

FIGURE 9.7 CinemaFX for Video uses multiple effect categories to keeps things organized.

FIGURE 9.8 You can combine up to three effects at a time.

FIGURE 9.9 Each effect can be adjusted or removed.

For example, let's say I wanted a warm, dreamy look with a subtle vignette. I might start by adding an Elf Glow effect to soften things up ('cause that's how I roll). After that, I'd pick the Egyptian Gold effect to add some warmth. Finally, I'd add the Vignette effect to darken the edges. Each time I add an effect, a representative icon appears under my clip, and the video updates to reflect the change (**FIGURE 9.8**).

Now that I've added the maximum of three effects, I can tell things aren't looking quite right. It's not soft enough, and the gold tint is overwhelming. As easy as effects are to add, they're even easier to adjust. By simply tapping the effect's icon once and then tapping ⊜, the bottom portion of the interface slides away, revealing simple controls to manipulate the selected effect. Using these controls, I can increase the Elf Glow's overall effect ('cause that's how I roll) and decrease the amount of Egyptian Gold being applied (**FIGURE 9.9**). Perfect!

Double-tapping the preview lets you switch between before and after views. If you're satisfied with what you've created, you can render the new clip in a variety of sizes. Sadly, render and export resolutions top out at 720p. 1080p export is not an option, even on iPhones that shoot 1080p. Once the clip is rendered, it can be exported to your camera roll, e-mailed, and uploaded to YouTube.

The only other significant drawback is the app's inability to save custom effect combinations for use with other clips. Until that feature is added, CinemaFX for Video provides beautiful results, one clip at a time.

More Options

Before moving on, four other color correction apps deserve a mention.

If you're using a Mac along with Apple's Color to correct your footage, check out vWave-Lite. This free app turns your iPad into a wireless, virtual, three-trackball remote control surface for Color. By comparison, physical control surfaces can cost thousands of dollars, so I'd say free is a pretty good deal.

If you're working in Cineform's First Light and you have $80 to spend, take a look at Gradiest. It also turns your iPad into a virtual control surface, but this one is *loaded* with impressive extras.

Not to be outdone, Nattress has released Chromagic for iPad. This free app provides a set of virtual trackballs, dials, and sliders that can remotely control Chromagic FXPlug, the company's $25 color correction plug-in for Final Cut Pro 7 (available at www.nattress.com).

VWAVE-LITE

iPad iPhone

- Tangent Wave Ltd.
- free
- hhhlinks.com/ nbv1

GRADIEST

iPad iPhone

- Act Focused Media LLC
- $79.99
- hhhlinks.com/ p2zf

Chromagic
www.nattress.com

Pixel Farm's AirGrade
www.airgrade.co.uk

CHROMAGIC

| iPad | iPhone |

- Nattress Productions Inc.
- free
- hhhlinks.com/ nOcm

AIRGRADE

| iPad | iPhone |

- The Pixel Farm Ltd
- free
- hhhlinks.com/ 5kel

AirGrade for iPhone is another free virtual trackball app, but this one works in conjunction with a free Mac client app (available at www.airgrade.co.uk). By using the two together, you can color correct a still image on your Mac and then export the correction settings in the industry-standard ASC file format for use in a professional color correction system. Neat!

And, if you're a seasoned pro, take some time to learn about Gamma & Density's 3cP / Image Control Pro. This iPad app is part of a larger on-location color correction system that allows directors and cinematographers to define their correction settings before ever leaving set.

EDITING FOOTAGE

Now comes the really fun part—whittling down oodles of raw footage into a single, cohesive, meaningful whole. This is when your project truly comes to life.

It doesn't matter if you're editing a feature comedy, a dramatic podcast, an informative news story, an inspiring sales reel, or your family's day at the beach—something incredible happens when two or more shots are thoughtfully strung together. They become more than the sum of their parts, capable of packing a surprisingly emotional punch.

Even more surprising is that you can now edit video on the same devices you might use to get driving directions.

iMovie

Leave it to Apple to craft a fuzzy-wuzzy app that strips all complexity out of the video-editing process. Clearly inspired by their equally elegant Mac app of the same name, iMovie for iPhone and iPad makes cutting your project a relatively painless process. The app has some limitations that will certainly pester professionals (we'll get to those), but for basic editing tasks with minimal fuss, iMovie has no equal.

When you launch the app, you'll be presented with a scrolling list of your existing projects, each represented by a separate movie poster (**FIGURE 9.10**). Tap a poster to open its project, or tap ➕ to create a new project from scratch.

iMovie is a universal app, so you can buy it once and use it on your iPhone *and* iPad. While the layout varies slightly between these two devices, the app's operation remains fairly consistent.

FIGURE 9.10 iMovie will help you cut your film for less money than it costs to see a film.

3CP/IMAGE CONTROL PRO

iPad | iPhone

- Gamma & Density Co.
- $399.99
- hhhlinks.com/wm59

Like most consumer-grade products from Apple, iMovie uses themes. Each of the eight bundled themes includes custom graphics, titles, transitions, and music. Some of the themes are quite professional (Modern, Bright, News), and some are downright silly (Neon, Playful, Travel). You can pull up a list of available themes (and other options) by tapping the Project Settings button in the upper right.

I avoid using themes because I don't want my videos looking like everyone else's. That said, when used sparingly, some theme elements (lower third titles, for instance) can add a little polish to your project.

iMOVIE

iPad | iPhone

- Apple
- $4.99
- hhhlinks.com/bd94

After creating a new project (or opening an existing project), you'll be brought to iMovie's editing interface (**FIGURE 9.11**). On an iPad, you'll find your media browser in the upper right (switchable between video, photos, and audio), the video preview area in the upper left, and the timeline across the bottom. On an iPhone, the video preview area takes the top half of the screen, and the timeline lives on the bottom. Because of space limitations on the iPhone's screen, the media browser is called up separately by tapping 🎬.

Any video clips you've shot or imported onto your iOS device (using the techniques I described earlier) should appear in your media browser, along with your photos and audio files. In addition, iMovie comes with a decent library of sound effects and "theme music."

Starting a cut could not be simpler. Just tap a desired video clip in the media browser, define the portion of the clip you'd like to include by dragging the yellow *in* and *out* trim handles, and then tap that clip's Insert icon to have it dropped into the timeline (**FIGURE 9.12**). Photos and audio clips are added in much the same way, although you won't be given the option to trim in and out points.

FIGURE 9.11 iMovie's editing interface is simple and elegant.

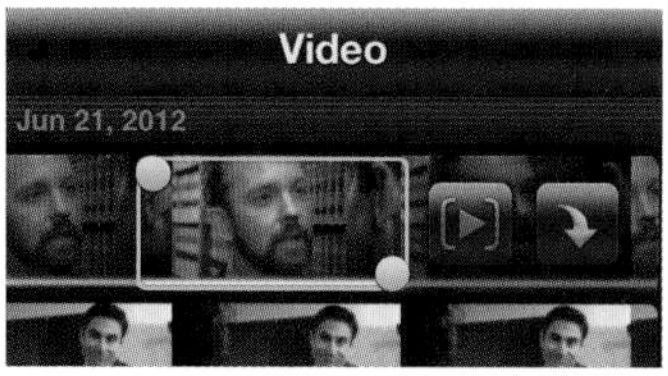

Back to Project Library | Help | Preview Area | Unto/Redo | Project Settings

Media Library — Audio — Photos — Video —

Timeline | Show/Hide Audio Waveforms | Playhead | Play | Record Audio | Record Video or Photo

FIGURE 9.12 You can select an entire clip in the media library or select a specific range by dragging the yellow trim handles.

There's only one track of video, so you won't be doing any complex compositing. On the bright side, the app does allow for three simultaneous audio tracks (useful for sound effects and voiceovers) *plus* a background music track. That's on top of any audio already contained within the movie clips.

You can shoot video straight to the timeline by tapping ▣, but the camera functionality is limited. If you're serious about capturing high-quality video, stick with one of the camera apps I mentioned in Chapter 6, and then access your footage within iMovie's media browser.

As video clips are added to the timeline, so are default cross-dissolve transi-tions indicated by a  icon. Double-tapping the icon presents options for switching the transition type. You can make it a cut (which I *really* wish was the default transition) or a more elaborate theme-based transition.

You can rearrange clips in your timeline by simply tapping and holding on a clip for a moment and then dragging from one position to another. If you drag it off the timeline, it will remove it from your edit (but not from your device). All clips (except for background music) can be trimmed by tapping them once and then adjusting their yellow in and out trim handles. Background music is automati-cally placed at the head of your cut, and as I mentioned, it cannot be easily trimmed or repositioned.

To play back your edit in the preview area, just tap ▶. While most video will play back in real time, you will no doubt experience the occasional glitch. Don't worry; those all get smoothed out during the final render. To rewind or fast-for-ward, simply drag your entire timeline back and forth. Whatever appears under the timeline's stationary playhead is exactly what you'll see in the preview area. Speaking of the timeline, it can be zoomed in or out with basic pinch gestures. If you haven't already caught on, iMovie is *very* into gestures…like New York taxi drivers.

Video clips can be assigned a title style, which is how you add theme-based graphics and titles. For instance, if you wanted to add a lower third (a title that sits in the lower portion of the frame and displays the name of the speaker) to some interview footage, you'd double-tap the interview clip to open its set-tings. From there, you would tap Title Style and then Middle, which is essentially a lower third. The new title is instantly superimposed over the selected clip (**FIGURE 9.13**). Naturally, the text can be customized.

FIGURE 9.13 Titles and graphics are applied directly to clips already in the timeline.

FIGURE 9.14 The Precision Editor facilitates independent trimming of a clip's video and audio content.

A common complaint I hear from iMovie users is that lower thirds can't be trimmed. Instead, they remain on-screen for the entire duration of their related clips. This isn't a problem on short clips, but if you have someone talking for 20 seconds, do you really want their name on-screen the entire time? Probably not.

Fortunately, there's an easy workaround. Before adding your lower third, slide the timeline so the red playhead sits directly over the point at which you'd like your lower third to *end*. Then tap the clip once (so its yellow trim handles appear), and then drag your finger down the playhead. This splits the clip in two at that exact point. Then, just add the lower third to the first chunk of the clip. It will fade out before the new edit point. Done!

iMovie has plenty of other features (audio waveforms, freeze frames, clip rotation, quick-navigation gestures, geotagging in titles, and so on), but I believe one new tool deserves your complete attention. By pinching apart over a transition icon, you'll open its transition editor. Here you can make far more precise editing decisions, but more importantly, you can independently edit the in and out points of your video clip's *audio* track (**FIGURE 9.14**). This allows for "J" and "L" cuts (edits in which the video and audio cut at slightly different times). Professionals use J and L cuts *all the time*. Sadly, this is currently an iPad-only feature. Perhaps that will have changed by the time you read this.

When you're ready to share your completed edit, you can upload a rendered video to YouTube, Facebook, Vimeo, and CNN iReport. Additionally, you can output it to your device's camera roll and even export the *entire project* via iTunes File Sharing for continued refinement on another iOS device running the app or in the Mac version of iMovie.

In addition to the basic editing workflow I've described, the app also boasts a semi-automated, semi-entertaining movie trailer maker. I'm not going into details because frankly, this feature is aimed at consumers, not filmmakers.

But, just in case you're curious, here's how it works: Pick theme, type text, add video, render trailer. Yawn.

For some reason, the trailer feature is available only for the iPhone 4 and newer, the iPad 2 and newer, and the fifth-generation iPod touch. If you're sporting an older device and can't use the trailer feature, I wouldn't lose any sleep over it. It's just another reason to upgrade…as if you needed another reason.

Pinnacle Studio

"Editing video on an iPad? Yeah, right. iMovie? Pffft. Whatever. Let me know when Avid makes an iPad app! Because that's when I'll start taking mobile editing seriously."

OK, cynical editor guy, it's time to get serious!

Originally designed and released by Avid (one of the leaders in professional nonlinear editing systems), Avid Studio turned an iPad 2 (and newer) into a slick video editor. Strangely, not long after its initial release, the app was sold to Corel, Inc., and renamed Pinnacle Studio. Why? No idea. Perhaps it had something to do with Avid's less-than-stellar financial state. Fortunately, the app has remained largely unchanged during the transition. While it suffers from some of the same limitations as iMovie, it packs enough power to warrant a closer look.

The layout is very similar to iMovie. In the upper left, you'll find the media library filled with thumbnails representing your videos, photos, and music. The preview area resides in the upper right, and the timeline sits below.

Like iMovie (and most nonlinear editing systems), this app lets you drag and drop your media to the timeline. Unique to Pinnacle Studio, however, is something called the *storyboard* (a strip of small square thumbnails that sits directly over the timeline) (**FIGURE 9.15**). In the storyboard strip, users can quickly tap and drag clips to reorder them, while keeping an eye on an overview of the entire project. While that sounds simple enough, most iPad and iPhone video editors lack this ability. Typically, users have to zoom into or out of the timeline in order to re-orient themselves.

Pinnacle Studio doesn't offer too much in the way of themes, but it does provide a decent variety of sound effects, transitions (dissolves, pushes, wipes, and so on), static and animated text effects, and what it calls *montage* clips. These are predefined (and somewhat editable) graphic animations and picture-in-picture effects that provide drop zones for your own content (**FIGURE 9.16**). Most are quite good-looking, but a few suffer from "templatitis." So, while Pinnacle Studio has the same single-video-layer restriction as iMovie, montage clips provide a workable workaround.

PINNACLE STUDIO

iPad iPhone

- Corel Inc.
- $9.99
- hhhlinks.com/
  2rm7

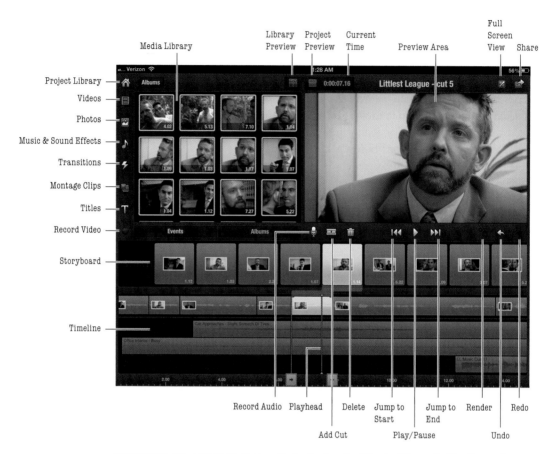

FIGURE 9.15 Although it may look similar to iMovie, Pinnacle Studio packs more options into its interface.

FIGURE 9.16 Drop your own footage into a montage clip in order to create multilayered video effects.

Like iMovie, Pinnacle Studio allows you to shoot video and record audio directly to the timeline, but as I've mentioned, you'll get better video with a dedicated camera app. If you're all about the audio, you'll be happy to know that the time-line supplies three additional audio layers for your dining and dancing pleasure.

Editing is done in much the same way as iMovie. You can drag clips to rearrange them, tap them to reveal trim handles, and double-tap them to call up extra options. Thankfully, Pinnacle Studio doesn't follow iMovie's lead and automatically add transitions between clips. If you want a transition on your timeline, you'll have to add it yourself. Thank goodness.

All of your edits can be fine-tuned (down to the frame) using the app's built-in precision editing tools; however, there's currently no support for J or L cuts. Your project can be played back at any time in the preview area, and you can even zoom playback to full screen by tapping ▣. While most edits can be played back without rendering, complex effects (such as montage clips) will require processing before they can be played back smoothly. The app functions equally well in portrait and landscape mode, although landscape does allow for a wider view of your timeline.

Once you're satisfied with your cut, you can render and upload a finished video to YouTube, Box, and Facebook. You can also export renders to your camera roll and via e-mail. Lastly, you can export the entire project for use within the Windows version of the app.

Overall, I really dig Pinnacle Studio and have no problem recommending it. However, there is one troubling issue that I'd like to put on your radar. When using iMovie, your videos, photos, and audio clips are available right away (after a brief loading period). In Pinnacle Studio, your media must first be cataloged in an internal media database it calls its *library*. It's a fully automated process that, depending on how much media you have, can take quite a while to complete (**FIGURE 9.17**). Normally, I'd say this isn't a big deal. However, any time you shoot a new photo or video clip and want access to it within Pinnacle Studio, the app will need to "rebuild its library." On my iPad 3, it takes almost two and a half minutes every single time. Ideally, this process will get a speed boost in future versions.

FIGURE 9.17 Any time you add media to your device, Pinnacle Studio will need to rebuild its media library.

DROP'N'ROLL

iPad | iPhone

- New Photographers Burning Factory Ltd.
- free
- hhhlinks.com/5mwf

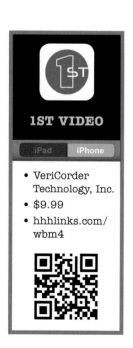

1ST VIDEO

iPad | iPhone

- VeriCorder Technology, Inc.
- $9.99
- hhhlinks.com/wbm4

Drop'n'Roll (formerly V.I.K.T.O.R.)

As much as it pains me to say this, most iPhone and iPad owners are not actually filmmakers. And, despite my best efforts, at least a few of them are likely to remain not-filmmakers. Heathens.

Despite their questionable lack of filmmaking ambition, most of them will shoot video at some point. I think it's safe to say that at least one of them will shoot *way* too much video, not think about editing any of it, and then force you to watch all of it. It's the digital video equivalent of having to sit through someone's vacation slides.

The next time this happens to you, I suggest you have your overshooting friend download a nifty little app called Drop'n'Roll!

This consumer-oriented gem will *automatically* edit video previously shot and stored in the user's iPhone's camera roll. For some cosmic reason, a slew of automatic video editors appeared in the App Store right around the same time. While a few of the others are quite capable and enjoy some unique features, I find that Drop'n'Roll produces the highest-quality results.

The app automatically selects clips from your camera roll (or lets you pick your own) and applies a user-selectable theme (**FIGURE 9.18**). When it's done, it has turned your footage into an entertaining montage complete with a zippy soundtrack, tight editing, and visual punch. You can control the duration, add color effects, and customize titles. If you like the finished edit, the app can share it via YouTube, Facebook, and e-mail.

If your friend balks at the idea of buying an app to edit their footage, tell them Drop'n'Roll is *free* and comes standard with an excellent theme. Additional themes can be obtained via an in-app purchase and range in price from $0.99 to $1.99. Purchasing themes can be a little confusing. You actually have access to *all* the themes right from the start. You can create and preview your movies

FIGURE 9.18 Drop'n'Roll uses predefined themes to automatically edit your footage.

using *any* of the themes. But if you want to render, save, and share a movie longer than 20 seconds, you'll need to purchase the theme you've selected. So, you can preview any theme at any length, but you'll have to pay to keep the longer results. Currently, Drop'n'Roll won't let you import your own music, but that makes sense since the app's automatic edits are perfectly timed to its included music.

I'll admit I was not terribly interested in Drop'n'Roll when I first read about it. Typically, apps that claim to do things *automatically* usually do them *sucktasticly*. However, in this case, the results are consistently and surprisingly impressive.

Make no mistake; this app is not for professional filmmakers. So, why am I including it in the book? Because, as a filmmaker, you will enjoy your friend's home videos far more (or at least be able to tolerate them better) after this app has turned two hours of your friend's dull footage into an exciting, great-looking two-minute music video. You're welcome.

Other Options

As much as I dig the editing apps I've just described, there are a couple more options worth checking out before spending your hard-earned cash.

1st Video was the first app to take video editing seriously. In fact, I'd still say it's one of the most professional video apps residing in the App Store. The app's unusual interface is like nothing you've ever seen, and for that reason, it has a curvier learning curve than most other editing apps. Visit Hand Held Hollywood to see the app in action (http://hhhlinks.com/1stv).

If you're looking for something a little less complex, take a peek at Splice. The app offers a simple interface with some decent features, but it has never quite won me over. That said, I've spoken with plenty of people who *swear* by this app. I'll tell you what I told them. Stop swearing.

COMPOSING THE SCORE

How's your edit looking? Does it feel a little dry? Maybe your show needs a theme song? Perhaps your narrative scene would pull more heartstrings if it were accompanied by actual strings. If you want to create a truly unique finished project, consider giving it some custom music.

While there are a bazillion (or less) music composition and virtual instrument apps available, I'm going to point out two of my personal favorites. After that, if

1ST VIDEO FOR iPAD

iPad | iPhone

- VeriCorder Technology, Inc.
- $19.99
- hhhlinks.com/aclc

1st Video on HHH
hhhlinks.com/1stv

SPLICE

iPad | iPhone

- Path 36, LLC
- $3.99
- hhhlinks.com/j9od

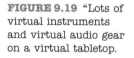

you're hungry for more musical goodness, take a spin over to PalmSounds.net, a blog devoted to iOS audio apps and accessories. One word of caution: If you spend more than a few minutes scanning its posts, you'll likely be spending way too much on awesome music apps. I know. I've been there.

Tabletop

As a loyal, loving, and dangerously obsessed fan of the desktop music-authoring application Reason, I've long hoped it would make its way onto the iPad. This Mac- and Windows-compatible composing tool provides users with a virtual rack that can be filled with virtual audio gear, which gets patched together with virtual cables. It's virtually awesome. While Propellerheads, the developers of Reason, do have a few apps floating around the App Store, it has yet to release Reason for iOS.

Thank goodness there's Tabletop!

Like Reason, Tabletop presents a virtualized music-authoring environment based on, you guessed it, a tabletop. After creating a new table (or using one of the app's many starter templates), you add virtual equipment, one piece of gear at a time (**FIGURE 9.19**).

FIGURE 9.19 "Lots of virtual instruments and virtual audio gear on a virtual tabletop.

Twenty-five different devices are available, 11 of which come with the app (Gridlok: Pad Sampler, M8RX: Tone Matrix, RS3: Polyphonic Stereo Keyboard, Mr. O: Master Output, Goblin MX8: 8-Channel Mixer, SpinBack: Turntable Player, Recorder M2: All-Purpose Input Recorder, Filtr LP: Low-Pass Filter Effect, 3Q: 3-Band Equalizer, X2: Splitter Unit, T101 - Triggerator: Sequence and Perform). The remaining devices (such as a TT-303 Baseline Sequencer and the T-Pain Effect) can be purchased from the Device Store as needed with prices ranging from $0.99 to $9.99. You may also be given the opportunity to purchase a bundle of devices at a big discount. Because the app is modular in nature, I have no doubt that new "devices" will be added over time.

Before I go on, let me just say that I friggin' love this app! I had originally planned on mentioning that as part of the wrap-up, but I couldn't contain my excitement.

As you add gear to your table, virtual patch cables are automatically added when appropriate. For instance, when you add a Stereo Keyboard, the app will automatically connect it to the mixer (**FIGURE 9.20**). That said, all of the cables are editable. After tapping [icon], you'll have the freedom to re-patch all of the virtual equipment however you'd like. This allows for seemingly infinite creative possibilities.

Every piece of gear you add provides its own appropriate controls. Virtual keyboards can be played, drum machines can be poked, mixer knobs can be turned, and so on. By filling your tabletop with just the devices you need, you can create your very own personalized recording studio. And, if you ever get lost, several demo songs (and tables) are provided along with a complete in-app user guide. Trust me, once you get the basics, you'll be jamming in no time.

Finished tracks can be saved as WAV audio files available via iTunes File Sharing or uploaded directly to SoundCloud. However, if you plan on mixing your project within Auria, an incredible multitrack mixing app I'll be covering shortly,

TABLETOP

iPad   iPhone

- Retronyms
- free
- hhhlinks.com/l2j6

FIGURE 9.20 New devices are automatically routed with virtual cables.

your best option may be to use AudioCopy, an interapp audio copy-and-paste technology developed by Sonoma Wireworks and Retronyms. Using Audio-Copy, you can simply copy your song from Tabletop and then paste it into Auria (or any AudioCopy-compatible app).

Tabletop isn't for everyone. It produces decidedly electronic sounding music. Furthermore, its reality-based interface might prove to be distracting for users simply looking to load a keyboard and play. That said, if you're a fan of synthe-sized instrumentation and you dig the idea of working with "real" gear, then you should stop what you're doing and download Tabletop.

Oh, I forgot to mention this little factoid. *Tabletop is free!* While you can pur-chase the extra gear if desired, the app comes with more than enough "equip-ment" to start recording custom music for your productions.

GarageBand

GARAGEBAND

iPad   iPhone

- Apple
- $4.99
- hhhlinks.com/ 69v6

You know what? I really don't feel like writing about Apple's GarageBand.

Not because it isn't awesome, but because it's *extremely* awesome. Over the past few years, this Mac-iLife-application-turned-iOS-app has received more coverage than Lindsay Lohan's court appearances...and there have been a *lot* of those. Frankly, I'm tired of GarageBand! You could spin a dead cat (wow, another truly grotesque cat expression; it's a good thing I hate cats) and hit another fan of this incredible app. I'm sick of it! In fact, I'm not going to willfully add my voice to the cattle call of praise-dispensing hacks. Instead, I'm going to point out all its faults. Ready?

The fact that this insanely inexpensive app will allow you to record multiple tracks of high-quality audio and mix them with studio quality sampled instru-ments totally sucks (**FIGURE 9.21**). The massive library of versatile and well-produced built-in music loops, along with the app's wide variety of virtual synths, sucks even more. Don't even get me started on the amazing stringed instruments and drum samples. Total crap.

Oh! I just remembered the app's horrendously brilliant use of the iPhone's and iPad's motion sensors to help replicate touch-sensitive pianos, drums, and more. Yuck.

I think the thing I hate the most about GarageBand is its ability to let anyone create professional-sounding music with its innovative "Smart" instruments. Ha! More like stupid, dumb-head, jerk instruments.

Throw in a variety of killer effects, a simple-to-use sequencer, fully editable per-formances, compatibility with external MIDI keyboards, its ability to sync and

FIGURE 9.21 This is GarageBand. Why don't you own it yet?

jam with other iOS devices on the same wireless network, and all of its other "features," and you've got one of the best, I mean worst, $5 investments you can possibly make.

There. I feel better. Now, if you'll excuse me, I need to go play with GarageBand, I mean my dog.

MIXING YOUR AUDIO

Once you have a *locked cut* (a final picture edit that won't be changing), it's time to mix (and fix) your audio. Along with color correction, audio mixing is a step that many amateurs skip, and like a scene that's way too purple, poorly mixed audio can easily wreck your work.

Generally speaking, there are two types of audio-editing applications. *Wave-form editors* are used to perform precision edits on a single audio file, while *digital audio workstations* (DAWs) are multitrack systems used for mixing entire projects, handling *many* audio files at once.

There are reasons for having both types of apps on hand, and they are often used in tandem. For example, while mixing your film's multiple audio tracks (music, dialogue, sound effects, and so on) in your DAW, what happens if you come across a bit of dialogue that contains an occasional distracting click sound? You could use your DAW's automated volume features to lower the sound level every time the click is heard, but it might be easier to transfer that dialogue file into a waveform editor where the offending clicks could be completely removed. Then, you could return a click-free version of the sound file back to the DAW and move right along with your mix.

Another significant difference between the two app types is that waveform editors perform destructive edits (permanently changing the audio files), while DAWs are typically (but not always) nondestructive (changing how the audio files are played back while leaving the original files unaltered).

Fortunately, several terrific audio tools are available to iOS users, including an awesome waveform editor and a mind-blowing Digital Audio Workstation.

TwistedWave Audio Editor

TWISTEDWAVE
AUDIO EDITOR

| iPad | iPhone |

- TwistedWave
- $9.99
- hhhlinks.com/ g3jd

TwistedWave is a simple but powerful audio waveform editor for your iPhone and iPad, based on the Mac application of the same name.

To get the ball rolling, you can open an existing audio file from the app's library, create a new, empty sound file (mono or stereo), or import an existing audio file from one of several sources (iTunes File Sharing, your device's music library, the app's built-in web server, and more). To import properly, audio files must be in one of the app's accepted formats (AIFF, AIFC, MP3, MPEG4 [AAC], AU, or SD2).

The app's main window is clean and intuitive (**FIGURE 9.22**). Toward the top you'll see your entire waveform stretched to fill the width of the screen. Below that is your primary editing area that can be zoomed in and out with simple pinch gestures. When zoomed in, a red range indicator appears over the top waveform, giving you an idea of what portion of the waveform you're currently viewing in the edit area. You can quickly navigate through the waveform with left and right swipes. To the right of the waveform you'll find an audio level meter (remember to keep your levels out of the red).

Basic playback controls can be found on the left side of the bottom toolbar. In addition to buttons for rewind, play, and fast-forward, there's also a button for recording new audio directly from your device's microphone (or external mic).

To begin editing a sound, select a desired region of the audio waveform by double-tapping in one position and then dragging to another. The size of the selected region can be altered by moving the range indicators found on either side of the current selection.

FIGURE 9.22 TwistedWave can help you make precise edits in your sound files.

FIGURE 9.23 Fix problems and get creative with the app's built-in effects.

With a region selected, use any of the tools on the bottom toolbar to modify the waveform. TwistedWave provides buttons for cut, copy, paste, fade up, fade down, undo, redo, and crop. There are also buttons for looping playback and accessing the app's wide range of effects (**FIGURE 9.23**).

Like Tabletop, TwistedWave supports AudioCopy for quickly moving audio between compatible apps. In fact, it's this feature that allows it to work hand in hand with Auria (the DAW I'll be describing in just a moment). Using AudioCopy, you could copy a segment of audio from within Auria, paste it into TwistedWave, edit it, copy it again using AudioCopy, and then paste it back into Auria. It's the quickest and easiest way to have these apps interact.

In addition to AudioCopy, there are plenty of other ways to get your work out of TwistedWave. You can export it via iTunes File Sharing, ship it off via e-mail, or upload it to an FTP server, Dropbox, or SoundCloud. You can send it directly to another app on your iOS device or make it available for download within the app's built-in web server.

I was already a fan of TwistedWave, but it wasn't until I used it in conjunction with Auria that angels began to sing. At least I think those were angels. I'll get back to you on that.

AURIA

iPad   iPhone

- WaveMachine Labs, Inc.
- $49.99
- hhhlinks.com/ 6tsw

Auria

146 pages. That's the size of the Auria User Guide.

Auria is a massive digital audio workstation with a ridiculous feature set that easily rivals many DAWs I've used on Macs and Windows machines. I'd say it deserves its own book, but with a 146-page manual, it already has one!

Clearly, there's no way I can briefly describe every function found in this absurdly powerful app (especially if I continue to use such effusive adjectives). So, instead, I'm going to give you the basic idea and then focus on a feature that seems tailor-made for filmmakers.

Auria turns your iPad into a professional, *48-track* digital audio workstation. Wait a second. Forty-eight tracks? That can't be right. It must be a typo. Let me try that again.

Auria turns your iPad into a professional, *48-track* digital audio workstation. Holy cow, it's true! As you might expect, an app this powerful requires serious horsepower. You'll need an iPad 2 or newer to access all 48 tracks, but the iPad 1 still provides a mind-bending 24 tracks.

If you've ever worked with high-end computer-based DAWs like Pro Tools, many of Auria's interface elements will feel familiar. You can record one track at a time, or up to 24 tracks simultaneously using a supported USB audio interface and the USB to 30-pin adapter from Apple's Camera Connection Kit. Like many DAWs, Auria provides two primary views: the Mix window and the Edit window.

Within the Mix window, each track is given its own channel on a virtual mixing board (**FIGURE 9.24**). Here you can adjust each track's volume, pan, auxiliary sends (for routing audio signals to virtual effects processors), subgroup assignments (for mixing related tracks in groups), fader and knob automation, signal processing, and more. On the far right side of the mixing board (revealed by swiping your entire mixing board to the left), you'll find your subgroup channels and master fader.

In the Edit window, you can modify and reposition all of your individual sound files (each of which is represented by a separate, colored waveform), define volume and pan curves, set up crossfades, and much more (**FIGURE 9.25**). Both views share a toolbar that contains access to the app's various commands, settings, and transport controls.

In addition to the basic signal processing provided to every track via virtual expanders, multiband EQs, and compressors, Auria supplies several additional built-in effects units, including delays, reverbs, choruses, and a pitch corrector. When you outgrow those, additional effects and app functionality can be purchased a la carte at prices ranging from $4.99 to $29.99.

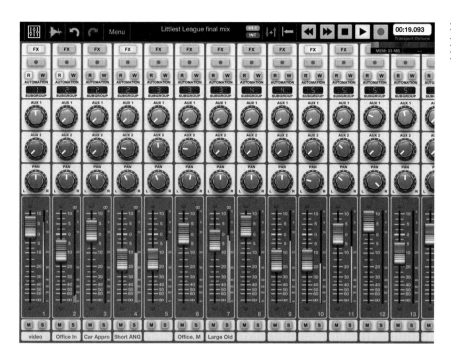

FIGURE 9.24 Auria provides 48 tracks of pure mixing madness.

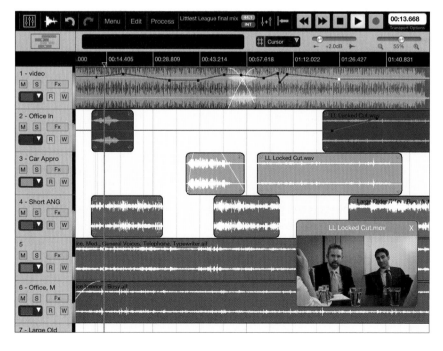

FIGURE 9.25 Manipulate your project's audio while watching video playback in the Edit window.

There's one item in the Auria store that's an absolute must-buy, and that's the Video Import add-on. It's this optional feature that turns Auria into a true film-making app. Here's how it works...

You begin by creating a new project and then importing a video clip (**FIGURE 9.26**). Unfortunately, Auria can't load movies directly from your iPad's camera roll (a strange oversight). Instead, movies (along with any audio files you'd like to add to your mix, such as sound effects and music) will need to be imported into Auria via iTunes File Sharing. Alternatively, the app can also access your files via Dropbox.

FIGURE 9.26 Using the optional Video Import add-on, Auria can import, play back, and export videos.

When Auria imports your video, it will extract the audio and place it on its own track, keeping it in sync with the video, which appears in a small floating win-dow. Double-tapping the video window brings it full-screen. As you play back the audio, the video plays right along with it. This means you can mix your audio while watching your edited video. Rad!

Since your video's original audio is now accessible on a track, you can adjust its volume over time, apply EQ to clean up any rogue frequencies, use filters to modify the sound, and use AudioCopy to transfer sections to TwistedWave for detailed editing.

More importantly, you can now add additional tracks for ambience, sound effects, music cues, replacement dialogue, and anything else you need to enhance your scene—all of which can be mixed, filtered, and automated.

When you're happy with your mix, you can export everything out as a sound file, *or* you can render out a *new video file that contains your brand new mix*! That blows my mind.

There are so many features I haven't even touched on, like the app's abil-ity to share audio "sessions" with professional DAWs like ProTools or its 96KHz recording on iPads 2 and 3, not to mention a 64-bit double-precision floating-point mixing engine, Track Freezing for minimizing CPU usage, WIST support for wireless syncing of other compatible music apps, and much more.

A DAW this complete could easily cost hundreds on other platforms. As I write these words, Auria will set you back $49.99—a price I suspect will rise at some point in the future. Tack on another $5 for the video import add-on (purchased within the app). While $55 may seem high to some, I bet it feels like a bargain to anyone who's used it, myself included.

Now that you're somewhat familiar with the most kick-butt mixer available on the iPad, perhaps you should give some thought to improving the way in which you get sound in and out of your iPad. If only there were a book that included... oh, wait!

Alesis iO Dock

If you're ready to go all-out, grab the bull by the horns, step up to the plate, do some other clichéd thing implying proactive improvement, and take your mixing to the next level, you're ready for the Alesis iO Dock.

This small wedge-shaped device looks utterly bizarre at first, like a piece of gear that left the factory before it was completed. But, slide your iPad (1, 2, or 3) into its front panel, and suddenly you have an iOS-powered audio and MIDI interface with a laundry list of impressive features (FIGURE 9.27).

The iO Dock doesn't rely on its own app. Instead, it works hand-in-hand with a wide variety of existing audio apps, giving them access to professional audio and MIDI connections.

Why is this important? Well, let's revisit the Auria mixing session. Ideally, while mixing your project, you're listening to everything through a good sound system. Sure, you can use your iPad's built-in speaker, but it's mono, can't

ALESIS iO DOCK

iPad   iPhone

- Alesis
- $399 (around $185 street price)
- hhhlinks.com/ sw8m

FIGURE 9.27 The Alesis iO Dock appears to have eaten my iPad.

reproduce a full tonal range, isn't especially loud, and just sorta sucks. When inserted into the iO Dock, your iPad's audio is pumped through a pair of ¼" audio output jacks (with volume control), perfect for connecting to a professional sound system. The iO Dock also provides a separate ¼" headphone jack with independent volume control.

Next, let's look at bringing sound *in*. The iO Dock sports two audio inputs that will accept either ¼" plugs or XLR connectors (used by professional microphones), each with its own gain (input volume) control (**FIGURE 9.28**). One of the inputs can be switched to Guitar, which is perfect when using guitar amp simulation apps. The iO Dock even has a phantom power option, allowing you to use professional phantom-powered microphones (such as my Sennheiser ME66/K6P shotgun mic).

While I love using the iO Dock for music composition, audio mixing, and voiceover recording, it can be used just as easily on a shoot to record live audio tracks. Just remember that the device requires AC power to operate, so it's a little less "run and gun" than the audio solutions I discussed in Chapter 7.

Lastly, let's explore the iO Dock's Musical Instrument Digital Interface (MIDI) functionality. Most professional music keyboards, drum machines, and other related devices include five-pin MIDI ports that allow them to connect to a computer in order to record performances and play virtual instruments. The iO Dock brings that capability to the iPad. Here's how I make use of the technology: After attaching my Akai MPK 49 MIDI keyboard to my iO Dock (using a standard five-pin MIDI cable) and launching GarageBand on my iPad, I'm able to hear the app's virtual Grand Piano (or any other sound) while playing on my Akai keyboard. For experienced musicians who simply can't tolerate playing a virtual keyboard on a touchscreen, MIDI is a lifesaver. Since the iO Dock supports Core MIDI, it should work with hundreds of MIDI-compatible audio apps available in the App Store.

On the side of the iO Dock, next to the standard five-pin MIDI connectors is a small port labeled USB MIDI (**FIGURE 9.29**). The purpose of this port is often misunderstood and has led some iO Dock owners to become frustrated. Allow me to clear it up. The USB MIDI port is *not* for connecting to external USB-compatible keyboards. It's meant to connect the iO Dock to a computer, for use

FIGURE 9.29 The iO Dock's MIDI connections, including an often-misunderstood USB port.

with desktop MIDI-based applications. The iO Dock has no ports for specifically connecting directly to USB-based MIDI keyboards. Now you know.

Truth be told, the Alesis iO Dock has received mixed reviews over the years, but I suspect the harshest words are coming from audio pros who are used to working on equipment costing thousands of dollars...or maybe not. I can only speak to my own experiences with the iO Dock. I've used it, I've relied on it, and I've loved it. And, I'm pretty sure it loves me, too.

EDITING EXTRAS

Just because you've decided not to color, cut, or score your latest project on your iPhone or iPad, that doesn't mean these devices should be dormant during the postproduction process. Quite the contrary!

Your iOS devices can help you take cut notes quickly and efficiently, calculate and convert timecodes, determine media storage requirements, and even remotely control your computer.

Without further ado, here are some great ways your iOS devices can help you "fix it in post."

Cut Notes

Cut Notes is a brilliant app for producers, directors, and anyone else who must regularly watch rough cuts and give notes.

Before Cut Notes came along, the note-taking process went something like this: With pen and paper in hand, you begin playback of the rough cut (usually provided on a DVD or as a digital video file). As the cut plays, a small timecode counter progresses in the corner of the image. When you come across something noteworthy, you stop playback, write down the current visible timecode, and scribble your note (for example, "cut this shot," "can't hear her line," or "add reaction shot"). Then, you restart playback and repeat the procedure until you've made it all the way through the cut.

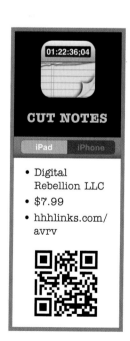

01:22:36;04

CUT NOTES

iPad   iPhone

- Digital Rebellion LLC
- $7.99
- hhhlinks.com/avrv

With Cut Notes on your iPad, the entire process has been digitized.

After launching the app, you'll find a timecode display above 12 large buttons, each containing a small bit of text. What text you ask? Cut notes (**FIGURE 9.30**)!

Each button contains a single cut note (such as "Cut Shot," "Too Slow," "Too Quiet," and so on). The idea here is to have a button for every note you might typically give while watching a rough cut. To that end, every button's text can be customized. For example, if you typically give the note "Find an alternate take," make a button for it! Likewise, if you typically give the note "That shot makes me itchy," make a button for it. If you run out of buttons, don't sweat it; you can always add more.

With your buttons customized, it's time to take some notes! Here's how.

Play and then pause the rough cut as soon as its visible timecode begins to roll. Then, tap the timecode within Cut Notes once to make it editable. Enter the current timecode from your paused rough cut, and tap Done. Now, just tap ▶ next to the timecode display while simultaneously starting the rough cut. Both timecodes should start rolling in sync (they won't match perfectly, but they'll be close enough).

FIGURE 9.30 Cut Notes will help you take notes faster by placing often-used bits of text inside tappable buttons.

FIGURE 9.31 You can always add a custom note simply by sliding the buttons to the right.

Now, as your cut plays and you see something noteworthy, just tap the appropriate button, and your note will be recorded at the current timecode. No stopping and no writing. Sweet! What if you want to add a note that isn't already assigned to a button? Just swipe the buttons to the right to reveal a text field. Type in your custom note and hit Return (FIGURE 9.31). It gets added to your list using the timecode from when you *started* typing the note. Sweet some more!

If you *must* stop playback for any reason, just tap ❚❚ to pause the timecode in Cut Notes. When you're ready to restart, just resync the timecode at the current position (the same way you did it before), and you're good to go.

By rotating your iPad into portrait orientation, you'll find a complete list of your notes that can be edited and deleted (all without stopping the timecode).

When you're done, you can export your notes in a wide variety of formats, including Final Cut Pro Marker lists and Avid Locators. With the help of a free Mac application available on the developer's website, Final Cut Pro (6, 7, and X) editors can import your notes directly into their timelines! Avid editors have it even easier since they can import the notes without the help of an additional desktop application.

Amazing, right? Yes, but not quite as amazing as what I've saved for last.

If you're watching a rough cut directly from a timeline in Final Cut Pro 7 (rather than a DVD or video file), you can set Cut Notes to automatically receive accurate timecode from your computer. You'll never have to enter timecode again! You can even start and stop Final Cut's playback from within Cut Notes. Sadly, this feature isn't available in Final Cut Pro X...at least, not yet.

Cut Notes is a killer app that hasn't left my iPad since the day it came out.

TIMECODE

- Panoptik
- $6.99
- hhhlinks.com/vg0a

Timecode

Years ago, when I was working as an assistant director at Fox Television, one of my responsibilities was to sit in the control room and time the shows. That meant quickly calculating exactly when to break for a commercial, when to come back, and how long each act needed to be in order to end the show on time. Since all professional video is based on timecode, a standard calculator wouldn't have worked (not easily, anyway). So, I used a timecode calculator.

Back then, they were clunky, expensive, ugly, and difficult to use. My, how times have changed. While there are many timecode calculators available in the App Store, my current favorite is called Timecode. Since that might be difficult to remember, I'll say it again. It's a timecode calculator called Timecode. Glad I could help.

Not only can this elegant and intuitive app quickly perform basic timecode calculations (addition, subtraction, multiplication, and division), it displays your results in four different user-selectable formats at once! For example, you could be performing your calculations in NTSC 29.97fps drop-frame (or non-drop) timecode but have your results simultaneously displayed in three other formats as well, such as HD 23.98fps timecode, PAL 25fps timecode, and 35mm film feet and frames (**FIGURE 9.32**). Why is that a good thing? Because it adds another valuable function to your timecode calculator: instant format conversions!

There's more to the app, but frankly, describing a calculator is about as exciting as using a calculator. So, I'll simply say that if you need to perform any timecode (or film) calculations or conversions, Timecode should be on your shopping list.

FIGURE 9.32 My timecode calculator can beat up your timecode calculator.

Editmote

Editmote is a very clever app that transforms your iPhone or iPad into a customizable remote control for your computer's nonlinear editing system. It performs this magic with the help of a free client app that gets installed on your computer and runs in the background to facilitate communications with your iOS device. Currently, the Editmote client is available only as a preference pane for Macs (**FIGURE 9.33**), but a Windows version is in active development and may be available by the time you read this.

Out of the box, the Editmode client app can control Final Cut Pro (7 and X), Avid Media Composer, Adobe Premiere Pro, After Effects, QuickTime Player (7 and X), and VLC. However, additional apps can easily be added. The beauty of the client is that it knows which app your computer is currently using and adjusts its controls accordingly.

Launching Editmote on your iOS device brings up a list of available controllable computers. If you installed and activated the client app on your Mac, it will now be listed here. Keep in mind that your computer and iOS device must be on the same Wi-Fi network. Tapping your computer's name initiates the connection. From there you're brought to the main remote-control screen.

When using Editmote on an iPhone, you'll have access to 26 different customizable buttons. On the iPad's larger screen, that number goes up to 50!

By default, you're given all the buttons you'd expect, such as play/pause, fast-forward, fast-rewind, frame forward, frame backward, and so on (**FIGURE 9.34**). There are even buttons for setting in points, out points, and

EDITMOTE

iPad | iPhone

- Digital Rebellion LLC
- $4.99
- hhhlinks.com/go9q

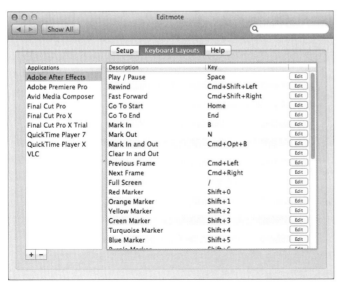

FIGURE 9.33 The Editmote preference pane running on a Mac computer.

FIGURE 9.34 Editmote turns your iPhone (or iPad) into a customizable remote control for your computer.

markers. While you can't drag buttons around the screen, you can change what each button does. After entering edit mode, tapping any button brings up a list of all the available options. There are 37 available commands, although not all of them are available in every computer application. Picking a command assigns it to that button. It's a very simple process. There's no need to customize the remote if you prefer its default settings, but it's nice to know the option is available.

Using the virtual remote is completely intuitive. Tap the play button on your iOS device, and your computer starts playing your video. Tap the Set In-point button, and your computer sets the in point. So, now that you know how easy it is, let's ask the big question: Why would you want a remote control for your computer?

Let me answer that by telling you how I've used the app. While watching hours of interview footage in Final Cut Pro, I like to sit on my sofa across the room and use the remote to control playback. While the clip rolls, I set markers when I hear something I want to return to later. It's a lot nicer than sitting in an office chair all day.

Ultimately, each user will likely find their own uses for Editmote. It's the sort of app that solves problems you didn't know you had.

AJA DataCalc

Before launching your next major production, you should take a moment to make sure you have enough hard drive space to store the assets you'll be generating and collecting (video, production audio, music, sound effects, graphics, and so on). Even as drive capacities expand (and prices fall), without proper planning you will very likely find yourself a terabyte short at a critical moment.

Designed by AJA, one of the leaders in desktop and professional video hardware, AJA DataCalc is a free iPhone app that helps you easily estimate your storage needs. To perform the calculations, simply enter the combined duration of all the footage you expect to shoot, how many audio channels that footage will contain, the format you're shooting on, and the codec that will be used to encode the footage (the app provides a long list of format and codec options). As you alter these values, the Total Data Storage estimate at the top of the screen updates to reflect the changes (**FIGURE 9.35**).

For example, let's assume you were about to shoot a feature film and you plan on shooting a total of 20 hours of raw footage (a little over a 10 to 1 shooting ratio). We'll assume your camera records at 1080p24 (full HD resolution, at 24 frames a second), with 4 channels of audio. You plan on encoding to Apple's ProRes HQ codec. Based on these numbers, DataCalc tells us we need 1.8 terabytes of storage. Does that mean you'll be fine with a 2 terabyte drive? Not necessarily. Depending on your workflow, you may need extra room for renders, visual effects, foley and automatic dialogue replacement (ADR), and more. I tend to multiply drive space estimates by a factor of 1.5 or more. If you decide to shoot at a higher resolution, or encode to a less compressed codec, just dial in your changes to get a revised storage estimate.

For finer control, the app lets you adjust your audio's sample rate and bit depth. There's also a very nicely laid out Summary screen containing all the current calculations. You can even share this data via e-mail.

AJA DATACALC

- AJA Video Systems, Inc.
- free
- hhhlinks.com/ qitn

FIGURE 9.35 I knew I should have purchased another terabyte!

Now that you know how much storage you're going to need, you have two choices. You can pick up a few more drives to store under your desk, or you can free up some existing space by finally deleting that 6-terabyte Chuck Norris photo library you've been hiding all these years.

LEARNING MORE

Have you recently come across a little extra space in your brain that doesn't seem to be doing very much? Don't let it go to waste! The following educational apps can help fill that space with valuable postproduction information!

Your brain will thank you for it.

- Anywhere-Education Inc.
- free
- hhhlinks.com/bc15

Larry Jordan Training for Final Cut Pro X

In addition to hosting the popular *Digital Production Buzz* podcast, Larry Jordan is one of the world's best-known, and most trusted, Final Cut Pro instructors.

The man has authored books, produced videos, led webinars, and presented at industry trade shows far and wide. Since I do quite a bit of presenting as well, I've had the pleasure of sharing the stage with Larry on several occasions, and he's never failed to impress (or educate) me.

Now, Larry has turned his sights on the App Store with a new app called Larry Jordan Training for Final Cut Pro X. Can you guess what it's for? That's right! Taco recipes! And Final Cut Pro X instruction! OK, mostly Final Cut Pro X instruction.

The app provides access to 10 hours of in-depth video-based training. It includes 90 individual tutorials organized into 11 chapters that cover everything from basic interface use to advanced editing techniques. To get you started, the first three chapters (containing 20 tutorials) are provided free of charge. After that, individual chapters can be purchased from within the app for $22 apiece, or you can purchase the entire course for $100 (a savings of $76).

Since the app downloads and stores its content on your iOS device, you don't need to be connected to the Internet in order to view the lessons. That's great news, unless you have limited storage space available. You might have to do a little media management before downloading the entire course.

Speaking of the course, Larry's tutorials are top-notch. He's a seasoned pro who knows how to make complex ideas seem simple. On top of that, his voice has the silky smooth tones of an easy-listening radio DJ. In fact, it wouldn't surprise me if he stopped halfway through a tutorial in order to "send out a very special long-distance dedication."

I have only one issue with the app, and that is its confusing interface—an unintuitive jumble of menus, submenus, pop-ups, and settings. I'll simply say that Larry's excellent tutelage is *well* worth the extra effort the app's less-than-excellent interface requires.

iKeysToGo: Final Cut Pro 7

I admit it. I've been using Final Cut Pro 7, Apple's nonlinear editor, for years, but I've only ever memorized about 20 keyboard shortcuts in total. Unfortunately, this means I often find myself poking through the app's dense manual, a process that's never quite as easy as it should be. That's why I'm glad I found iKeysToGo: Final Cut Pro 7.

This app provides quick access to concise descriptions (and keyboard shortcuts when applicable) for all 840 of Final Cut Pro's commands (**FIGURE 9.36**). This vast amount of data is organized into three easy-to-navigate views. You can skim through all commands sorted in an alphabetical list, find related commands grouped together by topic (such as Audio, Editing, and Importing), or navigate through commands organized using Final Cut Pro's own menu structure (File, Edit, View, and so on). Of course, you can always perform a search.

If you find a command you'd like to save for later reference, you can save it as a favorite. And, if you find a command that doesn't have a keyboard shortcut, the app provides instructions on how to assign one.

While it's true, Final Cut Pro 7 is no longer being developed and has been replaced with the radically redesigned Final Cut Pro X, many editors are sticking

FCP 7

IKEYSTOGO: FINAL CUT PRO 7

iPad | iPhone

- Weynand Training
- $2.99
- hhhlinks.com/ n3nj

FIGURE 9.36 iKeysToGo will help you master Final Cut Pro's keyboard shortcuts.

with the older version until Apple works out the kinks and brings back a few missing features. If you're among the version 7 loyalists, check out iKeysToGo: Final Cut Pro 7.

I'm sure this isn't what the developer wants to hear, but the app also makes for excellent bathroom reading.

EDITCODES

| iPad | iPhone |

- Digital Rebellion LLC
- $2.99
- hhhlinks.com/ 4z91

EditCodes

Has this ever happened to you? You're sitting in front of an Avid Media Composer, piecing together the final moments of your climactic scene when suddenly, *Whamo!* You're hit with an "Error -111." No? Yeah, me neither. But, if you *were* sitting at an Avid and you *did* get that code, would you have any idea what to do about it? No? Yeah, me neither.

Many of the professional desktop video tools we use on a regular basis (Adobe Premiere Pro, Final Cut Pro 7, Final Cut Pro X, DVD Studio Pro, Avid Media Composer, and so on) routinely dish up cryptic error codes that mean nothing to us mere mortals. Thanks to EditCodes, an iPhone-based directory of video application error codes (**FIGURE 9.37**), you no longer have to wonder what messages like "NSURLDomainError -1012" means (that's Final Cut Pro X telling you that it had trouble logging into a third-party service, such as YouTube or Vimeo, because of an incorrect username or password).

In addition to helping you translate baffling error codes, the app also provides suggested actions to help remedy the situation! How cool is that?

FIGURE 9.37 EditCodes. Because every editor should know what an "omfiHPDomain_Bad_Magic" error actually means.

Sure, you could do a Google search for your error code, but this app has done such a nice job of consolidating the information into an alphabetically sorted, easily searchable database, that you'll find your answers with far less frustration. To save you even more time, the app allows you to hide all the codes from the desktop applications you don't use.

On the rare occasion you find yourself faced with an error code that is *not* contained within the app's database, you can easily submit it to the developer, and it will be included in the app's next update.

By the way, "Error -111" is caused by a corrupt title. But, you already knew that. Right? No? Yeah, me neither.

Moviola's Pro Video Guide

Pro Video Guide is a well-organized, fact-filled reference manual that covers all the important technical aspects of modern digital video workflows. The main guide is broken down into five primary sections: Library, Glossary, Organizations, Bookmarks, and History.

The Library section offers useful, easy-to-understand explanations of complex topics (such as video signal standards, bit rates, color space, and so on) (**FIGURE 9.38**). The information is broken down by category and relevant subcategories. When necessary, images are also provided to further explain or demonstrate a concept.

MOVIOLA'S
PRO VIDEO
GUIDE

iPad   iPhone

- Moviola Studios
- $2.99
- hhhlinks.com/
  gg2d

FIGURE 9.38 Pro Video Guide is a professional video guide about video...for pros.

The Glossary section provides a comprehensive list of terms along with excellent, to-the-point explanations. You can scroll up and down through the terms or narrow down the list by using the search box (which remains fixed at the top of the screen, a thoughtful touch).

The Organizations tab provides lists of unions, guilds, groups, and forums. Each entry includes a brief description (sometimes too brief) and a URL. It even has a section for filmmaking-related blogs that very wisely includes a link to HandHeldHollywood.com, the greatest website ever to be shamelessly promoted by a self-serving author.

You can bookmark any entry in the Library, Glossary, and Organizations sections for later review. Unfortunately, the app offers no way to delete an individual bookmark. You can only choose to clear your entire bookmark list. The History tab shows where you've been in the app, like the history section of a web browser. Not much else to say about that.

Moviola's Pro Video Guide isn't a perfect app. It doesn't get updated very often and therefore lacks a few of the most recent technological advancements. That said, if you're working with brand new gear and implementing cutting-edge techniques, you're likely not someone who would be reading this guide in the first place. More likely, you'd be *writing* it!

Whether you're a tech-head or a video newbie, Pro Video Guide will make a worthy addition to your iPhone arsenal. And at $2.99, it's a significantly better investment than Burp and Fart Piano.

Side note: If you are 10 years old, please disregard the previous statement. For you, absolutely nothing is better than Burp and Fart Piano.

BURP AND FART PIANO

iPad   iPhone

- Sam Meech Ward
- free
- hhhlinks.com/ 55am

CHAPTER 10

IT'S DONE! NOW WHAT?

Congratulations! You've managed to guide your project from concept to completion. Your finished feature film or short film or documentary or corporate industrial or music video or wedding video or home video or other video is truly a unique work of art.

It's time to relax and enjoy a much-deserved rest. You've earned it.

Break time over! I hope you made the most of that tranquil moment. That was more time than some working filmmakers get.

What good is your finished work if no one else gets to see it? Did you just spend months of your life, and possibly a bucket of cash, on a private diary entry? Of course not! It's time to let the world see what you've done!

YOUTUBE, VIMEO, AND FACEBOOK

I'm guessing you don't need me to tell you that social video-sharing websites are the best way to reach the widest possible audience. But just in case you do, social video-sharing websites are the best way to reach the widest possible audience. Sites such as YouTube, Vimeo, Tumblr, and Facebook have made it absurdly easy to upload and distribute video.

When I set out to write this book, I figured I'd have a section on uploading to video-sharing sites. However, as I tunneled my way through the chapters, I realized that uploading video had become so automated and ubiquitous that there was no need to cover the topic in any great detail.

If you've shot and edited your project using traditional gear, you'll likely be uploading it from a desktop computer using each website's upload options (click, upload, done). If you've shot and/or edited your project on an iOS device, you'll be happy to know that nearly all the camera and editing apps I've mentioned have the built-in ability to easily upload to a variety of these video-sharing services (tap, upload, done) (**FIGURE 10.1**).

FIGURE 10.1 FiLMiC Pro, like many of the other apps in this book, make it easy to upload video to the most popular destinations.

Easy uploading has its advantages, but it's also the reason so many good projects get lost on these sites. If you can upload easily, so can everyone else. In fact, according to YouTube's own statistics page, more than 70 hours of video is uploaded every minute!

Don't let that statistic discourage you. Just make sure you keep an open mind about other forms of distribution. Speaking of which…

SELLING YOUR WORK

After putting so much of yourself into your finished production, wouldn't you like to get something back? But what exactly? Let's break it down.

> You put in *hours*. You certainly won't be getting those back.

> You put in *sweat*. You don't really *want* that back, do you?

> You put in *money*. Hey! Now, *that's* something you may be able to get back!

You have two primary choices when it comes to selling your films. You can partner with a distribution company, or you can self-distribute. Nearly all film-makers prefer the first option, but it can be downright brutal finding a reputable company that feels as passionately about your work as you do. Depending on the perceived commercial appeal of your work, finding a distributor can be harder than making the movie itself.

As I write this, I'm in the process of trying to find a distributer for my most recent work. Like most indie filmmakers, if I can't find a distribution partner, I'll be wading into the murky waters of self-distribution—a vast, bottomless ocean awash with opportunities…and piranha.

Self-distribution can involve everything from selling Blu-rays of your film at fes-tivals and art-house screenings to finding innovative, out-of-the-box ways to reach a mass audience. It's about pursuing any and all ways of recouping what you've spent and funding what's yet to come.

In this section, I'm going to show a few two iOS-based solutions that can help you sell your work at both ends of the self-distribution spectrum.

Put It in the App Store

There's no denying it: iPhones and iPads have revolutionized the way we make films, but consider how they've changed the viewing experience as well. While the world was busy doing other things, Apple managed to sneak portable movie screens into hundreds of millions of pockets, purses, and backpacks, providing today's filmmakers with an enormous potential audience.

You could try to get your film into the iTunes movie section, where it will join thousands of other titles. Or you could take a bold step into an entirely new distribution model. You could sell your movie *as an app*!

"That's totally insane!" says the traditional film distributor.

"Is it totally insane? Or is it *brilliant* and totally insane?" asks the author of this book. Why brilliant? I'll give you two reasons.

Reason 1: *It's cool!* How many filmmakers can claim to have their own app? Wait! Before you dismiss this whole idea, let me say that I agree with you: Being "cool" is not a good enough reason to go down this path.

Reason 2: When your movie is purchased or rented within iTunes, it is watched and then it is…um…well, that's it really. It's just watched. But if your movie were enclosed inside an app, the user experience would not have to end when the closing credits roll. Instead, you could offer all sorts of additional goodies, such as the bonus features found on DVDs and Blu-ray Discs. You might include behind-the-scenes videos, cast interviews, a director's commentary, photo albums, and up-to-date news about the film. You could even build a social presence around your app, letting your fans share their thoughts.

Did I say two reasons? I meant three.

Reason 3: Because your app will include awesome bonus features that aren't available on other platforms, you can charge a premium!

Keep in mind that building an app in no way guarantees that anyone is going to purchase it. You'll still have to do plenty of legwork, including marketing your app and spreading the word. You'll also have to give up 30 percent of your sales to Apple. That's Apple's standard percentage rate for all apps appearing in the App Store.

If you're not comfortable with the idea of your film existing *only* as an app, there's no rule that says you can't also make it available as a downloadable movie in iTunes. In fact, you could place an ad for the app after your movie's end credits, inviting fans to learn more about the film and to join its app-based online community. Neither of the two companies I'll be discussing in a moment requires exclusive rights to your film, so you're free to sell it in as many forms as you'd like.

Unless you know how to code your own app, you'll likely be searching for a company that already specializes in this sort of thing. Finding one might be hard. But finding *two*, well, that's easy! Just keep reading!

MoPIX

Think of MoPIX as a self-service distribution channel for independent filmmakers.

It has been helping customers turn their movies into apps since early 2011, and it has already completed 30 conversions. If that doesn't impress you, perhaps this will: MoPIX currently has 200 more films in its conversion queue! Does that mean you'll be waiting behind 200 other filmmakers before it's your turn? Nope!

MoPIX has managed to radically increase the speed of its app production process by developing an intuitive, web-based system that lets *you* perform most of your own setup work (**FIGURE 10.2**). I'm guessing this is how it has managed to keep its prices low (more on that in a moment). Using MoPIX's system, you can upload your content, pick your desired features, and tweak the overall look by adjusting the app's fonts, colors, background images, and layout (to a lesser degree).

The movie apps can include videos, images, and even PDF documents (great for sharing screenplays within the app). You can also add strong social network integration. For example, if a user likes an image in your behind-the-scenes photo album, she can share that image on her Facebook page.

When MoPIX first started making apps, it included all of the media within the app itself. That made for a smooth user experience, but it took up *way* too much storage space. Now, its apps are relying more heavily on streaming content. This way, the app itself can be kept smaller and more manageable. That said, there's one issue to consider.

Users will need an Internet connection to stream the content. Without a connection, all they'll be watching is their own frustrated expressions reflected on their touchscreens. It's a minor detail, considering the exponential expansion of always-connected technology, but it is worth keeping in mind.

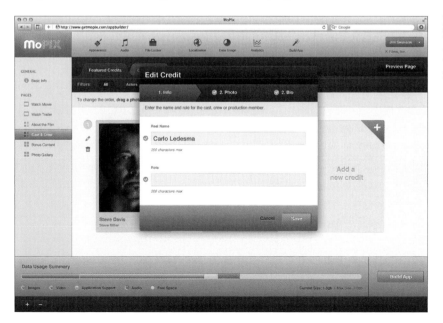

FIGURE 10.2 MoPIX has built a gorgeous web app that can help you turn your finished film into a finished app.

FIGURE 10.3 Design and preview your new app while keeping costs down.

FIGURE 10.3 Design and preview your new app while keeping costs down.

The sales model for these apps has been pretty consistent. Give the app away for free, but include an in-app purchase option to buy the film and extra content. This way, users can download the app and get a taste of things to come (watch the trailer, check out a few preview photos, and so on) and then pay for the movie if they so desire.

Fortunately for us, MoPIX has worked very hard to automate a large part of the app-making process (**FIGURE 10.3**). This allows MoPIX to provide its services as inexpensively as possible. For a typical conversion, prices start at around $500. If you know anything about app development, you already know that $500 is *wicked cheap*. Naturally, the more features you want to include in your app, the higher the price will climb.

In addition to the initial build cost, MoPIX also collects a percentage (somewhere between 10 and 30 percent) of your app's total sales. The best way to get the *real* numbers is to start a conversation with MoPIX by visiting its website (http://www.getmopix.com).

By now, you're probably wondering when you are going to get *your* money from the sales of your app. MoPIX pays out sales revenue to filmmakers on a quarterly basis.

What's next for MoPIX? Total world domination! Bwahaha! But, it is going to start by expanding its reach into other dedicated platforms (such as Roku). In fact, MoPIX should already have movie apps available for Android by the time you read this.

MoPIX
www.getmopix.com

Stonehenge Productions

Much like MoPIX, San Diego–based Stonehenge Productions can transform your film into an engaging, feature-packed app for iOS and Android devices around the globe. However, this company takes a different, more personal approach.

Before I delve into the specifics, let me give you a quick bit of history.

Mark Smillie, the company's founder, has been developing iOS apps for years. After witnessing several great films fade into obscurity because of a lack of proper distribution, Mark was struck with the idea to turn films into apps. Two weeks after creating his first movie app for a film called *geek-mythology* (directed by Phil Hwang), Apple released the iPad—the perfect movie-viewing device. Shortly after that, Mark and Stonehenge Productions were featured in the *Wall Street Journal*, spurring his company's growth. Thus far, the company has produced around 50 movie apps (**FIGURE 10.4**).

In addition to the features I've already mentioned (bonus videos, photo albums, and so on), Stonehenge has created some very cool custom features for its clients. For example, it's added a quiz to a movie app called Sync or Swim and a drumming game to another called Adventures of Power. It has even added video upload features to apps containing documentaries, giving viewers the ability to support the film's causes by adding their own videos and voices to the film's YouTube channel. It's app-enhanced social activism! Obviously, custom features like these will drive up the app's creation costs.

Speaking of costs, what's it gonna cost?

Because each iOS (or Android) app is custom built to the filmmaker's specifications, Stonehenge's services cost a bit more, starting at around $2000. The

FIGURE 10.4 Two of the many movie apps created by Stonehenge Productions.

process is pretty straightforward. After discussing the project with Stonehenge, you'll be asked to provide all of the available assets. This could include the film, Photoshop artwork (posters, logos, and so on), behind-the-scenes videos, photo albums, video diaries, relevant social links, and more.

Stonehenge will then create an app design for you to review. If you like what you see, the app gets built. If you want to make a few changes to the design first, Stonehenge will work with you until you're happy. Once the app is coded, it's sent to Apple for approval. Assuming Apple signs off, your app will appear in the App Store, ready to be purchased. Easy peezy.

Unlike MoPIX, Stonehenge Productions doesn't take a percentage of your sales. It receives payments from Apple and turns it all around to you (after your app revenue hits the $100 mark).

Now that you understand exactly how it's done, let me tell you how it's all about to change. Mark has decided to take Stonehenge Productions in a very interesting direction, one that will allow your movie app to reach a much wider audience.

While his company will continue to create and support iOS (and Android) apps for filmmakers who request them, Mark is now developing movie apps using the HTML5 web standard. In other words, he's building *web apps* that look and behave just like native apps, with some advantages (and disadvantages).

By building apps with HTML5, build costs are greatly reduced (starting at around $800). As with iOS apps, pricing is flexible based on the filmmaker's desired features. Once the app is done, it's available on *any* modern mobile platform (Android, Windows Phone, and so on). Build it once, and it works everywhere! That's another major cost savings. Furthermore, you can completely bypass Apple's approval process, which at times can be a little overly subjective. Because the entire app is streamed, you can make changes at any time. Want the best news? You get to keep 100 percent of the sales revenue. All of it. Nobody else gets a cut. All payments are instantly deposited into your PayPal account. Sweet!

Stonehenge Productions
www.stonehenge productions.com

Web apps aren't all peaches and cream. There are a few downsides to consider. First, web apps don't appear in the App Store. This means you'll have to find another way to get your app in front of your audience (not always an easy task). Because web apps can't tie into hardware as effectively as native apps, some bonus features may be limited (camera- and geolocation-based features, for example). Also missing are push notifications. Limitations aside, HTML5-based web apps are an interesting alternative worthy of consideration.

To learn more about the process, visit the Stonehenge Productions website (http://www.stonehengeproductions.com).

PayPal, Square, and Intuit

This solution is for filmmakers who travel with their movies (attending festivals and art-house screenings) and want to sell DVDs, Blu-rays, and related merchandise along the way.

Naturally, you don't *need* an iOS device to sell your work. People have been bartering for thousands of years, trading livestock for goods and services. Fortunately, many consumers now use cash instead. But what happens when a potential customer isn't carrying any paper-based currency? Unless you want to trade your film for three chickens and a goat, you might consider employing an iOS-based credit card reader.

In the past, swiping credit cards involved bulky equipment, special bank accounts, and excessive fees. These days, all it takes is a tiny plastic doodad plugged into your iOS device's headphone jack (**FIGURE 10.5**). The best part is that these devices are being given away for free by several companies who want your card-swiping business. Currently, the biggest players in the iOS mobile payment arena are PayPal, Square, and Intuit.

For all three companies, the process is the largely the same. Download their free app, set up a free account, request their free card reader, and start selling!

Of course, the service itself isn't free. You'll be charged a small percentage of every sale you make. This percentage will be higher if you tap in your customer's credit card number manually (using the app's on-screen number pad), rather than using the free accessory to swipe the customer's card. As an added treat, you'll also be charged a small per-transaction fee when entering numbers manually. With a lower percentage rate and nonexistent per-transaction fees, swiping plastic is clearly the way to go. Two of the services (Square and Intuit GoPayment) also offer alternative plans in which you can pay a monthly fee in exchange for reduced percentage fees.

When you're preparing to sell your work, make sure you've collected all the necessary talent and location releases, along with any required music and copyright clearances. It's also worth noting that not all festivals and theaters will permit you to sell your merchandise. Some may allow it but may ask for a percentage of sales. Others may permit it but ask that you keep it low-key (no sale signs and such). Make sure to get all the details before setting up shop.

TABLE 10.1 shows a basic breakdown of how each company charges for its services. Because fee structures change all the time, you should do a little research to make sure these numbers are still accurate.

PAYPAL HERE

iPad | iPhone

- PayPal, an eBay Company
- free
- hhhlinks.com/e9t9

FIGURE 10.5 The PayPal credit card reader plugs right into your device's headphone jack.

SQUARE CARD READER

iPad | iPhone

- Square, Inc.
- free
- hhhlinks.com/irus

INTUIT GOPAYMENT

iPad | iPhone

- Intuit, Inc.
- free
- hhhlinks.com/7dpf

TABLE 10.1 iOS-Based Credit Card Services

Service Name	Monthly Fee	Swipe Fee	Manual Entry Fee
PayPay Here	$0	2.7%	3.5%+15¢ per transaction
Square	$0	2.75%	3.5%+15¢ per transaction
Square (monthly)	$0	2.75%	3.5%+15¢ per transaction
Intuit GoPayment	$0	2.7%	3.7%
Intuit GoPayment (monthly)	$12.95	1.7%	2.7%

Transaction fees aside, there are other factors to consider when picking a service, such as the speed at which you actually get the money from your sales.

PayPal is the fastest, depositing the money directly into your PayPal account within minutes. If you already have a PayPal debit MasterCard, you can spend your money as soon as it hits your account. That's especially awesome if you just sold 20 copies of your film and feel like celebrating with a steak dinner!

Square sends your payments to a linked bank account, usually by the next day. Intuit lags behind, depositing your money in your bank account within two to three days. Not only are they the slowest, but I've heard a few complaints about Intuit's tendency to surprise sellers with extra fees.

iPHONE FILM FESTIVALS

With the rapidly rising popularity of the iPhone and iPad, there has been a sharp increase in the number of young and independent filmmakers using these devices as their primary cameras. If you count yourself among them, you'll be delighted to learn that iOS-specific film festivals are now popping up from Singapore to San Francisco.

While one of these festivals features public screenings and the other two are purely virtual (existing exclusively online), they all help to support and promote the growing iOS filmmaking movement.

Let's take a look at a few of the most interesting festivals.

The Original iPhone Film Festival

Founded by Matt Dessner and Corey Rogers, the Original iPhone Film Festival was conceived to support the rapidly growing iPhone filmmaking community and to showcase its emerging talent. It's the first iPhone festival that hit my radar, and as such, it holds a special place in my heart. I've spoken with Matt a few times, and he never fails to reenergize me when we discuss the iPhone film-making revolution.

When you enter the Original iPhone Film Festival, your work is judged by a panel of true heavyweights. For example, 2011's panel included names like Caleb Deschanel (legendary cinematographer) and David Pogue (the personal-technology columnist for the *New York Times*). Winners will enjoy prizes donated by several top-notch tech sponsors.

Original iPhone Film Festival
www.original iphonefilmfest.com

Entering the Original iPhone Film Festival is free, so there's no reason not to enter! Visit the festival's website to learn more, and check out all the rules.

If you're wondering why this festival has the word *Original* in its title, perhaps it has something to do with this next festival.

www.originaliphonefilmfest.com

The iPhone Film Festival

The iPhone Film Festival was created by filmmakers *for* filmmakers.

Entry is free, but they're selective about which films they'll accept. Aside from requiring that the films be shot entirely on an iPhone, iPad, or iPod touch, their rules are fairly relaxed, with one important exception: You may not submit your film to any other iPhone/mobile festivals until six months after this festival's winners are announced. This is not a huge deal, but it's something to keep in mind as you plan your festival road map.

iPhone Film Festival
www.iphoneff.com

The festival is judged by a panel of working producers, directors, actors, and more. Winners get a pile of great filmmaking gear from the festival's sponsors.

www.iphoneff.com

The Disposable Film Festival

The Disposable Film Festival celebrates the democratization of cinema. Not limited to iPhone footage, this festival welcomes any film shot on what they call "disposable" devices, such as mobile phones, pocket cameras, DSLRs, and so on.

Launched in 2007, this festival takes place every March in San Francisco and then travels to various cities around the world. I dig this fest because it's about actual screenings (along with workshops, competitions, panels, and other educational events). As much as I love the idea of millions of people enjoying my work in the privacy of their own living rooms, nothing beats the thrill I get

Disposable Film Festival
www.
disposablefilmfest.
com

watching an audience watch my film. It's always an exhilarating and informative experience.

Of the three festivals I've mentioned, this is the only one that charges an entry fee. But, it's only $0.99, so I think you can manage (just hold off on buying that $0.99 virtual mustache app you've had your eye on). If your film is shorter than ten minutes, you should absolutely check out this fest.

www.disposablefilmfest.com

PUTTING IT ON-SCREEN

We've explored putting your movie on the Internet, in film festivals, and within its own full-blown app. But what if your immediate goal is to simply put it on your television? No problem. Here are a few ways you can connect your tech to your tube.

Apple TV and AirPlay

APPLE TV

- Apple
- $99
- www.apple.com

Adding an Apple TV (second generation or newer) to your home television system is by far the fastest and easiest way to transmit content from your iPhone or iPad directly to your big screen. Closely resembling a squared-off hockey puck (**FIGURE 10.6**), this $99 small black box is a multipurpose marvel, bringing a wide range of audio and video resources to your television.

After connecting the Apple TV to your HDTV via a single HDMI cable (not supplied), it will allow you to purchase and enjoy movies (which can also be rented), recent and not-so-recent TV shows, and music. It can stream videos, photos, and music directly from networked Mac or Windows machines running iTunes. It even taps into online services like YouTube, Vimeo, and Flickr. If you pay a little extra, you can receive content from Netflix, Hulu Plus, the MLB, NBA, and the NHL. This is only scratching the surface! It also offers access to movie trailers, podcasts, Internet radio stations, and photos from your iCloud Photo Stream. And, since the Apple TV is running a modified version of Apple's iOS, it's very likely that it will soon be able to download additional third-party apps!

FIGURE 10.6 Connect an Apple TV to your HDTV, and you'll be able to wirelessly transmit video (and audio) from your iPad or iPhone directly to your television's display.

While all of those features are nifty, they have nothing to do with my reasons for including the Apple TV in this chapter. For me, one feature in particular makes this device a must-have, and it's called AirPlay.

Using AirPlay, your iPhone or iPad can wirelessly transmit its audio and video content straight to your Apple TV and HD television. I'm continually amazed by how many people own an Apple TV and *don't* know about this amazing feature.

As long as your Apple TV and iOS devices are on the same wireless network, making the connection is a snap. Using an AirPlay-compatible app such as the built-in Photos app, load a video and look for ▣. This is the AirPlay icon. Tapping it once will bring up a list of all the available AirPlay devices on your network (**FIGURE 10.7**). Look for your Apple TV on the list, tap it once, and you're done!

FIGURE 10.7 After setting up your Apple TV, it will magically appear on your iOS device as a new AirPlay destination.

Playing the video on your iOS device will now stream it live to the Apple TV and to your connected HDTV. Most, but not all, iOS devices are compatible with AirPlay. If you own any model iPad or an iPhone 3GS (or newer), you're all set. Original iPhone and iPhone 3G owners, you've just encountered another reason to upgrade.

If you've purchased a new Mac computer within the past few months, and it's running OS X 10.8 (Mountain Lion) or newer, there's a decent chance it can also take advantage of AirPlay, letting you send videos and music from your computer straight to your HDTV via the Apple TV box. If Apple ever chooses to release its own television set (the subject of rumors for the past three years), you can be sure AirPlay is going to play a major part.

How much do I *love* Apple TV (and AirPlay)? Why not ask any of my three Apple TV boxes stationed around my home. They'll tell you. It's a lot.

Video Cables

No AirPlay? No problem! May I offer this far less sexy alternative: cables. They cost less, are more portable, don't require a network, and work just as well, if not better in some situations.

Apple makes three video cables that can be connected directly to your iOS device's standard 30-pin dock connector, assuming your device actually has a standard 30-pin dock connector.

As I mentioned in Chapter 7, beginning with the iPhone 5, all new iOS devices will feature a redesigned, much smaller dock connector that Apple has dubbed *Lightning*. If you're lucky enough to have a Lightning-compatible device, these three cables won't work for you, but don't fret. Apple is already working on new Lightning video cables (which may be available by the time you read this). In the meantime, Apple TV and AirPlay are your best options.

**APPLE
DIGITAL AV
ADAPTER**

- Apple
- $39
- www.apple.com

Apple Digital AV Adapter

If you own an iPad (1, 2, or 3) or an iPhone (4 or 4S) and you want to connect it to an HDTV, this is likely the cable you'll want (**FIGURE 10.8**).

One end of the adapter slips into your device's dock connector, and the other features a female HDMI port, which means you'll also need your own HDMI cable to run from the adapter to your television. While HDMI cables are available at major electronics stores like Best Buy, I highly recommend you pick up your HDMI cables on eBay. The build quality won't be quite as nice, but they'll cost you about one-tenth the price.

FIGURE 10.8 The Apple Digital AV Adapter makes it easy to connect your compatible iOS device to an HDMI input.

Apple's Digital AV Adapter also provides a second female dock connection, allowing you to plug in a standard Apple 30-pin charger, keeping your device's battery happily charged. This is great news since you don't want your iPhone or iPad conking out right in the middle of your movie.

Once the adapter and HDMI cable are connected, you'll be able to view your movies on your HDTV just by playing them on your iOS device. Furthermore, if you have an iPhone 4S or 5 or an iPad 2 or 3, this cable also provides live mirroring. This simply means that everything on the connected device's display will also appear on your HDTV. It could not be simpler. However, while mirroring provides resolutions up to 1080p, movies will always play out at a maximum of 1280x720 (720p).

I'd like to spend the next few pages discussing the intricacies of using this cable, but there aren't any intricacies. So, I guess we'll have to move on.

Apple VGA Adapter

This slightly less expensive cable provides an easy way to send video *but not audio* to a VGA-equipped projector or monitor (**FIGURE 10.9**).

Just like the Digital AV Adapter, the VGA Adapter plugs into your device's doc connector. But, as you probably already guessed, instead of a female HDMI connection, the VGA adaptor supplies a female…wait for it…VGA connection. I hope you packed a separate VGA cable in your overnight bag.

Although this adapter can't carry an audio signal, it handles video in the same way as the Digital AV Adapter. Just plug it in, play a movie, and you're good to go! While iPhone 4S and newer and iPad 2 and newer owners will enjoy video mirroring with this adapter (at resolutions up to 1080p), iPhone 4 and iPad 1 owners will have to be satisfied with video playback only (at a maximum resolution of 720p).

Because VGA cables carry an *analog* signal, the picture will not be as crisp as what you'd see when using the HDMI adapter, which carries a digital signal. Since this is a video-only cable, you might want to have an external speaker on hand to amplify your device's audio.

APPLE VGA ADAPTER

- Apple
- $29
- www.apple.com

FIGURE 10.9 Send video (without audio) from your compatible iOS device to a VGA-ready device (such as an office projector or computer monitor) with Apple's VGA Adapter.

Apple Composite AV Cable

As the oldest cable in the group, I'd recommend using the Composite AV Cable (**FIGURE 10.10**) only if you have an older model iPhone or a monitor that only accepts composite input. It's compatible with every 30-pin bearing iOS device dating back to the original iPhone and also supports a *wide* variety of iPods.

I'm not going to spend much time on this cable…because it kinda sucks. It carries an outdated, analog signal that doesn't support high-definition video. The only reason to use it is if you're connecting to a piece of equally outdated, analog equipment. In those extremely rare instances when you find yourself staring at a composite connection, you'll be glad this cable exists, but until then, forget about it.

APPLE COMPOSITE AV CABLE

- Apple
- $39
- www.apple.com

FIGURE 10.10 Need to connect your compatible iOS device to a VCR? Get this cable…and then get rid of your VCR.

THE LAST APP IN THE BOOK

I wanted to wrap up the book with an app that represented the end of the film-making journey, one that would provide the most benefit *after* your film made it into movie theaters. I deliberated all the possibilities.

Should it be an app that looks up local movie times? Perhaps one that provides in-depth reviews? Or maybe it should be the official IMDB (Internet Movie Database) app? None of them felt right. I finally decided to go with an app that would bring joy and comfort to every filmmaker (and every filmgoer) around the world.

That app is RunPee (**FIGURE 10.11**).

RunPee allows you to quickly search through a huge database of films (including new releases) to find out exactly when it's safe to run to the bathroom. Yes, really.

While you're taking care of business, the app will display a synopsis of the scene you're currently missing so you'll be all caught up by the time you return to your seat. As if that weren't enough, the app also provides a recap of the film's first few minutes (just in case you're running late to the theater) and even lets you know about any extra scenes during or after the end credits.

RunPee takes all the stress out of movie theater bathroom breaks.

I can't think of a more appropriate app with which to end our journey.

RUNPEE

iPad | iPhone

- polyGeek
- free
- hhhlinks.com/
  k9pc

FIGURE 10.11 RunPee provides a unique and valuable service. Just get it.

ADDITIONAL RESOURCES

We've covered a lot of ground in these 350+ pages. But, truth be told, there's far more to the mobile filmmaking revolution than could ever be contained in a single book. For that reason, I thought I'd make a few suggestions about where you can turn to continue your journey.

Hand Held Hollywood

Hand Held Hollywood explores how iPads, iPhones, and other iThings can be used to aid nearly every aspect of film and video production.

If you dug this book, you'll dig the website that inspired it. If you hated this book, I strongly suggest reading it again while drinking heavily. You're welcome.

www.HandHeldHollywood.com

Prolost and *The DV Rebel's Guide*

Stu Maschwitz is a remarkably talented filmmaker who has his fingers in just about everything. Prolost is his blog, and it's a must-read for any and all filmmakers. He doesn't post often, but when he does, you can be sure it will contain something thoughtful, insightful, and inspiring (and occasionally, iOS related).

Back in 2006, one year before the birth of the iPhone, Stu wrote *The DV Rebel's Guide* (Peachpit Press). While this terrific, action-oriented filmmaking tome doesn't include a shred of iPhone goodness, it's been the first book I recommend to all filmmakers. However, now it will be the second. Tough break, Stu.

http://prolost.com

http://hhhlinks.com/rebel

Film Riot

I *love* this show/podcast because it focuses on low-budget production and out-of-the-box thinking while *never* taking itself too seriously. They cover iOS stuff on occasion, but that's not why I'm recommending it. The bottom line is it's fun, it's educational, and it's mildly idiotic in an awesome way. For new filmmakers, this show is a must-watch.

http://revision3.com/filmriot

Hand Held Hollywood
HandHeld Hollywood.com

Prolost
prolost.com

The DV Rebel's Guide
hhhlinks.com/rebel

Film Riot
revision3.com/ filmriot

Indie Mogul
www.youtube.com/
user/indymogul

Indie Mogul

Similar in tone and substance to Film Riot, Indie Mogul helps new filmmakers wrap their heads around the basics, while keeping things wonderfully unprofessional. They're also a *great* source for do-it-yourself film gear.

www.youtube.com/user/indymogul

EVERYBODY OFF THE BUS!

While I hope you enjoyed reading the book, I'd be happier knowing that it changed the way you think about your iOS devices. Actually, scratch that. I think I'd be happier knowing that you enjoyed reading the book, but the other thing is important, too. Now, where was I?

I hope you've found some new ways to incorporate your iPhone and your iPad into your creative workflow. I hope you feel empowered knowing that you already own the most versatile filmmaking tool on Earth. And, I hope that you have been filled with an overwhelming desire to buy me a beer should we ever meet. If I've earned even one free beer (and maybe a plate of chicken fingers), then writing this book will have been worth it.

Now stop reading, wrap up your game of Fruit Ninja, and go make a movie!

INDEX

NUMBERS

1st Video, 320–321
2× telephoto lens, 221
8mm and 8mm HD video camera, 195–196
60fps, shooting, 191
180-degree rule, applying in Shot Designer, 153–154

A

Abrams, J.J., 198
accessories. *See* extras; iPad accessories; iPhone accessories
Action Cart table dolly, 239–240
Action Movie FX video camera, 199–200
Adobe Story, 62–63
Adonit's Jot Pro stylus, 56, 137–139
agreements. *See* contracts; release forms
AirGrade for iPhone trackball app, 312
Airplane Mode, switching to, 169–170
AJA DataCalc app, 338–340
Alesis iO Dock
    audio connections, 332
    MIDI functionality, 332
    USB-MIDI, 332–333
Almost DSLR video camera app
    controls, 181–182
    exposure, 182
    focus, 182
    free version, 182
    launching, 181
annotating screenplays
    Adobe Story, 62–63
    GoodNotes, 60–61
    GoodReader, 57–58
    PDF Expert, 54–58
    PDFPen, 58–60
Apple's Camera Connection Kit, 301
apps, removing from iOS devices, 170. *See also* websites
Artemis Director's Viewfinder, 147–151
    indicating lens sizes, 149
    switching modes, 149–150
    workflows, 148–149
Artemis HD, 147–151
audio
    FiRe 2, 207

Hindenburg Field Recorder, 204–206
    overview, 200–201
    Pro Audio To go, 202–203
    Voice Memo app, 207
audio accessories, 322
    adapter cables, 243–244
    AR-41 stereo microphone, 247–249
    iXZ microphone adapter, 245–246
    Tascam iM2 stereo mic, 249–250
    VideoMic Pro shotgun mic, 244–245
audio mixing
    Alesis iO Dock, 331–333
    Auria, 328–331
    overview, 325–326
    TwistedWave Audio Editor, 326–327

B

Baby names + app, naming characters, 21
the bible production directory, 88–89
blocking shots
    MagicPlan floor plan, 161–164
    OmniGraffle, 156–160
    Shot Designer, 151–156
    TouchDraw, 160–161
Bluetooth keyboards
    Apple Keyboard Dock, 38
    Belkin YourType Keyboard Folio, 36–37
    cases, 35–38
    Kensington KeyFolio case, 37
    Logitech Ultrathin cover, 38
    pairing, 34–35
    Targus Versavu case, 35–36
    using, 33–35
    ZAGG Folio case, 36
brainstorming, with iThoughtsHD, 5–6
budgeting, overview, 127
Burp and Fart Piano, 344

C

calculator, pCAM Film+Digital, 265–268
call sheets
    doddlePRO, 107–109

FilmTouch, 112–113
    Lua, 113
    Pocket Call Sheet, 109–112
Camera app, built in, 183–184
camera calculations
    overview, 264–265
    pCAM Film+Digital Calculator, 265–268
    Toland ASC Digital Assistant, 268–270
Camera Connection Kit, 301
Camera Order tech scouting, 96–98
Campbell, Joseph, 14–15
cards, using to define story structure, 16–19
Casablanca script, accessing, 67
Celtx Scout resource collection tool, 165–166
Celtx Script, 22–24
    button bar, 23
    context-sensitive shortcuts, 23–24
    versus Storyist app, 25–26
character archetypes
    Martyr, 15
    Orphan, 15
    Wanderer, 15
    Warrior, 15
characters, naming, 20
Chromagic for iPad, 311
Cinema Forms, 119–121
CinemaFX for Video, 310–311
CinePro video camera app, 179–181
    filters, 180
    flaw, 180
    settings screen, 180
clappers. *See* slates
CollabraCam video camera, 184–187
    Director mode, 185
    overview, 184–185
    starting sessions, 186
color correcting footage
    AirGrade for iPhone, 312
    Chromagic for iPad, 311
    CinemaFX for Video, 310–311
    Movie Looks HD, 308–309
    overview, 305–306
    VideoGrade, 306–308
    vWave-Lite, 311
Common Lighting Setups, 175

composing scores
  GarageBand, 324–325
  overview, 321–322
  Tabletop, 322–324
computer
  importing footage to iPad,
    302–305
  importing footage to iPhone,
    302–305
Contour story development tool,
  14–16
  The 4 Questions, 15
  character archetypes, 15
  movie examples, 15
contracts. *See also* release forms
  Cinema Forms, 119–121
  Form Tools PDF, 117–119
  overview, 113–114
Corkulous Pro app. *See also* mind
  mapping
  benefits, 10
  corkboards, 9
  features, 9
  organization, 9
  syncing with iCloud, 9–10
Cosmonaut stylus, 139
credit card services, iOS-based,
  354
Croma LED lighting panel, 236–237
The Cube video encoder, 283–285
Cut Notes app, 333–335. *See also*
  notes

D

The Daily Script, 66
database of films, searching
  through, 360
DataVideo website, 262
del Carmen, Louie, 134
Denecke Slate, 280
Dictabulus, 42–43
dictation. *See* voice dictation
DiffCase conversion lenses,
  224–226
digital audio workstation, Auria,
  328–331
digital video workflows, reference
  manual for, 343–344. *See also*
  video
digitizing paperwork
  DodScanner, 125–126
  Doxie Go hardware scanner,
    121–124
  Eye-Fi, 124
  overview, 121

director's viewfinders
  Artemis, 147–151
  overview, 147
Disposable Film Festival, 355–356
doddle production directory, 89–91
doddlePRO call sheets, 107–109
DodScanner app, 125–126
Doering-Powell, Mark, 266–268
Doxie Go hardware scanner,
  121–124
Dragon Dictation app, 41–42
Drew's Script-O-Rama, 66
Dropbox, 81–83
Drop'n'Roll app, 320–321
DryCASE, using for underwater
  shooting, 231
DSLR Camera Remote HD, 285–286
The DV Rebels Guide, 164, 361

E

Easy Release forms, 115–117
editing extras
  AJA DataCalc, 338–340
  Cut Notes, 333–335
  Editmote, 337–338
  Timecode, 336
editing footage
  1st Video, 321
  Drop'n'Roll, 320–321
  iMovie, 312–317
  Pinnacle Studio, 317–319
editing while shooting, 190
Editmote app, 337–338
educational apps
  EditCodes, 342–343
  iKeysToGo: Final Cut Pro 7,
    341–342
  Larry Jordan Training for Final
    Cut Pro X, 340–341
  Moviola's Pro Video Guide,
    343–344
El Mariachi, 164
Elite Prompter teleprompter,
  255–257
  downside, 257
  Remote, 257
error codes directory, EditCodes,
  342–343
Evernote app. *See also* mind
  mapping
  creating notes in, 10–11
  uploading scans to, 124
exposure, 174
external keyboards
  Apple's Wireless Keyboard,
    33–34

  Bluetooth, 33–35
  wired, 38–39
extras
  LED lighting panels, 235–237
  mobislyder, 237–238
  sliders, 237–238
  SuctionClip, 242
  table dollies, 239–241
Eye-Fi card, 124

F

Facebook, 346
FAQ app, 84–85
FDX Reader, 50–51
Field, Syd, 12
field monitors, 283–286
file storage, Dropbox online, 81–82
files and folders, managing with
  iFiles, 83–84
film database, searching through,
  360
Film Riot, 361
FiLMiC Pro video camera app,
  176–179, 346
  audio meter, 177–178
  changing encoding rate, 178
  exposure reticle, 177
  locking focus, 177
  popularity of, 178
  setting exposure, 177
  shooting with, 177
FilmTouch call sheets, 112–113
Final Cut Pro keyboard shortcuts,
  mastering, 341–342
Final Cut Pro X, Larry Jordan's
  training for, 340–341
Final Draft, 28–29
Final Draft Reader, 46–50
FiRe 2 audio, 207
floor plan, MagicPlan, 161–164
Florida 411 production directory, 89
focus, 174
folders and files, managing with
  iFiles, 83–84
footage. *See* color correcting
  footage; editing footage; importing
  footage
Form Tools PDF, 117–119. *See also*
  PDF Expert
forms. *See* contracts; release forms
Fountain, 29–32
  conversion methods, 32
  downsides, 31
  previewing documents, 32
  screenplay formats, 31–32
  syntax, 30–31

G

GarageBand, 324–325
Glif tripod mount, 175, 219–220
GoodNotes, 60–61
GoodReader, 57–58
GorillaMobile for iPhone 4/4S, 229
Gradiest color correction app, 311
Gruber, John, 29

H

Haase, Eric, 262–264
HandBrake video converter, 303
Helios Sun Position Calculator, 290–291
The Hero with a Thousand Faces, 14
Highland app, 32
Hindenburg Field Recorder audio, 204–206
    adding markers to timeline, 204–205
    dual system setup, 205–206
    editing recordings, 205
    mono files, 206
    Play mode, 205
    Record screen, 204
    reviewing recordings, 205
    stereo files, 206
Holga iPhone lens, 226–227
Hollywood Camera Work, 152
Holmes, Per, 151

I

iBooks, importing PDF scripts into, 51–53
iBookstore scripts
    Casablanca, 67
    Inception, 67
    Inglourious Basterds, 67
    Star Wars: Episode III, 67
ideas, defined, 4. *See also* mind mapping
iFiles app, 83–84
ikan website, 262
iKeysToGo: Final Cut Pro 7, 341–342
iM2 Tascam stereo microphone, 249–250
imagery
    downloading still images, 79–80
    downloading video, 79–80
    finding, 79–80
images, loading to iOS devices, 71
Imagine 300 website, 264
iMovie app
    editing interface, 314
    movie trailer maker, 316–317
    overview, 312–313

playing back edit, 315
Precision Editor, 316
rearranging clips in timeline, 315
reducing rolling shutter with, 173
sharing edits, 316
shooting video to timeline, 314
title styles for video clips, 315
trimming lower thirds, 316
importing footage
    from computer to iPad, 302
    from computer to iPhone, 302–305
    HandBrake video converter, 303
    from iPhone to iPad, 300
    Permute app, 303–304
    from video camera to iPad, 300–302
Inception script, accessing, 67
index cards, using to define story structure, 16–19
Indy Mogul prompter mount, 262, 362
Inglourious Basterds script, accessing, 67
instant dailies, 283–286
The Internet Movie Script Database, 66
Interrotron, creating, 262–265
iOS devices
    determining space on, 170
    footage requirements, 169
    freeing up memory on, 172
    as light sources, 294
    loading files to, 71
    loading images to, 71
    making space on, 170–172
    prepping, 169
    removing apps, 170
    streaming music on, 172
    switching to Airplane Mode, 169–170
    video capabilities, 168
iOS Dictation, 40–41
iPad
    importing footage from computer to, 302–305
    importing footage from video camera to, 300–302
    lighting with, 291–292
iPad accessories
    Movie Mount, 232–233
    Padcaster, 233–234
iPhone
    importing footage from computer to, 302–305
    importing footage to iPad, 300

iPhone accessories
    2× telephoto lens, 221
    DiffCase conversion lenses, 224–226
    Glif tripod mount, 219–220
    Glif+, 219–220
    GorillaMobile for iPhone 4/4S, 229
    Holga iPhone Lens, 226–227
    iPhone Lens Dial, 227–229
    iPhone SLR mount, 217–219
    iPro Lens, 220–222
    mCAM and mCAMLITE, 212–217
    mCAM Neck Strap, 217
    Olloclip, 222–224
    OWLE Car Mount, 217
    Phocus for iPhone, 217
    shooting underwater, 230–231
    SLR mount, 217–219
    Steadicam Smoothee, 210–212
    Turtlehead mount, 217
    websites, 217
iPhone film festivals, 354–356
iPhone Lens Dial, 227–229
iPhoto app, 70–73
iPod touch video capabilities, 168
iPro Lens, lenses, 220–222
iThoughts app, versus MindNode, 7
iThoughtsHD app
    child topics, 6
    concept, 4
    features, 7
    grouping topics, 6
    mind mapping, 4–7
    topics, 5
    using in brainstorming, 5–6
iTunes File Sharing interface, 47–48
iXZ microphone adapter, 245–246

J

Jordan, Larry, 340–341
Jot Pro stylus, 56, 137–139

K

Kaminski, Dave, 262
keyboards. *See* external keyboards
Keynote application, 75–77
The Kick Plus, 294–295

L

LA 411 production directory, 88–89
Lawrence, David H XVII, 65
LED lighting panels
    Croma, 235–237
    Micro, 235–237

lenses
   2x telephoto, 221
   DiffCase conversion, 224–226
   Holga iPhone, 226–227
   iPhone Lens Dial, 227–229
   iPro, 220–222
   Olloclip accessory, 222–224
Light Iron website, 284
light meter app, audiences for, 288
light meters
   incident type, 288
   reflected type, 288
   spot type, 288
light sources, iOS devices as, 294
lighting, learning about, 174–175
lighting with iPads, 291–292
light-related apps
   Helios Sun Position Calculator, 290–291
   The Kick Plus, 294–295
   Photo Soft Box Pro, 293
   Pocket Light Meter, 287–290
   using iPads, 291–292
List Sender tech scouting, 98
LIVE PLAY website, 284
location scouting
   Map-A-Pic Location Scout, 94–95
   Panascout, 92–93
Lua call sheets, 113
Luma video-stabilizing camera app, 193–195
   real-time filters, 195
   settings, 194–195
   zooming in and out, 195

M

Magic Bullet Arsenal, 73–74
MagicPlan floor plan, 161–164
MamboFrame, 280–281
Map-A-Pic Location Scout, 94–95
MarineCase, using for underwater shooting, 230
Markdown, 29
markers. See slates
Maschwitz, Stu, 29, 164, 361
The Master Course In High-End Blocking & Staging, 151
mCAM and mCAMLITE, 212–217
   1/4-20 mounts, 213
   availability, 215
   combo lens, 213
   comparing, 214
   EnCinema SLR lens adapter, 215–217
   external microphones, 214

mCAM Neck Strap, 217
ME66/K6P shotgun microphone, 246
memorizing screenplays, Rehearsal 2, 63–65
memory, freeing up, 172
Micro LED lighting panel, 235–236
microphones
   adapter cables, 243–244
   AR-4i stereo, 247–249
   G3 wireless lavalier, 243
   iXZ adapter, 245–246
   KV Connection, 244
   ME66/K6P shotgun microphone, 246
   shotgun, 244–246
   Tascam iM2 stereo, 249–250
   TRRS connector, 243
   VideoMic Pro shotgun mic, 244–245
mind mapping. See also Corkulous Pro app; Evernote app; ideas concept, 4
   iThoughtsHD app, 4–7
   MindNode app, 7–8
   topics of trees, 4–5
   as tree, 4–5
MindNode app
   benefits, 8
   desktop version for Mac, 8
   versus iThoughts, 7
   mind mapping, 7–8
   text outline, 7
Mini Cart table dolly, 241
mixing audio. See audio mixing
mobislyder, 237–238
mounting system, GorillaMobile for iPhone 4/4S, 229
mounts, SuctionClip, 242
Movie Looks HD, 308–309
Movie Magic Scheduling To Go, 100–102
Movie Mount for iPad, 232–233
Movie★Slate
   exporting shot log, 274
   metadata for history log, 273
   syncing with TimeCode Buddy, 277
   timecode display, 271–273
   time-of-day timecode, 274
   wireless transmission, 274–275
Moviola's Pro Video Guide, 343–344
music, streaming on iOS devices, 172
music-authoring, Tabletop, 322–324

N

naming characters, 20
New Mexico 411 production directory, 89
Noir Photo, 143
Nomad Brush stylus, 140
notes, creating in Evernote app, 10–11. See also Cut Notes app
NY 411 production directory, 88

O

Olloclip lens accessory, 222–224
OmniGraffle, 156–160
   adding objects, 157–158
   blocking diagrams, 157–159
   Pen tool, 157–158
   stencils, 157–159
online file storage, Dropbox, 81–82
OnOne Software website, 286
overcranking, explained, 191
OWLE Bubo, 212–213
OWLE Car Mount, 217

P

Padcaster frame for iPad, 233–234
Palmsounds.net blog, 322
Panascout location scouting, 92–93
Paper app, 135–136
pCAM Film+Digital Calculator, 265–268
PDF Expert, 54–58. See also Form Tools PDF
PDF scripts, importing into iTunes, 51–52
PDFPen, 58–60
Penultimate note taker, 133–134
Permute app, 303–304
Phocus for iPhone, 217
Photo Soft Box Pro, 293
Photos app, 70–73
Pinnacle Studio
   editing in, 319
   features, 317
   interface, 318
   media library, 319
   montage clips, 317–318
   storyboard, 317
pitches, following up on, 80–85. See also presentation apps
Pocket Call Sheet, 109–112
Pocket Light Meter, 287–290
presentation apps. See also pitches
   iPhoto, 70–73
   Keynote, 75–77
   Magic Bullet Arsenal, 73–74
   Photos app, 70–73
   Presentation Link, 77–79

Presentation Link, 77–79
Previs app, 136–137
Pro Audio To go audio, 202–203
production directories
  the bible, 88–89
  doddle, 89–91
  Florida 411, 89
  LA 411, 88–89
  New Mexico 411, 89
  NY 411, 88
Prolost website, 134, 361
Prompter People website, 262
ProPrompter HDi Pro2, 259–261
ProPrompter teleprompter, 252–255
  customization options, 254
  downside, 254
  remote-control cable, 254–255
ProPrompter Wing, 257–259

Q

QRSlate, 281–283

R

reading screenplays. *See also*
  screenplays
    FDX Reader, 50–51
    Final Draft Reader, 46–50
    iBooks, 51–53
Rebel Without a Crew, 165
recorder, Pro Audio To Go, 202–203
reference manual, Moviola's Pro
  Video Guide, 343–344
Rehearsal 2 script-reading app,
  63–65
release forms. *See also* contracts
  Easy Release, 115–117
  overview, 113–114
remote control converter, Editmote,
  337–338
remote control surface, vWave-Lite,
  312
resource collection tool, Celtx
  Scout, 165–166
Ritt Labs, 295
"The Rodriguez List," 164–165
rolling shutter, 172–174
  avoiding whip pans, 173
  reducing with iMovie, 173
ROLLINGSHUTTER plug-in, 174
Rosten, Jesse, 291–292
RunPee app, 360

S

Save the Cat! story development
  tool, 12–14
  assigning tags to scenes, 14
  beat sheet, 13

The Board, 13–14
  litter box, 14
  logline, 13
  tracking story structure, 14
scanning documents
  DodScanner, 125–126
  Doxie Go hardware scanner,
    121–124
  Eye-Fi, 124
  overview, 121
scenes, representing on index
  cards, 20
scheduling
  Movie Magic Scheduling To Go,
    100–102
  overview, 99–100
  Shot Lister, 105–107
  ShotList, 102–104
score composition
  GarageBand, 324–325
  overview, 321–322
  Tabletop, 322–324
Screenplain website, 32
Screenplay app, 28
Screenplay book, 12
screenplay writing
  Celtx Script, 22–24
  Final Draft, 28–29
  Fountain, 29–32
  Screenplay, 28
  Scripts Pro, 26–27
  ScriptWrite, 27
  Storyist, 24–26
screenplays. *See also* reading
  screenplays
    annotating, 54–63
    The Daily Script, 66
    Drew's Script-O-Rama, 66
    finding, 65–67
    iBookstore, 67
    The Internet Movie Script
      Database, 66
    memorizing, 63–65
    Scripted iPad app, 66–67
    Simply Scripts, 66
Screenplays for You, 66
Scripted iPad app, 66–67
scripts. *See* screenplays
Scripts Pro, 26–27
ScriptWrite, 27
selling films
  in App Store, 347–352
  Intuit, 353–354
  iOS-based credit card services,
    354

PayPal, 353–354
Square, 353–354
shooting underwater
  DryCASE, 231
  MarineCase, 230
Shot Designer, 151–156
  180-degree rule, 153–154
  adding cameras, 153
  adding objects to diagrams, 153
  animation system, 156
  blocking scenes, 155
  building sequences, 154
  creating diagrams, 152
  future versions, 156
  viewing axis lines, 153–154
Shot Lister scheduling, 105–107
shotgun microphones
  ME66/K6P, 246
  VideoMic Pro, 244–245
ShotList scheduling, 102–104
shots. *See* blocking shots
Simply Scripts, 66
SketchPad Pro app, 136
slates
  Denecke Slate, 280
  MamboFrame, 280–281
  Movie*Slate, 271–275
  overview, 270–271
  QRSlate, 281–283
  TimeCode Buddy, 275–277
  T-Slate, 277–279
SloPro slow-motion app
  complaints, 193
  launching, 191
  overcranking, 191
  recording video, 191
  rendering method, 192
  shooting 60fps, 191
  speed options, 192
slow-motion footage, using,
  190–193
Snyder, Blake, 12
sound files, editing with
  TwistedWave, 327
Splice app, 321
stabilization, activating in Luma, 194
Star Wars: Episode III script,
  accessing, 67
Steadicam Smoothee, 210–212
still images, downloading, 79–80
storage needs, estimating, 339
story structure
  Baby names +, 21
  Contour, 14–16
  index cards, 16–19

Save the Cat! 12–14
StorySkeleton, 19–20
Syd Field Script Launcher, 12–13
three acts, 12
Storyboard Composer HD, 141–144, 150
  adding camera moves, 143
  Panel view, 142
  sharing boards, 143
  taking photos, 142
  viewing animated shots, 143
storyboarding
  for artists, 132–133
  Cosmonaut Stylus, 139
  Jot Pro Stylus, 137–139
  Nomad Brush, 140
  for non-artists, 140–141
  Paper, 135–136
  Penultimate, 133–134
  Previs, 136–137
Storyboards 3D, 144–147
  closed system, 146
  rendering styles, 146
  thumbnails of actors, 146
Storyboards Premium, 146
Storyist app, 24–26
  button bar, 25
  versus Celtx Script, 25–26
  index card system, 26
  project folders, 24
  screenplay functions, 25
Storyist for Mac, 32
StorySkeleton app
  export formats, 20
  index-card interface, 19–20
  preparing for pitch meetings, 20
streaming music, 172
structuring stories. See story structure
styluses
  Cosmonaut, 139
  Jot Pro, 56, 137–139
  Nomad Brush, 140
SuctionClip, 242
Super 8 app, 198–199
Syd Field Script Launcher, 12–13

T

table dollies
  Action Cart, 239–240
  Mini Cart, 241
Tabletop music-authoring environment, 322–324
Tascam iM2 stereo microphone, 249–250

tech scouting
  Camera Order, 96–98
  List Sender, 98
  overview, 95
  TechScout Touch, Lighting Edition, 96–97
telephoto lens, 2x, 221
teleprompters
  DataVideo website, 262
  DIY $5 Prompter, 263
  Elite Prompter, 255–257
  ikan website, 262
  Prompter People website, 262
  ProPrompter, 252–255
  ProPrompter HDi Pro2, 259–261
  ProPrompter Wing, 257–259
  through-the-glass, 259–260
  websites, 262
television
  AirPlay, 356–357
  Apple TV, 356–357
  video cables, 357–359
TeraCentral app, 283
text snippets, creating library of, 84–85
Three Point Lighting, 175
three-act structure, 12
through-the-glass prompters, 259–260
TimeCode Buddy, 275–277
  syncing with Movie*Slate, 277
  WiFi Master, 276–277
Timecode calculator, 336
Toland ASC Digital Assistant, 268–270
TouchDraw, 160–161
trackball app, AirGrade for iPhone, 312
transcription. See voice dictation
tripod mount, Glif, 175
TRRS connector, using with microphones, microphones, 243
T-Slate, 277–279
Turtlehead mount, 217
TwistedWave Audio Editor, 326–327
  AudioCopy support, 327
  exporting files from, 327

U

underwater shooting
  DryCASE, 231
  MarineCase, 230
  pCAM Film+Digital Calculator, 268

V

video. *See also* digital video workflows
  downloading, 79–80
  uploading with FiLMiC, 346
Video Camera app
  adding elements, 189
  controls, 188
  editing while shooting, 190
  interface, 187
  LiNE (live nonlinear editing), 187
  record button, 188
  settings screen, 190
  transitions, 189
video camera apps
  Almost DSLR, 181–182
  built-in, 183–184
  CinePro, 179–181
  FiLMiC Pro, 176–179
video cameras
  8mm and 8mm HD, 195–196
  Action Movie FX, 199–200
  CollabraCam, 184–187
  importing footage to iPad, 300–302
  Luma Camera, 193–195
  SloPro, 190–193
  Super 8, 198–199
  Video Camera, 187–190
  Vintagio, 197–198
  Vizzywig, 187–190
video capabilities
  resolution and frame rate, 168
  storage requirements, 168
video encoder, The Cube, 283–285
VideoGrade color correction app, 306–308
VideoMic Pro shotgun mic, 244–245
video-stabilizing camera app, Luma, 193–195
Vimeo, 346
Vintagio app
  altering speed, 197
  Express Mode, 197–198
  Pro Mode, 198
  rendering, 197
Vizzywig video camera, 187–190
voice dictation
  Dictabulus, 42–43
  Dragon Dictation app, 41–42
  iOS Dictation, 40–41
Voice Memo app, 207
vWave-Lite color correction app, 311

W

websites, 217. *See also* apps
1st Video, 320
8MM and 8MM HD, 195
Action Cart table dolly, 239
Action Movie Fx, 199
AJA DataCalc, 339
Alesis iO Dock, 331
Almost DSLR video camera app, 181
Apple Keyboard Dock, 38
AR-4i stereo microphone, 247
audio apps and accessories, 322
Auria digital audio workstation, 328
Burp and Fart Piano, 344
Celtx Scout resource collection tool, 165
Chromagic for iPad, 311
CinemaFX for Video, 310
CinePro video camera app, 180
CollabraCam video camera, 184
Common Lighting Setups, 175
Croma LED lighting panel, 236
The Cube video encoder, 284
Cut Notes app, 332
The Daily Script, 66
DataVideo, 262
del Carmen, Louie, 134
Denecke Slate, 280
Dictabulus, 42–43
DiffCase conversion lenses, 224
DIY $5 Prompter, 263
Drew's Script-O-Rama, 66
Dropbox online file storage, 82
Drop'n'Roll app, 320
DryCASE, 231
DSLR Camera Remote HD, 285
EditCodes directory, 342
Editmote app, 337
Elite Prompter teleprompter, 255
EnCinema SLR lens adapter, 215
Film Riot, 361
FiLMiC Pro video camera app, 176
Final Cut Pro X training by Larry Jordan, 340
Fountain, 31
GarageBand, 324
Genius Pro, 278
Glif tripod mount, 219
GorillaMobile for iPhone 4/4S, 229
Gradiest, 311

HandBrake video converter, 303
Helios Sun Position Calculator, 290
Highland app, 32
Hindenburg Field Recorder audio, 204
Holga iPhone lens, 226
ikan, 262
iKeysToGo: Final Cut Pro 7, 341
Imagine 300, 264
Indy Mogul, 262, 362
The Internet Movie Script Database, 66
iPhone Lens Dial, 227
iXZ microphone adapter, 245
Jot Pro Stylus, 56, 138
The Kick Plus, 294
KV Connection, 244
LA 411 production directory, 88
Light Iron, 284
LIVE PLAY, 284
Luma Camera, 193
MarineCase, 230
mCAM and mCAMLITE, 212
ME66/K6P shotgun microphone, 246
Micro LED lighting panel, 235
Mini Cart table dolly, 241
mobislyder, 237
Movie Looks HD, 308
Movie Mount for iPad, 232
Movie*Slate, 271
Moviola's Pro Video Guide, 343
Noir Photo, 143
NY 411 production directory, 88
OnOne Software, 286
pCAM Film+Digital Calculator, 265
Permute app, 303
Phocus for iPhone, 217
Photo Soft Box Pro, 293
Pinnacle Studio, 317
Pocket Light Meter, 287
Previs app, 136
Pro Audio To go audio, 202
Prolost, 134, 361
Prompter People, 262
ProPrompter HDi Pro2, 259
ProPrompter teleprompter, 252
ProPrompter Wing, 257
QRSlate, 281, 283
Rehearsal 2 script-reading app, 65
ROLLINGSHUTTER plug-in, 174

RunPee app, 360
Save the Cat! 12
Screenplain, 32
Screenplay, 12
Screenplays for You, 66
Simply Scripts, 66
SloPro video camera, 190
Splice app, 321
Steadicam Smoothee, 210
Storyboard Composer HD, 141
Storyboards 3D, 145
Storyboards Premium, 146
Storyist for Mac, 32
SuctionClip, 242
Super 8 app, 198
Tabletop music-authoring environment, 343
Tascam iM2 stereo microphone, 249
teleprompters, 262
TeraCentral app, 283
Three Point Lighting, 175
TimeCode Buddy, 275
Timecode calculator, 336
Toland ASC Digital Assistant, 268
TouchDraw, 160
T-Slate, 277
Turtlehead mount, 217
TwistedWave Audio Editor, 326
VideoGrade color correction app, 306
VideoMic Pro shotgun mic, 244
Vintagio app, 197
vWave-Lite app, 311
white balance, 174
Wireless Keyboard, Apple's, 33–34
wireless lavalier microphone, using, 243
wireless scanning, 124
writing screenplays
Celtx Script, 22–24
Final Draft, 28–29
Fountain, 29–32
Screenplay, 28
Scripts Pro, 26–27
ScriptWrite, 27
Storyist, 24–26

Y

YouTube, 346